ROUTLEDGE LIB

HISTORY OF MONEɪ, ᴅᴀɪ̠ɴᴋɪ̠ɴ̠ᴜ ᴀᴎᴅ

FINANCE

MW00782037

Volume 8

FINANCE AND TRADE UNDER EDWARD III

FINANCE AND TRADE UNDER EDWARD III

Edited by
GEORGE UNWIN

Routledge
Taylor & Francis Group

LONDON AND NEW YORK

First published in 1918 by the Manchester University Press

This edition first published in 2018
by Routledge
2 Park Square, Milton Park, Abingdon, Oxon OX14 4RN

and by Routledge
711 Third Avenue, New York, NY 10017

Routledge is an imprint of the Taylor & Francis Group, an informa business

Reprinted in 1962 by Frank Cass & Co. Ltd

British Library Cataloguing in Publication Data
A catalogue record for this book is available from the British Library

ISBN: 978-1-138-70169-4 (Set)
ISBN: 978-1-315-10595-6 (Set) (ebk)
ISBN: 978-1-138-05763-0 (Volume 8) (hbk)
ISBN: 978-1-138-05766-1 (Volume 8) (pbk)
ISBN: 978-1-315-16479-3 (Volume 8) (ebk)

Publisher's Note
The publisher has gone to great lengths to ensure the quality of this reprint but points out that some imperfections in the original copies may be apparent.

Disclaimer
The publisher has made every effort to trace copyright holders and would welcome correspondence from those they have been unable to trace.

Finance and Trade under Edward III.

FINANCE AND TRADE
UNDER EDWARD III

EDITED BY
GEORGE UNWIN

FRANK CASS & CO. LTD
1962

First published in 1918
by the Manchester University Press

Published by Frank Cass & Co. Ltd
10 Woburn Walk, W.C.1

FIRST EDITION 1918
REPRINTED 1962

Printed in Great Britain by
Taylor Garnett Evans & Co. Ltd
Watford

PREFACE.

Some five or six years ago a plan was formed to illustrate a dozen or more different aspects of 14th century history by the publication of work done by graduates of the History School of Manchester University. The war has seriously hindered the realization of the project, and this volume represents merely an instalment of it. Apart from my own contributions, each of the studies here presented is based on a thesis prepared for the History Schools of 1911 and 1912. Their separate publication in advance of the rest may plead the justification of a certain unity of subject. They deal with various economic aspects of the reign of Edward III, and the writers, with one exception, were members not only in Professor Tout's honours class in the "Early part of the reign of Edward III," but of my honours class in Economic History. It has thus fallen to my lot to advise their postgraduate researches and to edit this volume.

The two articles on " The Social Evolution of Mediæval London " and " London Tradesmen and their Creditors," though falling somewhat outside the scope of the book as indicated by its title, have been included in the hope that they might supply a broader introduction to some of the special problems dealt with in the subsequent studies. As will perhaps be apparent to the critical reader, they were both originally prepared for oral delivery—the former as one of the Warburton Lectures of 1911 and the latter as a paper read before the Manchester University Historical Society in the following session.

Of the remaining articles, that on " The Estate of Merchants " was the last to be written, and aimed, along with the Introduction, at providing a tentative survey of the reign as a whole.

The full treatment of the Staple has been facilitated by the thesis of Mr. L. H. Gilbert, B.A. (now in France) on the History of the Staple, 1313—1353, which it has not been found practicable to include in this volume. It should also be added that Mr. Sargeant's article on " The Wine Trade with Gascony " had to be completed amidst the distractions of barrack-life in Ireland, and since the author's removal to France, has been deprived of the full advantage of the author's revision.

I desire to express my deep obligations to my colleagues, Professors Tout and Tait, whose knowledge of fourteenth century history is far greater than my own, and whose numerous suggestions and corrections I have been grateful to adopt.

In the somewhat laborious task of preparing the book for the press, I have been much assisted by my wife, and by Mr. H. M. McKechnie, the Secretary of the University Press, to whose experienced judgment and untiring care I owe more than I can adequately acknowledge.

GEORGE UNWIN.

The University,
    Manchester,
        January 'IIth, 1918,

CONTENTS

INTRODUCTION.

I.

The reign of Edward the Third is one of the longest in history, and long reigns tend to possess an interest which is even more than proportionate to their length. It is, however, an interest that springs not so much from unity as from contrast and change; the beginning and the end of such a reign lie in different worlds. The three visitations of pestilence in 1349, 1361 and 1366 make this especially true of the reign of Edward III; few of those who were born before its stormy opening can have lived to see its disastrous close, and the contrast between the England of 1377 and that of 1327, whether in regard to its external relations, its constitutional development or its social and economic conditions, must have been scarcely less striking than the more familiar contrast between the beginning and the end of the Victorian era.

In approaching the detailed study of such a period we need the help of all the large landmarks that are available; and it so happens that the fifty years of the reign divide themselves naturally into five epochs—each of which is almost exactly a decade. The commencement of the Hundred Years' War marks the close of the first decade. The second decade ends with the victory of Crécy and the Truce of Calais. The middle period, which is rather longer than a decade, opens with the Black Death in 1349, and after a renewal of the war in 1355, and the victory of Poitiers in 1356, closes with the siege of Paris, the dictation of terms and the imposition of an indemnity in the form of a ransom by the treaties of Bretigni and Calais in 1360. The fourth decade is one of nominal peace with France, and the fifth, which opens with the second renewal of the war in 1369 is one of continuous military disaster and of increasing economic exhaustion.

With this broad outline of the military history of the reign in mind we are better able to map out its constitutional history and to link together those aspects of its economic history

—mainly fiscal aspects—which are studied in this volume. Every campaign was preceded or accompanied by recourse to unconstitutional forms of supply, and every truce was followed by a Parliamentary crisis—the truce of Esplechin by the crisis of 1340-1, the truce of Calais by the crisis of 1348, the treaties of Bretigni and Calais by the decisive constitutional victory of 1362, and the truce of Bruges by the Good Parliament of 1376.   A less obvious and equally significant fact is that each of these constitutional crises is followed by a reshaping of what becomes in the course of this reign one of the central fiscal organs of the government— the Staple.   As far as the present volume of studies is concerned, the three principal epochs of the reign are marked by the definite constitution of the Foreign Staple at Bruges in 1343, the establishment of the Home Staples by the ordinance of 1353, and the setting up of the Calais Staple in 1363.

The significance of the development as a whole may perhaps be made clear by drawing a very broad analogy with a more familiar period of fiscal history.

The seventeenth century, like the fourteenth, witnessed a transformation of the system of national finance. The two main features of change were in both cases a great and permanent extension of indirect taxation and the creation of a new form of national debt.   In the seventeenth century, as in the fourteenth, both these innovations were initiated by the Crown, and were strenuously resisted by Parliament, which as the price of its final authorisation of them claimed and secured an increased measure of control over national finance. The reader who is sufficiently forewarned of the limited value of historic analogies will find it helpful to compare the wool subsidy of the fourteenth century with the excise of the seventeenth, and to think of the Governor and Company of Staplers at Calais as the forerunners of the Governor and Company of the Bank of England.

II.

The most serious attempt hitherto made to deal comprehensively with the commercial policy of England in the reign of Edward III is undoubtedly that of Dr. Cunningham.   In view of this fact, and of the great authority accorded to Dr. Cunningham's conclusions, it is desirable to have those conclusions clearly before us and to use them as a basis from which any further discussion of the subject may set out. The most fundamental position, as stated in the third edition of Dr. Cunningham's " Growth of English Industry and Commerce," is admittedly a hypothetical one.   It is that " the wars of Edward III were not dictated by personal ambition. . . . but that his policy was thoroughly English, and that he aimed at the development of the national resources and increase of the national power."

" The main object of Edward's continental wars was to establish national industry and commerce upon a wider territorial basis.   To have established a firm hold upon Gascony, Flanders and England would have been to create a remarkably powerful commercial federation. . . . . it was a thoroughy statesmanlike plan and would justify the reputation Edward III enjoyed as the Father of English Commerce."   " This must, of course," says Dr. Cunningham, " be mere hypothesis, as we cannot hope at this distance of time to become thoroughly acquainted with the precise motives which influenced the King, but it is an hypothesis as to his political intentions which has much in its favour since it renders his attitude towards industry and commerce intelligible."[1]   But if we cannot now discover the King's political motives, what clues have we to his attitude towards industry and commerce ? Dr. Cunningham finds these in the Parliamentary enactments of the reign.   " The *Dialogus* assumes that prosperity is a good thing, but Edward III's legislation implies definite schemes as to the best way of promoting that end. . . . He endeavoured (a) to foster foreign commerce, (b) to foster industry, and (c) to check extravagance by sumptuary legislation. . . . He desired to increase the volume of trade, and he legislated in the interest of the consumer and in disregard of the claims of particular classes. . . . He endeavoured to develop a manufacture for which the country was specially suited, and to do so he showed himself somewhat cosmopolitan in inviting artisans from the Continent. . . He set himself

1. *Growth of English Industry and Commerce during the Early and Middle Ages.* Third Edition, 1896, pp. 266, 269.

to encourage thrift among the labouring population—more it
is true by precept than by example. . . . The necessity of
procuring large supplies forced him at times to make severe
demands from the commercial classes, and to levy heavy taxes
either in money or in kind; but he did not consciously and
habitually subordinate economic to political interest, in fact
it would be more true to say that, as in modern times, his
policy was very greatly determined by a desire to promote
economic interests." [1]

In a later passage which has had considerable influence on
the subsequent writing of economic history, Dr. Cunningham
in describing the development of mercantilist aims in
the parliaments of Richard II, sets those aims in
sharp contrast to the policy which he had previously
attributed to Edward III. "Edward had legislated in the
interests of the consumers and with the view of providing
plenty; the parliaments of Richard II took another turn and
insisted on introducing conditions which, eventually, as they
were worked out in subsequent centuries favoured the growth
of English power. . . . To some extent plenty is a condition
of power, and the two policies may have much in common :
but whereas Edward III desired to see large cargoes, whoever
brought them, *i.e.* plenty, the Ricardian Parliament desired
to have more English ships, even if the home consumers were
for a time badly supplied with wine."[2]

It is very instructive to note the modifications of these
views which further investigation and study have led Dr.
Cunningham to adopt in the more recent editions of his work.
He has come to take a less favourable view of the statesmanship of Edward, and is inclined to regard the hypothetical
scheme of a great commercial federation as "highly
ingenious" rather than as "thoroughly statesmanlike." He
now considers that while "Edward may possibly have recognised the cohesive power of commercial intercourse, his plans
were not farseeing, and they broke down because he failed to
bring conflicting interests into harmony." "The privileges
he conferred on Flemish merchants roused the jealousy of
English subjects : while the arrangements which were favourable to sheep farmers and to consumers in this country proved

1. *Ibid.*, pp. 298–9, 310–1.
2. *Ibid.*, pp. 470–1.

to be injurious to English shipping."[1] Not only therefore was Edward's commercial and industrial policy inconsistent with his supposed scheme for commercial federation but the several parts of that policy did not form a consistent whole.

This view is much more in accordance than the earlier one with the estimate formed of Edward III by the other historians. Professor Tout, who is perhaps the most appreciative of the strong points in Edward's character, considers that " he lacked the self-restraint and sense of proportion which would have prevented him from aiming at objects beyond his reach. The same want of relation between end and means, the same want of definite policy and clear ideals, marred his statecraft." [2] The judgment of Stubbs is more decisively unfavourable. " Edward III was not a statesman, although he possessed some qualifications which might have made him a successful one. He was a warrior; ambitious, unscrupulous, selfish, extravagant, and ostentatious. His obligations as a King sat very lightly on him. He felt himself bound by no special duty either to maintain the theory of royal supremacy or to follow a policy which would benefit his people. Like Richard I, he valued England primarily as a source of supplies. . . . A King whose people fly from his approach, a King overwhelmed with debt, worn out with luxury, the puppet of opposing factions such as Edward in his later years became, is a very different thing from the gentle, gay, and splendid ideal King of chivalry." [3]

The reader of the studies contained in this volume is likely to admit the wisdom of Dr. Cunningham's later reservations as to the statesmanship of Edward III, and may even be disposed to go much further in the same direction. Dr. Cunningham still holds that the hypothetical federation was a highly ingenious plan and would justify the reputation Edward III enjoyed as the Father of English Commerce. But, after all, nothing but the clearest facts could warrant us in imputing to Edward, whether as depicted by Froissart or by Stubbs, an economic policy of such scope and elaboration that it anticipated the views of Cobden on the one hand

1. *Growth of English Industry and Commerce during the Early and Middle Ages.* Fifth Edition, p. 266.
2. Tout. *Political History of England,* 1216–1377, p. 313.
3. Stubbs, II, 393–4.

and those of Frederick List on the other; and the facts seem
to indicate that the first of the aims attributed to Edward—
his desire to " foster foreign commerce shown by legislation
in the interests of the consumer and in disregard of the claims
of particular classes"—his policy of plenty rather than power
is as hypothetical as his scheme of commercial federation.
It rests on the assumption that Acts of Parliament are a sure
indication of royal policy—an assumption no more justifiable
in the reign of Edward III than in that of James I. The
" free trade " enactments of Edward III's reign were carried
in response to urgent petitions of the Commons. In the
two leading instances of 1335 and 1351-3 they imply the
reversal of a restrictive policy previously adopted by the King
without parliamentary sanction. It is true that Edward in
making these concessions contrived in some cases to combine
them with arrangements that would equally serve his fiscal
purposes. But the fact that he knew how to make ' free trade '
pay when driven to adopt it is no reason for crediting him
with a policy of ' plenty rather than power.' When acting
on his own responsibility Edward persistently returned to a
policy of restriction and monopoly for the simple reason that
this policy enabled him to borrow, and he could only borrow
by heavily discounting the resources of the future.

The second imputed object of policy—the fostering of
national industry by prohibiting the exportation of wool and
the importation of cloth and by inviting Flemish manufacturers to settle in England, whilst it accords much less than
the policy of " free trade " with the supposed scheme for commercial federation with Flanders, has somewhat more claim
to be connected with the personal initiative of the King
because the measures that purported to carry it into effect were
royal letters patent,—some of which were issued in advance
of the parliamentary enactments. But when the whole
circumstances of the case as recorded in the studies on the
' Taxation of Wool ' and the ' Estate of Merchants ' are duly
considered, the part played by Edward in fostering English
industry is reduced to comparatively small proportions.

The statute embodying the supposed industrial policy of
Edward III was passed in the spring of 1337. At that
moment his intended war with France gave the King two

strong preoccupations—to raise money at home and to get allies in the Low Countries. In conjunction with a group of English merchants he was organising a monopoly in the exportation of wool which was meant to serve both his fiscal and diplomatic objects; and a temporary prohibition on the exportation was an essential part of the scheme. The prohibition on Flemish cloth and the invitation to Flemish clothworkers were meant to intensify the diplomatic pressure on Flanders, whilst they might serve to mitigate English objections to restrictions on the exportation of wool. This combination of devices was not new; it was one that tended to recur whenever friction arose between England and Flanders. Its embodiment in a Parliamentary statute and the fact that a number of Flemish clothworkers availed themselves of the invitation have given it in this instance an altogether undue prominence in English industrial history. That it did not represent any serious industrial policy in the mind of the King is shown by the fact that it was deliberately intended to lead—and did lead—to an alliance with Flanders by which Flemish industry secured a predominant hold on the English wool supply.[1] The Flemish alliance, which thus involved a reversal of the industrial policy attributed to the King, might in itself have been part of a scheme for a commercial federation; but there is no evidence to show that this was actually the case, and the subsequent history of the alliance is much more intelligible in the light of the " dynastic ambition " hypothesis.

In regard to the third aspect of the policy attributed to Edward—" he set himself to encourage thrift among the labouring population "—the discrepancy between precept and example, though bizarre and even ludicrous, is not on that account incredible. The hearts of princes are unsearchable, and stranger contrasts are fully vouched for in the records of mediæval psychology. Two questions however need to be asked. Was the encouragement of thrift of such a sustained and serious character as to deserve the name of policy, and does the evidence warrant us in attributing it to the King rather than to Parliament? Of the only two recorded instances of this policy, in 1336 and 1363, the first occurred

---

1. See article on Estate of Merchants, pp. 186-7.

at the opening of the great war, when taxation was reaching a maximum,[1] and the second some years after the conclusion of peace, when a recurrence of the plague had added to the exhaustion caused by the war, and the Commons were struggling to reduce taxation and to prevent a natural rise of wages and prices.   In both cases the 'encouragement' is embodied in an Act of Parliament and is easily explicable as the product of a transitory movement of public opinion.   The petitions of the 1336 Parliament are not extant, but those of 1363 show that the statute of that year was based on the demands of the classes represented in Parliament.   The Commons show that "divers victuals within the realm are greatly enhanced in price by reason that divers people of divers conditions use divers apparel not belonging to their estate," and the statute made in response to this petition proceeds to regulate the dress of every rank up to that of a knight, whilst in the more important matter of diet its restrictions apply only to labourers in husbandry, journeymen and other servants, or to those who have not goods and chattels to the value of forty shillings.[2]

From the standpoint of recent experience it is not difficult to realise the mood of the governing classes which finds expression in this legislation.   At a time of national exhaustion, vividly depicted for us in the sixth Passus of *Piers Plowman*, when victory had been speedily followed by plague and famine, when the freebooters who had wasted France for twenty years had returned to pillage their peaceful neighbours,[3] at a time when all classes were demoralised and the restraints of custom and religion were widely disregarded, there was a demand for national reformation in which all classes except the nobility and the higher clergy were to share.   But whilst there was no effective guarantee that knights and their ladies would amend their lives and their households at the bidding of an Act of Parliament, the clauses that affected the labourer were an addition to a code of class legislation for the enforcement of which special machinery had been provided, and the stringency of which

1. See below, p. 186.
2. *Rot. Parl.*, II, pp. 278–9.
3. C. G. Crump and C. Johnson. "The Powers of Justices of the Peace," in *Eng. Hist. Rev.*, xxvii, 228.

had been greatly increased at the conclusion of the war. The Statutes of Labourers have been defended on the ground that they provided for the regulation of prices as well as of wages. But whilst wages were fixed at a definite and impossible maximum, prices were only required to be "reasonable "; and whilst the penalisation of excessive wages was universal and drastic, the penalisation of excessive prices could only · be occasional and ineffective. It fell upon the class of small traders which was least responsible, if any class was responsible, for the increased cost of living; and which was little better represented in Parliament than the journeyman or the labourer.[1] Perhaps it was a sense of the futility and injustice of this procedure that led to the inclusion in the Statute of 1363 of the clause which aimed at checking the monopoly of large importing merchants by restricting every merchant to one branch of trade.[2]

A single year of experience sufficed to show that these measures of national reconstruction, however disinterested in intention, had in fact served to increase the evils they professed to cure; whilst they threatened to subject the nation to a new and intolerable servitude. The restriction of merchants to one branch of trade had been made the basis for the bestowal of chartered monopolies by the King which had raised prices thirty per cent higher than before. The Commons therefore prayed that the whole statute might be repealed, that the charters might be annulled, and " that all people of whatever estate or condition may freely order their sustenance, in food and apparel, for themselves, their wives, children and servants in manner as seems to them best."[3]

III.

When we speak of the economic policy of Edward III or of his parliaments we make what is a natural but at the same time a questionable assumption. The word *policy* implies a continuous unity of purpose in public affairs or an attempt to achieve such a unity. Even the attempt is a late product of

---

1. B. H. Putnam. *The Enforcement of the Statutes of Labourers,* Appendix, pp. 322–99.
2. *Rot. Parl.,* II, p. 277.   3. *Ibid.,* p. 286.

historical development. It implies the control of legislation and of administration through a consciousness of the interests of the nation as a whole, guided by more or less adequate ideas, and capable of restraining and subordinating the operation of lesser interests. Now the records of Parliament in the fourteenth century, and indeed in many later centuries, contain ample evidence of the effective operation of a multitude of minor interests, and when we speak of national policy we assume the existence of a national interest through whose activity the partial interests of classes, or localities are to some extent harmonised and controlled. Have we any evidence of this in the records of Edwardian Parliaments?

A near approach to it may perhaps be found in the petitions to the King, frequently adduced as the ground of legislation, which claim to express the views of the Commons or the " poor Commons" or " the Community of the Realm." The demands embodied in many of these petitions represented interests wide enough to be called national, and they were maintained with sufficient continuity to constitute a policy if they were harmonious and effective. The widest of these interests was that of the taxpayers resisting the enormous increase of taxation made necessary by the war with France. This was indeed the most universal, powerful and continuous interest operative in Parliament throughout the reign, but it did not produce continuous effects in economic policy. On the contrary it tended, in conjunction with the King's increasing demand for increased supplies of money, to produce a marked discontinuity of policy in regard to the wool trade. Unwillingness to grant direct taxes at first induced the Commons (1340) to legalise for a limited time not only a very high export tax on wool, but also the exercise of a royal monopoly in the export trade; but a few years' experience of the evils of these methods of taxation led them (1344) to offer a grant of direct taxation on condition of the withdrawal of the monopoly and of a speedy diminution of the wool tax. Later on (1353), finding it impossible to get rid of the high export tax, the Commons returned to the policy of withholding direct taxes and of resisting the exercise of monopolies in the wool trade.

But the petitions of the Commons reveal other widespread economic interests which had more direct and continuous effects upon fiscal policy. The largest of these interests was that of the wool producers—a body that must have included the great majority of those who found representation in Parliament. Their first wish was to have no tax on wool, but, if a tax must be laid, they desired that a minimum price might be set on the various kinds of wool which it was hoped would have the effect of throwing the tax on the foreign consumer. In the same way they were opposed to any staple restrictions on the export of wool, but they preferred a number of staples, where there would be comparatively free access of both home and foreign buyers, to a single foreign staple which was avowedly set up in the interests of royal and mercantile monopoly.

Quite apart from and often opposed to the interests of the grower were the interests of the dealers in wool. These did not all run in one channel. At least three distinct bodies of mercantile interest can be observed in operation, each of them associated with one of the three alternating staple policies of the reign. One body of merchants clearly agreed with the growers in supporting the entire abolition of all staples so as to have free access to upland supplies. Another set of trading interests favoured the establishment of home staples which enabled them to reap a preferential advantage out of their local connections; whilst the various monopoly projects based upon the maintenance of a foreign staple attracted the support of a small class of wealthy exporters.

Numerous attempts were made during the first period of the French war by the fiscal opportunism of the King to ally itself with various combinations of the two interests last named. The failure of these attempts owing to the opposition of the Commons, the persistent bad faith of the King and the conflict of the interests with which he sought alliance; and the success of Parliament in absorbing most of these interests, in defining its constitutional status and in formulating and enacting a measure that had some claim to be considered a national policy—have been fully described in two of the studies contained in this volume. The taxpayers, the wool growers and the smaller merchants were united in opposition to the continuance of the monopoly embodied in the staple at Bruges. Fifteen years' experience of a succession of syndicates of native monopolists led them to demand the exclusion of English capitalists from the export trade and the re-establishment of the home staples through which it was hoped both the grower and the small dealer would get the benefit of the free access of foreign capital. The King in return for his abandonment of a bankrupt monopoly system received a grant of wool subsidy for three years, and willingly consented to an exclusion of native exporters which secured him a higher rate of export tax from aliens.

But if the regulation of foreign trade in the middle decade of Edward's reign exhibits a marked tendency towards a national policy, there are two assertions that may be clearly made about that policy. It was not an Edwardian but a parliamentary policy; and it was not a mercantilist policy; *i.e.*, it did not aim at the protection of native merchants, manufacturers or shipowners against foreign competition. Indeed it might be considered as anti-mercantilistic were it not that mercantilism as a policy had scarcely as yet found articulate expression. The parliamentary policy arose in deliberate opposition to methods of fiscal opportunism practised by the King which had very much in common with the methods of later mercantilism. Edward III has no claim at all to the title "Father of Commerce," but he would have a genuine claim to be considered as the Father of Mercantilism, if his fiscal and diplomatic devices had sought justification on broad grounds of national interest. Mercantilism became a policy when the merchants and manufacturers became strong enough in Parliament to represent their interest as the national interest. The attempts of Edward III to bargain separately with the merchants show that in the early half of his reign the interests of the landed classes as taxpayers, producers and consumers were still predominant in Parliament.

Nevertheless there is one phase of national policy closely associated with the mercantilism of later reigns of which the distinct beginnings are to be found in the legislation of this period. One of the main motives of the establishment of the home staples as set forth in the ordinances was a desire ' to replenish the realm with money and plate of gold and silver,'[1]

---

1. *Rot. Parl.*, II, 6, 247.

and this is too much in accordance with earlier petitions of the Commons to be attributed solely to the fiscal exigencies of the Crown. The popular remedy for the evil of a disappearing currency had been found in the enactment in 1340 that two marks of silver should be deposited at the Tower for every sack of wool exported,[1] and an equivalent requirement formed the central feature of the staple at Calais when Parliament had become reconciled to it as a permanent institution and had authorised its regulation. Bullionistic policy was no doubt motived largely by fiscal needs, but it was supported by popular opinion; and this opinion, if it was a delusion, was not an abstract or theoretical delusion.[2] When papal taxation was levied and the King's foreign allies subsidised in English wool, it seemed a practical remedy for an actual grievance to insist on cash payment for the chief national export.

The matter was indeed not so simple as this. Inadequate ideas on the nature of money and the almost universal dishonesty of governments at a time when the operations of international finance were rapidly extending and a bi-metallic system was everywhere in course of adoption, had reduced the currency and the foreign exchanges to a state of permanent confusion. But it has not been sufficiently realised by historians that the evils for which the governments of the middle ages continually professed to be seeking a remedy were to no small extent the consequences of their own actions. Edward I, for instance, is represented as struggling in 1299 heroically but vainly against the outflow of his own and the inflow of foreign coinage. But the outflow of good English coin was the result under " Gresham's law " of the King's having begun in war time to coin money of a lower standard, whilst the foreign money that flowed in was to a large extent the exported English silver reminted into coin which was quite equal to the King's new standard but upon which the King's heavy charge for recoinage had not been paid.

1. 14 Edw. III, c. 21.
2. For the close connection between papal taxation and the policy of bullionism, *cf.* W. E. Lunt, "Papal Taxation in England in the Reign of Edward I," in *Eng. Hist. Rev.*, xxx, 410.
3. Cunningham. *Growth of English Industry and Commerce during the Early and Middle Ages*, par. 102.
4. C. G. Crump and H. Hughes. "The English Currency under Edward I," in *Economic Journal*, v, p. 62.

Similar complaints of the outflow and inflow of currency became a normal incident of war finance under Edward III. And if the Commons did not fully grasp the causes of these phenomena their demands were generally reasonable and to the point.   It was not unreasonable at a time of social unrest and of unstable prices to ask that the government should not further dislocate the whole range of public and private contracts by tampering with the currency.   Nor was it unnatural to expect that the government should receive as taxation the inferior coinage with which it had been paying its debts; or to demand that when money had lost a third of its former value the prices paid by the royal purveyors for the people's wool should be raised to a corresponding degree.[1]

It seems then that there is little ground for attributing any definite economic policy to Edward III except the one implied in the judgment of Stubbs, " Like Richard I he valued England primarily as a source of supplies."   If any distinctive policy is to be associated with the reign it must be attributed to the action of Parliament.   This, however, only serves to bring into greater relief the contrast that has been made, in regard to economic policy between the reign of Edward III and and that of his successor.   The change from a ' policy of plenty ' to a ' policy of power,' so far as it took place, corresponded to a change in the mind of Parliament itself, and was not due to the passing of a monarch of exceptional economic genius, who had anticipated the views of Cobden and Gladstone.   It is not unreasonable to expect that the studies collected in this volume should afford some new light as to the reality, extent and significance of this important change in public opinion; but as they are concerned with only one of the contrasted periods, we need to be furnished in advance with fairly accurate conceptions of the other period.

Some of the leading elements of the " policy of power " or mercantilism are undoubtedly to be found embodied in the Acts of Richard the Second's Parliaments; but it would be an entire mistake to suppose that Parliament during the reign of Richard the Second consistently and continuously pursued either a mercantilist or any other form of economic policy. Almost every session of Parliament witnessed a reaction and

1. *Rot. Parl.*, II, 105, 137–8.

sometimes a violent reaction from the policy of the previous session. The Parliament of 1381 passed the first Act for the protection of the native shipping interest. The Parliament of 1382 practically repealed this Act, which had been supported largely by the fishmongers, and passed an Act for securing free trade in fish; which in the following Parliament was in its turn repealed. The same contrast is to be found between the ' free trade ' policy of 1391 and the anti-alien legislation of 1393. Taking the reign as a whole we have to recognise a distinct development of mercantilist opinion and policy in Parliament, but the opposition continues to be active and frequently successful.[1]

But what of the other side of the contrast—the policy of plenty or of free trade pursued by the Parliaments of Edward III ? As far as the mind of Parliament may be said to constitute a policy we have here something much less ambiguous. The demand for ' free trade,' *i.e.* the relaxation of staple restrictions and the free intercourse of alien exporters and importers with native producers and consumers or their agents—finds repeated and increasingly emphatic expression throughout the first four decades of the reign and is embodied at long intervals in the ' free trade ' enactments of 1335, 1351 and 1365, as well as in that great commercial code—the Statute of the Staple 1354. There is, moreover, no general body of opposition to set off against this consistent and continuous expression of Parliamentary opinion. Nevertheless it would be a serious mistake to take the ' free trade ' enactments as constituting in a practical sense the policy of the reign. In point of fact they were little more than protests, and for the most part ineffectual protests, against the administrative and fiscal action of the King. Within a year of its enactment each of the statutes of 1335, 1351 and 1365 had become a dead letter. The opposing force that served to nullify them lay in the ever present exigencies of war finance. In actual practice there was probably less realisation of the policy of free trade in the reign of Edward III than in that of Richard II. The contrast between the two reigns is not one of policy in the sense of governmental practice, but one of policy in the sense of the reasoned basis of statecraft. It

1. Unwin. *Gilds and Companies of London*, chap. x.

implies a new growth of opinion and theory, and a new growth of organised interests represented in Parliament, through which the new opinions find effectual expression. Such a growth is, however, to be traced not merely by contrasting the two reigns, but also by comparing the successive decades of the reign with which the following studies are especially concerned.

G. UNWIN.

ABBREVIATIONS.

A. M. Bord. - - - - *Archives Municipales de Bordeaux.*
Atton and Holland- - *The King's Customs,* 1908.
Baker, and Baker *Chronicon of Geoffrey le Baker,* edited Sir
  Chronicon - - - - E. Maunde Thompson.
Beaven - - - - - - *The Aldermen of the City of London, temp.*
  Henry III to 1908, *with Notes on the parlia-*
  mentary representatives of the city, by A. B.
  Beaven, 1908.
Bond - - - - - - - *Extracts from the Liberate Roll relative to*
  Loans by Italian Merchants to the kings
  of England in the 13th *and* 14th *centuries,*
  with an introductory memoir, by E. A. Bond,
  Archæologia, vol. xxviii, pp. 207–326.
Bk.A.B.C. etc. - - - *Calendar of the letter books of the city of*
  London, edited by R. R. Sharpe.
C.C.R. - - - - - - *Calendar of Close Rolls*
C.F.R. - - - - - - *Calendar of Fine Rolls.*
C.P.R. - - - - - - *Calendar of Patent Rolls.*
Cal. Wills - - - - - *Calendar of Wills proved and enrolled in the*
  court of Husting, London, edited by R. R.
  Sharpe, 1889.
Cunningham - - - - *Growth of English Industry and Commerce,*
  by W. Cunningham.
Daumet - - - - - - *Calais sous la Domination Anglaise,* by G.
  Daumet.
D. N. B. - - - - - *Dictionary of National Biography.*
Dowell - - - - - - *A History of Taxation and Taxes in England,*
  by S. Dowell, 1888.
Foed. - - - - - - Rymer's *Foedera* (*Records Commission edition.*)
Froissart - - - - - *Oeuvres de Jean Froissart,* edited Kervyn de
  Lettenhove.
Hall *Customs* - - - - *A History of the Customs Revenue in England,*
  by Hubert Hall, 2 vols, 1885
I. S. Gironde - - - - *Inventaire Sommaire des archives departe-*
  mentales de la Gironde.
Jullian *Hist. de Bord* *Histoire de Bordeaux,* by C. Jullian.
Knighton - - - - - *Chronicon of Henry Knighton (Rolls Series).*
Le Bel - - - - - - *Chronique de Jean le Bel,* edited J. Viard
  and E. Duprez, 1904.
Le Muisit - - - - - *Chroniques et Annales de Gilles Le Muisit,*
  edited H. Lemaitre.
Liber Albus - - - - *Liber Albus, The White book of the City of*
  London, translated by H. T. Riley, 1886.
Lib. Cust. - - - - - *Liber Custumarum,* in vol 4 part 1 of *Muni-*
  menta Gildhallae Londiniensis.
Lords Report - - - - *The House of Lords' Reports on the Dignity of*
  a Peer, vol iv, 1826.
Michel - - - - - - *Histoire du Commerce de Bordeaux,* by F.
  Michel.

xxix

Murimuth - - - - - *Continuatio Chronicarum*, by A. Murimuth (*Rolls series*), edited Sir E. Maunde Thompson.

Nichols - - - - - - *Chronicles of Calais* (Camden Society), edited J. G. Nichols.

Peruzzi - - - - - - S. L. Peruzzi, *Storia del Commercio e dei Banchieri di Firenze, etc.*

Ramsay - - - - - - *The Genesis of Lancaster*, by Sir J. H. Ramsay.

Rhodes " Italian *Italian Bankers. in England and their Loans* Bankers in England"- *to Edward I and Edward II*, by W. E. Rhodes, in *Historical Essays by Members of the Owens College*, 1902.

Riley *Mem.* - - - - *Memorials of London and London Life in the 13th, 14th and 15th centuries*, by H. T. Riley.

Rot. Parl. - - - - - *Rotuli Parliamentorum.*

Rot. Scot. - - - - - *Rotuli Scotiae.*

Rot. Vasc. - - - - - *Rotuli Vasconiae.*

Scalacronica - - - - *Scalacronica*, by Sir T. Gray, edited J. Stevenson, (*Maitland Club*), 1826.

S.R. - - - - - - - *Statutes of the Realm.*

Stow - - - - - - - *A Survey of London*, by J. Stow, edited C. L. Kingsford, 1908.

Stubbs - - - - - Stubbs, *Constitutional History of England.*

Tout - - - - - - - *The History of England from the Accession of Henry III to the Death of Edward III* (1216–1377), by T. F. Tout, in *Longman's Political History of England.*

Unwin *Gilds.* - - - - *The Gilds and Companies of London*, by G. Unwin.

Villani - - - - - - *Croniche de Firenze*, by Giovanni Villani.

Yver - - - - - - - *Le Commerce et les Marchands dans l'Italie méridionale au xiiie et au xive siècle*, by G. Yver.

SOCIAL EVOLUTION IN MEDIÆVAL LONDON.

Any town that has a past has a natural history no less interesting than that of an anthill or a beehive—if only it could find a Lubbock to unravel the long evolution of its social instincts or a Maeterlinck to unfold its wealth of mystical suggestion. Readers of the autobiography of Goethe cannot easily forget his vivid account of his boyhood in Frankfort, of the endless delight which his already creative imagination took in the long vista of centuries which the daily sights and the immemorial customs of his native city opened up to him.

" The street in which our house was situated," he tells us, " passed by the name of Hirschgraben (Stag-ditch), but as neither stags nor ditches were to be seen we wished to have the expression explained. They told us that our house stood on a spot that was once outside the city, and that where the street now ran had formerly been a ditch in which a number of stags were kept . . . because the senate every year, according to an ancient custom, feasted on a stag."

He tells us how he loved to wander over the fourteenth century bridge and to return by the ferry, with what reverence he gazed on the Saalhof, which stood where the palace of Charlemagne had been, how he lingered to spend his pocket-money in the mediæval market that crowded the space in front of St. Bartholomew's Church, how he roamed at will (as the privileged grandson of one of the city magistrates through the ancient vaults of the Römer (the City Hall), was shown the three benches on which the three estates of citizens—the magistrates, the middle class and the craftsmen—sat separately on Council days, and how he listened with boyish delight in the Election Chamber to the story of emperors who had been chosen in that very room and whose portraits adorned its walls. He describes the bustle and excitement of the great fairs,—the whole city pouring forth to meet the procession, the solemn ceremonies of the Pipers' Court, the weird music of the shawm, sackbut and the oboe, the symbolic gifts of pepper and gloves.

"But what chiefly attracted the child's attention," says Goethe, "were the many little towns within the town, the fortresses within the fortress; viz., the walled monastic enclosures and several other precincts remaining from earlier times and more or less like castles—such as the Nuremberg Court, the Compostella, the Braunfels, the ancestral house of the von Stallburg family, and several strongholds which had been transformed into dwellings and warehouses. . . . Everything bore witness to a remote past when the town and its neighbourhood were seldom free from strife. Gates and towers still remained to mark the limits of the older city, and beyond these a new line of gates, towers, walls, bridges, ramparts encompassed the later growth."

The title which Goethe chose for his autobiography— *Poetry and Truth*—is at once elucidated and justified by this account of the environment of his childhood. With a sure instinct for what was essential and an imagination admirably balanced between the demands of science and of art, he has sketched, in a few broad but effective strokes, not only the outer Frankfort of his boyhood, but the inner life of an earlier time in which his own genius had its roots. Most striking of all perhaps is that last touch about the surviving mediæval enclosures,—the little towns within the town, the deserted shells in which the patrician burgher, the monastic community, the company of foreign merchants had been held aloof by a spirit of social exclusiveness. Of this spirit the boy still beheld a living instance as he gazed in fear and wonder through the gate of the Jewish quarter at the abodes of a people whose history had deeply impressed his growing mind. These survivals were not only well adapted to captivate the romantic imagination of a young poet; they bodied forth the earliest phase of the mediæval city; they furnish me with my clue, the starting point of my essay.

If we go back five centuries, from the middle of the eighteenth to the middle of the thirteenth century, and betake ourselves from Frankfort to London, we shall find the living world represented by the survivals of Goethe's boyhood. Let us suppose a knight from the country on a visit to his cousin, a London alderman, and riding in with him through the western suburbs of the city. As they pass through the Abbot of Westminster's lands at Kensington the alderman talks of business matters, and the knight is surprised to find how extensive and complicated the affairs of a London alderman are. He knew, of course, that his cousin, though, like himself, of mixed Saxon and Norman descent on one side, was descended on his mother's side from a well-known Jewish banker of King John's time, that he had married the daughter of a worthy Provençal knight, who had followed the Queen Eleanor into England. He knew also that his cousin had inherited several manors in Kent and Surrey, the produce of which was brought to the London market in his own barges, that he was a purveyor to the King and the nobility, and that he carried on a small loan office under forms adapted to the prejudices of the age. But he was not prepared to hear that the alderman was nearly as much in Southern France, where he bought wine for the King, as in England, that he was a farmer of the tolls at Queenhithe, and that he was about to have a share, along with an expert Italian, in coining the new gold pennies with which the King had resolved to celebrate his reign. A man of such high connections is evidently the right person with whom to see the town.

They make a slight detour to see the sights of Westminster. All at once they come to a great field filled with an immense crowd of traders of all nations, buying and selling at endless rows of stalls, eating and drinking, listening to jongleurs or friars. This is the Abbey Fair, and the King has compelled all the citizens of London to close their shops for a fortnight and to come and trade in the fields. The citizens are enraged and swear they will not come next year, but the King is determined to find money to finish the great abbey church which you can see a-building yonder. And so they pass the Abbey through a crowd of debtors, beggars and outlaws huddled within its precincts, and the great hall of Rufus, where the King's three chief judgment seats are set, where he lately kept the marriage-feast of his brother with thirty thousand dishes of meat, and where he has on occasion fed six thousand poor people at Christmas. "The citizen who gets

c

the contract on these occasions," says the alderman, "may make a fortune, but is as likely to lose one." They pass more houses of great magnates, then the King of Scotland's town house, and reach Savoy House, a palace newly built for the Queen's uncle. "A great household this," says the worthy citizen. "I supply them with a ton of tallow candles yearly and eighteen hundredweight of wax." Along the Strand facing the river are the Bishops' town houses,—Worcester Inn, Bath Inn, Chester Inn, Exeter Inn, and each has a little population of retainers, servants and craftsmen attached to it. When they reach the great establishment of the Knights Templars they find a crowd collected. A waggon of the King's treasures, guarded by men-at-arms, is passing through the gate. The Temple, in fact, serves as the national bank. They turn up the New Road (our Chancery Lane), pass Chichester House (lately the residence of the Chancellor, Ralph Nevill), and come to the house of the Black Friars, who have not yet transferred their site to the Earl of Lincoln for his New Inn and moved within the city wall. Then, turning the corner, they ride along Holborn with the Abbot of Malmesbury's town house on their right and the Bishop of Ely's town house on the left. As they descend the hill to cross the river Fleet the alderman points out the towers of the Knights Hospitallers across the fields at Clerkenwell, with the nunnery beside it, and around both a hamlet of settlers. There, too, they catch a glimpse, across the open ground of Smithfield, of the Priory of St. Bartholomew, with the beautiful church that still remains to us, and of the hospital, and the alderman would talk of the recent struggles of the city with the Prior about St. Bartholomew's Fair, and how the Priory was like to rob the city of the cloth trade unless it were sharply looked after. And now they have climbed Snow Hill and entered Newgate. The half-finished walls of the Grey Friars rise to their left. The choir is already built, by an alderman of the city, but three other aldermanic benefactors who are destined to furnish the chancel, the dorter and the chapter house are still in their cradles. "The builder of that choir," says the alderman, "my old friend William Joynour, God rest his soul, was a right worthy man. Although he had been in the King's service, as we aldermen all are

sooner or later—our trade wouldn't prosper if we were not,—
yet when he was mayor in '39 he stood manfully for the
liberties of the city against the King, who wished to force
a sheriff upon us." "Ah," says the knight, "that will be the
affair of the 'commune' I heard some talk of." "No,"
replies the alderman, somewhat disconcerted; "that is another
matter. That was a mere dispute we had with the riff-raff
of the city."

Threading their way across the market, in front of St.
Nicholas' Church, they pass the gate of the sanctuary of
St. Martin-le-Grand, through which they can see a whole
street of craftsmen's stalls, and behind them lodgings for
refugees, and so come to the open space on the north-east
side of St. Paul's, with St. Paul's Cross in the midst of it,
and the city belfry at one corner. "This is the place of the
Folkmoot," explains the alderman, "where the people of
London assemble to meet the King, or to hear a Pope's bull,
or to proclaim an outlaw. It would be better," he adds, "if
this old custom were allowed to drop. It is but an occasion
of turbulence, and all the serious business of city government
has long been transferred to the hands of the aldermen in
their separate wardmotes or collectively in their Court of
Husting at the Guildhall. But when the King, to serve his
own ends, has the bell sounded to summon the folk a great
crowd of pedlars and tinkers get together, and fancy that their
'Yea, Yea!' and 'Nay, Nay!' is to settle everything, and
that they are the commune of the city. Now, I need not tell
you, that it is we men of substance who are the commune,
we men of good birth and knightly breeding, who are
aldermen and the sons of aldermen, who know the law and
custom of the city, who own the land and carry on the trade.
It was we who gained the commune and the mayoralty from
King Richard, and it is only our wary policy that can preserve
them, for the King could easily persuade the crowd to shout
their liberties away.

"But, come," says the alderman, "lest you should think we
citizens were all a set of base handicraftsmen, let me show
you our place of arms." And he led the way to the open
space before the west end of the cathedral. "Here the men
of London meet to go forth to battle. And the lord of Castle

Baynard, whose towers you see near the river yonder, claims an hereditary right to marshal the host and lead it forth. On occasions of war he comes riding with nineteen mounted followers, and the mayor and aldermen coming forth from the west door, fully armed, deliver to him the banner of the city which bears the image of St. Paul in gold, but the face, hands, feet and sword are of silver. Even in time of peace the castellan of Castle Baynard has the whole parish of St. Andrew under his special supervision, with a court and stocks and prison of its own, and the mayor must summon him to all great councils and must rise to meet him and set him by his side, and as long as the castellan remains all judgments must be delivered by his mouth."

Then the alderman leads his companion between the bakehouse and the brewhouse, whence 40,000 loaves and 60,000 gallons of beer are provided for the great household of St. Paul's every year, down to Paul's Wharf, where the supplies from the manor houses are landed, and so along Thames Street to the Bridge and the Tower. Here the knight marvels at all the sights and sounds of a great port; but what surprises him most is to find how little of the river-side appears to be in the hands of the citizens themselves. Where the Fleet entered the Thames were the corn mills of the Knights Templars, then the wharf of the Archbishop of Canterbury, then Castle Baynard Wharf, then Paul's Wharf. Queenhithe, where all the corn supplies that came by water were landed, had just been secured for the city from the Earl of Cornwall by an enterprising mayor. The trade of Vintry was still mostly in the hands of Flemings and Gascons, and that of Dowgate was dominated by the German merchants, who had their gildhall in the Steelyard there. The bridge itself was controlled by wardens appointed by the King; and the wool exporters, whose business occupies the river front from Billingsgate to the Tower, were largely companies of Flemings and Italians. When the knight went to see the Guildhall he would find it in the centre of a quarter peopled by a separate community of Jewish bankers ruled by their own rabbis and controlling much of the finance of the city.

Nor was this atmosphere of exclusion and privilege confined to foreigners—to religious communities, to feudal magnates. The very fishmongers and weavers were not, in their trade matters, under the control of the city. Each of these trades had, like the Castellan and the Bishop, the Abbot and the Knights Templars, a law of its own and a special court to itself.

These feudal forms were in fact a survival from what had been till recently the dominant element in the constitution. At the beginning of the thirteenth century the King's letters to London had been addressed to the barons and citizens, and down to the middle of the fourteenth century there appeared at the funeral of an alderman a rider on a caparisoned horse, arrayed in the armour of the deceased and bearing his banner and shield, as at the burial of a baron of the realm. A class of similar pretensions were the landlords and the rulers of all the continental cities. They lived in fortified stone houses, fought on horseback, held office in royal or episcopal households and inter-married with the territorial nobility. If we seek an illustration, what better could we have than that of the first Mayor of London, Henry FitzAylwin, and his immediate descendants. Henry died possessed of broad lands in Middlesex, Kent, Surrey and Hertfordshire. His son married the heiress to an estate in Surrey held by a service of serjeantry in the King's kitchen. Joan, the daughter of this marriage, married Ralph the Furrier, a serjeant of the King's Chamber, upon whom the King bestowed various houses in London and Winchester, and who combined a lucrative trade in foreign skins with the management of an estate in Norfolk. Robert, the son of Joan, and the grandson of a FitzAylwin, who inhabited his grandfather's mansion near London Stone, married the daughter of the Earl of Derby, turned his grandmother's Surrey manor house into a castle, was lord of the hundred of Lambeth and a privy councillor. Many of the parish churches of London had been built by the early aldermen as private chapels and chantries, and half a dozen still bear their names.

These examples clearly explain the nature of the power exercised by these early rulers of the city. It rested primarily on the ownership of land, official position, and family connection; trade was only a secondary, though no doubt an important, source of wealth. This is true also of the great continental cities. In some cities trade became important very early, as at Venice and in Flanders. But even in the Flemish cities, whose mercantile origins M. Pirenne, their historian,[1] has clearly demonstrated, the traders became powerful through land ownership and official power.

The mediæval city owed nearly as much to this patrician class as it had done to its early bishops. What M. Pirenne says of their achievements in the great Flemish cities, Bruges, Ghent, Ypres, Douai, etc., might be applied with little modification to the early aldermen of London. They gave urban civilisation a permanent shape. They set up a system of municipal administration, of finance and taxation, of halls and markets, in which the democracy that followed them found little to alter. They built solid walls, constructed ports, cut canals, dredged rivers, established a water supply, organised transport and postal service, created a civic bureaucracy and inaugurated municipal records. But their greatest service was political. By dint of skilful negotiation, timely pressure and the judicious use of their opportunities and resources they laid a firm foundation for civic independence. The aldermen of London might claim with some justice that it was they who had won the liberties of the city. Undoubtedly there was another side to the matter. Towards the end of their régime, in the second half of the thirteenth century, a universal cry goes up from all the cities of Western Europe denouncing the abuse of magisterial power by the civil oligarchies. They are accused of keeping all civic offices in the hands of a clique, of laying all the taxes on the poorer citizens, of creating trade monopolies for themselves, of building their mansions on public land, of sitting in judgment on their own causes.

But whether used well or ill, their control over the destinies of the city during the twelfth and thirteenth centuries is undoubted. How did it pass from their hands?

The story of how this was accomplished is the story of the growth of the commune, upon which recent historical investigation has shed much new light. At the end of the eleventh and beginning of the twelfth century there was a widespread rising of the French cities against their episcopal

1. *Belgian Democracy : Its Early History* (Manchester, 1915), p. 119.

lords. The inhabitants swore a secret oath to live and die together, and took up arms in defence of their common liberties. The King of France favoured the movement as tending to weaken the feudal power of the bishops and to strengthen his own, and supported the commune by swearing to it himself. Thus there arose a new form of municipal independence in close connection wth the royal power.

The early historians of the communal movement—French scholars with popular sympathies—looked upon it as a great democratic upheaval—the first rising of the Third Estate. We now know that this was far from being the case. The communal movement was in fact carried to success by men of that very patrician class I have just been describing. Without their leadership success would have been impossible, and as a rule they retained control of the new political instrument they had created. But in one important respect their rule differed from that of the patricians. In the hour of common peril all classes of inhabitants—knights, clergy and citizens—had sworn the oath. They had all a tacit claim to share in the commune. That claim was full of possibilities.

The famous case of the London commune is the best example of this development. The policy of Henry II had seriously diminished the civic liberties which the patrician class had won for London, and they seized the opportunity presented by the absence of Richard to extort the grant of a commune and a mayor from John. But for all practical purposes the government of London remained the same. The aldermen presided in their ward-motes, gave judgment in the husting and chose the mayor and the sheriffs. Only under royal compulsion did they take any counsel with the rest of the citizens. But whenever a popular protest is heard it takes the form of an appeal to the communal ideal. "We are the Commune of London, and we ought to elect the mayor and the aldermen."

In that cry we seem to hear the first expression of the spirit of modern democracy. But democracy, ancient or modern, has done nothing without party discipline, and party discipline needs a basis in social organisation. If, therefore, we find the commune ultimately widened, we look for the social forces that achieved this result; and if the social forces from below were not strong enough we must examine those that were operating within the patrician class itself. It was for the purpose of gaining a brief preliminary survey of those forces that we accompanied the knight and alderman in their ride into the city of London.

We found the early civic community closely hemmed in by an environment—partly consisting of feudal households, but still more of communities in whose life its own life was very closely intermingled—bodies of monks and cathedral clergy, of templars and hospitallers, and foreign merchants. The period during which the city had been acquiring its political independence on a patrician basis had been marked by an immense growth of communities representing nearly every variety of religious, social and economic aim. There were communities of ecclesiastical and social reformers, of popular preachers, of slum workers, communities to house the pilgrim, to visit the prisoner, to tend the leper, to nurse the sick, to console the dying; communities of adventurous younger sons such as now go to the colonies or join a filibustering raid, communities of alien merchants, and last, but not least, communities of students of theology, and the arts, of law and medicine.

Yet, in spite of this extreme variety of membership and of purpose, most of these communities had some striking characteristics in common. They almost all represented at first an upgrowth from below; the powerful spontaneous impulse of new religious, social and economic forces to re-shape the old order, or to transfuse it with a new spirit. They were nearly all international organisations, and most of them united within a single community members of widely different social ranks and origins. The living principle of their organisation was in every case that of the religious fraternity, whilst its external and legal aspect was almost as universally that of a collective feudalism.

The functions which the gilds performed in the later period of civic development were performed by these communities for the city of the patrician period. They were largely recruited from the patrician class, and served as the natural organs of its expansion. The class out of which the early oligarchies of the cities were formed was increasing by additions from above and from below much too rapidly to find room within the limits of what was becoming more and more a close coterie of families. It cast off swarms in every direction—swarms of monks, of knights, or scholars, of merchant adventurers, and the communities which we find filling so large a space in city topography and operating so powerfully upon it as an environment were settlements from these swarms.

It is one of the many merits of Dr. Rashdall's *History of the Universities in the Middle Ages* to have emphasised the close analogy between those earlier associations and the later gilds. The rise of the universities, he says, was " merely a wave of that great movement towards association which began to sweep over the cities of Europe in the course of the eleventh century." Only a wave, but surely the most influential wave and also the most significant. For with the rise of universities the meaning of the whole movement becomes clear. It is laying the foundations of the liberal and learned professions, just as the later gilds were to lay the foundations of the mercantile and industrial professions. It may be a matter of dispute which group was the more important of the two, but both were undoubtedly essential to the fully-developed city, and still more to the realisation of that national life of which the city was to be the organ.

The direct control exercised over city life by these non-civic communities was very great. Monastic and clerical bodies and universities have ruled or dominated cities like Oxford, Cambridge, Bologna, Rome. Alien merchants were the earliest rulers of Prague and Stockholm, and still dominate the life of many a city in the East of Europe to-day. Acre and Tyre and Antioch during the rule of the crusading knights, were full of palaces, on whose roofs noble ladies walked with crowns of gold, whilst knights hospitallers from Yorkshire were collecting rents in the villages of the Archbishop of Nazareth. The Teutonic Order of Knights, turning aside from the failure of the crusades to Germanise Slavonic Europe, founded and ruled a group of Baltic cities that grew into a powerful commercial state. And three great orders of knights who dwelt in Castilian cities from which they had expelled the Moors almost constituted a separate estate in all the later monarchies of Spain.

But it is with the indirect effects of this stimulating environment on the growth of the city that I am chiefly concerned.

When we read the biographies of the men who played a leading part in the twelfth century we realise how much of the industrial freedom, the social fluidity, the *carrière ouverte aux talens* which we associate with city life could be attained by a skilful use of the opportunities offered by the earlier communities. Thomas " à Becket," born in Cheapside, the son of a London citizen, is educated by a community of monks, at Merton, enters a community of students at Paris, serves for a time as a civic official, acquires the accomplishments of knighthood, joins the feudal household of the Archbishop of Canterbury, enters deacons' orders, and enjoys a plurality of living, qualifies as a lawyer at the University of Bologna, becomes an Archdeacon, a clerical emissary to Rome, a royal favourite, Warden of the Tower of London, Chancellor of the Realm, Archbishop. The rungs in this astonishing ladder of promotion are furnished by the great households and the great communities. Or, to take another familiar instance— Carlyle's Abbot Sampson. He was not fortune's favourite like Thomas; he made his own way, and all the rungs of his ladder were provided by the Abbey at Bury St. Edmunds. Yet what a remarkable range of talents—none of them of a religious kind—does this monastic community find scope for. In the obscure poverty of his youth and early manhood, Sampson sees the world as a student at Paris, as an emissary at Rome. Later on he is an estate agent, an improving landlord, an architect, an acute financier, the progressive autocrat of a thriving town, the lord of fifty knights, a peer of Parliament, a Royal Commissioner.

Thomas of London and Abbot Sampson reached the goal of their ambition, but very few of the thousands who were thronging the Universities of Bologna and Paris or returning from an adventurous but profitless youth spent in the Crusades could hope to become archbishops and abbots. The applicants for what we may call Civil Service appointments must have been numerous, and one of the chief avenues to that service was controlled by the patrician oligarchy in the city. When that oligarchy showed signs of becoming an hereditary caste of inter-related families the discontent of outsiders of the same class must have been great. But discontent might have a nobler motive. The aldermen were oppressing the poorer citizens, and a fervent religious sympathy with the wrongs and sufferings of the poor was one of the strongest characteristics of the best minds of that age—the age of Arnold of Brescia, Peter of Lyons, and Francis of Assisi. The rising of London under William FitzOsbert in 1196 is best explained by a combination of both these motives. Only five years before the patricians had invoked all the forms of a popular insurrection to secure a restoration of civic independence on a firmer basis. John had sworn to the commune. The aldermen who held office for life as rulers of the wards and judges and administrators in the Court of Husting, had elected Henry Fitz-Aylwin to be mayor on the same tenure. There is no evidence that they gave the rest of the citizens any share in the constitution. Indeed, ten years after FitzOsbert's rising, and fifteen years after the grant of the commune, we find King John commanding the city to elect a special council of twenty-four to enquire into the wrongs inflicted by those who are set over the administration of the law and over the assessment and collection of taxes, and over the government of the city, who are accused of collecting much money from the common people and of withholding it from the King.

But the most definite and the most interesting things we know of FitzOsbert's rising relate to FitzOsbert himself. He had fought as a crusading knight in Portugal. He was learned in the law, and equally learned in the Scriptures. He preached to the people in the streets and open spaces—in St. Paul's itself. He took his texts from Isaiah, and declared it to be his mission to save the poor from the oppression of the rich. When he was dragged from sanctuary and hanged the common people accounted him a martyr. Such was London's first demagogue. But he was himself an alderman, a patrician, a knight, a learned man. In this class also belonged the later leaders of the commons of London, Thomas FitzThomas, Walter Hervy. The patricians were divided amongst themselves.

If we look around the cities of Western Europe in the latter half of the fourteenth century, a great revolution appears to have been accomplished. Instead of the hereditary rule of a score of families who circulated the offices amongst themselves, we find in some of the greatest cities a well-organised democracy. In place of or beside a court of land-owning magistrates, aldermen with feudal pretensions and aristocratic connections holding office for life, we find a Council elected annually from tradesmen by tradesmen. The increasing list of trades which share in this right of election shows the growing organised political power of the once despised craftsmen. Indeed, it is often enacted that no one can acquire the position of a citizen without being a member of a trade gild. The old patricians held craftsmen in contempt, and regarded commerce mainly as an official perquisite; their politics were of a feudal cast, they backed one episcopal candidate—one royal pretender—against another. The new civic community shuts its gates on feudal anarchy, and puts trade and industry frankly in the first place. How has this great change been effected? It looks at first sight as if the organised trades and handicrafts had gone up against the patrician stronghold, and carried it by storm.

But closer study does not confirm this notion. The great families still remain, or others have taken their place. Their collective hereditary control is gone, but their social prestige is still great, and they fill many elective offices both in the city and the gilds. In their style of living and dying they are as feudal as ever. Sir John Pulteney, who was Mayor of London in the middle of the fourteenth century, and lived in the mansion vacated by the Earl of Norfolk, endowed by his will seven priests to sing in a new-built chapel for his soul, and bequeathed ruby and diamond rings to his friends, the Bishop of London and the Earl of Huntingdon, that they might see his wishes properly carried out. Richard Whittington of famous memory made a similar will.

The trade gilds, on the other hand, when we know more about them, do not appear likely to have contrived the over-throw of the patricians. The poorer gilds are not strong enough, the more powerful gilds not sufficiently democratic. These greater gilds, indeed, had always been full of patrician members. If the gilds have conquered patrician feudalism in any sense, it can only have been by absorbing it. There has been no abrupt transition, no complete displacement of the knightly class by the bourgeois. The patricians have been gradually transformed from within.

Much of this gradual transformation is no doubt to be attributed to the gilds, but not by any means all of it. They came into the field when the work was already half done. Friendly societies of craftsmen had indeed probably existed here and there since Roman times, but these could not overthrow or undermine a strong patrician society. The gilds of merchants which were very active in the twelfth century cities, were certainly one of the chief means of transforming the garrisons of knights and officers into a mercantile community. But the merchant gild was so far from destroying the exclusiveness of the patrician class that it had become one of its chief organs. Its rules strictly forbid the admission of craftsmen—"men with blue nails." The craft gilds did not win collective recognition or play any effective part in political life till the end of the thirteenth century. Even then they won but partial and temporary victories, and they fought under patrician leaders.

And now let us suppose ourselves out for a final ramble through the city at a period part way between the Middle Ages and our own time—the end of the sixteenth century—the time of Shakespeare. We might have many guides who know and love every inch of the ground, but before all others we should be wise in preferring old John Stow, tailor, antiquarian, annalist, chronicler. We shall naturally find a great change from the thirteenth century. The population is at least five times as great; the shops and houses—especially those of the middle-class citizens—are immensely improved. If we could peep inside we should notice more improvement still. Tapestry, Turkey work, pewter, brass, fine linen and costly cupboards of plate worth £500 or £600. "For such furnishing," we are told, "is to be seen in the houses of knights, gentlemen, merchant men and other wealthy citizens." Most of the houses are the timber structures we think of as Elizabethan, but a few of the older stone houses that were inhabited by the city magnates of our earlier time still remain to attract the gaze of the curious and the study of the antiquarian. It is even more interesting to find the old feudal halls with their enclosures still shutting out the intrusion of the crowded city; the houses of kings, nobles, bishops; of monks, friars, hospitallers and Templars. Most of these appear to preserve a life that is modelled on the social ideals of the past, the style of the great household of the feudal baron.

We turn aside into one of these mansions—for our guide seems to take a certain affectionate pride in it. Here is a group of buildings in which a prince of the blood need not be ashamed to dwell—a great banqueting hall that will seat two hundred guests, with windows of Flemish glass and tapestries like those at Hampton Court. A chapel, a portrait-gallery, a king's chamber, an exchequer chamber, a treasury, a wardrobe, a pantry, a buttery, a larder, a kitchen, a store-house, a bakehouse, a brewery, a gardener's house and stables. Near the gateway stand a row of cottages. "These," says our companion, "are the company's almshouses, and yonder livings," he adds, pointing to the steeples of several adjacent churches, "are in the company's gift." "The Company." What company can this be? But we have no time to ask questions, for we are hurried in by our eager companion to see the records, and from these we only gather that the company is a fraternity of St. John the Baptist. In a great scroll under a baronial coat-of-arms, magnificently emblazoned, consisting of "Argent, a tent royal between two parliament robes, gules, lined ermine, on a chief azure a lion of England; crest the Holy Lamb in glory proper, supporters two camels; motto *concordia parvae res crescunt*." On the scroll we see a list of honorary members embracing seven kings, two princes, and bishops, dukes and earls by the score. The ordinary leading members we find are aldermen and sheriffs, baronets and knights, merchant princes and lawyers, whose sons and brothers hold high office in church and state. We are still puzzling over the social basis of this remarkable company, when, as we are examining the rich treasures of its wardrobe and, amongst other things, a richly-embroidered hearse-cloth —where pascal lambs alternate with heads of John the Baptist—we notice with some surprise several embroidered pairs of scissors. A light strikes us—the meaning of the " Parliament robes, lined ermine," clears up. " What company did you say this was?" we ask our companion. —John Stow draws himself up in astonished pride. " *My* company—the honourable Merchant Taylors."

We explain our former bewilderment and how we took this for a great baronial mansion. " There is no marvel in that," replies Stow; " it was once the house—though then much smaller—of Sir Oliver de Ingham, the Seneschal of Gascony under Edward III." He proceeds to show us parallel cases. Here is St. Helen's Priory, inhabited by the Leather-sellers. There is the mansion of the FitzWalters, taken over by the Grocers. Yonder the manor-house of the Nevilles, occupied by the Pewterers. And each of these communities appears to be a microcosm of the social life of the great city. Beneath the top dressing of aldermen, merchants and professional men there was a main body of wealthy shop-keepers, a large contingent of master craftsmen, a following of journeymen and apprentices, who in their spare hours read the chap-book lives of Sir John Hawkwood and Sir Richard Whittington—and aspire to marry their master's daughter and become Lord Mayor.

Gravely pondering on the social transformation that has been thus gradually wrought we pass out of Newgate—along Holborn—down Chancery Lane. Here, we remember, were formerly houses of chancellors, justices and bishops, and also the great community of Knights Templars. These we now find inhabited by gilds of lawyers, which together make up a great legal university. In all outward respects these communities resemble those we have left behind, in their feudal style, halls, gardens and chapels, arms and liveries and hierarchies of classes. But the residents are not all of civic extraction; indeed, one of their number has just written a book to prove the direct contrary. This is John Ferne of the Inner Temple, and his work is entitled " The Glory of Generosity." " Nobleness of blood," says he, " joined with virtue, counteth the person as most meet to the enterprising of any public service, and to that cause it was not for naught that our ancient governors in this land did with a special wisdom and foresight provide that none should be admitted

into the house of Court except he be gentleman of blood.''
Yet, notwithstanding this pardonable vaunt, we shall find the
sons of citizens mingling with the sons of gentry of every
degree in this training-ground of the statesmen and the
administrators of the growing nation.

NOTE.—The statement made on p. 13 about the constitution
of London in the reign of John is based upon a writ printed in
Rotuli Litterarum Clausarm, Vol. I, p. 64 (ed. 1833), which
appears to have been overlooked by the historians of London.

LONDON TRADESMEN AND THEIR CREDITORS.

Amongst the most valuable material for the economic history of the middle ages are the recognisances of debt which are frequently to be found in great numbers in the public archives of states and municipalities. As, however, the obligations thus recorded obviously partake in many cases of the nature of legal fictions, the interpretation of them is not a task that can be lightly attempted, except in cases where they constitute such a close sequence amongst themselves as to cast light upon each other, or where they can be brought into intelligible relations with the data of the same period. Both these conditions are fortunately fulfilled in the case of a series of recognisances contained in the " Letter Books " of the City of London, and in the following essay an attempt will be made to use this material as a means of illustrating the relations existing at the end of the thirteenth and the beginning of the fourteenth centuries between the shopkeepers of London in a variety of trades and their creditors.

Let us begin with the trade in wine, which is the foreign commodity that bulks largest in early commerce. Wine was the one article of daily consumption—for the middle and upper classes a necessity rather than a luxury—that had to be brought from abroad. It came chiefly from Gascony and the Rhineland. The *Liber Custumarum* preserves a vivid picture of the arrival of the Lorraine merchants with the wine fleet. They raise their ensign and sing *Kyrie eleison* as they approach London Bridge. There they may broach a tun of wine and sell it at a penny a stoop retail. After passing the Bridge they must wait two ebb-tides and a flood so that the Sheriff and the Chamberlain may come and have the first pick of their wares on behalf of the King; for the ships may be bringing not only wine from the district of Cologne and Mainz, but also gold and silver cups and precious stones, fine textiles and coats of mail that have come from Constantinople by the Rhine route. A London jury of goldsmiths, drapers and mercers will set a price on such of these wares as the King may fancy. Then when the Sheriff

D   19

and Chamberlain have claimed two tuns of wine below the mast and one before the masthead for the King's use at reduced prices, the Lorrainers are free to sell by wholesale first to the merchants of London, then to those of Oxford and Winchester, and afterwards to other merchants and the general public. If they wish to seek customers on shore they must first take registered lodgings and pay extra custom. In forty days they must depart, unless a storm or their debtor detain them.[1]

Acknowledgments of debt in the " Letter Books " show us that not only noble and rich merchants but also well-to-do craftsmen bought their wine direct at these times from the foreign merchant. Brokers were appointed by the city to facilitate the bargains, and credit was given for three or six months. Wine could be readily stored : it was as good as money : fines were generally levied in it in settling trade disputes. For this reason a class of native wholesale wine merchants was slow to develop ; especially as the Gascons, with the King's connivance, frequently ignored the restrictions set on their stay in the country. The King, through his officers, the Sheriff, the Chamberlain and Butler, dominated the wine market, both as a buyer and as a seller. He caused much of the inferior wine levied as custom to be sold, and bought large quantities of superior vintages. Gregory Rokesley and Henry le Waleys, who between them held the mayoralty for ten years under Edward I, began their careers as buyers of the King's wines. But as this was only one of their many mercantile interests they cannot be styled vintners. Matthew of Colombiers, who continued to be King's Chamberlain of London for twenty-one years, at the same period was a vintner of the official type. He sold the King's wines. Through his connections we may get a glimpse of the wine trade in general. One of Matthew's clients was a young citizen, Henry of Arras, who, despite his French name, had inherited rents and tenements in London, a manor in Buckingham, and a mill at Ware. But his wine business had not prospered ; in 1287 he owed Matthew of Colombiers 75 marks. To make matters worse, he had two younger brothers and two sisters upon his hands. While in these

1. *Lib. Cust.*, I, 61.

difficulties he made proposals 'of marriage to the daughter of a more successful wine merchant, William of Barage. William received him with words to the following effect: " Well, Henry, Philippa seems to have taken a fancy to you, and I've nothing against you as a son-in-law, but you've clearly no notion of business as yet. I'll tell you what I'll do. If you'll let me manage all your property for the next eight years, I'll pay your debts, I'll find jobs for your brothers, and husbands for your sisters, I'll back you with my credit, and I'll teach you the business."[1]

Now we know enough of William Barage's business to satisfy us that it was worth learning. It was evidently very extensive. In 1283 we hear of one of his young men, after transacting successful business as a commercial traveller in the North of England, being robbed of thirteen marks at Lichfield. In 1286 we find two of his agents setting out with a cargo for Norway. In 1287 and 1288 William himself was summoned across the Channel to transact some business for the King in Gascony.[2] But it is with the London business that we are especially concerned. This was of a very varied character. William acted as the London agent for a Gascon firm, and collected the instalments of their debts. He also lent his credit to back the bills of less substantial merchants than himself. He did the same for retailers of wine. Here is a case in point. Allan of Suffolk is a neighbour of William's, a taverner of Vintry Ward. His moveables are assessed at 5/- (William's at 20/-),[3] and his credit with Gascon firms is limited. On one occasion he buys £8 worth of wine in August, and arranges to pay £2 at Xmas and the rest by quarterly instalments of 30/-. When therefore we find Allan and William Barage acknowledging a joint debt of £38 to a Gascon firm we may be sure that William is lending Allan his credit for a consideration.[4]

William also bought extensively from the Gascon merchants on his own account. In November, 1282, for instance he orders from a Gascon firm seventy tuns of wine, worth £84, to be paid for next midsummer. The wine is

1. *Bk. A.*, pp. 95, 95, 102, 103, 118, 164.
2. *C.P.R.*, 1286, p. 249; 1287, p. 289.
3. Subsidy Roll of 1290, Public Record Office.
4. *Bk. A.*, pp. 71, 87.

apparently at Portsmouth. A week later a skipper from that port presents a bill for freight amounting to £24. William has not so much cash in hand, and it will take him a fortnight to collect it. He goes with the skipper to the Guildhall, acknowledges the debt, promises to pay it in fourteen days, and agrees to give the skipper fourpence a day with which he may have a good time in London whilst waiting.[1]

In the meantime William must get his wine landed from the Portsmouth vessel lying at Vintry Wharf. There are four gangs of winedrawers of twelve men each, for the union rule is that there shall never be less than twelve men to a job of this sort. Wine, like meat, should be " led, not drove." William, we will suppose, engages the " skip up " gang (their name promises alacrity), and their registered tariff is 2½d. for every tun carried into any of the lanes near the wharf where William has his cellar. But some of the tuns will no doubt have to pay the higher tariff of 8d. that they may be carried to William's customers, the taverners of the city. These are evidently sometimes indebted to the vintner, not only for their wine, but also for other stock-in-trade.—thus resembling the " tied houses " of our own day. Cristian the Taverner, for instance, acknowledges " that he has received from William Barage six casks of wine for sale, worth £13, which is stored in the cellar of Walter of Berden. Also four silver cups, weighing 40/3, which he would account for when he sold the wine."[2] It was unlawful for the wholesale merchant to retail wine on his own account. When the wine was delivered at the taverner's, the official searcher would come round and mark the end of the cask, after testing its quality, with the price at which it was to be sold. In 1311 the price of best wine was fivepence a gallon, of seconds fourpence, of the rest threepence. The cellar door was to stand open so that the customer might see that his wine was drawn from the right cask. In 1331, twenty-nine taverners closed their shops as a protest against unfair prices fixed by the authorities.[3] In 1364 a taverner who had sold unsound wines was condemned to " drink a draught of the same, and to have the remainder poured upon his head and to forswear his calling for ever unless the King will pardon him." [4]

1. *Bk. A.*, p. 55.   2. *Bk. A.*, p. 41.
3. Riley, *Mem.*, p. 182.   4. *Ib.*, p. 318.

A vivid picture of a tavern interior is presented by the verdict of a coroner's jury in 1277. On December 6 the keeper of a tavern in Ironmonger Lane was heard quarrelling with his man; and as they slept in the same room alone in the house, the man arose in the night, murdered his master, and hid the body in the coalhole. For two days afterwards he sat at the bench and sold wine; then he departed, taking with him all the portable property—a silver cup, a robe and some bedclothes. Three weeks later the vintner who had supplied the wine called for the money, and, finding the debtor gone, took all his stock-in-trade—a tun and a half of wine, worth fifty shillings, some small tables, cloths, gallons and wooden potels, worth two shillings. Not till the following Easter, when the landlord, Master Robert the Surgeon of Friday Street, set the shop to a new tenant was the murder discovered. The murderer was never caught. Chattels, adds the jury, he had none.[1]

Though the corn supplies of London did not arrive with the same pomp and ceremony as the wine fleet, their coming was not without a certain picturesqueness of its own. Most of it must have been brought from the ports on the East Coast in barges not unlike those that still make the same voyage and that lend the Thames so much of its charm to the eye of the artist. On its arrival at Queenhithe it must be measured by the cornmeters. There were eight of these officers, each of whom had three servants, and each servant one horse and five sacks. Bakers and brewers who came to buy their corn were charged $\frac{3}{4}$d. or 1d. for measuring and carriage of every quarter, according to the distance. We know many bakers acted as their own corn-merchants, since we find them forbidden to go out and forestall supplies. But more often a corn-monger intervened—" blader " was the term used—and played the same part in relation to the baker that the vintner bore to the taverner.[2] In 1301, for example, Thomas Lef, baker, acknowledges a debt of £35 to a blader, to be paid in instalments of £4 or £5, lasting over several years.[3] To take another more interesting case. We find a certain Henry

1. *Ib.*, p. 12.
2. *Liber Albus*, trans. by T. Riley, pp. 212, 229.
3. *Bk. B.*, p. 111.

le Coupere, baker, has run up a debt in 1301 of forty-three marks
to a goldsmith—who seizes his body, lands and tenements in
satisfaction—but who, finding this satisfaction very imperfect,
makes over the whole bad debt to a blader, Roger the Palmer,
on condition of receiving twenty-five marks in two years'
time; and Henry le Coupere completes the arrangement by
leasing his bakehouse to the blader. Obviously the corn-
monger intends to run the bakehouse on capitalist lines.[1]
Now, in the year 1310 Roger the Palmer, by virtue of his
office as Sheriff of London, is recorded as having arrested
a whole cavalcade of market-women who were bringing in
bread from Stratford and of condemning it as being of light
weight. The jury found that the bread was weighed when
cold and had therefore been condemned unjustly; but, as a
warning to the offenders, it was ordered that three halfpenny
loaves should be sold for a penny; whilst as an act of mercy
the bakeresses aforesaid should this time have such penny.[2]
A cynic might be tempted to infer that Roger's bakehouse
speculation had deflected his judicial mind from the strict
course of equity.

Let us descend one step in the scale to the baker who was
a substantial tradesman, using his own capital. He must
make his choice between brown bread and white. He must
not sell bread in his own house, but might either have it
hawked about by " regratresses," or sell it from a hutch in
the market twice a week—Wednesdays and Saturdays. He
was forbidden to deal with the breadwomen on any other
footing than thirteen to the dozen, and he must not give a
woman credit who owed debts to his neighbour. He must
stamp all his bread with a seal, and he might fatten swine
on his husks so long as he reared them in his own house
or elsewhere, and not in the streets or lanes of the city.[3]

The business of the trading baker was moreover elaborately
regulated by the Assize of Bread. According to the custom
of London this was made at Michaelmas by four sworn men,
who were to buy three quarters of corn—one in Cheapside,
one at Grasschurch or Billingsgate, and one at Queenhithe—
of which they were to make wastel bread, light bread and

1. *Bk. B.*, 40, 42, 43, 114.   2. Riley, *Mem.*, pp. 71-2.
3. *Liber Albus*, pp. 231-2.

brown bread, and to present the loaves while hot to the Mayor and Aldermen, who weighed them and fixed the weight of the halfpenny and farthing loaves for the year. Eightpence a quarter was allowed for expenses of baking The halfpenny loaf of best bread—called *demeine* bread or *simnels*—only weighed as much as the farthing loaf of wastel or seconds.[1]

The nature of the penalties by which these regulations were to be enforced was one of the most disputed points of mediæval municipal policy. An aldermanic chronicler lays it to the charge of the Earl of Gloucester's unconstitutional government of the city in 1258, that, instead of placing bakers in the pillory he exalted them in the tumbril. But he is still more scandalised by the leniency of Walter Hervy, the revolutionary Mayor of 1271, who let bakers off scot free, though every loaf was a third short weight.

Below the class of independent tradesmen who sell their own bread, there was a lower rank of bakers who worked upon the materials supplied by their customers. It has been a matter of lively dispute amongst those interested in mediæval origins, which of these two classes developed out of the other; but the evidence seems to point to their simultaneous existence in the earliest times. Sometimes both modes of business were combined, but there were obvious reasons why the municipal authorities should desire their separation. There is a case on record which not only serves as an admirable illustration of this point, but also proves beyond a doubt that the " public baker " was a widespread institution in mediæval London.

In 1327 John Brid, baker, " was attached to make answer as to certain falsehood, malice and deceit by him committed to the nuisance of the common people in that he did skilfully and artfully cause a certain hole to be made upon a table of his called a moulding-board pertaining to his bakehouse after the manner of a mouse-trap; there being a certain wicket warily provided for closing and opening such hole. And when his neighbours and others who were wont to bake their bread at his oven came with their dough—such dough having been placed on the aforesaid table, the said John had one of his household sitting in secret beneath the table who carefully

1. *Liber Albus*, pp. 402–4.

opened the hole and bit by bit craftily withdrew some of the dough aforesaid, falsely, wickedly and maliciously."

The Serjeant-at-mace and the Sheriff's Clerk who discovered this atrocity, having made a raid on the public bakehouses of the city, found no less than nine others provided with fraudulent tables, beneath which in many cases lay an accusing litter of dough. The sentence passed by the civic jury on these malefactors was a fine specimen of mediæval justice. All the bakers with dishonest moulding boards were to stand till vespers in the pillory : and those under whose tables dough was found were to have a quantity of dough suspended from their necks. Two women bakers were reprieved for a time because they declared that they had husbands, and that the deed was not their deed.[1]

As in the case of the vintner so in that of the goldsmith, we have a profession whose free development was overshadowed and retarded by the dominance of official privileges. Many of the early mayors and sheriffs of London had been at one time or another goldsmiths as well as vintners. They minted the King's money, acted as his exchangers, undertook the repair of the crown jewels or negotiated for a new supply, generally with the technical and financial assistance of Italian experts. In this sense Gregory de Rokesley, Mayor of London 1275–81, was a goldsmith. But he was also, as we have seen, a vintner, and he dealt largely in wool. We are concerned here with the goldsmith's trade as a distinct profession. It had been organised as a powerful gild in the twelfth century, and there are abundant evidences of its activities in the Letter Books dating from the end of the thirteenth century. First and foremost, the goldsmith was a highly skilled craftsman. He did not necessarily own the precious materials in which he worked. We find him going to the Guildhall to acknowledge the receipt of articles of plate entrusted to him by royal or noble personages for his manipulation. But more often he was a dealer as well as a worker in the precious metals. The first charter of the craft (1327) authorises the goldsmith to buy gold and silver plate, but only in the row of shops called Goldsmiths' Row, in Cheapside, where their work may be overlooked, and not in back streets where stolen

1. Riley, *Mem.*, pp. 162–5.

goods might be received. Other sources show us that the goldsmith's profession embraced men of every degree of wealth—from the merchant of aldermanic status to the poor craftsman, and the charter gave to the select body of dealers who had shops in Cheapside the control of the trade. It is, however, with other aspects of the goldsmith's calling that we are here more especially concerned. Before their expulsion in 1290 Jews had often followed the goldsmiths' profession, and in their hands it embraced the functions of the banker, the moneylender and the pawnbroker. During the civic revolutions that accompanied the Barons' Wars we see the Jews, who were frequently harried by the London mob, hastening to deposit their store of pledges with Gentiles who were not always faithful to the trust reposed in them. Did this side of the goldsmiths' calling disappear along with the Jews? It is often assumed that it did, and that the banking carried on by the seventeenth century goldsmiths was a " new-fashioned mystery." I think there is good reason to doubt this.

We shall see presently, from an examination of the acknowledgments of debt, that the lending of money and of credit was carried on in an occasional way by many of the wealthier merchants of all trades, and the same evidence seems to show that the goldsmiths, as was natural, specialised in this direction, and acted as channels through which both ready money and credit might flow. We find that a certain wealthy fishmonger named John Sterre was in the habit of advancing £2 to £5 in money to butchers, who no doubt needed short credit with which to buy stock and who came in little groups of twos and threes for a loan in common. Now John King, who twice forms one of these groups of borrowers, comes a third time accompanied by a goldsmith, Robert le Gloucester.[1] Why should a goldsmith be borrowing money along with a butcher? Is it not more likely that he is merely guaranteeing the butcher's solvency, " for a consideration "? But then we find Robert de Gloucester and other goldsmiths several times borrowing on their own account from the fishmongers. And moreover on looking further we find these same goldsmiths borrowing, about the same time, considerable sums from a

1. *Bk. B.*, pp. 163, 176, 150.

variety of people—Gascon wine merchants, Spanish leather merchants, London aldermen, corders, ironmongers, country gentry and clergy.[1] It seems difficult to account for these loans otherwise than as deposits. The sums vary from £3, or £4 to £25, and are generally entrusted to a group of two or more goldsmiths, who are jointly responsible for their repayment. It is not, I think, an extravagant inference to suppose that foreign merchants or country gentlemen should have left their surplus cash at the goldsmith's, who may possibly have encouraged the practice by acknowledging a debt of the deposit plus a small amount for interest. They might thus manage to borrow in spite of the usury laws; and by reversing the process they could contrive to lend at a profit; but as I find them borrowing oftener than lending, I imagine that their loans may have taken the form of purchasing articles of plate below cost price and holding them as pledges.

This form of banking, if it existed at all, was rudimentary. Most of the advances of capital on which London commerce and industry in the thirteenth or fourteenth century were dependent were made by merchants in the ordinary course of business, and as the way in which this was done has an important bearing on the social and constitutional history of London it will be worth while to follow it in some detail. The classification of London citizens made by Miss Curtis on the basis of the subsidy roll of 1332, will be found of great value in interpreting the data given by the acknowledgments of debt; and will enable us to realise with some clearness the economic relations of the several classes to the foreign capitalist and to each other.[2]

The foreign merchants who periodically visited England, whether they were drapers from Louvain and Douai, dealers in the light fabrics of St. Omer and Cambrai, mercers of

---

1. *Bk. B*, pp. 20, 30, 53, 70, 88, 113, 135, 137, etc., etc.
2. See later, pp. 44-5. The classes distinguished by Miss Curtis are here given for convenience of reference [Ed.].

Class.	No. of taxpayers in class.	Amount of tax.	Assessed value of property.
A.	16	£4 and upwards	£60 and upwards
B.	172	£1 — £4	£15 — £60
C.	141	10/- — £1	£7 10s. — £15
D.	253	5/- — 10/-	£3 15s. — £7 10s.
E.	502	1/4 — 5/-	£1 — £3 15s.
F.	543	8d. — 1/4	10/- — £1

Paris, Gascon wine merchants, or Spanish leather merchants, were apparently prepared to give from three months' to twelve months' credit (or even more) to all who could offer sufficient security. We may roughly distinguish—merely by their size—two kinds of "transactions," the larger of which—£20 to £80—we may call a "shipping order," and the smaller— £1 to £10—a wholesale order. But there were half a dozen kinds of transactions by which these two kinds of orders might be fulfilled. A foreign merchant might (1) supply a shipping order to the value of £30 or more on the single security of one of the larger merchants (classes A and B). Or (2) he might give credit for that amount to a shopkeeper (class C) if backed by the additional security of a merchant (class B), or (3) for a lesser amount on his own security. Or (4) he might accept the joint shipping order and joint security of half a dozen small traders (classes C and D). Or, finally, a merchant who had obtained credit from a foreigner for a shipping order might proceed to give a number of shopkeepers credit for wholesale parcels ordered from himself.

The two most significant records of the dealings of London tradesmen with foreign merchants and with each other are that of the cordwainers and that of the potters. The term " cordwainer " was applied in the thirteenth century to men of widely different social status. Early in the middle ages Cordova acquired a wide reputation for the leather which its craftsmen prepared from goats'-skins, and the manufacture, which afterwards spread to Barcelona, Northern Spain and Provence, supplied one of the main articles of commerce at the Champagne fairs. The merchants who dealt in it were called cordwainers. Gervase the Cordwainer, who was King's Chamberlain of London in 1227, and Sheriff ten years later, derived his name from the cargoes of Spanish leather which he brought to London. At the end of the thirteenth century the merchants of Northern Spain or their agents visited London and the English fairs with great regularity, and the leading cordwainers or skinners of London gave them " shipping " orders and received credit for sums of from £30 to £75. Besides these there were lesser merchants who took smaller parcels worth from £5 to £10, and occasionally as much as £15. But by far the commonest form of transaction was from two or three, four or five, six or eight of these lesser merchants and shopkeepers to combine for the purpose of buying a cargo. We have a record of nearly a score of these bargains stretching over a period of three years. The first is the most remarkable. A merchant of Spain, named John de la Founs, had brought, in August 1276, a cargo of leather valued at £133, and sixteen of the cordwainers of London arranged to buy it between them. They divided themselves into two groups—one of seven, the other of nine— and each became jointly and severally ´responsible for half the cargo, *i.e.* £66. This was equivalent to the purchase by each member of the smaller group of over nine pounds worth of leather, and by each member of the larger group of seven pounds worth. In the later transactions the groups were generally smaller and the average share larger. A fortnight later five members of the larger group combined to buy a second lot of £78 from a Gascon firm, whilst the leading member of the smaller group bought on his own account a large parcel of £30.[1] We do not know anything about the internal arrangements of these groups of cordwainers, but we may safely infer that they were mainly composed of traders and manufacturers of classes C and D, who, by co-operation, were enabled to put themselves on a bargaining level with importing merchants of classes A and B.

But most of the cordwainers of the fourteenth century were small craftsmen and shopkeepers of class E, and we get a glimpse of their economic status in the recorded transactions of Ralph Poyntel, a well-to-do leather merchant and currier, who acted as a middleman between the foreign merchants and the craftsmen. He buys a lot of £20 and sells it in parcels of from 25/- to £5. One of the largest of his customers is a certain cordwainer John Tilli, who buys, in 1281, a parcel of leather worth £7. 10s. John Tilli's affairs seem to have prospered (in 1290 he belonged to class C, being assessed at 13/4 in Cordwainer Street Ward), and he wished to extend his business. The gild rules generally forbade a member to have two shops, but this obstacle could be surmounted by setting up a man of straw. In 1286, therefore, John Tilli joins with Ralph Poyntel in setting up a certain

1. *Bk. A.*, pp. 8–9.

Richard " the Sewer " with a stock worth £11. 13s. Richard covenants to remain in their service three years, to render a yearly account of all money and goods received and profits made, whilst Ralph and John agree to provide Richard with all necessaries and to pay him a yearly stipend of one mark for his service.[1]

Here we have a situation parallel, only with harder conditions, to that of the taverner in the tied house, and such arrangements were common in other trades.

Let us now transfer our attention to the economic conditions of a craft which possesses much æsthetic and antiquarian interest—that of the potter. The potters of the fourteenth century London were not makers of earthenware, but workers in copper and brass, and bell-founders. The early potters, like the early cordwainers, were importers of foreign goods—mostly kitchen utensils known as *dinanderie*. The brasswork of Dinant, near Namur, had acquired a European reputation, and a class of wealthy exporters had arisen in that city, of whose mercantile operations M. Pirenne, the historian of Belgium, has recently made an interesting study. These *marchands batteurs*, as they were called, brought large quantities of their wares to England and took back English wool and tin. Two wealthy London merchants, Walter the Potter and Richard the Potter, who made their wills in 1280 and 1281, in all probability derived their names from their extensive dealings in *dinanderie*. Walter the Potter, senior, was an alderman, and built the Chapter House of Grey Friars. Richard the Potter lived in Cheapside and had much property in London besides a shop at Bury St. Edmunds and land at Boston and Winchester. Richard's nephew, Walter the Potter, junior, and Henry, Walter's brother, to whom he left the shop and the land, were extensively engaged in the same business, as was also Alan the Potter, another nephew. The merchant of Dinant, who appears to have done most of the English trade at this time bore the rather invidious name of Aubrey le Pecherous; and in 1287 we find Walter the Potter, junior, and Henry, his brother, giving him a shipping order for £34 worth of *dinanderie* to be paid for in four instalments at the fairs of St. Ives, St. Botolph's, and Winchester.[3]

1. *Bk. A.*, pp. 26, 41, 97, 141.
2. *Bk. A.*, p. 106. 3. *Cal. Wills*, I, 49.

In this transaction Walter and Henry were only receiving the ordinary mercantile credit. The case of another of Aubrey's clients is more interesting because it not only shows us how a London merchant might become dependent upon foreign capital, but also reveals the process by which the possession of real property on which the power of the aldermanic class was originally based, was gradually dissipated in unsuccessful trading operations. The Durhams were one of the ruling families of London during the thirteenth century. They were connected by marriage with the Viels, the Basings and the Buckerels.[1]. William of Durham, Alderman of Bread Street Ward, who died in 1283, had apparently lost much money in trade. Two years before his death he was obliged to hand over for eight years' occupancy some valuable property near London Bridge to Richard the Potter, to whom he owed eighty marks.[2] The assumption that William had been a potter—a dealer in *dinanderie*—is strengthened when we find his widow, Sabine, shortly afterwards marrying Adam le Potter at the sign of the Rose. Now Sabine (née Viel) had some real property in her own right, and soon after this second marriage we find her going with Adam the Potter to convey this property for a term of years to Aubrey le Pecherous, in return for which he supplied them with capital to the extent of forty-six marks. This was in 1284.[3] In 1287 and 1288 Aubrey supplied Adam the Potter on credit with two lots of £20 each.[4] On the first of these occasions credit was given for a fortnight only; but, on the second, payment had to be arranged for by twelve instalments spread over four years, and two other potters had to provide security for Adam's debt. Adam is evidently steadily going downhill. Sabine Viel's second marriage has been more unfortunate than her first. We should not be surprised to find the pair going, later on, to one of the aldermanic moneylenders. And we actually do find that in 1311 their son Adam has become a desperate character, has made a murderous attack on Alderman Richard of Gloucester, and has had to be bailed out by several more prosperous members of his father's calling.

So far the potters we have met with have been dealers

1. *Cal. Wills*, I.
3. *Bk. A.*, p. 158.
2. *Bk. A.*, p. 153.
4 *Ib.*, pp. 105, 109.

in foreign goods. But a home industry has been growing up, and we can watch its beginnings. In 1277 Walter the Potter, senior, the alderman, helped to set up a working coppersmith named Nicholas of Stortford by advancing him £5 in money and copper. Nicholas had no security to offer but his tools and his workshop, and he undertook not to alienate either of these till the debt was paid.[1]

Another working craftsman of this trade, John the Potter, was a man of more resources. In October 1288 he undertook a contract with the Abbot and Convent of Ramsey, in Huntingdonshire to make a new lavatory for them "of good and durable metal, thirty-three feet long and two and a half feet high, with sixteen copper keys (clavifus) of subtle design and richly gilt, and fillets through the centre." For this piece of work he was to receive £30 and a gown. A third of the money was to be paid in advance to enable him to get materials, a third in six months' time, and a third when the work was completed. John was to ride down to Huntingdonshire with his two journeymen. The Abbey would find food for horses and men whilst they stayed. Master and men were each to have two loaves of bread and two gallons of beer, a dish of meat or a dish of fish every day; but one of the master's loaves was to be "monks' bread," and both his gallons were to be drawn from the Convent cask, whilst his men were to be content with the bread and beer given out in the hall to the servants of the Abbey.[2]

Richard of Wymbush—a third working potter of our acquaintance—was probably even better off than John the Potter. His credit was good with various aldermen for £9 or £10, and we find a tiler owing him twenty marks.[3] He had formerly cast a bell for Holy Trinity Priory, near Aldgate, and in 1312 he contracted to supply another as nearly as possible in tune with the first. The second bell, though not so large as the first, was to weigh over a ton. Richard was to have six months to complete the task, and the Priory was to lend him the first bell to work by. We are glad to hear that the job was finished to the Prior's satisfaction.[4]

Such great contracts as these do not of course represent

1. *Bk. A.*, p. 15.
2. *Ib.*, p. 172.
3. *Bk. B.*, pp. 54, 129.
4. Riley, *Mem.*, p. 100.

the everyday work of the potter, but they show that London craftsmen were by this time capable of large undertakings. We may get an idea of the nature and value of the more ordinary productions of the potter from a list of household utensils seized in 1303 for arrears of taxes. The cooking pot and other kitchen utensils were the readiest articles to the hand of the tax collector, and three potters, including Richard of Wymbush, were upon the jury specially appointed to value the goods, which included :—

One brass pot, weighing 14 lbs., value 21d.

One brass pot weighing 18 lbs., value 2s. 6d.

One kettle, value 14d.

One brass posnet, weighing 6 lbs., value 10½d.[1]

This record may fitly conclude with a document that shows us the London potters on the point of organising themselves as a craft. In 1316 a number of those engaged in making and selling brass pots came before the mayor and aldermen to complain of the abuses perpetrated in their trade. Many persons, they declared, who busied themselves in buying and selling brass pots, and especially a certain Alan the Shopper, were in the habit of buying pots of bad metal and then putting them on the fire that they might sell them as good second-hand pots on Sundays and other feast days in Cheapside; and these pots when exposed to great heat melted and came to nothing. They received permission to elect eight men to make an assay to determine how much lead should go to the hundredweight of copper; and it is of special interest to note that four of these men chosen are described as " dealers in the said trade," and the other four as workers and founders of pots.[2]

G. UNWIN.

1. Riley, *Mem.*, pp. 47–9.
2. *Ib.*, p. 118. The founders are all on the tax roll of 1319. One belonged to Class F, one to Class E, two to Class D. The dealers in pots on the tax roll belonged to Classes B and C.

THE LONDON LAY SUBSIDY OF 1332.

I. THE TAX AND ITS ASSESSMENT.

The London Lay Subsidy Roll of 1332 is to be found in the Public Record Office. It consists of seven sheets of parchment; the entries are made in double columns, and all the sheets, except the seventh, are written on both sides. The roll is in a state of good preservation; only eleven items are missing. In Cordwainer Ward the pence are torn off in two of the amounts; in Farringdon Without the sums paid by four persons, and in Cripplegate Within, those of five people are wanting.

The value of the roll may be realized when it is stated that there is only one subsidy roll of London in print—that of the lay subsidy of 1411–12.[1] The earlier roll is of greater importance since it shows the incidence of the normal form of taxation— a fraction of moveables, while the later one is a record of an exceptional impost on rents.

The year 1332 is memorable in the history of taxation. The disputed right of the King to tallage was then probably claimed for the last time. Tallage had not been expressly forbidden in the "Confirmatio Cartarum," and was levied in 1304 apparently without opposition. In 1312, however, London and Bristol made a strong resistance to a similar demand by Edward II. The Londoners finally escaped payment by raising two loans amounting to £1,400, which were to be allowed for in the collection of the next general aid. The tax apparently proved unprofitable, and was not revived for twenty years.[2] Then Edward III issued letters for the collection of tallage on June 25th, 1332.[3] The next Parliament did not meet till September 9th, and the subject of taxation was almost immediately opened up. "They granted the King one Disme and one Fifteenth to be levied of the Laity, so as the King will live of his own, without grieving his subjects with outragious prises and such like."[4] The King

1. Edited by J. C. L. Stahlschmidt. *Archæologia*, XLIV, 56–82.
2. Stubbs, II, 545–8.   3. *Rot. Parl.*, II, 446.
4. "Cotton's Abridgement of Records," quoted by Rylands, *Lancs. and Cheshire Record Society Miscellanies*, II, vi.

in return recalled the commissions for the collection of tallage.[1]

The grant that replaced the tallage was a fraction of moveables, which, known in England as early as 1166, had been a frequent form of taxation since Henry III's reign.[2]

But whilst in similar grants previous to 1332 the fractions had varied from a fortieth to a fourth, after that date they were always a tenth and a fifteenth, as in 1332. Moreover this was the last time that in London[3] and many other places the amount of taxation due from them was fixed by the valuation of goods. In 1334 (professedly owing to complaints of the strictness of the 1332–3 collection, more probably in order that the King might know beforehand how much a subsidy would yield, and not be the loser through any misdeeds of the collectors, since the fixed amount could be demanded from each district), the writ ordered, that in place of assessment, the royal commissioners should treat with the men of the different districts for a composition for a tenth and a fifteenth. The method of assessment was only to be used in case of a refusal to compound, and the amount levied was not to exceed the sum assessed in 1332.[4] The settlement made in 1334 proved permanent, and accordingly the fractions of moveables were stereotyped as a tenth and a fifteenth. This arrangement made the tenth and fifteenth merely a name for a tax levied as in 1334, and known to yield from £38,000 to £39,000.

The difference in the fractional amounts of the subsidies originated in the payment of tallage.[5] The ancient demesne of the Crown with the boroughs contributed in a larger proportion than the counties. London, however, obtained the privilege from Edward III in 1327 of being assessed with the counties at a lower rate.[6]

Edward maintained the concession, though he seems to have regretted his generosity. In a writ to the Mayor and

1. *Rot. Parl.*, II, 66.
2. There were four taxes on moveables in Henry III's reign; nine in Edward I's reign. *Cf.* J. F. Willard, *Roy. Hist. Soc. Trans.*, 3rd Series, Vol. VII, p. 168.
3. *Bk. F.*, p. 68. In December 1335 London is said to have compounded for the fifteenth.
4. *Rot. Parl.*, II, 447.   5. Dowell, I, 58.
6. *Liber Albus*, pp. 146–7. It was renewed by Henry IV, *ib.*, p. 168. Stubbs, II, 545, gives the reference, but writes Richard II in place of Henry IV.

Aldermen in 1335 he signified his readiness to accept the sum fixed according to the county rating, " although inadequate." [1]

There were other advantages in being assessed with the counties. The exemption of goods from taxation was much larger in their case. In the boroughs the only exemptions in 1332 were " a dress for the man, and one for the woman, and a bed for both, a ring and a chain of gold or silver, and a girdle of silk that they use every day ; and also a goblet of silver or mazer from which they drink." [2] But in the counties, armour and riding horses, all the jewels and dresses of the man and his wife, and their vessels of gold and silver were exempted.

These exemptions were considerable when we remember that people spent their money in the middle ages on ostentatious personal display, on rich garments and jewels and vessels of gold and silver, rather than on costly furniture. [3] This is proved by the wills of the Londoners. A bed is almost the only piece of furniture which was ever bequeathed. Their treasured possessions appear to have been exactly those mentioned in the list of exemptions, with the exception of riding horses and perhaps armour. [4] To take one example. Richard Constantyn left to his son two goblets of silver, a silver water vessel, a sapphire of value and a silver ring with a precious stone. To his daughters he bequeathed a silver goblet each, and to his wife all his vessels of silver. [5] The value of the Londoners' clothes may be judged by the fact that a third best robe sometimes formed a separate bequest.

An additional privilege which London secured in being taxed with the counties was that no payment was demanded from those whose possessions were worth less than ten shillings, whereas the limit in the boroughs was six shillings [6] in 1332.

The ways of the mediæval taxgatherer were marked by a

1. *Bk. F.*, p. 68.
2. *Rot. Parl.*, II, 447. Also *C.P.R.*, quoted and translated by Rylands. *op. cit.*, p. xi. The exemptions of 1332 were the same as those of Edward I's reign from 1283 onwards, with the exception of 1301. Prof. Willard, "Taxes upon Movables in Edward I's reign," *Eng. Hist. Rev.*, July 1913, p. 517.
3. Rylands, *op. cit.*, II, xi.
4. Robert de Lincoln and Thomas Corp left armour, however, *Cal. Wills*, I, 477 and 624.
5. *Cal. Wills*, I, 482. 6. *Rot. Parl.*, II, 447.

leisureliness which must have been trying to a King in need of supplies. In the case of the grant made in September 1332, although Edward was in great need of money owing to the Scotch war, the tax was not paid into the Exchequer till 1334. The dates for the delivery of the money at the Exchequer were fixed in the first place as February 3rd and May 31st, 1333. These were the times named in the writs of appointment of collectors, issued on September 16th, 1332.[1] But the writs ordering the assessment were not issued apparently till 1333, and in them the dates for the payment of the tenth and fifteenth were postponed to April 4th and September 30th, 1334.[2]

The method of assessing the taxation was the same for the boroughs and counties. It was usual to have two chief taxers for each district; but in 1332 the first intention seems to have been to associate two high officials with two men of the city. John de Stonore, second justice of the King's Bench, and William de Denum, baron of the Exchequer, were appointed with Richard de Hakeney and John de Preston,[3] aldermen of London[4] as collectors of the fifteenth for London. But eventually the two latter were alone entrusted with the duty.[5] The chief taxers were commanded to choose four or six, or more if required, from the most lawful and most esteemed men of each district.[6] The administrative divisions of London naturally formed the districts for the assessment of the taxation. The wards, at this time twenty-four in number, presented no great inequality of size, except those which stretched beyond the walls of the city. With regard to those to the east of the Walbrook (the natural division of the city), the scantiness of the population counteracted the extent of the wards. But in the west, the large size and population of Farringdon and

1. *Foed.*, II, ii, 845. The day after the Purification and the day after Trinity Sunday are the dates given.
2. This postponement may not apply to the whole country. It appears in *C.P.R.* 1330–4, p. 484, for Northumberland. Northumberland was in an exceptional position owing to the disturbances of the Scotch War and the death of one of the collectors. But in the assessment writ in *Rot. Parl.*, II, 447, which appears to have a general reference, the later date is given for payment, and Sharpe refers to it as if it were identical with the London writ, *Bk. F.*, p. 290. (The dates are the day after the close of Easter and the day after Michaelmas.)
3. *C.P.R.*, 1330–4, pp. 357–9.
4. Beaven, *Aldermen of London*, pp. 22, 137.
5. *C.P.R.* 1330–4, p. 359. Also see the heading of the roll.
6. *Rot. Parl.*, II, 447.

Cripplegate made it convenient to divide them into a ward within and a ward without for the purposes of taxation.[1] The size of the ward would doubtless determine the number of collectors; in 1319, six or more were selected from each ward for the collection of a twelfth.[2]

The status of the taxers seems to have varied considerably. Henry de Preston, collector for Dowgate in 1334, possessed goods of the value of £20 in 1332, but William de Sabrichesworth in Limestreet[3] had moveables worth only twenty shillings.

The deputy assessors had to swear by the Holy Evangelists to state fully what goods the inhabitants of each district possessed and to tax them at their true value. The Parliamentary grant was a fraction of the moveables possessed on September 29, 1332, but in the writ for the collection it was stated that all goods acquired since that date had also to be taxed. The collectors were to proceed hastily with the assessment, and "reduce it into writing and put it in a roll written quite plainly." They were to deliver one roll to the chief taxers and retain a duplicate themselves.

The business of the chief taxers was to check the work of their subordinates, and report any misdeeds to the Treasurer and Barons of the Exchequer. As soon as they received the indentures of the collectors they were to cause the tax to be raised. The chief taxers drew up two rolls; one they retained to raise the taxation, the other was presented at the Exchequer with the first payment of the tax. It is one of these two rolls that has survived. The collectors were taxed by the chief taxers, and their names are doubtless entered in the roll. But the taxation of the chief taxers and their clerks was reserved to the Treasurer and Barons of the Exchequer, so they were not enrolled with other Londoners.[4]

The collectors would probably proceed according to parishes, but it is impossible to prove this, as the residences of the men whose names are enrolled can seldom be discovered. They may have conducted their inquiries on a plan like that

---

1. For further proof of what is found in the roll, see *Bk. F.*, pp. 4, 9, 27, 33. In the case of Farringdon the custom was extended by the Statute of Richard II, and since 1394 Farringdon has been represented by two aldermen (Beaven, *op. cit.*, p. 144), but Cripplegate has never attained to this dignity.

2. *Bk. E.*, p. 123.   3. *Bk. F.*, pp. 33-4.

4. *Rot. Parl.*, II, 447.

adopted at Colchester in 1301.[1] The taxers there visited the treasure-chest first, then the chamber and the rest of the house, passing from the kitchen to the brewery, larder and granary, when the houses contained these offices. Afterwards they directed their attention to the stock-in-trade or implements of handicraft, and, lastly, to the animals, hay and fuel.[2] The tax collectors valued each article separately in 1301; in 1332 they probably made a rough estimate of the goods, as the items are not enrolled. The large number of round sums suggests this. Fractional amounts are not found in five of the wards, and they only occur once in seven wards. The collectors in Bassishaw and Walbrook appear to have done their work more thoroughly as fractional sums ranging from £4 8s. 10¾d. to 9¾d. are common.

The assessment was apparently not strict, as the highest amount paid was only £8, whereas in 1319 several citizens paid £20. Also London paid only £670 7s. 5¾d. according to the roll, although 1332 is supposed to have been a heavy year,[3] and yet paid £733 6s. 8d. in later years. The small payment was not due to an inability to meet the demands of the collectors,[4] as in the case of John de Triple, who at his death owed £53 16s. 8d. for divers assessments,[5] since it has already been seen that the rolls were drawn up from the assessment and not the levy of the tax.[6] This is further proved by the 1319 roll (also probably by the 1334 roll),[7] where there is a memorandum, at the end of the account of some of the wards, of the amounts which had been assessed and collected, and the sum which consequently still remained to be paid. The total of the separate items equals the amount of the assessment. The smallness of the amount paid may be accounted for in the following ways. Some of the wealthy

---

1. The poll tax of 51 Edward III was drawn up according to parishes.
2. Dowell, I, Appen. II, p. 232. He translates and arranges the information given in *Rot. Parl.*, I, 243 *seq.*
3. *Ib.*, I, 86, says it seems to have been heavier than the last grant of a fifteenth and tenth, but contrast the larger amounts paid in Edward I's reign. Willard, *Eng. Hist. Rev.*, July 1913, pp. 517 *seq.*
4. *C.P.R.* 1338–40, p. 76. This appears to have been one of the causes of Essex being in arrears in taxation in April 1338.
5. *Bk. E.*, p. 198.
6. *Ante*, pp. 11–12; c.f. Willard, *Eng. Hist. Rev.*, July 1913, p. 517.
7. *Bk. F.*, p. 3. See such entries as "John Lovekyn and his fellow collectors of the Ward of Bridge £51 18s. 8d., viz. of £53 assessed in the said ward."

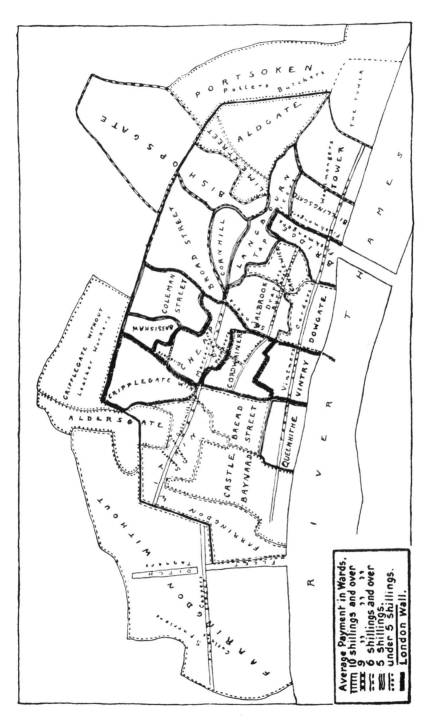

THE RELATIVE WEALTH OF THE LONDON WARDS AS SHOWN IN THE SUBSIDY OF 1332.

London citizens gained exemption from taxation, while the aldermen seem to have been persistently guilty of attempts at evasion. Edward II and Henry IV had to command that the property of aldermen should be taxed in aids, tallages and contributions by men of the wards in which such aldermen resided in the same manner as the property of other citizens.[1] The names of seven of the twenty-three secular alder- men of the city are absent from the 1332 roll. The assessors were also usually dishonest. In 1334 there were complaints that the collectors in 1332 had con- nived at evasion, and applied to their own use great sums which they had extorted.[2] This accusation has no special reference to London, but the morals of the city were evidently not superior to other parts of the country. In 1346 in the assessment for the loan of 3,000 marks to the King, one hundred and sixty-two men, many of them assessors, had their payments increased, or they were inserted where they had previously been omitted, by order of the King's writ.[3]

Before leaving the taxation of London it is interesting to consider the proportion which it bore to the taxation of the whole country. This cannot be definitely stated for 1332, as there is no evidence how much the subsidy yielded in that year. But it is probable that the amounts paid by different parts of England were in the same ratio as in later years. The average yield of a tenth and fifteenth after 1334 was from £38,000 to £39,000[4] and the amount which London had compounded for in 1334 was £733 6s. 8d.[5] This is the sum which the city paid in 1373 according to the subsidy roll of that year, which is the only printed roll, showing the taxation of the whole country under Edward III.[6] It affords a means of comparing the amounts contributed, and consequently the wealth of London with other parts of England. Only three

1. *Liber Albus,* pp. 144 and 167.
2. *Rot. Parl.,* II, 447.
3. *Bk. F.,* pp. 148–9 n. The increase varied from 20/- to £25. They are in many cases the same men as were enrolled in 1332.
4. Dowell, II, 86. In 1344 it appears to have fallen as low as £28,682. Ramsay, *The Antiquary,* I, 158. The amount was £38,170 9s. 2½d. in 1373. *Archæologia,* VII, 337–47.
5. *Bk. F.,* p. 68. The King says they had compounded for 1,100 marks. *Bk. F.,* p. 4, also shews that this was the amount paid in 1334.
6. .*Archæologia,* VII, 337–47, edited by Topham.

other towns were assessed separately, like the counties, and their payments are insignificant in comparison. The largest city of the North, York, was assessed at £162; the flourishing port of Kingston-on-Hull paid only £33 6s. 8d., and Bath £13 6s. 8d. It is with counties that London must be compared; in the fourteenth century Leicestershire, the West Riding of Yorkshire and Nottingham had almost the same taxable capacity.

II. The Size, Wealth and Occupations of the Population of London in 1332.

The question of the size and wealth of the population of London naturally arises, when the amount which London contributed to the exchequer is under discussion. It is certain that London, like other mediæval cities,[1] was much smaller than has generally been supposed; it is not yet possible, unfortunately, to estimate the exact size of the population. There is no record of the population of London till the poll tax of 1377,[2] and it is difficult to reconcile the numbers given there with the 1,636 names contained in the subsidy roll of 1332. In 1377 there appear to have been 23,314 lay persons over 14 in London, which suggests a total lay population of about 30,000.[3]

In normal times London might double her population in a generation. But in the forty-five years between 1332 and 1377 there were three visitations of the pestilence. The excessive number of deaths might be regarded as counteracting any increase of population; but the flow of outsiders into London was no doubt accelerated in these years. It is well known that many villeins left the homes of their predecessors at this time. Great numbers of them would doubtless be attracted to the capital. On the other hand, artisans from

1. *Cf.* Pirenne, *Les Anciennes Démocraties des Pays Bas*, pp. 129–135.
2. Topham, *Archæologia*, XLIV, 237, shows that the roll is not accurate. 1,376,442 are stated to have paid the tax in the whole country, but the sum paid, £22,607 2s. 8d., contains only 1,356,428 groats. The clergy were entered on a separate roll.
3. This number is obtained by reckoning the children as 30 per cent. of the total, the most moderate estimate that can be allowed for the period. Joseph Cuvelier, *Les Dénombrements des Foyers en Brabant*, pp. xci–xcii, points out that a higher percentage is probably more correct for the middle ages, when births and deaths were of more frequent occurrence than in modern times.

other towns and younger sons of yeomen who would usually account for much of the increase of London's population, would probably have little incentive to leave their homes, now that the scarcity of labour brought them higher wages. This suggests that the population in 1332 cannot have been much smaller than the 30,000 of 1377, but the numbers given in the roll would seem to preclude the possibility of so large a population. It must be remembered, however, that some evaded taxation, and that many were exempt from payment, by the limit of ten shillings. In 1301, when there was no exemption, 33 per cent. of those who paid the tax in Colchester [1] possessed goods of less value than ten shillings. The number would be larger in London, and may perhaps be reckoned as 50 per cent. This would raise the number of householders to 3,272. The number of women, children and servants who were not taxed is problematic. Authorities on the subject usually reckon about five to a household, which brings the total lay population of London in 1332, up to 16,360. This is the largest computation that can be made on the basis of the subsidy roll, and if correct, it would follow that London must have doubled its population between the years 1332 and 1377.

The roll affords a means of judging how the wealth of the city was distributed among those who possessed goods of greater value than ten shillings. The taxpayers may conveniently be divided into six classes according to the amount of their assessments.

A statement in tabular form giving the numbers of each class as found in the roll will indicate the social stratification of the city.[2]

A.   16 with possessions of value of £60 or more, paying £4 and over.

B.   172 with possessions of value of £15—£60, paying between £1 and £4.

C.   141 with possessions of value of £7 10s.—£15, paying between 10s. and £1.

D.   253 with possessions of value of £3 15s.—£7 10s., paying between 5s. and 10s.

1. *Rot. Parl.*, I, 243 *seq.*
2. See also the analysis of the payments in the wards, p. 57.

E. 502 with possessions of value of £1—£3 15s., paying
between 16d. and 5s.

F. 543 with possessions of value of 10s.—£1, paying
between 8d. and 16d.

To interpret this list we need to know the callings of those
who composed the various classes. The roll itself does not help
much, as the trades are only given in two of the smallest
wards, Candlewick and Portsoken, and occasionally in a few
other wards.

The information about individuals contained in the London
records makes it possible however to discover the occupation
of more than a quarter of the people, whose names are contained in the roll.

The members of the top classes, A, B and C, are naturally
those whose names frequently found their way into the
records, and consequently the trades of more than half of
them are known. The amount of information decreases as
the men become poorer. In the classes D and E it has been
possible to discover the craft of about a third of their members,
but in F the proportion falls as low as one-seventh.

The material is therefore insufficient to give statistics of
the relative numbers of the different crafts, but it allows
generalizations to be made as to the composition of the various
classes.

The mercantile element of the population, as might
naturally be expected, is shown to be the wealthiest. In
class A there were four pepperers (later known as grocers),
but the highest amount, £8, was paid by a mercer
and vintner.[1] The other members of this class were another
mercer, two woolmongers, a draper, a vintner, a blader, and a
butcher. It is rare to find a butcher in the highest rank;
the butchers are much more numerous in the lower classes.
But Nicholas Crane evidently resembled the other men of class
A rather than a shop-keeping butcher of class E. He is
spoken of as a " merchant of England."[3]

1. Three others paid £8, but their occupations have not been found.
2. *Cf.* Paris. " Au-dessus s'élevait une sorte d'aristocratie bourgeoise.
Certaines familles étaient arrivées à une grande fortune dans les industries de
luxe ou dans le commerce en gros. Les changeurs, orfèvres, huchiers
pelletiers, drapiers, merciers, épiciers, étaient les corporations où l'on trouvait
le plus de richesses." Lavisse, *Histoire de France*, IV, pt. i, p. 25.
3. *C.C.R.*, 1337–9, p. 124.

With the exception of the butchers, and vintners, who supplied a small number to each class, the occupations found in class A formed the majority in class B. They were present in decreasing numbers in the other classes. The only considerable element in B were the fishmongers, who formed a large proportion of all the classes below B.

The goldsmiths, skinners, and different types of leather-workers (cordwainers, saddlers, girdlers, a tanner and a whittawyer) were the other members of B. These men were shop-owners, and possibly did not engage in the industry themselves but acted as middlemen to the poorer members of the same craft.

All these types occur again in C, but in D there is a change. The number of butchers increases, and the craft element appears more strongly. In addition to the handicrafts already mentioned, there are ironmongers, plumbers, an armourer and a shipwright.

The change becomes more pronounced in E and F. The number of victuallers is much increased. There are fourteen butchers and eleven brewers. The skinners and leather workers are also far more numerous.

The information that can be gathered about class F suggests that they were not the poorest class of people in London. Richard de Swanlond, fishmonger, who paid twelve pence in 1332, leased a house and shop only two years before, at three shillings a year, and also a tenement with houses and shops over it at a rent of twenty shillings.[1] The girdler, Thomas West, who was assessed at sixteen pence, leased a tenement with shops, a postern and a garden in 1339.[2] There is evidence, also, that only the better class of victuallers were in class F.

John Scot, who is known to have been a poulterer from the roll paid the smallest amount of taxation, but in 1328, he had with another man, supplied the city with bitterns, herons and capons for a present to the King, and with pheasants and swans for the Queen.[4]

The craftsmen of the lowest class in the roll were also of

1. *Bk. E.*, p. 251.　　　2. *Bk. F.*, p. 35.
3. See Cheap Ward.　　　4. Riley, *Mem.*, p. 170.

sufficient status to be appointed wardens of such crafts as the saddlers, [1] cordwainers and armourers.

It is certain, therefore, that there was a large number of people (perhaps 50 per cent., as already suggested), poorer than the lowest class enrolled for the payment of the tax.[2]

It has already been indicated in this brief analysis that some crafts had a membership representing the different classes to a fairly equal extent. The various ranks in such trades were filled by men who were occupied in different functions of the trade. The fishmongers provide the best illustration, as they formed the most numerous body of craftsmen in London; and consequently the most information can be collected about them.

The richest of them were called "merchants of the city of London," and evidently did the wholesale buying for the trade. In 1318 a number of them received safe-conduct for a journey to Lincoln, Norfolk and Suffolk "to buy stockfish, salt-fish, herrings and oil to take it to London."[3]

Some of them, like John de Mokkyng, owned a house in Great Yarmouth,[4] and would obtain supplies of red-herring there, which they would land on their own wharf in London.[5]

These wealthy merchants often owned shops near to their wharves. John de Mokkyng,[6] John Lambyn,[7] and John Leche,[8] for example, had shops in Bridge Street. In some cases the shop might be the chief source of their wealth, but all the richest shopkeepers, like Geoffrey Aleyn in Langbourne, would have their own wharf at the river side.[9]

The fishmongers who paid below £1 included the various ranks of shopkeepers.[10]

Some of the poorer fishmongers seem to have purchased

1. John de Hereford and William de Blithe, paying 16d., and Maurice de Herlawe, 12d. *Bk. E.*, p. 232.
2. Contrast Professor Unwin's conclusions from the 1319 roll, *Gilds of London*, p. 75. He seems to suggest that all the poor craftsmen were assessed. It is true that the limit in 1310 was lower than in 1332, 6/8 instead of 10/- (*Bk. E.*, p. 122), so about 300 more people were assessed.
3. *C.P.R.*, 1317–21, p. 215.   4. *Cal. Wills*, I, 499.
5. Stephen Lucas leased a wharf in St. Magnus, *Bk. E.*, p. 252. Walter Turk leased several wharves, *Bk. E.*, p. 246.
6. *Cal. Wills*, I, 499.   7. *Ib.*, I. 582
8. *Ib.*, I, 584.   9. *Ib.*, I, 461.
10. William Turk, 6s. 8d., shop in Bridge Street, *Ib.*, II, 56. Hugh de Mokkynge, 5s. 4d., cellar and shop in Croked Lane, St. Margaret de Bridge Street, *Bk. E.*, p. 253. Nicholas Madefrey, 16d., shop in Eldefish Street, *Cal. Wills*, I, 552. Richard de Swanlond, *Bk. E.*, p. 25.

their supplies from local fishermen. They were occasionally summoned to give evidence if fishing-nets were false.[1] Some like Richard de Lambeth[2] and Henry Graspays,[3] owned fishing-ships and " batells," while others combined in the possession of a boat.

There was no sharp distinction between the different classes. The highest class stood somewhat apart, but the members of the classes B to F, performed the same kind of duties. They are found together policing the city, or in attendance at the Gildhall, or in the government of the misteries. Classes B and C, however, provided the majority of those engaged in this way.

There is not much information of general application that can be found about the lower classes. The greater part of it is not very creditable to the persons concerned, since it tells of the infringement of the rules which it was the business of the mediæval gild to draw up and enforce. The fishmongers and butchers were frequently punished for refusing to bring their goods to be sold at the regulated market. The favourite offence of the shoemakers was to mix good and inferior leather (bazen and cordwain), and the butchers continually attempted to sell putrid meat.

It is only in classes A and B that the men are found who made any mark on the history of their times. The high officials of the city, mayors, sheriffs and aldermen, were drawn from these two classes, as were also men of national importance. They were frequently members of Parliament, and there was a possibility under Edward III., as there had been under Edward I., of the merchants forming a new estate. Edward III. more than once summoned them to a separate council,[4] and negotiated with them to increase the revenue from wool. The London merchants were naturally prominent in these councils. They also acted frequently as agents for the King, in his pre-emption of wool, or as his financiers, recouping themselves out of the customs. Two London merchants, who were pre-eminent in such transactions, John Pulteney and Richard de la Pole, were aldermen in 1332,

1. *Bk. F.*, p. 111.
2. *Cal. Wills*, I, 549.　　　　3. *Ib.*, I, 627.
4. For example, twice in 1336 (Stubbs, II, 398) and twice in 1337 (*C.P.R.* 1337-9, pp. 615 and 621).

although their names are not to be found in the roll, but Reginald de Conduit, paying only 35s. 6¾d., was partner in many of their undertakings.

The London merchants were a useful source from which the King could draw loans to carry on his wars. In 1339, for example, he borrowed several sums ranging from £100 to £30.[1]

They were enabled to meet the demands of the King owing to the extent of their business concerns. They did not confine themselves to trade in one class of goods. Doubtless many of the wealthier merchants shared in the export of England's staple product—wool. The pepperers seem to have used it as an outgoing cargo; John de Grantham was exporting wool in 1324[2] and Andrew Aubrey was buying wool in Wales in 1350.[3]

The import of wheat also attracted merchants. John de Causton, a mercer, bought corn in Dublin.[4] Richard de Hakeneye, a woolmonger, procured " protection for himself and servants who were buying corn, wares and other things in divers parts of the realm and bringing them to London to make profit thereon."[5]

John Lovekyn, a fishmonger, was one of the early importers of sea-coal from Newcastle into London.[6] The extent of the business of some of these wealthy merchants may be discovered from the notices of debts due to them in the Close Rolls. Their debtors were in all parts of England, and owed them such large sums as £400. John de Oxenford, a vintner, and one of the richest men in London, seems to have supplied a great many of the monasteries in the country with large quantities of wine.

These wealthy merchants were able to maintain a considerable social status. At the same ceremony at which seven earls were created in 1337, the London mayor, John Pulteney, was made a knight.[7] Many others probably possessed the

1. *C.P.R.* 1338–40, p. 405. There are numerous other cases, *e.g.* Aubrey, *C.P.R.* 1341–3, p. 495; Causton, *C.P.R.* 1338–40, p. 313.
2. *C.C.R.* 1323–7, p. 115.
3. *Calendar of Letters to the City of London*, pp. 3, 7–8
4. *C.C.R.* 1330–3, p. 94.
5. *C.P.R.* 1334–8, pp. 384 and 572.
6. *Calendar of Letters to City of London*, p. 94.
7. *Annales Paulini*, p. 366.

required conditions for knighthood. Some like Henry Darcy obtained special pardon from the King for not having taken the burdensome honour, and received a respite therefrom, which would be renewed on its expiration.[1] The faltering tone in which the reply was made in 1344, that none had £40 a year in lands or rents for certain; the plea that was made, that tenements often stood empty or were burnt, seems to prove that many had the stated possessions[2] and shirked the attendant duty.

The wealthy citizens not only possessed tenements in all parts of the city,[3] but owned and rented manors in the country, where they appear to have resided,[4] at least in their old age.

Like the knightly class, many of them had the leisure and means to make the shorter pilgrimage to St. James of Compostella,[5] and Edward III. did not consider it beneath his dignity to entertain the wives of the wealthy London burghers to supper and assign them their places at table.[6]

It is evident, therefore, that the rulers of the city in the fourteenth century were almost as aristocratic as the feudal nobles they had replaced.[7] The great difference was that they had a close bond of union with the poorer classes of the city through their common membership in a craft-gild.

The line of cleavage in the city was no longer between rich and poor, at least not as such, but between craft and craft. The causes of the disputes between them in Edward's reign are as yet little understood, but their comparative wealth, as revealed in the roll, combined with other facts, may help eventually to provide an explanation.

1. *C.P.R.* 1334–8, p. 253. *Ib.* 1338–40, p. 254.
2. *Bk. F.*, p. 105.
3. This is shewn by the wills, *e.g.* John de Grantham, *Cal. Wills*, I. 475. Richard le Lacer, *Ib.*, II, 59.
4. Simon Dolseley and Richard le Lacer dated their wills from their manors, *Ib.*, II, 59, 75.
5. Andrew Aubrey, *C.P.R.* 1348–50, p. 561 ; Richard Hakeneye, *Ib.* 1330–4, p. 259; John Oxenford, *Ib.* 1348–50, p. 560.
6. Murimuth, p. 155.
7. *C.f.* Paris. " Cette aristocratie nouvelle cherchait à imiter les nobles et un chroniquer parisien nous a laissé le curieux récit de grande joutes organisées par les Parisiens en 1330," etc. Lavisse, *Hist. de France*, Vol. IV, pt. I, p. 24.

III. The Wealth and Trades of the Wards.

Tax-rolls are frequently described as directories of the districts which returned them. It is fortunate that there is one of these directories for mediæval London, which makes it possible to reconstruct the city as it was six hundred years ago. Such a reconstruction is particularly interesting after a study of the crafts, since it shews where they were located.

As in other mediæval cities, the members of the same trade were gathered together in one district, probably to simplify the enforcement of the regulations, and the toll-taking which were prominent features of the gilds.[1]

Some crafts however, especially the victuallers who were indispensable in all quarters of the city, were not confined to one district. But many trades were particularly associated with one ward.

In the river-side wards it was naturally the mercantile element which predominated. From Vintry to Tower stretched a line of wealthy wards, through which the imports and exports of the city passed.

These wards resemble each other in the numbers who paid the taxation, about seventy-five in each, and the average amount paid, about ten shillings a head, except Vintry, the second richest ward in London, which, with only forty assessed, contributed £37.

The trade which employed the greatest number of people in these wards was fishmongering. It occupied the inhabitants of Bridge, rich and poor, almost exclusively. In Billingsgate and Queenhithe also the majority of the people appear to have been fishmongers, and in the other three wards a minority. The fishmongers of Billingsgate were doubtless conterminous with those of Bridge; several of them had shops in Bridge Street.[2]

Even more important to England than the import of fish was the export of her wool. Tower and Billingsgate were

---

1. Unwin, *Gilds*, pp. 31–3. See his map of localized trades in mediæval London. *Cf.* Lavisse, *Hist. de France*, IV, pt. i, p. 24.
2. William Turk, *Cal. Wills*, II, 56, and John Leche, I, p. 584, described as "fishmonger of Bridge Street." Thomas de Brayneford evidently lived near the boundary of the two wards, as his house was opposite St. Magnus the Martyr, *Ib.*, I, 465.

F

the wards through which large quantities of it passed.   It was evidently a profitable trade, as the three richest men of Tower ward, all of them aldermen, were wool-mongers.[1]

Vintry, as its name suggests, had the wine trade of the city, which was then passing into English hands.   One of the richest men in London, John de Oxenford, was a vintner. The four other aldermen in this ward had other occupations.[2]

The distinctive trade in Dowgate appears to have been that of a corder.   There were doubtless many corn and wood-mongers in these river-side wards, but few have been discovered.   Shipbuilding would also be carried on along the banks of the river, but apparently by men not important enough to find their way into the city records.   Only one shipwright has been found in the roll, Alan le Palmere, who lived in Petty Wales near the Tower.[3]

All the occupations that have been mentioned, from their nature had their headquarters in these wards.   But there were also, along the river-side, wealthy members of misteries which centred in other parts of London.   These, like Benedict de Fulsham,[4] the pepperer, and Robert le Callere,[5] the mercer in Vintry, and John de Caustone[6] in Billingsgate, doubtless imported ware for their own shops, and for the purely shop-keeping members of their misteries.

Of the other rich wards of London, which clustered together behind Vintry and Dowgate, Cordwainer was by far the wealthiest.   Cheap, a thickly-peopled ward, with about twice the number assessed, contributed only about the same amount. In Cripplegate Within and Bread Street both population and assessment were about one-half those of Cheap.

It is more helpful in explaining these facts, not to confine the attention too strictly to the wards.   The wards had no bounding walls restricting men within their limits.   Many of the great highways of London, running from East to West,

1. William de Briklesworth, Henry de Combemartyn and John Priour senior. Beaven, *op. cit.*, 382, 383, 385. The alderman, Richard de Hakeneye, who was a collector of the subsidy, was a woolmonger, so probably belonged to one of these wards. *Ib.*, p. 382.
2. Walter Nel, blader; Walter Turk, fishmonger; Benedict de Fulsham, pepperer, and Robert de Callere, mercer.
3. *Cal. Wills*, I, 412.   4. Beaven, *op. cit.*, p 383.
5. *Ib.*, p. 382.
6. *Cal. Wills*, I, 672. He had tenements in all parts of London and shops in Thames Street.

retained the same name in different wards. Thus it was with West Cheap, and round it the richest shop-keeping district of London centred. This wealthy area apparently widened in the East, including all Cordwainer, and South Cheap, while it probably comprised those parts of Cripplegate, Bread Street and Farringdon Within, which bordered more nearly on West Cheap. In this district were pepperers, mercers, drapers, and hosiers.

The pepperers were specially connected with one street which ran at right angles to West Cheap. John de Grantham of Cordwainer Ward was one of the " good folk of Soperes-lane of the trade of pepperer."[1] They were settled here till the reign of Henry VI., when they removed to Bucklersbury.[2]

The Mercery of London was on West Cheap,[3] round the great shed which it came to include in Henry VI.'s reign, which Edward III. built by the church of St. Mary le Bow, in order to " behold the justings and other shewes."[4] Not far away was the great seld which had belonged to Roesia of Coventry, near to which William de Causton, one of the richest men in London, had his houses and shops.[5]

The mercers were also found as far north in Cheap as Catte Street—where Henry le Chener (taxed in Cripplegate Within) had five shops.[6] The drapers probably occupied the same district, but not stretching so far into Cheap.[7]

Passing further West, goldsmiths were among the wealthy shop-keepers. They also centred round West Cheap. John Makeheved in Bread Street had his shop opposite to the Stone Cross,[8] and those in Cripplegate and Farringdon Within had

1. Riley, *Mem.*, p. 120. Thomas Corp also had a shop in Sopers Lane. *Cal. Wills*, I, 477.
2. Stow, I, 26.
3. Richard le Lacer had a seld near West Cheap (*Cal. Wills*, II, 59); John Knopwed (*Ib.*, I, 448), and Richard Scarlet received a grant of " a mansion and shop near West Cheap " (*Bk. F.*, p. 155); Simon Fraunceys leased a cellar there (*Bk. E.*, p. 224).
4. Stow, I, 257.
5. *Cal. Wills*, I, 680. "A seld was an extensive warehouse open at the sides, sometimes containing shops within and room for wholesale stowage." Riley, *Mem.*, p. 22.
6. *Cal. Wills*, I, 462.
7. Only one draper has been found in Cheap, and he is called "mercer or draper." In Cordwainer Richard de Berkyng had tenements in the parish of St. Mary le Bow, some of them in Goose Lane, which ran along the south side of that church. *Ib.*, I, 687.
8. *Ib.*, I, 587.

their shops in the parishes of this neighbourhood—St. Peter de Woodstreet,[1] St. Matthew Fridaystreet,[2] St. Michael le Quern [3] and St. Vedast.[4]

In the goldsmiths' charter it was stated that " it had been ordained that all who were of the Goldsmith's trade were to sit in their shops in the High Street of Cheap, and no silver-plate, nor vessel of gold or silver ought to be sold in the city of London except at our Exchange or in Cheap among the Goldsmiths." [5]

The only other rich men in these wards appear to have been some girdlers in the North part of Cheap.[6]

It has not been possible to discover the occupation of many of the poorer inhabitants of the wards. In Cheap, however, various trades were practised.[7]

A large number of the men in Farringdon Within were saddlers and cordwainers. The richest members of these crafts, like Robert de Bristoll [8] and William de Mymmes,[9] were, however, in West Cheap.[10]

Passing out of these wards beyond the walls of London, the shop-keeping element is left behind. Cripplegate Without was a poor ward, paying only £7 with forty-three assessed. The trade of nine men only is known. They are all workers in leather, probably dependent on the saddlers to supply them with work.

Farringdon Without, a somewhat richer ward, also contained many leather workers, of a different type however. Tanning was one of the chief industries of the ward. It was

---

1. Simon de Berkynges (Bread St.), *Cal. Wills*, I, 542.
2. Robert le Bret (Cripplegate Win), *Ib.*, I, 410. William de Ippegrave (Farringdon Win), *Bk. F.*, p. 222.
3. Henry le Gloucestre (Farringdon Win), *Bk. G.*, p. 44.
4. John de Mallyng and Richard Denys had tenements in "Goderoneslane," *Cal. Wills*, I, 437, 457.
5. Unwin, *Gilds*, p. 79.
6. John Potyn owned 8 shops in St. Michael de Bassishaw (*Cal. Wills*, I, 383); Thomas West and Nicholas de Reygate also had tenements in that parish, *Bk. F.*, 70; *Cal. Wills*, I, 556.
7. A butcher, cordwainer and a chaundeler paying over £1; a glover, baker, cheesemonger, armourer, purser, coffrer paying over 10s.; chaundeler, two armourers, an ironmonger, a cutler; a purser, a coffrer and saddler; two tailors. a fuller, two apothecaries, three brewers and an "ymginour" paying smaller amounts have been found.
8. *Cal. Wills*, I, 507.   9. *Ib.*, I, 405.
10. *Cf.* Unwin, *op. cit.*, p. 53. The saddlers had their shops at the N.W. corner of Cheap, near the ends of Foster and Gutter Lanes.

carried on in the neighbourhood of the Fleet Ditch.[1]   These tanners carried their hides for sale to the " Tannereselde in the forum of West Chepe in St. Mary le Bow," where many of them would have a place and table.

To this region of the Fleet valley, the Cutlers also, whose earlier settlements were near the Conduit in Cheap and in St. Magnus' parish near the Bridge, had for some time past been overflowing.[2]

The cappers appear to have been as closely connected with Fleet Street as the pepperers were with Sopers Lane.[3]

Walbrook is the only one of the remaining wards, which is certainly known to have been almost entirely inhabited by a set of craftsmen peculiar to it.   In point of numbers it comes after Farringdon Within and Cheap, and resembles the former ward in contributing about £20 less than the latter. It was pre-eminently the skinners' ward.   Twenty-one in the roll have been found to be skinners, including all classes from John de Oxenford and Simon de Thorpe paying sixteen pence each to John de Cotum paying 35s. 6¾d.

The skinners would no doubt have their works along the Walbrook; the name Budge Row[4] suggests that they were also on the Cordwainer side of the stream, but only one skinner has been discovered in that ward.

In the case of Walbrook and the neighbouring ward of Candlewick, a street is again the centre of an industry.   The cloth of the burlers of Candlewick Street was noted; in 1322 some was purchased for the King from Thomas de Wynchestre among others.[5]   There are only two burlers in Candlewick Ward, but five have been found in Walbrook.   The majority of them paid small amounts (2s. 8d. and 16d.), and it is probable that the great number of burlers were too poor to be assessed.

They were doubtless provided with work by the rich drapers of the district.   One of these drapers, Richard de

1. Richard Ussher's shops were in the parish of St. Sepulchre, some of them in a "little lane opposite the Flete Prison," others in "lanes called Sacollane and Wandayeneslane " (*Cal. Wills*, I, 439).   Walter Ussher's were in the same parish (*Ib.*, I, 420).

2.   C. Welch. *History of the Cutlers' Company*, I, 36–42.

3.   In addition to the three hatters indicated in the roll, there are Richard de Luton and Alan de Wight.   They are spoken of as "capellarii de Flete Street " in *Munimenta Gildhallae Londoniensis*, II, pt. i, 430.

4. Stow, I, 250.   5. *Bk. E.*, p. 171.

Torinton, was the richest man in the Candlewick Ward, and John de Somersham in Walbrook lived in Candlewick Street.[1]

Twelve wards still remain, but they must unfortunately, through lack of information about them, be dismissed in a few words. On the outskirts of the city were the poor, thinly-populated areas, in the East, of Portsoken, Aldgate and the diminutive Limestreet; and in the West, of Castle Baynard and Aldersgate.

Slightly richer, and containing more inhabitants, were the wards of Langbourne, Cornhill, Coleman Street, Bassishawe and Queenhithe, which bordered on some of the richest wards of the city.

The potters carried on their handicraft in Portsoken,[2] and the tapicers were apparently located in Langbourn.[3]

The study of the individual wards suggests to the mind the main features of mediæval London. The impression which it leaves is of rich mercantile wards on the river bank in the East which were easily accessible to sea-going ships.   In their Western rear was a shop-keeping area which formed a wealthy centre, from which radiated districts of poorer shops, and then of workmen, poor in the North, but richer in the West and East, till the poor, thinly-populated districts of the East were reached.

1. *Cal. Wills*, I, 441.
2. See the roll.
3. The only men whose trade has been found in Langbourne were tapicers. John de Bromhelm, Walter de Stepenheth, Richard Frere, Richard Merk presented the ordinances of the tapicers (Riley, *Mem.*, p. 179).   William Palmer was also a tapicer (*Bk. F.*, p. 122).

Note.—Since the above was written, Prof. Willard has contributed a note on the taxes upon Movables of the Reign of Edward III to the *English Hist. Rev.*, XXX, p. 69.

MARGARET CURTIS.

ANALYSIS OF THE PAYMENTS IN THE WARDS.

Ward.	Amount paid. £	s.	d.	Nos. in ward.	Nos. paying £1 & +	10/- & +	5/- & +	Between 5/- & 16d.	Between 16d. & under.
Aldgate	5	9	9½	21	2	—	3	15	1
Aldersgate	5	17	11¾	43	—	—	4	22	17
Bassieshaw	4	14	11¼	18	1	2	2	4	9
Billingsgate	24	10	2¾	49	8	6	14	11	10
Bishopsgate	22	6	6¾	47	5	2	2	13	25
Bread St.	23	16	4¼	77	6	9	13	25	24
Bridge	47	12	10½	72	19	8	6	18	21
Broad St.	33	7	9¾	74	10	6	8	25	25
Candlewick	13	15	9½	45	4	2	6	27	6
Castle Baynard	8	3	10	46	—	1	12	20	13
Cheap	67	3	1½	127	20	23	16	35	33
Coleman St.	16	18	4¼	59	4	6	8	16	25
Cordwainer	62	13	1¾	73	18	13	19	16	7
Cornhill	12	0	5½	43	—	8	13	13	9
Cripplegate Within . (5 amounts missing.)	36	10	6¾	74	13	9	11	15	21
Cripplegate Without	7	9	9½	43	1	2	7	12	21
Dowgate	30	18	9½	85	14	3	14	24	30
Farringdon Within .	48	8	4	130	16	7	14	50	43
Farringdon Without (4 amounts missing.)	31	19	2¾	98	7	6	21	19	41
Langbourn	18	17	8	77	5	4	9	14	45
Limestreet	2	6	2½	18	1	—	—	4	13
Portsoken	5	7	7¾	23	1	1	5	4	12
Queenhithe	20	19	4¼	74	4	4	14	17	35
Tower	34	6	4	73	9	5	7	34	18
Vintry	37	10	0	40	7	4	8	14	7
Walbrook	47	2	4	107	13	10	17	35	32
	£670	7	5¼	1,636	188	141	253	502	543

THE CRAFTS IN THE DIFFERENT CLASSES.

(The scanty information given in the roll has been supplemented by
search in the London records.)

Amount for
  which
assessed.
£4 & over.

4 pepperers, 1 vintner, 1 butcher.
2 mercers, 2 woolmongers, 1 draper.

Between
£1 & £4.

20 fishmongers; 7 pepperers; 3 butchers; 3 vintners.
6 mercers, 4 woolmongers, 12 drapers, 2 tailors, 1 haber-
dasher, 2 burlers, 1 dyer.
7 skinners, 1 tanner, 3 cordwainers, 1 saddler, 1 whittawyer, 2 girdlers, 1 bookbinder.
7 goldsmiths, 6 bladers; 1 woodmonger, 1 chandler, 1
painter.

Between
10/- & £1.

9 fishmongers, 1 pepperer, 6 vintners; 3 butchers, 2
cheesemongers, 1 salter, 1 cook, 1 baker, 2 apothecaries.
1 chaucer, 5 mercers, 2 woolmongers, 2 drapers; 2 tailors,
1 burler, 1 dyer, 1 fripperer.
5 skinners, 1 tanner, 4 cordwainers, 1 glover, 1 girdler.
2 bladers, 1 woodmonger, 3 ironmongers; 1 plumber,
1 armourer, 1 spurrier; 1 mason, 1 tiler; 1 shipwright,
1 corder.
1 barber, 1 clerk.

Between
5/- & 10/-.

15 fishmongers, 1 pepperer, 2 spicers; 11 butchers,
4 vintners, 1 brewer, 1 cook, 1 salter.
3 woolmongers, 1 draper, 2 tailors, 1 weaver, 1 tapicer,
1 fripperer.
8 skinners, 3 tanners, 2 curriers, 4 cordwainers, 1 purser,
1 cofferer.
4 goldsmiths, 3 carpenters, 3 ironmongers, 1 plumber,
1 tiler, 1 armourer, 1 potter; 2 chandlers.
1 clerk, 1 horsedealer.

Between
5/- & 16d.

11 fishmongers, 2 grocers, 14 butchers; 1 pork butcher,
4 vintners, 7 brewers, 1 taverner, 1 hostler, 4 drawers,
2 cornmongers, 1 fruiterer.

3 woolmongers, 2 drapers, 4 tailors, 2 haberdashers, 5 burlers, 1 fuller, 1 tapicer, 4 hatters, 1 hosier, 2 fripperers.

12 skinners, 6 tanners, 8 saddlers, 1 fuster, 4 cordwainers, 1 bracer, 3 girdlers.

10 goldsmiths, 4 bladers, 3 ironmongers, 1 armourer, 1 bowyer, 1 spurrier; 1 cutler; 1 brassour, 1 joiner, 2 potters, 2 corders; 2 chandlers, 2 cirgers; 3 image-makers.

Between 16d. & 8d.

6 fishmongers, 10 butchers, 2 vintners, 6 brewers, 1 taverner, 1 cook, 2 bakers, 1 fruiterer, 1 poulterer.

1 woolbroker, 1 draper, 1 mercer, 4 tailors, 6 weavers, 1 shearman, 1 burler, 1 dyer, 4 tapicers, 2 hatters, 2 hosiers.

9 skinners, 2 tanners, 1 currier, 1 leather merchant, 5 cordwainers, 1 saddler, 1 fuster, 2 girdlers.

5 goldsmiths, 3 armourers, 1 spurrier, 3 cutlers, 2 carpenters, 1 plumber, 1 coppersmith, 1 smith, 1 ironmonger, 1 pavier, 3 chandlers, 1 cirger.

1 barber.

NOTE I. WOMEN IN THE CRAFT GILDS.

Dr. Cunningham in a passage on the position of women in the craft gilds [1] says that in the case of the London weavers, the weaver's rights descended to his widow, but that this seems to have been exceptional.

But in the case of five men in the roll, of four different trades, they expected their wives to carry on their business, as they left to them the remaining term of an apprentice. Thomas de Worstede, mercer, left also to his wife, six chests in a seld,[2] and another mercer, Henry le Chener, left to his wife, his shop in the great seld of London, and also the remaining term of two apprentices [3]; John Trapp, a skinner [4]; Simon de Turnham, a fishmonger,[5] and John de Somersham, draper,[6] each assigned one apprentice to his wife.

It might be contended that though this was done, the custom had no sanction from the craft or city authorities, but it is stated in the will of Simon de Turnham that his wife or his executors shall present the apprentice, "at the end of his term in the Gildhall, as a good and faithful apprentice, as is the custom, and make him free and lawful, according to the custom of the city for apprentices." There is evidently no doubt of the wife's power to do this, or the duty would have been left to the executors alone.

So the widow's rights seem to have been of the fullest kind, extending even to those which belonged to to the members of the craft gilds as burgesses.

1. *Growth of English Industry and Commerce*, I, 352.
2. *Cal. Wills*, I, 489.   3. *Ib.*, I, 462.   4. *Ib.*, I 475.
5. *Ib.*, I, 495.   6. *Ib.*, I, 441.

NOTE II. THE TRANSLATION OF ALDERMEN.

The translation of aldermen from one ward to another was frequent in the fourteenth as in later centuries. Mr. Beaven makes some comments about it, but he gives no reason for the translations.[1]

The roll, by indicating the man's residence, makes it possible to suggest an explanation.

In the cases where an alderman was not translated he was generally living in the ward that he was elected by in the first instance. This is true of John de la Rokele (Dowgaté), William de Briklesworth (Tower), Ralph de Upton (Coleman Street), and John de Cotoun (Walbrook).

But it would frequently happen that there was no vacancy in the ward of residence of the man who wished to become an alderman. In such cases, he would represent another ward, and might in time be elected to the ward he lived in. This appears to have been the case with Andrew Aubrey and John de Grantham, who were translated from Bread Street and Cornhill respectively, to the aldermancy of Cordwainer. Richard Constantin was probably translated from Aldersgate to Cripplegate,[2] and Bartholomew Deumars was translated from Bishopsgate to Dowgate; and Henry Combemartyn from Aldgate to Tower.

In all these cases the aldermen served first for poor wards which would always be dependent on the richer wards for their aldermen. But translation was as frequent from the rich wards as from the poor.[3]

NOTE III. THE MYSTERY OF BLADERS.

On page 233 of *Letter Book E* there is evidently a misreading or a misprint of " beader " for " blader." The wardens here mentioned are elsewhere called blader—*e.g.* Hamo le Barber in *Bk. F.*, p. 220, *Cal. Wills*, I, 533, and John Ate Loke, *Cal. Wills*, I, 544.

1. *Aldermen of London*, 240–1.   2. *Ib.*, 385.   3. *Ib.*, 241.

PARTICULE COMPOTI JOHANNIS DE PRESTON ET RICARDI DE KAKENEYE, COLLECTORUM QUINTE-DECIME REGI A LAICIS ANNO SEXTO CONCESSE IN CIVITATE LONDON DE EADEM QUINTADECIMA.

Sma tot . . . xv inhuc vij rot . . . dclxxj li vij s̄ v d̄ qᵃ p.b̄.

WARDA TURR.[1]

Will Haunsard	xl s̄
Johñs Priour, Senior	xiij s̄ iiij d̄
Johñs Priour, Junior	vj s̄ viij d̄
Henri de Combemartyn	cvj s̄ viij d̄
Henri Wymond	liij s̄ iiij d̄
Walt le Meleward	vj s̄ viij d̄
Simon Turgis	xl s̄
Henr Cros	xxvj s̄ viij d̄
Nichi de Bray	xiij s̄ iiij d̄
Will Bon	xxvj s̄ viij d̄
Adam Hurel	iiij s̄
Ricūs de Preston	iiij s̄
Will Priour	ij s̄
Johñs Gouge	iiij s̄
Radūs Cosyn	xiij s̄ iiij d̄
Will de Brikelsworth	cvj s̄ viij d̄
Gocelinus de Clyne	xxvj s̄ viij d̄
Edmundus de Saunford	vj s̄ viij d̄
Vincencius Sefoul	ij s̄
Alex Maunsshipe	iiij s̄ iiij d̄
Petrus atte Vyne	iiij s̄
Rogur atte Ponde	vj s̄ viij d̄
Galfs Turgis	ij s̄
Johñs Benro	xij d̄
Wills de Ho	iiij s̄
Simon de Wymondham	ij s̄
Nichs Totyngham	xvj d̄
Johñs le Hurer	ij s̄ viij d̄
Johñs atte Made	ij s̄
Robtus le Brewere	vj s̄ viij d̄
Alanus le Palme	vj s̄ viij d̄
Ricūs de Talworth	ij s̄
Radūs le ffruiter	iiij s̄
Martinius le Palme	ij s̄ viij d̄
Thomas Potyn	xiij s̄ iiij d̄
Ricūs de Pelham	v s̄ iiij d̄
Godwinls Turk	xiij s̄ iiij d̄
Johñs de Sudbery	ij s̄
Will Swote	iiij s̄
Hamo ffaber	xvj d̄
Johes de Combe	ij s̄
Johes Smart	ij s̄ viij d̄
Johes Ballard	xij d̄

1. Tower.

Will de Litton	ij s	
Stephus de Hakeneye		xvj d
Symon de Dalyngg		xvj d
Johes Mouce		viij d
Nichus atte Boure	ij s	viij d
Will Turk		ij s
Johes de Kyngeston	ij s	viij d
Ricus de Kent	iiij s	
Robtus de Chigwell	ij s	viij d
Robtus Waldecard		xvj d
Nichus le Blake, Tavner	iij s	iiij d
Wills le Chaundeler		xvj d
Ricus Comsedieu	ij s	
Radus le Massoun		xvj d
Ricus Alisaundre		xvj d
Johns Godchep	ij s	
Waltus le Brewere		xij d
Phus le Wolleberere		xvj d
Ricus le Pakkedrawere		xij d
Adam de Gloucestre		xij d
Alic. relict. Willi. de Braye	ij s	viij d
Johna. Relict. Johis. Cosyn	iiij s	
Amicia relict. Alexi. Pyk		xij d
Johna de Stodle		xvj d
Margareta de Barton	ij s	
Ricus Asselin	xxix s	iiij d
Waltus le Hurer	iiij s	
Wills Cros. Cristemasse	ij s	viij d
Wills de Preston		xvj d

Sm^a. xxxiiij li vj s. iiij d, p.b.

LYMESTRETE.

Clemens le Keu	ij s	viij d
Johes de Topesfeld	xxvj s	viij d
Ricus Walram		xx d
Symon de Houndesdich		xij d
Henr de Habyngdon		xij d
Waltus de Chelmesford		xvj d
Robtus de Kelbourne	ij s	
Simon de Sendale		xx d
Wills de Maldon		viij d
Petrus ffourner		viij d
Johns de Grenewich		viij d
Rad de Rothyng		viij d
Johes le Pessoner		xvj d
Robtus Greylond		viij d
Henr. le Herrere		viij d
Robtus. de Kent, Cordewan		viij d
Wills. Sabrichesworth		xvj d
Wills. de Alegate		x d ob

Sma. xlvj s. ij d. ob. p.b.

PONT.

Johs de Herkstede	ij s	
Thomas de Ware		xvj d

Wiłłs. de Braughyñg	xvij ꝣ iiij ꝺ
Simon de Broune	xxix ꝣ iiij ꝺ
Gilbtus de Mordone	xxvj ꝣ viij ꝺ
Wiłł. atte Lavende	xvj ꝺ
Radus Lucas	iiij ꝣ
Raꝺ de Loune	xxvj ꝣ viij ꝺ
Stepħs Lucas	xxvj ꝣ viij ꝺ
Agnes Lucas	xl ꝣ
Robtus Swote	xiij ꝣ iiij ꝺ
Rob de Thorneye	xl ꝣ
Robtus de Eure	ij ꝣ viij ꝺ
Thomas atte Wich	xxxvj ꝣ
Joħs le Parker	xvj ꝺ
Waltus de Mordone	lxvj ꝣ viij ꝺ
Wiłłs de Witheresfold	xxvj ꝣ viij ꝺ
Joħ Lovekyn	liij ꝣ iiij ꝺ
Petrus de Ware	xvj ꝺ
Adam Lucas	xvij ꝣ ix ꝺ ob
Robtus de Mordoñ, Wiłłs frater ejus	Liij ꝣ iiij ꝺ
Wiłłs Oliver	ix ꝣ iiij ꝺ
Wiłłs Ralot	viij ꝺ
Riꝅ de Esseẍ	xiij ꝣ iiij ꝺ
Henꞃ Sterre	xiij ꝣ iiij ꝺ
Joħs Turk	xiij ꝣ iiij ꝺ
Riꝅ de Brisyngham	iiij ꝣ
Joħ Lambyñ	liij ꝣ iiij ꝺ
Thomas Pikeman	ij ꝣ viij ꝺ
Roᵹus Aleyn	vj ꝣ viij ꝺ
Roᵹus le Chaundeler	xl ꝣ
Wiłłs Gaudre	ij ꝣ viij ꝺ
Adam Reson	xvj ꝺ
Radūs Gaudre	xxvj ꝣ viijꝺ
Joħes de Tramhale	xij ꝺ
Thomas atte Naye	ij ꝣ viij ꝺ
Wiłłs le Tablettere	ij ꝣ
Robtus Abel	ij ꝣ
Deonisius le ffourbour	ij ꝣ viij ꝺ
Riꝅ le Gloucestre	v ꝣ iiij ꝺ
Hugh de Bonberry	ij ꝣ
Riꝅ Paterlyñg	xvj ꝺ
Waltus Paterlyñg	xxvj ꝣ viij ꝺ
Joħns de Mokkyng de Soṁset	liij ꝣ iiij ꝺ
Joħs de Croydon	xxvj ꝣ viij ꝺ
Joħs atte Wode	xvj ꝺ
Riꝅus Horn	xvj ꝺ
Nicħus le Chaundeler	xvj ꝺ
Joħ le Litle	ij ꝣ viij ꝺ
Gaefꞃ ffairher	xiij ꝣ iiij ꝺ
Riꝅ Sterre	xiij ꝣ iiij ꝺ
Thomas de Bery	lxvj ꝣ viij ꝺ
Robtus le fflourmakere	iiij ꝣ
Joħēs Horn de Southwark	xvj ꝺ
Nicħus atte Brodegate	xvj ꝺ
Arnold le Chaundeler	ij ꝣ viijꝺ
Roᵹus de Notyngham	xij ꝺ
Jacobus atte Pire	xvj ꝺ

Wiłłs. Amys	ij ß	viij ₫
Riĉ. de Boterwiꝁ		xij ₫
Bordinius ffader		xvj ₫
Joħ. atte Gatte		xvj ₫
Symon de Berdefeld	ij ß	
Joħ le Hostiler	iiij ß	
Henř. Graspays	iiij ß	
Thoᵐ. Lambyn̄	viij ß	
Roḃtus Baudri		xvj ₫
Jacobus Waꝸbak		viij ₫
Joħ. Oliver	v ß	iiij ₫
Hug̃ de Mokkyng̃	v ß	iiij ₫
Joħ Cotekyn		xvj ₫

Smᵃ. xlvij li. xij ß. x ₫. oḃ. p.ḃ.

WARDA DE CORNHULLE.

Ric de Yeting	viij ß	
Roḃtus de Ravenston	ij ß	viij ₫
Wiłłs de Manhale	x ß	viij ₫
Paulinus le Auntermaker	vj ß	viij ₫
Riĉus le Stoler	iiij ß	
Hugo de Berkyng	ij ß	
Joħes de Parys	vj ß	viij ₫
A₫ de Wodehous		xvj ₫
Gilbtus de Brauncestro		xvj ₫
Rog̃us de Shorne	x ß	viij ₫
Thomas Leggy	xiij ß	iiij ₫
Stepħs atte Holte	ix ß	iiij ₫
Joħes Wodehous	ij ß	
Hugo de Rothingg	x ₫	oḃ qᵃ
Rog̃us le Draper	vj ß	viij ₫
Riĉus Swyft	iiij ß	
Galfridus le Keu	ij ß	
Roḃtus le Laten̄		xvj ₫
Bartholomeus le Bordesle	x ₫	oḃ qᵃ
Roḃtus le Conduyt	vj ß	viij ₫
Joħes le Knyght		xvj ₫
Ricus Huggele	viij ß	
Nicħs Seman	x ß	viij ₫
Joħns Roumhale	vj ß	viij ₫
Joħes Owayn	xij ß	
Joħes Cristemasse		xvj ₫
Wiłłms Brangwayn	xiij ß	iiij ₫
Joħes Leflyt	ix ß	iiij ₫
Joħes de Salesbury	vj ß	viij ₫
Edmunds Mohaut	viij ß	
Thomas le Northerne	v ß	iiij ₫
Gerardus le Laton̄	xiij ß	iiij ₫
Roḃtus Kyngesbury	ij ß	viij ₫
Wiłłms de Grenestede	xiij ß	iiij ₫
Wiłłms de Grauntebrigge	viij ß	
Wiłłms le Stokfishmong̃r	ij ß	viij ₫
Roḃus de Caimmpes	ij ß	viij ₫
Roḃus de Arderna		xvj ₫

Johes Wychberd	ij s̄ viij d̄
Amicia ate Holte	iij s̄ viij d̄
Juliana le Joignour	xvj d̄
Johes del Brendeswode	iiij s̄
Wiltms Deer	ij s̄

p.b. Sm^a xij li v d̄ ob.

WARDA DE CANDELWYKSTRETE.

Thomas de Wynchestr, burler	xx s̄
Hugo Bener, viniter	xxvj s̄ viij d̄
Johes de Wynchestr, plomer	xiij s̄ iiij d̄
Ric̄us de Torinton, draper	xliiij s̄ v d̄ ob
Henr̄c̄ de Braghing, stokfishmongere	xl s̄
Hug de Craye, blader	iiij s̄
Johes Gubbe, stokfishmon̄ḡ	v s̄ iiij d̄
Hen̄r̄ Rumbold, hostiler	ij s̄ viij d̄
Ric̄o de Herkestede, blader	iiij s̄
Mat̄hus Abraham, skinner	xvj d̄
Robs le Chaundeler	xvj d̄
Wiłłs de Mercheye, cornm̄oḡe	iij s̄ iiij d̄
Robts le Mazerer, brewere	ij s̄ viij d̄
Joħs Odicrue, bocher	xiij s̄ iiij d̄
Ricus Cori, bocher	ij s̄ viij d̄
Wałtus de Dene, bocher	xvj d̄
Wiłłs Knyght, bocher	vj s̄ viij d̄
Johes Blod, bocher	v s̄ iiij d̄
Johes Lenman, bocher	iiij s̄
Gilbus ate fforde, bocher	iiij s̄ viij d̄
Johns Edward, bocher	iiij s̄
Johes Turgis, cir̄ḡ	ij s̄
Robt ate Dych, plom̄	ij s̄
Wiłłs de Bokkyng, plom̄	vj s̄ viij d̄
Ad de Pydington, plom̄	xvj d̄
Johes ate Hulle, webbe	xvj d̄
Galfridus Payn, webbe	ij s̄
Ric̄us de Caun̄tbur̄, plom̄	ij s̄
Johes ate Dyche, plom̄	ij s̄ viij d̄
Thomas Baud̄r̄, plom̄	iij s̄ iiij d̄
Wiłłs de Godalmyng, cordwan̄	ij s̄
Wiłłs de Walden, burler	ij s̄
Hugo le Tayllor, brewer	v s̄ iiij d̄
Thomas Knyght, peorker	ij s̄ viij d̄
Petrus de Grenewych, haberdassher	ij s̄ viij d̄
Wiłłs ate Noky, cir̄ḡ	xvj d̄
Galfridus le Brewer	iiij s̄
Ric̄us de Shenefeld	ij s̄
Johes de Croydone, senior, piscenar	ij s̄ viij d̄
Ad de Canefeld, bocher	v s̄ iiij d̄
Johes Gifford, brewer	ij s̄ viij d̄
Wiłłs Wynelyn	ij s̄ viij d̄
Henr ate Lanende	ij s̄
Henr le Rous	ij s̄
Joħes Honder, bocher	ij s̄

p.b. Sm^a xiij li xv s̄ ix d̄ ob.

WARDA DE DOUEGATE.

Henr̄ de Preston	xxvj s̄ viij d̄
Joħs de Swanlond, senior	xxvj s̄ viij d̄
Thomas de Swanlond	xxvj s̄ viij d̄
Wiłłs de Roskele	xij s̄
Joħ de la Roskele	xxvj s̄ viij d̄
Barth Denmars	xxvj s̄ viij d̄
Joħ de Weston	vj s̄ viij d̄
Wiłł de Maccyngg	iiij s̄
Joħ Picot	viij s̄
Roḃtus Daynesham	xxvj s̄ viij d̄
Roḡ de Waltham	ij s̄ viij d̄
Nicħ de Dunstapele, minor	xxj s̄ vij d̄
Ric̄us Chunet	xxx s̄ viij d̄
Johns de Swanlond, minor	vj s̄ viij d̄
Joħ Brutyn	iij s̄
Ric̄ Andrew	xxvj s̄ viij d̄
Thomas de ffriston, Sherman	xij d̄
Hermann le Shippere	xxvj s̄ viij d̄
Nicħus de Dunstapele, senior	xvj d̄
Thomas de Spayne	xvj d̄
Petr̄ Cosyn	viij s̄
Joħ de Prestoñ Gerdelere	viij s̄
Bn̄dc̄us de Southfolk	ij s̄ viij d̄
Joħes ffot	x s̄ viij d̄
Joħ Vanne, Barber	xiij s̄ iiij d̄
Ric̄ de Salworth	xxvj s̄ viij d̄
Ric̄ de Dittoñ	viij d̄
Wiłł de Wircestre	xxxiij s̄ iiij d̄
Tideman Couset	ij s̄ viij d̄
Henr̄ le Chaundeler	.ij s̄
Joħ de Shrovesberry	iiij s̄
Wiłłs de Hulte	vj s̄ viij d̄
Thomas le Brewere	vj s̄ viij d̄
Joħ de Baudon, Dyegher	iiij s̄
Wiłł de Croidon, Taverñe	ij s̄ viij d̄
Wiłł de Chesham, Dyegher	iiij s̄
Joħ de Tewkesbery	ij s̄ viij d̄
Stepħs de Durem, Scherman	ij s̄ viij d̄
Wiłłs Swyft	iiij s̄
Joħ Robert Sherman	viij s̄
Hugh de Spalding, Sherman	xvj d̄
Petrus Vinion	iiij s̄
Thomas de Dunstaple, ffelmonger	xij d̄
Wiłłs le Chaundeler de Douegate	ij s̄ viij d̄
Wiłł de Douegate, Peleter	ij s̄ viij d̄
Thomas le Coupe et Wiłłs le Coupe	ij s̄ viij d̄
Joħ Marler	xvj d̄
Roḃtus atte Mor	xvj d̄
Adam le Coupe	xvj d̄
Ric̄ atte Sole, Bakere	xvj d̄
David le Cordewan	iiij s̄
Marcius Pihan	xvj d̄
Alanus de Pynyngton, Tayllour	xij d̄
Beatrix de Dunstaple	xij d̄

Riĉ Deumars	vj s̃ viij đ
Joħ ate Gerere	viij đ
Roƀtus de Norampton	viij đ
Anselmus le Peleter	viij đ
Roƀtus de Makeseye	ij s̃ viij đ
Wiłłs de Stanford	viij s̃ x đ oƀ qᵃ
Wiłłs de la March	iiij s̃
Riĉ de Buterle	v s̃ iiij đ
Joħ Bussħ, Barber	xij đ
Riĉ le Barber	viij đ
Walt atte Wharf	vj s̃ viij đ
Wiłł Ralond	vj s̃ viij đ
Wiłł de Kershalton	xvj đ
Joħ Mast, pistor	viij đ
Joħ Poterel	xvj đ
Wiłł de Licchefeld, Allutar	x đ oƀ qᵃ
Wiłł le Keu, Brewer	ij s̃
Riĉ le Mazoñ, Allutar	xij đ
Simon le Keu	xvj đ
Joħ le Drawere	xij đ
Wiłłs de ffristoñ	vj s̃ viij đ
Riĉ de Wendone	viij đ
Joħ Baudri, Dyegħere	xvj đ
Galff de Wyntton	xxvj s̃ viij đ
Wiłł de Wandelsworth	iiij s̃
Simon atte Walle, Brewere	xij đ
Joħ de Kent	xxvj s̃ viij đ
Adam Lopechaunt, keu	xij đ
Ric ffevere	viij đ
Wiłł de Harewełł	ij s̃ viij đ

p.ƀ. Smᵃ xxx łi xviij s̃ ix đ oƀ p.ƀ.

WARDA DE WALEBROKE.

Joħns de Cotoun	xxxv s̃ vj đ oƀ qᵃ
Simon de Mereworth	v mar
Joħns Hamond	liij s̃ iv đ
Simon Dolsely	xxvj s̃ iv đ
Edmundus Cosin	iv s̃
Joħ de Somesham	xxxj s̃ j đ oƀ
Agnes Jakes	xx s̃
Gaefr. de Botelier	xiij s̃ iv đ
Matild de Caxton	liij s̃ iv đ
Wiłłs ffaunt	iv s̃ v đ oƀ
Wiłłs de Lavenham	v s̃ iv đ
Thomas de Cantuaȓ	xvij s̃ ix đ oƀ
Thomas de Soñset	viij s̃
Eustachius de la Bataill	ij s̃ viij đ
Torus Ody	liij s̃ iv đ
Roƀtus de Knapwell, minor	ij s̃
Gaefr. de Schrowesbury	viij s̃ ix đ oƀ qᵃ
Joħ de Bedeford	xiij s̃ iv đ
Joħ de Bery	iv s̃
Wałtus Page	xiij s̃ iv đ
Ricus de Carleton	viij s̃ x đ oƀ qᵃ

G

Robtus de Wodeford	xxj đ ob
Johs Cole	iv s̄
Johs Brode	iv s̄
Johns de Eynesham	ij s̄ viij đ
Gaefr de Notyngham	iv s̄
Elias Dicoun	xiij s̄ iv đ
Lauř de Exceshr	iv s̄
Simon de Thorp	xvj đ
Nichs Godwyne	v s̄ iv đ
Robtus Ilger	xiij s̄ iv đ
Roḡus de Netlested	xxvj s̄ viij đ
Wills de Lichebergh	vj s̄ viij đ
Gilbtus de Lincoln	vj s̄ viij đ
Robtus de Knapwell	vj s̄ viij đ
Ric. de Oxon	x đ ob qa
Joh. de Oxon	xvj đ
Lauř Sely	iv s̄
Will Cane.	liij s̄ iv đ
Simon de Pulham	v s̄ iv đ
Petrus de Noue Cast	iv s̄
Will de Consowe	ij s̄
Henr. de Shawe	ij s̄
Robtus de Brugges	ij s̄ viij đ
Adam de Massebury	xij đ
Adam le Hore	xij đ
Johns de Schorne	xij đ
Andre le Hore	xij đ
Petr. de Sandwico	iv s̄
Adam le Piemakere	iv s̄
Joh. de Chalneye	iv s̄
Reginald le Tawiere	vj s̄ viij đ
Robtus Pynchebaner	xij đ
Elias de ffarnham	xij đ
Joh le Neve	xxvj s̄ viij đ
Gaefr. de Haselwell	xvj đ
Ricus de Mereworth	xiij s̄ iv đ
Rič Ingelond	ij s̄ viij đ
Thomas de Bruges	xvj đ
Wills de Haselwell	xij đ
Will Stacy	vj s̄ viij đ
Thomas de Sewell	xiij s̄ iv đ
Petrus Estmar	ij s̄ viij đ
Rob de Dene	ix s̄ iv đ
Augnes de Wynton	ij s̄
Joh le Dobbere	xvj đ
Rid ffox	iv s̄
Henř Peche	xij đ
Henř le Neve	xiij s̄ iv đ
Will de Wedon	ij s̄ viij đ
Thomas le Coupe	x đ ob qa
Joh Petit	ij s̄ viij đ
Joh le Mareschal	v s̄ iv đ
Wills de Kent	xij đ
Henř le Brode	xvj đ
Gilbs de Bromle	ij s̄
Simon le Bakere	xxvj s̄ viij đ

Waltus le Hore	xvj đ
Joh Page	viij s̄
Henr. atte ffrith	v s̄ iiij đ
Nichs de Wight	xl đ
Ricus le Longe	liij s̄ iiij đ
Joh atte ffrith	iiij s̄
Joh Goldeneye	xij đ
Joh Donmowe	xvj đ
Robtus le ffoundour	vj s̄ viij đ
Ric. de Chesthunte	xvj đ
Thomas atte Bourne	xij đ
Wiłłs de Stanbourn	xij đ
Joh Joye	x s̄ viij đ
Ric̄ le Yonge	x đ ob q^a
Rogus le Peleter	vj s̄ viij đ
Isabell de Cheyham	xij đ
Wiłłs de ffarnhurst	ij s̄
Petrus Dauboneye	xij đ
Henr̄ le Taillour	x đ ob q^a
Wiłł de Bokebrok	xvj đ
Wiłł de Oxon	x đ ob q^a
Joh de Godefeld	xij đ
Adam de Bery	x đ ob q^a
Joh de St. Edmñd	x đ ob q^a
Burnett le Spicer	xx s̄ ij đ ob q^a
Joh le Carte	ij s̄ viij đ
Elias de Thorp	xxj đ ob
Thomas de ffarnham	iiij s̄
Robts de Hatfeld	ij s̄ viij đ
Wiłłs de Braghynggs	iiij s̄

p.b. Sm^a xlvii łi ij s̄ iiij đ

WARDA VYNETRIE.

Johñs Gisors	ij mar
Johñs de Oxenford	xij mar
Ric de Rodyngges	xij mar
Walt Turk	iiij mar
Henr Gisors	xiij s̄ iiij đ
Wiłłs le Tourñ	ij s̄ viij đ
Henr le Palñie	v s̄ iiij đ
Stephs. atte Conduit	ij s̄ viij đ
Joh le ffruter	iiij s̄
Robt Heryngkarterc	iiij s̄
Walt Nel	viij mar
Henr̄ Moukor	ij s̄ viij đ
Adam le Chaundeler	xij đ
Philipus de Shopdon	iiij s̄
scratched out	
Robts de Linc[oln]	ij s̄ viij đ
Michel Mynot	ij mar
Joh de Combe	v s̄ iiij đ
Gilbtus le Joignour	v s̄ iiij đ
Thomas le Lymbnere	xvj đ
Alanus atte Hethe	v s̄ iiij đ

Witts Claptons	ij mar
Bñdcūs de ffulsham	iiij mar
Robtus le Callere	vj s̄ viij đ
Joħ de Romeseye	xij đ
Witt Barri	iiij s̄
Joħ Psoun	x s̄ viij đ
Joħ Renaud, devant	vj s̄ viij đ
Witts le Gang	vj s̄ viij đ
Joħ le Gros	ij s̄ viij đ
Joħ de Wissaund	ij s̄ viij đ
fferand Mangon	xiij s̄ iiij đ
Robtus le Lenne	viij đ
Witt de Kent, tegulator	vj s̄ viij đ
Ric̄ Brid	ij s̄ viij đ
Joħ le Bakere	xvj đ
Joħ ffynch	xvj đ
Joħ de Cranstok	ij s̄ viij đ
Joħ de Swyndon	iiij s̄
Joħ de Cressyngham	ij s̄ viij đ
Joħ Hardel	viij đ

Smᵃ xxxvij łi x s̄ p.ƀ.

WARDA DE CORDEWANSTRETE.

Roḡ de Ely		xl s̄
Joħ Capel		ij s̄ viij đ
Matild le Bracer		ij s̄
Mauricius le Roper		ix s̄ iiij đ
Petrus de Kyngeston		vj s̄ viij đ
Joħ de Hurton		xvj đ
Petrus de Armurer		ij s̄
Ric de Breteigne	iiij łi	
Thomas de Upton & Robtus Austyn, Socius eius	iiij łi	
Nicħ de Sañdwic̄o		xvj đ
Joħs de Kent Sakkere		xvj đ
Johñs le Sakkere, senior		ij s̄ viij đ
Petr̄ le Keu		viij đ
Johanna Heiroun		vj s̄ viij đ
Thomas le Brus		ij s̄ viij đ
Tehobaldus le Chaucer		vj s̄
Will le Taverner Chaucer		xij s̄
Richd de Berkyng		xxvj s̄ viij đ
Stephūs de Berhge		vj s̄ viij đ
Thomas de Kent		xxvj s̄ viij đ
Robtus Grendel		iij s̄ iiij đ
Joħ de Berkyng		vj s̄ viij đ
Joħ de Beverle		vj s̄ viij đ
Robtus Jordan		iiij s̄
Rid Keselyngbery		xxvj s̄ viij đ
Joħ de Kelyngworth		xiij s̄ iiij đ
Radūs˙ de Coventre		xvj s̄
Witts de Bannebery		ix s̄ iiij đ
Alisia de Speresholt		vj s̄ viij đ
Joħ atte Gate, bracer		iiij s̄
Joħ de Ileford, peleter		iiij s̄

Petr de Ware	iiij s̃	
Rog de Athelby	xiij s̃	iiij d̃
Rid̃. de Wolleford	liij s̃	iiij d̃
Joh de Bredstrete	xiij s̃	iiij d̃
Witts de Anyngtoñ	vj s̃	viij d̃
Henr̃ le Callere	xiij s̃	iiij d̃
Rid̃. le Ruthyn	xvij s̃	ix d̃ ob
Theobald de Caustoñ	xvij s̃	ix d̃ ob
Witt de Caustoñ	viij ti	
Mich de Causton	xxvj s̃	viij d̃
Rich de Lyncotn	liij s̃	iiij d̃
Witts Broune	viij s̃	
Renndeus de Burdeux	ij s̃	viij d̃
Thomas de Depham	vj s̃	viij d̃
Johñs Nichole	iiij s̃	
Thomas de Basham	iiij s̃	
Joh de Grantham	cvj s̃	viij d̃
Joh Trapp	xvj s̃	
Joh Bole	xiij s̃	iiij d̃
Adam de Brastlingworth	xiij s̃	iiij d̃
Thomas de Herewold	xiij s̃	iiij d̃
Joh de Braibourñ	vj s̃	iiij d̃
Thomas atte Vyegne	viij s̃	
Joh de Pritewett		viij d̃
Joh de Strode	xxvj s̃	viij d̃
Witt de Waltham		xvj d̃
Witt de Chelree	ij s̃	
Andr̃ Aubrey	iiij ti viij s̃	x d̃ ob qᵃ
Petr̃ Vanne	ij s̃	viij d̃
Gilbtus Payn		xvj d̃
Nichus atte Merssch	xx s̃	
Joh de Garton	xxvj s̃	viij d̃
Thomas de Garton	xiij s̃	iiij d̃
Witt de Thorneye	iiij ti	
Thomas Corp	viij s̃	
Joh Pisselegh	viij s̃	
Simon Rote	vj s̃	v [torn]
Galff̃ de Haliwell	vj s̃	v [torn]
Walt de Blenkynglegh	xxx s̃	[torn]
Galff̃ Batoun	iij s̃	iiij d̃
Ric de Cotyngton	vj s̃	viij d̃

p.b̃. Smᵃ lxij ti xiij s̃ j d̃ ob qᵃ p.b̃.

WARDA FFORI.[1]

Johes de Paston	xiij s̃	iiij d̃
Thoñ de Cantebrigg	vj s̃	viij d̃
Johes Picot	vj s̃	viij d̃
Johs de Writhele	ij s̃	viij d̃
David de Tillebury	ij s̃	viij d̃
Johs de la Pole	ij s̃	viij d̃
Johes de ffalstede		viij d̃
Henr̃ de Staunton	xxvj s̃	viij d̃

1. Cheap.

Johes ate Bowe	viij ᵭ
Eds de Wiche	v s̄ iiij ᵭ
Johes le Botiller	xvj ᵭ
Johs de Romberwe	xxvj s̄ viij ᵭ
Wilłs de Skeltoñ	xiij s̄ xvj ᵭ
Thom̄ de Waledeñ	xiij s̄ iiij ᵭ
Johes de Carlel	v s̄ iiij ᵭ
Johes de Norton	xvij s̄ ix ᵭ ob
Johes Wroth	vj s̄ viij ᵭ
Roḡus de Astwode	xxxvj s̄
Walłs le Wayte	ij s̄ viij ᵭ
Johes de Bokeler	ij s̄
Henr̄ de Reigate	xvj ᵭ
Johs le Mirorer	xiij s̄ iiij ᵭ
Gaefr̄. la Mirorer [name added]	xiij s̄ iiij ᵭ
Walłs. de Cavendissh	xvj ᵭ
Nichs de Horton	viij ᵭ
Robts le ffoundour	viij ᵭ
Ric̄us le Lacer	viij mar
Walt Sprot	xvj ᵭ
Johes le Chaundeler	ij s̄
Thom̄ West	xvj ᵭ
Wilłs de Arderne	ij s̄ viij ᵭ
Johes ffaunt	viij ᵭ
Wilł de Shrowesbury	xij s̄
Ric̄us Startolf	xx s̄
Wilłs de Stebenheth	iiij s̄
Johes de Enefeld, Brewer	viij ᵭ
Ric̄us Sprot	xij ᵭ
Ric̄us de Gaunt	ij s̄ viij ᵭ
Johes Bussh, Baker	xiij s̄ iiij ᵭ
Johes de Ewelle, Senior	xvj ᵭ
Henr̄ ate Rothe	xxvj s̄ viij ᵭ
Rads Cirotecar̄	ij s̄ viij ᵭ
Johes ate Naxe	iiij s̄
Ric̄s Scarlet	xij ᵭ
Johes ate Rothe	xij ᵭ
Ric̄d le Mirourer	xiij s̄ iiij ᵭ
Thom̄ de Pykenham	xiij s̄ iiij ᵭ
Wilłs de Berkhampstede	iiij s̄
Regiñld le Chaundeler	viij ᵭ
Wilłs de Elsyng	xiij s̄ iiij ᵭ
Ricus Ailward	xij ᵭ
Johes Potyn	liij s̄ iiij ᵭ
Sibiłł Potyn	vj s̄ viij ᵭ
Johs le Brewere	ij s̄ viij ᵭ
Nichus Blosme	xiij s̄ iiij ᵭ
Wilłs de Braghyng	viij ᵭ
Robts de Hete	vj s̄ viij ᵭ
Wilłs de Grubbelane	xxvj s̄ viij ᵭ
Alardus Larmurer	x s̄ viij ᵭ
Alex̄ de Burgoyne	xiij s̄ iiij ᵭ
Wilłs de Lathe	iiij s̄
Thom̄ le Peautrer	iiij s̄
Wilłs de Louhthebourgh	viij ᵭ
Johes Gut, Spic̄	xxvj s̄ viij ᵭ

Johes de Bristowe		iiij s̄
Roḡus le Latoñ		xvj đ
Thoñ de Cavendissh	iiij ƚi	
Wiƚƚs de Sabrichesworth		xvj đ
Roḡus Deynes		vi s̄ viij đ
Simon le ffoundour		iiij s̄ iiij đ
Rics de Sabrichesworth		viij đ
Thoñ le Carpent		xiij s̄ iiij đ
Rics de Gloucestre		ij s̄ viij đ
Johes de Mymmes		iiij s̄
Ricus de ffarnebergh		vj s̄ viij đ
Waltus le Keu, brewer		ij s̄ viij đ
Wiƚƚs ate ffold		ij s̄ viij đ
Ad de Saint Alban		xxvj s̄ viij đ
Robts le Clerk		ij s̄ viij đ
Robtus de Bedeford		viij đ
Wiƚƚs Tythynglomb		xiij s̄ iiij đ
Thom. Camon		viij đ
Johes Scot, Pulter		viij đ
Henr̄ de Benendoñ		xvj đ
Simon le Heaumer		viij đ
Johes le Chaundeler		xvj đ
Ricus Baldewyne		viij đ
Galfrid de Wynchecombe		xxvj s̄ viij đ
Thoñ Deynes		ij s̄
Henr. de Horpel		iiij s̄
Roḡus Sauvage		xij đ
Curtius le Lombard		ij s̄ viij đ
Wiƚƚs le Peautrer		v s̄ iiij đ
Gore Lombard		xxvj s̄ viij đ
Johes Urlond Lombard		iiij s̄
Petr̄ de Tryple		xxvj s̄ iiij đ
Johes Pecche		xiij s̄ viij đ
Barths Thomasin		xxvj s̄ viij đ
Wiƚƚs de Stanes		xxvj s̄ viij đ
Nichus Guillem		xiij s̄ iiij đ
Petr̄ de Arras		vij s̄ viij đ
Johes de Writele, Spic̄		vj s̄ viij đ
Simon Hauteyn		xxvj s̄ viij đ
Thoñ Hauteyn		xxvj s̄ viij đ
Wiƚƚs de Sainte Elena		v s̄ iiij đ
Robts de Saint Noz		iiij s̄
Ricus le Coffrer		ij s̄ viij đ
Wiƚƚs de Saint Alban		viij s̄
Wiƚƚs Aylward		xiij s̄ iiij đ
Thom de Castevene		xij đ
Roḡs de la Marche		ij s̄
Johes Knapwed		xxvj s̄ viij đ
Nichs de Grenewych		xiij s̄ iiij đ
Johes de Balsham		xiij s̄ iiij đ
Wiƚƚs Courtoys		xiij s̄ iiij đ
Simon ffranceys		x mars
Nichs le Clerk		x s̄ viij đ
Wiƚƚs de Hauchunte		xij đ
Galfrđ le Blake		xvj đ
Thoñ de Matthyng		ij s̄

Joħes de Beseviħ	xiij ş iiij đ
Christina Saleman	viij ş
Alic que fuit ux̄ Salmoñ la Coffrer	ij ş viij đ
Thoñ de Maryns	iiij ş
Joħes atte Barnet	ij ş viij đ
Nicħus de Roygate	ij ş
Joħnes de Enefeld	ij ş viij đ

p.ħ. Smᵃ lxvij ħ iij ş j đ oħ.

WARDA DE FFARNDON EXTRA.

Roħts le Ros, Sporier	xiij ş iiij đ
Wiħs le Cotiller	vj ş viij đ
Alañ de Wight, Hatter	xvj đ
Joħes de Pelham	ij ş viij đ
Waħts le Mareschal, Bocher	vj ş viij đ
Wiħs a Codeshalf, Bocher	vj ş viij đ
Rads le Hattere	viij đ
Joħes de Amondesham, Hatter	xvj đ
Rois que fuit ux. Robi le fferñ	xiij ş iiij đ
Roğus Chauntecler	vj ħ xiij ş iiij đ
Thoñ de Chetindon	viij ş
Simon le Armurer	vi ş viij đ
Ricus de Wronyngham, Hatter	ij ş
Wiħs de Passtfeld, Sporier	xij đ
Wiħ de Wapenham, Sporier	ij ş viij đ
Joħes Trot, Vyneter	vj ş viij đ
Rađus de Hobeleє	ij ş
Nicħus le Sporier	v ş iiij đ
Wiħs de Waltham, Cordwaner	xiij ş iiij đ
Joħes de Hertepol, Coteler	xvj đ
Wiħs de Toppesfeld	ij ş viij đ
Joħes le Beel	iiij ş
Thoñ Ciles	xvj đ
Ricđ le Sadeler	viij đ
Waħts atte Stow	vj ş viij đ
Galfrid Lefhoğ	xvj đ
Joħes le Vannere	xiij ş iiij đ
Roħts le Mareschal	xvj đ
Ricħus le Cok	xvj đ
Robts Petit	ij ş
Joħs Elys	xvj đ
Hugo de Arderne	viij ş
Wiħs de Stanford, Cord	xvj đ
Thom de Northalle	ij ş
Joħes Rote, Skinnere	xvj đ
Joħes Crigge, Brewere	ij ş
Ricħ de ffourbour	xvj đ
Joħes de Donstaple, Taverner	ij ş viij đ
Thoñ le Chaundeler	viij đ
Ricħs le Armurer	viij đ
Petῆ le Quisshoner	xij đ
Joħes le Canet	viij đ
Anabilia la Coke	ij ş

Robts le Honde	ij ſ viij ď
Robts le Goldsmyht	v ſ iiij ď
Elena ffayrman	xvj ď
Robts de Wyke	xvj ď
Johes Tany	xij ď
Johes le Stynners	viij ď
Robs le Beste, Tanñ	vj ſ viij ď
Johes atte Belle	viij ď
Ricď de Ledrede	xvj ď
Robt atte Mulle	xvj ď
Walts de Mosehache, Tanñ	viij ſ
Johes de Neuport, Bokebynder	xx ſ
Johes de Blakewelle	xiij ſ iiij ď
Roḡs Power	xvj ď
Phus Dykeman	liij ſ iiij ď
Rďus ate Welhour	viij ď
Simon Picote	xxvj ſ viij ď
Hugh le Mareschal	xxvj ſ viij ď
Ricď ate Vyne	xij ď
Johs Spront	viij ſ x ď ob qa
Johes Myles	xx ſ
Walts de Harwedon, Coseour	xl ſ
Wills de Bolyngbroke	xij ď
Wills le Haftere	xvj ď
Lauŕ de Suttoñ	iiij ſ
Wills de Machyng	[torn]
Ad le Leure	[torn]
Robts de Kirkeby, Tanner	[torn]
Rics Dymenes	[torn]
Henŕ Bonmarche	vj ſ viij ď
Hugh le Hattere	xij ď
Simon le Cotiller	v ſ iiij ď
Galfrid ate Cherche	vj ſ viij ď
Rics le Ussher	iiij ſ
Walts le Ussher	xvj ſ
Reginald le Tannere	viij ď
Walts de Schenefeld	vj ſ viij ď
Roḡs de Schopstode	viij ſ
Wills de Chelchehuthe	ij ſ
Johes Swyft	v ſ iiij ď
Robtus de Sto Albano	ij ſ
Wills le fforest	iiij ſ
Johes de Hendonne	xij ď
Johes Prentys	xvj ď
Raďus le Cotiller	xij ď
Petŕ le Hornere	viij ď
Walts le Arblaster	viij ď
Johes le Walkerne	viij ď
Rics de Luton, hatter	viij ď
Johes' le Sadeler	viij ď
Reginalď de Thorp	ij ſ
Ricus ate Gate	v ſ iiij ď
Robtus de Affte	iiij ſ
Wills Viary	iiij ſ

p.b. Smᵃ **xxxj li xix ſ** ij ď ob qᵃ.

WARDA DE CREPELGATE EXa

Joħes Quilter	x s̄ viij đ
Wiħs Pecok	x s̄ viij đ
Tircener	v s̄ iiij đ
Robtus de ffynchyngfeld	iiij s̄
Rađs Picot	v s̄ iiij đ
Robtus de Brighull	iiij s̄
Rađus de St. Albano	iij s̄ vj đ ob qᵃ
Joħ de Kyngeston	xvj đ
Joħ atte Crouch	xvj đ
Walt. Pecok	xvj đ
Joħns le Brewere	ij s̄
Joħns Seman	vj s̄ viij đ
Robtus Picot	viij đ
Wiħs de Parkele	xvj đ
Robtus de Harengeye	vj s̄ viij đ
Adam Inchelane	xvj đ
Hugh atte Cok	vij s̄ iiij đ
Joħ le Kynky	xvj đ
Henr de Denecombe	xxvj s̄ viij đ
Wiħs de Berkynugg, fuster	viij đ
Adm le Nailere	iiij s̄
Rid de Enefeld	ij s̄ viij đ
Waltus Inchemore	v s̄ iiij đ
Rid de Stokwell	xvj đ
Roğus Stoppesle	x đ ob qᵃ
Symond Porkesle	viij đ
Rich de Newton	viij đ
Robtus Brokke	viij đ
Wiħs de Bedeford	viij đ
Symon Seman	ij s̄ viij đ
Joħns le Gardiner	viij đ
Walt Baudry	iiij s̄
Thomas de Kent	ij s̄ viij đ
Joħ Lynkthorn	ij s̄
Thomas de Braghinges	viij đ
Adam le Couere	xvj đ
Gilbtus le Chaloner	iiij s̄ iiij đ
Robtus atte Welle	viij đ
Walt le Cordewaner	xvj đ
Joħ le Glasenwiche	viij đ
Alic Podifat	v s̄ iiij đ
Gaefr̄ de Litlyngtoñ	xvj đ
Wiħ Baudry	iiij s̄

p.b. Smᵃ vij ħi ix s̄ ix đ ob.

PORTSOKNE.

Nicħus Dereman, Bocher	xiij s̄ iiij đ
Stepħus Talp, Brewere	iiij s̄
Joħs de Romeneye, Pottere	ix s̄ iiij đ
Joħs Hank, Drovere	xxvj s̄ viij đ
Waltus Cobbe, Bocher	vj s̄ viij đ
Alex̄ Cobbe, Bocher	vj s̄ viij đ
Thomas Cobbe, Bocher	iiij s̄

Martiñ Girdlere, Bocher	viij ß x ᵭ oƀ qᵃ
Joħns le Brewere	xvj ᵭ
Roƀtus de Stapelford, Brewere	xvj ᵭ
Laurencius le Meneter, Brewere	xvj ᵭ
Joħs atte Gate, Bocher	x ᵭ oƀ qᵃ
Hugh atte Banke, Bocher	xxj ᵭ oƀ
Rogus de Algate, Pottere	ij ß viij ᵭ
Waltus Andrew, Bocher	x ᵭ oƀ qᵃ
Waltus Cartere, ffrutrer	ij ß
Thomas de Caxton, Bocher	xvj ᵭ
Henr̄ de Swofham, ffruter	xvj ᵭ
Warinus Tasse	xij ᵭ
Robtus Tasse	xij ᵭ
Riċ Dun	xij ᵭ
Petr̄ de Weston	xvj ᵭ
Joħes de Stowe	x ᵭ oƀ qᵃ

Smᵃ cvij ß vij ᵭ qᵃ p.ƀ.

WARDA DE ALLEGATE.

Maurice Turgys	xxii ß viii ᵭ
Wiłłs. Shep	xx ß
Joħes de Newebery	v ß iv ᵭ
Riċus Tripet	ix ß iv ᵭ
Joħes Hadham	vi ß viii ᵭ
Thomas Savage	iv ß
Raᵭus de Kent	iv ß
Simon de Totynhale	iv ß
Riċus atte Baskette	ii ß viii ᵭ
Laur̄ Maushipe	ii ß viii ᵭ
Arnaldus Quilter	ii ß
Riċus le ffourbour	ii ß viii ᵭ
Wiłłs le Warner	ii ß viii ᵭ
Joħs le Coliere	ii ß viii ᵭ
Wiłłs Baudry	xvi ᵭ
Joħns de Grenewich	ii ß
Joħs Holyn	ii ß
Salemon le Pottere	iii ß iv ᵭ
Joħs Hardi	ii ß viii ᵭ
Roƀtus de Benstede	xxi ᵭ oƀ
Waltus Costantyn	ii ß viii ᵭ

Smᵃ C. ix ß ix ᵭ oƀ p.ƀ.

WARD DE BYLLNGESGATE.

Wiłłs Tropynet	xij ᵭ
Wiłłs Alisaundre	viij ß
Joħs Joye	xiij ß iiij ᵭ
Thomas atte Vyne	viij ß
Simon de Cantuar̄, carpent	viij ß
Huᵹ̆. Curteys, Taillour	xiij ß iiij ᵭ
Nicħ Deubeneye	xxij ß ij ᵭ oƀ qᵃ
Joħ de Causton	xvij ß ix ᵭ oƀ
Alanus Gille	lxvj ß viij ᵭ

Roḃtus de Hakeneye	xx s̄
Joħ de Londoneston	ij s̄
Gilbtus le Clerk	iiij s̄
Joħ de Navestoke	x ḋ oḃ qᵃ
Roḃt Scharp	xvj ḋ
Raḋ. att Pole	viij s̄
Henr̄. Beauflour	ij s̄ viij ḋ
Laur̄. de Ludelowe	x ḋ oḃ qᵃ
Joħ. de Baldok, chauṅdeler	xvj ḋ
Joħ. Wymark	v s̄ iiij ḋ
Alex̄. Lucas	iiij s̄
Wiłłs. Cros	xiij s̄ iiij ḋ
Roḃtus de Derby	iij s̄ iiij ḋ
Joħ de Dovenich	xxvj s̄ viij ḋ
Hugh le Hurer	iij s̄ vjḋ oḃ qᵃ
Adam Pikeman	liij s̄ iiij ḋ
Joħs Ruddok	iiij s̄
Joħs Greylond	v s̄ iij ḋ
Thomas de Lodrede	ij s̄ viij ḋ
Ric̄. Aleyn	v s̄ iiij ḋ
Thomas de Braynford	viij s̄
Joħ Leche	xx s̄
Roḃtus de Chidingfeld	xij ḋ
Thomas atte Grene	xvj ḋ
Ric̄. Double	viij s̄
Robtus Storm	xx s̄
Wiłłs Turk	vj s̄ viij ḋ
Gilḃtus Cros	ij s̄
Adam de Arderne, baker	xvj ḋ
Roḃtus Madour	xvj ḋ
Adam de Louth	iiij s̄ x ḋ oḃ qᵃ
Joħ Yoñ	xxvj s̄ viij ḋ
Joħ Cros	ij s̄
Joħ de Warefeld	xiij s̄ iiij ḋ
Wiłłs Beauflour	xiij s̄ iiij ḋ
Joħs Thomelyn	vj s̄ viij ḋ
Roḃ de Eboraco	v s̄ iiij ḋ
Ric̄ de Lamhuth	v s̄ iiij ḋ
John de Wrotham	iiij s̄ viij ḋ
Roḃtus le Ropere	viij s̄

Smᵃ xxiiij łi x s̄ ij ḋ oḃ qᵃ p.ḃ.

WARDA DE BISSHOPESGATE.

Roḡus le Mareschal	xvj ḋ
Joħes le Longe	xvj ḋ
Ric̄us le Mareschal	ij s̄
Walẗus de Lyndwode	xxvj s̄ viij ḋ
Cambyn ffolberd	xxvj s̄ viij ḋ
Joħes de Tholouse	viij mar
Ragate Lombard	x s̄ viij ḋ
Gilḃtus Aswote	xvj ḋ
Joħes Pedewardyn	xvj ḋ
Alanus Aspal	iiij s̄
Joħes Osekyn	xvj ḋ

Pelle Chaundeler	xij ᵭ
Johnes de Chesthunte	xvj ᵭ
Alan Prat	xvj ᵭ
Johnes Frere	vj ŝ viij ᵭ
Wiłłms ate Cokke	ij ŝ viij ᵭ
Wiłłms de Montagu	xij ᵭ
Ricus le Heymongŕ	ij ŝ viij ᵭ
Cristiana ate Gate	xvj ᵭ
Johnes Huberd	xvj ᵭ
Thomas le Chaundeler	xvj ᵭ
Wiłłms le Baker	xij ᵭ
Andreas Portenar	x mar
Symon le Barber	xvj ᵭ
Ricus de Swanlond	xij ᵭ
Thomas le Barber	ij ŝ viij ᵭ
Galfridus le Whytawyer	ij ŝ viij ᵭ
Johes Bryd	ij ŝ
Raᵭus Heyron	xiij ŝ iiij ᵭ
Wiłłs de Baldok, carnifex	xij ᵭ
Johes de Thilbournham	xij ᵭ
Galfridus Lyghtfot	xvj ᵭ
Johes Hering	v ŝ iiij ᵭ
Jacobus Mautel	xvj ᵭ
Johes Wysman	ij ŝ
Godfridus Lelly	iiij ŝ
Thoms le Gardener	viij ᵭ
Johnes Cosyn	viij ᵭ
Ričus le Brewere	viij ᵭ
Robus le Taverñ	x ᵭ oᵬ qᵃ
Ričus le Pakker	viij ᵭ
Thomas Mautel	viij ᵭ
Henricus Beumond	viij ᵭ
Nichs Pongg	iiij ŝ
Jacobus Sherman	iiij ŝ
Henric de Norhamton	iij ŝ
Wiłłs de Poumfreyt	iiij ma

p.ᵬ. Smᵃ **xxij ᵗi vj ŝ vj ᵭ oᵬ qᵃ** p.ᵬ.

WARDA DE BRADESTRETE.[1]

Johs Hauteyn	lxvj ŝ viij ᵭ
Henŕ Darcy	cvj ŝ viij ᵭ
Johs Poyntel	xxvj ŝ viij ᵭ
Johs Sok	xx ŝ
Johs de Herewarstoke	xxvj ŝ viij ᵭ
Huḡ. Dedham	xxvj ŝ viij ᵭ
Ricus de Staundon	xxxv ŝ vj ᵭ oᵬ qᵃ
Wiłłs. de Potenhale	xx ŝ
Raᵭs le Chaundeler	ij ŝ viij ᵭ
Johs Sefoul	v ŝ iiij ᵭ
Nichs le Songe	v ŝ iiij ᵭ
Petrus atte Reredore	xiij ŝ iiij ᵭ
Roᵬtus de Chesthunte	vj ŝ viij ᵭ

1. **Broad Street**.

Joħs le Chaundeler	vij s̄ ix d̄ oƀ
Wiłł le Bakere	iiij s̄
Wiłł de Schorne	vj s̄ viij d̄
Joħs de Notyngham	v s̄ iv d̄
Joħs de Lyndeseye	ij s̄
Stepħs le Coky	ij s̄ viij d̄
Thomas atte Rededore	xx s̄
Henr̄. Lauren	xiij s̄ iiij d̄
Roƀts de Witteneye	vj s̄ viij d̄
Adam de Ondeby	x s̄ viij d̄
Joħ de Oteswich	xiij s̄ iv d̄
Joħ de Berden	xiij s̄ iiij d̄
Elias le Coupe	vj s̄ viij d̄
Thomas Liouns	vj s̄ viij d̄
Joħs le Callere	ij s̄
Godefr de Eldyng	ij s̄ viij d̄
Katina de Hanham	ij s̄
Wiłł. de Castre	iiij s̄ iiij d̄
Roƀtus Chauntour	xxvj s̄ viij d̄
Simon le Wyttawere	xvj d̄
Joħ. Toinard	xvj d̄
David de Kyngeston	ij s̄ viij d̄
Wiłł. Terry	iiij s̄
Walt. de Oxenford	viij d̄
Ric̄. de Wynton	xvj d̄
Ric̄. de ffalstede	iv s̄
Hugh le Brewere	viij d̄
Wiłł le Gerdlere	viij d̄
Wiłł Prophete	viij d̄
Joħ. de Doune	x d̄ oƀ q̄ᵃ
Thomas de Newenton	viij d̄
Adam de Elmedon	x d̄ oƀ q̄ᵃ
Wiłł de Calvedon	xvj d̄
Pħus Swift	iiij s̄
Nicħus de Bery	viij d̄
Gaefr. le Armurer	viij d̄
Petrus le Chaundeler	xvj d̄
Stepħus de Hodosdon	xvj d̄
Roƀtus atte ffelde	ij s̄
Ric̄ de Chavering, uphelder	xvj d̄
Ric̄ de Cordewaner	xvj d̄
Roƀtus Gosebak	ij s̄ viij d̄
Roƀtus de Grantele	xvj d̄
Joħs de Rothynges, carpent.	viij d̄
Petr de Morpath	xvj d̄
Roƀtus de Canterburgh	ij s̄
Joħ le Sakkere	ij s̄
Roƀts de Rothyng	xvj d̄
Roḡus le Bere	xvj d̄
Wiłłs le Hore	xiij s̄ iv d̄
Wiłłs de Godeleston	iv s̄
Joħna de Herlawe	ij s̄ viij d̄
Joħ. le Barber	xvj d̄
Wiłłs atte Ponde	vj s̄ viij d̄
Joħna de ħarnebergh	iiij s̄
Thomas Poyntel	ij s̄ viij d̄

Roḡ Poyntel	ij ſ viij ɗ
Petrus. le Coffrer	ij ſ viij ɗ
Walꝫ. Muriet	xvj ɗ
Joħ. de Totynham, carpenꝫ	xvj ɗ
Walꝫ. de Lokkesle	viij ɗ

Smᵃ xxx ꝉi xvij ſ ix ɗ oꝺ qᵃ p.ꝺ.

WARDA DE LANGEBOURN.

de Hodesdon Cocus	ij ſ viij ɗ
⌐Document ⌐ btus Bourounci	xij ɗ
[torn] de Bradele	xiij ſ iv ɗ
de Takkele	iiij ſ
Joħ de Brstoll	viij ɗ
Robtus de Stratford	vj ſ viii ɗ
Robtus de Holewell	vj ſ viii ɗ
Rič Wilde	xij ɗ
Matild atte Vyne	xx ſ
Magister Henr le Mareschal	viij ɗ
Marger Albon	viij ɗ
Wiꝉꝉs de Dakenhale	xij ɗ
Henr de Webbele	xij ɗ
Thomas le Chaundeler	iiij ſ iv ɗ
Robtus atte Gate	iv ɗ
Nicħus atte fforde	xxj ɗ oꝺ
Joħ de Bromhelm	iv ſ
Wiꝉꝉs Cꝉicus	xij ɗ
Ric. ffrere	xij ɗ
Rich. de ffische	ij ſ
Robtus de Burgh	ij ſ
Joħs. Wyneman	viij ɗ
Joħ de Southereye	iv ſ
Rič Merk	v ſ iv ɗ
Johñ de Bokenham	xij ɗ
Wiꝉꝉs Palmē	xvj ɗ
Wills de Stanes	xij ɗ
Joħ Warntri	viij ɗ
Stepħ. Thomas, Pistor	viij ɗ
Wiꝉꝉs de Cornwaille	xvj ɗ
Wiꝉꝉs le Hattere	xvj ɗ
Joħ de London	xij ɗ
Walꝫ. Cocus	xvj ɗ
Wiꝉꝉ le Cordewañ	ij ſ viij ɗ
Rič attc Cocke	viij ɗ
Thomas Abel	xij ɗ
Wills le fischmonger	viij ɗ
Reginald de Conduit	xxxv ſ vj ɗ oꝺ q
Joħ Breynte	xij ɗ
Roḡus Cille	ij ſ viij ɗ
Robtus Coky	viij ɗ
Joħ Spronke	viij ɗ
Adam de Kelseye	viij ɗ
Gaefr. Aleyn	xxvj ſ viij ɗ
Rič le Taillour	viij ɗ
Isabeꝉꝉ Godchep	vj ſ viij ɗ

Barth. de Stanho	liij s̄	iv d̄
Thomas Godchep	xiij s̄	iv d̄
Robtus le Sadeler		xij d̄
Will de Croidon		xvj d̄
Hug de Kent		xij d̄
Robtus de Bristoll		xij d̄
Will Wastel		xvj d̄
Joh de Nonnes	vj s̄	viij d̄
Rob de Swalelme		xvj d̄
John Hablount	xiij s̄	iv d̄
Thomas atte Wode, pistor	ix s̄	iv d̄
Joh de Totenham	viij s̄	
Joh atte Belle	vj s̄	viij d̄
Eustachus Lombard		xij d̄
Robtus Crigge		viij d̄
Joh Alisaundre		xvj d̄
Radus Baret		xij d̄
John le Clerk, hodere	xxvj s̄	viij d̄
Laur̄ de Canefeld		xvj d̄
Rog̃ Godchep		xij d̄
Reynerus Barber		xvj d̄
Ivo le Coupe		xij d̄
Joh Ace	xvj s̄	viij d̄
Hugh Picard		xvj d̄
Nichs atte Marche		viij d̄
Mag̃r Henry de Lindesere		xij d̄
Wills Dereman		viij d̄
Thomas Otewy	xiij s̄	iiij d̄
Alex̄. de Watford	ij s̄	
Wills. de Wrotham	ij s̄	
Walt. de Stepenheth		viij d̄

p.b. Sm̃a xviij l̃i vij s̄ viij d̄ p.b.

WARDA RIPE REGINE.[1]

Alanus de Tichewell	xxvj s̄	viij d̄
Henr Chaundeler, fruiter	iiij s̄	
Thomas de Leddredre	viij s̄	
Joh le Coroner	v s̄	iiij d̄
Gilbtus Pany	xxvj s̄	viij d̄
Nichus de Burgh	xiij s̄	iiij d̄
Thomas Curteys	vj s̄	viij d̄
Joh Laudron	ij s̄	
Joh de Ditton	ij s̄	
Ric̄ le Rous	iiij s̄	
Henr le Keu		xij d̄
Will le Keu		xvj d̄
Thomas Squier		xvj d̄
Joh Pynne, fruiter		viij d̄
Joh de Hylaunde	v s̄	iiij d̄
Walt̄ Gardiner		xvj d̄
Joh Hosebonde		viij d̄
Will Palm̃e		xvj d̄
Ric̄ de Reynham	xl s̄	

1. Queenhithe.

Riē de Ware	ix s̄ iiij d
Wiłłs de Neuport	ix s̄ iiij d
Roḡ de Bedyngfeld	vj s̄ viij d
Thomas de Gloucestre	xiij s̄ iiij d
Joħ Wade	xvj d
Wiłłs Sterre, Taverñ	xvj d
Wiłłs de Stamstok	xvj d
Wiłłs de la Cornere	xij d
Agnes de Reygate	ij s̄ viij d
Riē Waldeschef	viij d
Nicħs le Orfevre	viij d
Riēs le Haymonger	xij d
Riē le Chaundeler	xvj d
Thomas atte Lose, Pessoner	ij s̄ viij d
Wiłłs de Worthstede	xvj d
Margeria le Vaus	viij d
Walt Harneys	viij d
Walt de Berham	xvj d
Matild de Berkyngg	viij s̄ x d oƀ qᵃ
Joħ le Haymongere	viij d
Agnes de Kent	iiij s̄
Roḡus de Bernes	viij s̄ x d oƀqᵃ
Stepħus de Staneford	xiij s̄ iiij d
Gilƀtus de Berkyngg	vj s̄ viij d
Wiłł Trigg	ij s̄ viij d
Galff Scot	xij d
Wiłł de ffulham	viij s̄ x d oƀ qᵃ
Riē de Stratford	vj s̄ viij d
Wiłłs Michel	xiij s̄ iiij d
Joħs de Bixle	xij d
Martinius de Chikewell	lxvj s̄ viij d
Wiłł de Ware	xxvj s̄ viij d
Roƀtus Bernard	viij s̄
Walt de Theydoñ, chaundeler	xij d
Reginaldus de Codyngtoñ	iiij s̄
Jacobus de Denham	viij d
Joħns de Balsham	xij d
Wiłł Taverner	xij d
Roƀtus de Richemond	ij s̄
Wiłłs de Berkyng	vj s̄ viij d
Stepħus Savage	viij d
Lenota le Bracer	viij d
Joħ de Saunford, chaundeler	xvj d
Matild Piebakere	xij d
Wiłłs Boteler	xij d
Joħ de Neutoñ	xij d
Joħ de Walpoł	ij s̄
Henf Hosebond	ij s̄ viij d
Adam le Traier	xvj d
Alicia Pipechese	xij d
Joħns Bran	iiij s̄
Joħ Page	xij d
Wiłł de Brynkele	iiij s̄
Riēus Edrop de Oxon	ij s̄
Huḡ le ffitz Roger	xij d

p.ƀ. Smᵃ xx łi xix s̄ iiij d qᵃ p.ƀ.

H

WARDA DE BREDSTRETE.[1]

Joħ de Dallynges	v ṡ iiij đ
Joħ Makeheved	iiij ṡ
Simon de Berkynges	v ṡ iiij đ
Alanus de Conductu	xxvj ṡ viij đ
Joħ de Conductu	iiij ṡ
Stepħus de Parys	ij ṡ
Wals de Skardeburgh	ij ṡ viij d
Joħ Sprot	xvj đ
Joħ Janyn	x ṡ viij đ
Joħ le Boteler	v ṡ iiij đ
Joħ Blank	ij ṡ viij đ
Joħ de Drayton	ij ṡ viij đ
Wiłł de Cheyham	xxvj ṡ viij đ
Osbeř de Braye	xiij ṡ iiij đ
Gilbtus de Fulham	viij đ
Wałt de Barkworth	viij đ
Robts de Hore	vj ṡ viij đ
Joħ le Noreys	xvj đ
Huḡ de Depedeñ	iiij ṡ
Wiłłs le Cirger	iiij ṡ
Adam de ffarndon	viij đ
Joħ le Lithyngtoñ	viij đ
Wiłł Daungre	iiij ṡ
Roḡ le Peutrer	vj ṡ viij đ
Robts le Brokesbourñ	xvj đ
Joħ atte Loke	iij ṡ iiij đ
Anthonius Citroun	xl ṡ
Thomas de Crokeslee	ij ṡ
Joħ Scot	xvj đ
Thomas de Scharnebrok	ij ṡ viij đ
Nicħus atte Rothe	ij ṡ viij đ
Joħ de Refham	ij ṡ
Wiłłs de Garton	viij đ
Stepħs le Palm̄	xvj đ
Gilbtus le Palm̄	x ṡ viij đ
Joħ de Eilesham	xiij ṡ iiij đ
Riċ de Stokebregh	xvj đ
Hamo le Barber	xiij ṡ iiij đ
Thomas Walpol	vj ṡ viij đ
Joħ Gubbe	viij đ
Ricus Gubbe	xxvj ṡ viij đ
Joħ de Denham	vj ṡ viij đ
Nicħs Madefrey	xvj đ
Joħes de Triple	xiij ṡ iiij đ
Hugħ Madefrey	ij ṡ viij đ
Rid Heigne	vj ṡ viij đ
Robtus de Stratford	viij đ
Wiłł de Berkyñḡ	ij ṡ
Joħs de Goucestre	xiij ṡ iiij đ
Petrus Warde	xvj đ
Wałt de Bampton	xvij ṡ ix đ oħ
Joħ de Stanstede	viij đ

1. Bread Street.

Joħ de Kent, faber	xij đ
Joħ de Tarente	viij s̃
Joħ atte Riole	ij s̃
Wiłłs de Hales	v s̃ iiij đ
m de Charnel	viij s̃
Baynard	xvj đ
[Hole.] de Kyngestoñ	xiij s̃ iiij đ
el le Kerner	ij s̃
de Bentlee	xvj đ
Joħ de Godestone	xx s̃
Petrus Bisshop	ij s̃
Galfr de Bodelee	ij s̃ viij đ
Wiłłs de Denham	ij s̃ viij đ
Christina la Thelmostere	ij s̃
Sabyna de Rodyñg	viij đ
Isabełł de Wybourne	ij s̃
Margeria Gubbe	ij s̃
Margareta Maderman	x đ oƀ qᵃ
Aliĉ de Bredstrete	viij đ
Joħna Lovekyn	viij đ
Agatha de Draytoñ	viij đ
Joħ Bovet and Thomas frat eius	xl s̃
Joħ de Ware	ix s̃ iiij đ
Riĉ de Kent	vj s̃ viij đ
Joħ de Tiffeld	ij s̃ viij đ

p.ƀ. Smᵃ xxiij łi xvj s̃ iiij đ qᵃ.

WARDA DE BASSIESHAWE.

Joħes de Dallyng	j mar
Laur le Botener	viij s̃ x đ oƀ qᵃ
Niĉħ de Caustone	j mar
Joħns de Ebor	ij mar
Riĉ de Hakeborn	viij s̃ ix đ oƀ qᵃ
Roƀtus de ffromele	xvj đ
Rogus de Dunkele	x đ oƀ qᵃ
Rogus Madour	iiij s̃
Simon de Levesham	iiij s̃
Joħ de Berdefeld	x đ oƀ qᵃ
Petr̃ de Tabelet	xvj đ
Wiłł Bateman	xxj đ oƀ
Jacobus le Kisser	xvj đ
Alanus de ffrestoñ	iiij s̃
Joħ le Honute, keu	x đ oƀ qᵃ
Rogus le Dallyng	xvj đ
Thomas atte Brom	xvj đ
Wiłłs ffurnivałł	viij đ

Smᵃ iiij łi xiiij s̃ xj đ qᵃ.

WARDA DE COLMANSTRETE.

Rads de Upton	xxxv s̃ vj đ oƀ qᵃ
Hugħ de Stokes	i mar
Ric de Reynham	ij mar
Stepħus le Coteler	xxxij đ

Waltus de Denesle	viij ꝺ
Joħ de Pottele	iiij s̃
Henr̄ de Waltene	iiij s̃
Thomas de Thorplond	xvj ꝺ
Adam le Selgraver	viij s̃
Joħs ffissch	viij ꝺ
Riꝺus Schordich	xvj ꝺ
Nicħus le Dubber̄	xij ꝺ
Joħ Deynes	i mar
Joħ Botild	xvj ꝺ
Wiꝉ le Chaundeler	xvj ꝺ
Henr̄ de Ware	i mar
Joħnes Priour	xij ꝺ
Hugħ le Carpenter	viij ꝺ
Joħ de Odyham	xvj ꝺ
Dionisia de Eynesham	x s̃ viij ꝺ
Joħns Starkulf	x s̃ viij ꝺ
Wiꝉ de Spondeñ	viij ꝺ
Wiꝉ atte Halle	xxj ꝺ oꝺ
More Kelendrer	ij s̃ viij ꝺ
Robtus Lychfot	vj s̃ viij ꝺ
Joħ le Chaundeler	ij s̃ viij ꝺ
Adam le Gerdler	viij ꝺ
Symon le Barber	i mar
Roḡus le Wirdrawere	xvj ꝺ
Henr̄ Hauberger	viij ꝺ
Margaret de Chesthunte	xvj ꝺ
Wiꝉs Martyn	iiij s̃
Wiꝉs le Dyere	ij s̃ viij ꝺ
Johns de Euelle	vj s̃ viij ꝺ
Hugħ de Stortford	viij ꝺ
Aliꝝ Warius	xij ꝺ
Simon le Skynñ	viij ꝺ
Cristina Caps	iiij s̃
Ricus ffruiter	viij ꝺ
Thomas le Coteler	viij ꝺ
Wariñ de Hodesdoñ	viij s̃
Rogus de Wistoñ	ij s̃ viij ꝺ
Huḡ Homle	xvj ꝺ
Stepħs Poyntel	vj s̃ viij ꝺ
Thomas Chescoumbe	vj s̃ viij ꝺ
Robtus Wynhelm	iiij mar
Laur̄ de Chayham	ij s̃
Joħna le Naile	viij ꝺ
Wiꝉ Purtere	ij s̃ viij ꝺ
Christina atte Brighous	viij ꝺ
Wiꝉs de Denham	vj s̃ viij ꝺ
Robtus le Raas	xvj ꝺ
Rid de Bottele	xx s̃
Wiꝉs Pope	iiij s̃
Joħ Gentyl	xvj ꝺ
de Herlawe	iiij s̃
[Torn.] ũs ffoundour	ij s̃ viij ꝺ
us le Kyng	ij s̃ viij ꝺ
Pħus Gentil	v s̃ iiij ꝺ

p.ꝺ. Sm^a xvj ꝉi xviij s̃ iiij ꝺ q^a p.ꝺ.

WARDA DE ALDRESGATE.

Henr̄ de Segford	vj s̄ viij d̄
Joħ de Champaigne	iiij s̄ iiij d̄
Roḡus de Woxebrugges	iiij s̄
Joħ Hugh	v s̄ iiij d̄
Simon le Goldbetr	iiij s̄
Riđus de Bernham	ij s̄ viij d̄
Thomas ffriday	iiij s̄
Radūs de Northfolk	xvj d̄
Emma atte Grove	xij d̄
Thomas Nichole	iiij s̄
Joħ Wyrhale	ij s̄ viij d̄
Joħ de Mymmes	xvj d̄
Thomas de Wilteshire	xij d̄
Joħns de Lillyngston	ij s̄ viij d̄
Negellus de Whatéle	v s̄ iiij d̄
Robtus le Reyntour	xij d̄
Roḡus Dun, peller	iiij s̄
Joħ de Kent	ij s̄
Joħ de Stokes	ij s̄
Adam le Pehemyn	ix d̄ oƀ qᵃ
Joħ Spray, junior	iiij s̄ iiij d̄
Wiłłs de Eton	xvj d̄
Emma de Burdene	ij s̄
Gaefr. de Harengeye	xvj d̄
Joħns le Peyntour	iiij s̄
Nichus de Rameseye	xvj d̄
Joħns de Thame	iiij s̄ iiij d̄
ffelicia de St. Albano	xvj d̄
Wiłłs de Som̃sete	ij s̄ viij d̄
Thomas de Chacombe	ij s̄
Wiłłs de Rameseye	xiij s̄ iiij d̄
Joħs le ffrensshe	xij d̄
Joħna de Berkynges	ix d̄ oƀ qᵃ
Andr. le Bocher	ij s̄ viij d̄
Wiłł Chaundeler	iiij s̄ iiij d̄
Rads. Neuman	xvj d̄
Joħns le Callere	xij d̄
Simon de Graston	xvj d̄
Joħ de Leycester	xvj d̄
Petr̄ atte Corner	iiij s̄
Gaefr. de Eston	ij s̄ viij d̄
Wills de Salesbery	xvj d̄
Thomas de Cantebrugḡ	ij s̄

p.ƀ. Smᵃ cxvij s̄ xj d̄ qᵃ oƀ p.ƀ.

WARDA DE CREPELGATE INFRA.

Nichus de ffarnđon	viij s̄ x d̄ oƀ qᵃ
Robts le Bret	xl s̄
Robts de Kelseye	vj s̄ viij d̄
Ad de Burgoyne	liij s̄ iiij d̄
Joħes de Hyngeston	xl s̄

Joħes le Younge	xiij s̃ iiij đ
Wiłłs Sporoun	xiij s̃ iiij đ
Thom le Werroun	ij mar
Joħes de Kyselyngbury	ij mar
Joħes de Pampesworth	xl s̃
Thoñ de Worstede	ij mar
Joħes Russel	xiij s̃ iiij đ
Joħes de Colwełł	ij mar
Wiłłs atte Spense	ij s̃ viij đ
Hamo de Toltham	xvj đ
Joħes de Mounguler	xvj đ
Petr̃ de Sellyng	v s̃ iiij đ
Roğs de ffrowyk	xiij s̃ iiij đ
Ric̃s le Disshere	ij s̃ viij đ
Thoñ de Porkelee	ij s̃
Nichus de Wyrlingworth	xiij s̃ iiij đ
Joħes de Wattoñ	x s̃ iiij đ
Gilbts Tymbermonğ	vj s̃ viij đ
Adam de Walpol	iiij s̃
Nichs de Hedyngdon	viij s̃
Joħes de Totenham, chaundeler	vj s̃ viij đ
Rađs le Gildere	v s̃ iiij đ
Galfrid le Goldbetere	vj s̃ viij đ
Reğin de S̃o Qutino	xvj đ
Robts de Pertenhale	xvj đ
Walłs le Cok	xvj đ
Hugo Otewy	xij đ
Joħ Coc̃ điu s. Willi de Everdon	xvj đ
Wiłłs le Couper	xvj đ
Robts le Sutton	xij đ
Ad le Chaundeler	xvj đ
Ric̃us le Hodere	iiij s̃
Rogs de Mymmes	xij đ
Joħes de Wynton	xx đ
Joħes le Hore	xiij s̃ iiij đ
Alic̃ Eypt	ij s̃ viij đ
Margia ate Welle	xij đ
Wiłłs de Pertenhale	xx s̃
Thoñ de Dallynğ	xiij s̃ iiij đ
Thoñ le Brewere	ij s̃ viij đ
Gilbtus de Salisbury	vj s̃ viij đ
Rađs ate Brome	xvj đ
Ric̃us Costontyn	liij s̃ iiij đ
Robt le Hosier	xvj đ
Petr̃ de ffulbourñ	iiij s̃
Henr le Cheyñ	xiij s̃ iiij đ
Jordañ le Taillur̃	xij đ
Wiłłs Joye	xvj đ
Joħes de Kendale	xvj đ
Nichus de Bradestoke	xvj đ
Robts de Northampton	ij s̃
Galfriđ de Weston	ij mar
ffabran le Taillur	ij s̃
Adam de Essex̃	xvj đ
Wiłłs de Wallyngford, Pelter	ij s̃ viij đ
Walłs de Dorset	ij s̃ viij đ

Johes le Kyng, Tayllour	ij s̄
Johs de Boseworth	xvj đ
Wills de Houghton	vj s̄ viiij đ
Johes Barry, Baker	
Johs de Donmowe	
Johs Broky	
Wills de Hederfott	
Wills le Doo	
Henr̄ ate Brome	xij đ
Johes Galoys	liiij s̄ iiij đ
Wills de Oxoñ	ij s̄
Simon de Gartoñ	ij mar
Thom Basset	v s̄ iiij đ

p.b̄. Sm^a **xxxvj li x s̄ vj đ** ob q^a p.b̄.

WARDA DE FFARNDON INFR.

Petrus le Convers	xvj đ
Walts ate Verne	xij đ
Nichs le Walssh	xvj đ
Thom Sporoun	xij đ
Nichus de Harwe	xvj đ
Thom de Weston	iiij s̄
Stephs ffrenssh	iiij s̄
Robts de Lesne, aurfaber	xx s̄
Robtus ate Condut	viij s̄
Johes de Honylane	v s̄ iiij đ
Jacobs de Thame	xij đ
Robts Horn, aurfaber	xx s̄
Johes de Taunton	xij đ
Walts Galle	ij s̄ viij đ
Thom̄ Warñ	xvj đ
Johes Perler	xij đ
Andr̄ de Essex	iiij s̄
Henr̄ Gloucestr	vj s̄ viij đ
Johes de Ivylane	ij s̄ viij đ
Johes de Causton	iiij s̄
Andr̄ de Sherford	vj s̄ viij đ
Galfriđ de Causton	xl s̄
John de Longe, hatter	iiij s̄
Wills Pycot, aurfaber	vj s̄ viij đ
Gawyñ aurfab	ij s̄ viij đ
Johes de Bermynghm	xiij s̄ iiij đ
Wills de Ippegave	ij s̄ viij đ
Stephs le ffrut	vj s̄ viij đ
Hugo le Brandon	xxvj s̄ viij đ
Johes de Yakesthorp	xvj đ
Mich le Hattere	iiij s̄
Stephus le Mazerer	xiij s̄ iiij đ
Jacobs le Corder	xvj đ
Wills de Shirwode	xvj đ
Nichs le Calicer	xiij s̄ iiij đ
Robts le Hornere de Luddegate	ij s̄ iiij đ
John de Waltham	v s̄ iiij đ
Walts de Shrowesbury	xvj đ

Thom̃ Edmond	ij s̄
Henr Kuyt	xvj d̃
Wiłłs de Gloucesf̃r	ij s̄
Robtus de Haselyngfeld	ij s̄ viij d̃
Rich̃s le Brewere de Luddegate	xvj d̃
Nich̃s le Bokebyndere	xvj d̃
Petr̃ de Mazoun	xij d̃
Joh̃es ffroyle, Chaundeler	iiij s̄ iiij d̃
John Horkesle	ij s̄ viij d̃
Ric̃ Sorel	xxvj s̄ viij d̃
Andr̃ de Salle	ij s̄ viij d̃
Joh̃es de Pykenham	vj łi xiij s̄ iiij d̃
Hugo le Marberer	liij s̄ iiij d̃
Robts Pursel	xiij s̄ iiij d̃
Joh̃es Pursel	ij s̄ viij d̃
John de ffelstode	ij s̄ viij d̃
Henr̃ le Sherman	xvj d̃
Nich̃us Crane	iiij łi
Joh̃es le Kyng	ij s̄ viij d̃
Rich̃ le Brewere	v s̄ iiij d̃
Rich̃ le Kyng	xxvj s̄ viij d̃
Wiłłs Abel	ix s̄ iiij d̃
Simon ate Gate	xij s̄
Roḡs de Hatfeld	xx s̄
Steph̃s le Plom̃	xvj d̃
Petr̃ de Russheleyr	xvj d̃
Gilbts le Hornere	iiij s̄
Steph̃us de Holande	xij d̃
Robts le Chaundeler	xij d̃
Joh̃es Smart	xiij s̄ iiij d̃
Robs de Langelee	ij s̄ viij d̃
Joh̃es Gerveys	ij s̄ viij d̃
Ric̃s de Herlawe	ij s̄ viij d̃
Rad̃s de Langelee	ij s̄ viij d̃
Thom̃ de Ware	vj s̄ viij d̃
Joh̃es Bacheler	iiij s̄
Wiłłs Clerk	xvj d̃
Joh̃s le Clerk	ij s̄ viij d̃
Joh̃es de Bristoll	xx s̄
Joh̃es de Breden	xij d̃
Rics Goldeneye	iiij s̄
Rad̃s le Kyng	xij d̃
Wiłłs de Wynton	ij s̄
Joh̃es Mounde	xx s̄
Henr̃ Soudan	xvj d̃
Sibilia Soudan	xij d̃
Joh̃es Spray	vj s̄ viij d̃
Robt Neucome	xij d̃
Thom de Depeden	xvj d̃
Joh̃es Daa	xij d̃
Henr̃ de Wymundham	xvj d̃
Joh̃es de Pr̃ston, aurfab	ij s̄ viij d̃
Joh̃es de Stafford	ij s̄ viij d̃
Wiłłs ate Barnet	xij d̃
Thom le Perler	xvj d̃
Joh̃nes de Hereford	xvj d̃

Wilłs de Blaneford	xvj đ
Wilłs de Blithe	xvj đ
Thom̄ de ffrechebok	xvj đ
Thom̄ Walssheman	xvj đ
Ric̄s de Arderne	iiij s̄
Joħes Sharp	xvj đ
Wilłs ate fforest	ij s̄ viij đ
Joħes de la Riote	xvj đ
Rad̄s Mordak	xij đ
Robs de Bristoll	iiij s̄
Alañ de ffrethebok	iiij s̄
Wilłs Pykerel	vj s̄ viij đ
Joħes de Ideshalle	ij s̄ viij đ
Joħ fil Alex̄r le Goldbeter	ij s̄ viij đ
Alex̄ le Goldbeter	xvj đ
Joħes de Richemond	xij đ
Ric̄us Denys	xx s̄
Joħs de Mallyng	ij s̄ viij đ
Mauric̄s de Herlawe	xij đ
Ralph de Blithe	xxvj s̄ viij đ
Rog̃us de Bardestaple	xij đ
Ric̄us de Honneye	iiij s̄
Wills de Iseldon	iiij s̄
Wilłs de Mymmes	xxvj s̄ viij đ
Wilłs de Enefeld	ij s̄ viij đ
Ric̄us Sire	xxvj s̄ viij đ
Nicħs Bouere	xvj đ
Alex̄ de Themasstone	ix s̄ iiij đ
Ric̄us Coteler	ij s̄ viij đ
Galfrid de Rokyngham	vj s̄ viij đ
Walt̄us le Blake	viij s̄
Joħes Hake	xij đ
Wilłs Bouere	ij s̄ viij đ
Joħes de Brigeford	iiij s̄
Thom̄ Hardy	iiij s̄
Rog̃us ate Belhous	ij s̄ viij đ

p.ħ. Sm̄ª xlviij łi viij s̄ iiij đ p.ħ.

WARDA CASTI BAYNARDI.

Joħns le Brewere	iiij s̄
Henr̄ Stokfisch	xvj đ
Wilł. le White	x s̄ viij đ
Adam ffairhod	xvj đ
Joħs de Hales	ij s̄
Joħ ffairhod	xij đ
Robtus le Masoun	xvj đ
Marg̃ia Sprot	iiij s̄
Thomas le Coo	iiij s̄
Rosia le Bowier	iiij s̄
Margareta de Essex	xvj đ
Wilłs le Hastere	vj s̄ viij đ
Joħns Sward	ij s̄
Joħ de Ryiton	xij đ
Elianora la Bakera	iiij s̄

Robtus Brongor	vj s̄	viij d̄
Nichus de Haleford	viij s̄	
Thomas de Cornubia	viij s̄	
Henr. de Cherryngworth		xij d̄
Rogus. de Hodele	v s̄	iiij d̄
Johes Gisors, armig̃	ij s̄	
Ricard de Pynnore	ij s̄	viij d̄
Hamond ffraunceis	iiij s̄	
Johna de Brghtewell	v s̄	iiij d̄
Margareta Selkewif	ij s̄	viij d̄
Thomas de Schene	ij s̄	viij d̄
Johns de Thamo		xvj d̄
Johns Maderman	iiij s̄	
Alanus Turk	vj s̄	viij d̄
Henr̄ Pelm̃, piscenar	v s̄	iiij d̄
Rid̄ Senglaunt		xvj d̄
Elias le Wodeberere		xviij d̄
Witts de Dorkyng		xvj d̄
Johns Lombard		xvj d̄
Henr̄ Breuge	iiij s̄	
Johns Tornegold	ij s̄	viij d̄
Henr̄ de Cofford	v s̄	iiij d̄
Dionis de Brokwode	iij s̄	iiij d̄
Edmund de Reynham	vj s̄	iiij d̄
Radus le Chener	ij s̄	viij d̄
Joh Cissor	v s̄	iiij d̄
Nich Cissor		xvj d̄
Simon de Turnham	ij s̄	viij d̄
Witt. de Sutton	vj s̄	viij d̄
Robtus de Raundes		xvj d̄
Rads. de Lennet	ij s̄	

p.b̄. Sm̃ᵃ viij l̃i iij s̄ x d̄.

THE SOCIETIES OF THE BARDI AND THE PERUZZI AND THEIR DEALINGS WITH EDWARD III., 1327-45.

At the beginning of the fourteenth century Florence was a city state, with a dependent territory somewhat less in extent than the county of York. Its merchant companies or societies had their agents in every important centre of population throughout Western Europe, and finding ample opportunity for the negotiation of loans, they had extensive dealings with the Papacy, the Plantagenets, the Valois, and the Angevins of Southern Italy. In fact, most of the business of Europe of this particular type was in their hands, and in many places their remarkable success procured for them cordial hatred.[1]

Everybody in Florence, from its merchant nobles downwards, is said to have been more or less engaged in the production of wealth. The mainstays of its prosperity were the extensive transactions in banking and moneylending already mentioned, and a flourishing cloth industry embracing manufacturing, dressing, and dyeing. The silk industry was probably not of first-rate importance till somewhat later. The gilds of the " Exchangers" or " Bankers," of the " wool merchants," and of the " merchants in foreign cloth " were the chief of the seven " Arti Maggiori " of the city.[2]

The " Arte del Cambio " seems to have been first concerned with the collection and transmission of dues from various princes to the Roman Pontiff, and it is probable that whilst thus engaged the merchants first realised the possibilities of this branch of their activities. The Societies of the Mozzi and Spini of Florence were famous papal bankers of the thirteenth century and farmers of the papal revenues; in the fourteenth century they had largely given place to the Bardi and Peruzzi, whose agencies were by then scattered widely throughout Western Europe.[3]

---

1. *The English Nouveaux-Riches in the Fourteenth Century*, by Alice Law. *Trans. Royal Hist. Soc. n.s.*, Vol. IX. See also S. L. Peruzzi, *Storia del Commercio e dei Banchieri di Firenze*, p. 177.
2. Ib., p. 58.
3. T. A. Trollope, *The Commonwealth of Florence*, II, 172.

For the " Arte della Lana " and the " Arte di Calimala "
the chronicler Villani gives·some interesting figures for the
year 1338.   He asserts that the former had more than two
hundred cloth manufacturing and dyeing establishments in
the city, that 70,000 to 80,000 " panni " or " pieces " of cloth
were produced annually to the value of 1,200,000 golden
florins, and that over 30,000 people were employed in the
trade.   The wool from which this cloth was made was imported mainly from Spain, Portugal, and England.   The
" Arte di Calimala " had, says Villani, no less than twenty
" fondachi " or " warehouses " importing over 10,000 panni
valued at 300,000 florins, all to be resold in Florence.[1]   In the
list of the names of the societies owning these warehouses
appear the Bardi, Peruzzi, Acciaiuoli, Alberti, and Bonaccorsi,
all of which at different times had their agencies in England.[2]

Side by side with this industrial and commercial prosperity
of Florence there existed social and political unrest, in which
usually the merchant societies were deeply involved.   A conspiracy, inculpating certain of the Frescobaldi, had been frustrated in 1323,[3] to be followed in 1325 by another equally unsuccessful.   Tommaso Frescobaldi had undertaken to betray
the city to Castruccio Castrucani of Lucca, and although
he escaped with his life, he was sentenced to perpetual
infamy and his property confiscated.[4]   War with Castruccio supervened in the same year, and the Florentine arms
endured severe defeat at Altopascio,[5] the enemy ultimately
reaching the very walls of the city.   The Duke of Calabria,
eldest son of the King of Naples, was made Lord of the City,
but not arriving at the stipulated time, he imposed the French-
man, Walter de Brienne, Duke of Athens, on the people, as
his Lieutenant.   The Emperor, Louis of Bavaria, also
appeared in Italy, and received the iron crown of Lombardy
at Milan in May, 1327, and the prospect was distinctly gloomy
for the Florentines.   The Duke of Calabria hurried south to
protect his father, leaving the Duke of Athens behind him.
He had done nothing whatever for the Commonwealth, but
his rule had entailed expenses to the extent of 900,000 florins.[6]

1. Villani, p. 827.   2. Peruzzi, p. 67.   3. Villani, ·p. 543.
4. Ib., p. 569.   5. 23 Sept., 1325.
6. Yver, *Le Commerce et les Marchands dans l'Italie méridionale, au xiii*
et au xive siècle, p. 316; but see Villani, p. 629, where the text mentions
400,000 florins, and a footnote states " più di ottocento migliaja di fiorini."

Relief, however, came unexpectedly—Castruccio died on the 3rd September, 1328, and the Duke of Calabria died also in November in the same year. The death of the latter, according to Villani, prevented an uprising against him in Florence.[1] The war with Castruccio had caused heavy expenditure, but the city was by no means at the end of its resources.

Passing over various intrigues, which centre round Lucca, the acquisition of which town was earnestly sought by the Commune of Florence, the city was next at war, from 1336 to 1339 with the powerful House of Scala. The exchequer being much depleted, a number of " wise and clever merchants " (of whom Villani is said to have been one) was summoned together and arrangements were made with the gilds by means of which 100,000 golden florins, and more as required, were to be provided at a stipulated rate of interest.[2] Florence was, however, duped by her powerful ally Venice, and reaped little from the war, other than a debt of over 450,000 florins, for the repayment of which the customs' dues of the city were pledged to private citizens for the next six years.[3]

One authority considers that this is the epoch which may be justly regarded as furnishing events signifying the beginning of the end for the financial and commercial prosperity of Florence.[4] During this period there developed a state of affairs inimical to the Commonwealth throughout the spheres of influence of her merchant societies. The Bardi and Peruzzi were probably the richest of these societies, and there is little doubt that they were heavily involved in the financial difficulties of the city at home. This in itself, however, would not have been serious, the very extent of their business activities throughout Europe would have provided, and in fact did provide them with the means of meeting their obligations for some years after 1339. The outbreak of war between England and France was the great calamity which ultimately ruined the merchants. They probably found it impossible to maintain friendly relations with both combatants; in any case the formal outbreak of the war in 1337 was accompanied by the arrest of the representatives of the Florentine societies

1. Villani, p. 670.   2. Ib., p. 786.
3. Ib., p. 822.
4. Yver, *Le Commerce et les Marchands*, etc., pp. 319, 320.

in France, the price of their release being huge loans to Philip of Valois.[1]   But what was still worse, the King of England, to whom they had made enormous advances, ceased in actual fact to make any adequate payment of his debts whilst all the time desiring to take up further loans.[2]

Added to all this there was further financial 'disaster in Florence itself, and also in the kingdom of Naples, where the merchants had much capital engaged.   This capital was, of course, not entirely their own property, but that of Florentines and others who had deposited with them.   Lucca was again the immediate cause of the crisis.   Disappointed at not having obtained possession of the town after the war of 1336 to 1339, Florence entered into further negotiations for its purchase, which ultimately involved her in war with Pisa.   After enduring a severe defeat in October, 1341, the Commonwealth appealed for aid to Robert, King of Naples, and, greatly angered by his apathy, it even turned momentarily to the Emperor, Louis of Bavaria.   Yver argues that the Florentine merchants used all their influence in the endeavour to secure the assistance of the King of Naples, and that they—the Bardi, Peruzzi, and their dependents—were the " certi savi amatori di parte guelfa "[3] of Villani, who, having much at stake in the Neapolitan kingdom, and being anxious not to alarm Robert, did their utmost to prevent the acceptance of the Emperor's terms.   The result was satisfactory to the merchants as regards the Emperor, but not so in the kingdom of Naples, where there occurred a run on the funds of the Florentine bankers which caused the immediate failure of the Bonaccorsi and several other of the smaller firms (1341).[4]   The greater companies, the Bardi and Peruzzi, had still sufficient political prestige at home, and sufficiently valuable property and possessions, and sufficient business reputation, to enable them, though severely shaken,[5] to combat fortune a little longer.

Florence suffered further defeat to her armies, and Pisa obtained possession of Lucca in July, 1342, after which Walter

---

1.   Yver, p. 319; and Villani, cap. 71; see pp. 98, 119, below.
2.   Peruzzi, p. 452; also pp. 471, 472.
3.   Villani, p. 863.
4.   Yver, *op. cit.*, pp. 320, 321.
5.   They encountered difficulties in their business enterprise even before this.   Cf. *C.P.R.* 1338–40, p. 391.

de Brienne, Duke of Athens, a French adventurer,[1] was chosen Lord of the City and made commander of the armies. He did not continue the war, but intriguing, in order to obtain supreme power, with the " grandi " and " popolo minuto " against the " popolani grassi," he succeeded rapidly in alienating all classes.[2] Many of the wealthier merchants, including the Bardi, Peruzzi, and Acciaiuoli, at first supported the Duke, hoping through him to re-establish their estate somewhat, but when he entirely repudiated the public debt, they realised their error and engaged in conspiracies against him.

In one of these, the Bishop of Florence, a Dominican of the family of the Acciaiuoli, and many nobles, including representatives of the Bardi and Frescobaldi families, were involved, but nothing came of the attempt.[3] The city, however, having first asked help from Siena and other neighbouring towns, rose against the tyrant on the 26th July, 1343. Some of the " popolo minuto" and a few of the great " popolano" families—the Peruzzi, Cavalcanti, Acciaiuoli, and Antellesi, at first tried to create a diversion in his favour,[4] but finding it quite useless they allied themselves with the majority of the citizens. By Monday, the 28th July, a Committee of fourteen citizens (seven " grandi " and seven " popolani," one of whom was named Simone Peruzzi) was deputed to reform the government of the city.[5] Barely escaping with his life, the Duke was smuggled out of Florence in the dead of night on the sixth of August. His rule had lasted a little over ten months, and had cost the city over 400,000 florins.[6]

After the expulsion of Walter de Brienne, those of the wealthier classes who had at first supported his aggressions were attacked by the populace. The main strength of the " grandi " was in the Oltrarno quarter of the city on the left bank of the river, where the houses or palaces of the Bardi, Frescobaldi, Rossi, Nerli, Mannelli, and others were situated.[7] The barricaded bridges over the Arno were stormed and

1. Villani, p. 871.
2. Ib., p. 879, mentions the indignation of the "grandi" because one of the Bardi who had strangled one of the people for insolence was fined 500 florins!
3. Ib., p. 887.   4. Ib., p. 890.
5. Ib., p. 892   6. Ib., p. 880.   7. Ib., p. 901.

carried on the 25th September, 1343, and the houses of the Frescobaldi and Rossi were soon captured and despoiled. The Bardi made a desperate resistance, but their palaces were sacked and burnt, and they themselves with difficulty escaped alive. From fifteen to twenty members of noble families were banished, and the loss of the Bardi alone on this occasion is said to have been over 60,000 florins of gold.[1] This was the " coup de grâce " to the Florentine merchant companies. They could not even appeal for aid to Robert, King of Naples, for whom they had done so much, for he had died in the previous January, and the treasure which he had amassed was being squandered by his successor. Robert had also, like Edward of England, though for other reasons, forborne to pay his debts, and was under obligation to the extent of 100,000 florins to each of the societies of the Bardi and Peruzzi.[2] He had been, during his long reign,[3] a means of their attaining opulence and power; he was also an instrument of their downfall. The crisis, from this moment, seems to have been inevitable; it was merely postponed for a few months longer, till the beginning of 1345, but their creditors were everywhere clamorous and their stability was destroyed. It is evident that in England their activities were seriously curtailed, and that they practically ceased to be of any vital financial importance after 1343. The affairs of Florence did not improve; the catastrophe of 1345 was followed by a failure of the harvest in 1346, and by famine in the following year. The feeding of the people is described by Villani, and he estimates the loss to the Treasury at more than 30,000 florins.[4] Worse than all this, in 1348 came the terrible devastation wrought by the Great Pestilence.[5]

The foregoing considerations may serve to establish the opinion that the failure of the Italian financiers is not solely to be attributed to the perfidy of Edward of England. It may, perhaps, be true that his were the most serious delinquencies,[6] yet the disturbed state of Florentine affairs and the expenses in which the merchants were there involved, the loss of property they sustained, their persecution in France,[7] and their

1. Villani, p. 902.
2. Ib., p. 934.   3.   1309 to 1343.   4.   Villani, p. 956.
5.   Villani himself was a victim of the pestilence, see the end of his Chronicle, p. 1002.
6.   Peruzzi, p. 477.   7.   Villani, p. 936.

repudiation by the King of Naples, must have been potent factors in the shattering of a business reputation, whose limits were alone determined by the civilisation of the age.

Most of the societies of Italian merchants that had been prominent under his father and grandfather had disappeared from the field of operations at the beginning of the reign of Edward the Third. Two great societies had already met with serious misfortune, the Riccardi under Edward the First and the Frescobaldi under his successor. The remaining companies were either involved in the ruin of the greater ones, or considered the risks too formidable, or perhaps they found the magnitude of the negotiations beyond their ability, and continued to trade in the country privately apart from the court. Whatever course they adopted, with two outstanding exceptions, they withdrew for the most part from the political arena. The exceptions, of course, were the societies of the Bardi and Peruzzi of Florence.

Of these two societies, that of the Bardi was much the more important at first. It appears indeed to have succeeded almost immediately to the position from which, owing largely to the antipathy which the English displayed in 1311 towards foreigners,[1] the Frescobaldi fell. The Bardi advanced at least £72,631 to the English Sovereigns between 1290 and 1326, and of this amount, only £4,926 was lent before 1311,[2] whilst the Peruzzi, on the other hand, are only recorded as having taken part in two transactions with the King, and are only involved to the extent of £900,[3] within the period above mentioned. There is, however, a tendency apparent by about the year 1337, for the two societies to act in concert. This has become the established custom by 1340, in which year the Treasurer and Barons of the Exchequer received orders to charge and discharge each society by itself in the accounts which they rendered for sums and things lent by them to the King and delivered to them by the King, "as they have begun to render their accounts together for such

---

1. Rhodes, "Italian Bankers in England, and their Loans to Edward I and Edward II," in *Historical Essays by Members of the Owens College,* p. 156.

2. Ib., pp. 163, 164, appendix N.

3. Ib., p. 163, appendix L. The dates of the two transactions are 1311 and 1315 respectively.

I

sums."[1] When the crisis came in 1345 both societies were irretrievably ruined.

By reason of their great wealth, their business capacity, the universal acceptability of the Florentine gold coinage, which was of absolute fineness and was never debased[2], and their advanced methods of international credit and exchange, the services of the Italian merchants became practically indispensable to several governments of their age.   They were not "mere merchants," but "bankers" also, exercising the double function of receiving and husbanding the funds entrusted to them by depositors, especially after the suppression of the Templars, and also of negotiating loans for clients who could offer reasonable security[3].   They were invaluable to the Papacy as collectors and transmittors of its revenues.

In the following attempt to estimate the extent of the services rendered to Edward III by the Bardi and Peruzzi, it is proposed that the Society of the Bardi shall be first dealt with, as they, without doubt, were the more important at the commencement of the reign.

The deposition of Edward II appears to have affected them but little.   They were extensively employed, both in France and England, by Isabella and Mortimer, and after the fall of the latter, still more by the youthful King.

A merchant operating alone, either for himself or as a representative of his society, had become somewhat of an exception—owing perhaps to the increasing magnitude and risk of the negotiations.   The tendency also to require some

NOTE.—As regards the £900 mentioned above, it is probable that it does not fully represent the activities of the Peruzzi prior to the fall of Edward II, for there are among the extracts from the Liberate Rolls given by Sir Edward Bond at the end of his article in *Archæologia*, Vol. xxviii, pp. 207–326, three entries ordering payment from the Treasury, under date 26 May 1324, to the Bardi, the Scali, and the Peruzzi respectively of over 1,000 marks, "because they have lent, for our business, to the Constable of Bordeaux" in each case over 3,950 florins of gold. (Bond, Appendices, clxiv to clxvi to the above-named article.) One of these societies, the Scali, had failed for more than 400,000 florins of gold prior to the accession of Edward III in England, on 31 July, 1326, the day after the entry of Charles, Duke of Calabria, into Florence, to assume the supreme authority in the city. (Yver, *Le Commerce et les Marchands*, etc., p. 317; Villani, p. 603, where he describes this failure as more unfortunate than such a defeat as that of Altopascio.)

1. *C.C.R.* 1339–41, p. 419.
2. W. A. Shaw, *The History of Currency, 1252—1894*, p. 302.
3. Yver, *op. cit.*, p. 351.

security for the monies advanced—the pledging of jewels, an assignment on some branch of the customs revenue, or the privilege of exporting free of toll, or at a reduced toll at least— was pronounced. A day for repayment was also often fixed, and gifts in money or kind were of frequent occurrence as compensation for failure to meet the obligation. The necessity to pay it was, indeed, instanced by the King as a hardship when writing, through his Chancellor, to the sheriffs and the collectors of the triennial tenth and fifteenth granted by the community of the realm in various counties. These officials had not been sufficiently prompt in rendering account of the monies received by them for the King's use. The King ordered arrest of the collectors and seizure of their lands and goods, unless his orders were at once complied with, " for," states the writ in question, " the King has learned that the collectors retain the money, devoting it to their own uses, not weighing the King's most urgent necessity for lack of money, which is notorious to all his subjects, by reason of the war, so that he has had resource to usury with several creditors."[1]

In connection with the Bardi the name of Taldo Valori appears in 1327. He did not apparently visit England after this date, although his death did not occur before 1344. He appears to have been dissatisfied with the conditions and vicissitudes of financial dealings with English Kings.[2] A detailed list of the names of members of the Society of the Bardi trading in England during the reign of Edward III is

1. *C.C.R.* 1339–41, pp. 175, 176; see Bond, p. 224, as to ways of circumventing the laws against usury; also see Rhodes, "Italian Bankers in England," etc., p. 140.

2. *Famiglie celebri italiane*, Conte Pompeo Litta, Vol. I, fasc. xiii, gives an account of the career of this important politician, ending with a reason for his withdrawal from activity in England. "Morì dopo il 1344. Come mercante fiorentino era stato ricchissimo, avendo prestato 30 mila fiorini d'oro ad Odoardo III re d'Inghilterra per la guerra contro i Francesi, ma non avendo riscosso i crediti, abbandonò disgustato i negozi."

Although Valori does not appear to have been actually in England after 1327, he did not withdraw from the Bardi. He had married Francesca de' Bardi, and he was a member or partner in the Society at the time of its liquidation; see Appendix, p. 133 below. Probably Litta's statement merely signifies that Valori had 30,000 florins of his own private capital invested in the Company, which of course he would ultimately lose.

Peruzzi, p. 456, has the following :—"... nella Storia Fiorentina dell' Ammirato si narra che Taldo Valori gonfaloniere di giustizia nel 1340 fu compagno della gran ragione dei Bardi in Londra : egli era sì ricco, che di sua proprietà, come apparisce nei libri di quella ragione, prestò 30 mila fiorini d'oro..."

given below, so far as they are indicated in the Patent and Close Rolls.[1]   Of these names the following recur most frequently :—Alessandro de' Bardi, Bartolommeo de' Bardi, Pietro Bene, Dino Forzetti, Giovanni di Francesco, Francesco Grandoni, Jacopo Niccolini, and Pietro Rinieri.

At the beginning of the reign of Edward III the Society was engaged in a not very important dispute with Thomas de Useflete, a former keeper of the Great Wardrobe, who had been ordered to account with Taldo Valori and his fellows for things bought and received by him for the late King's Wardrobe and to certify what was due to them or to the King.[2] This was followed by complaints from the Bardi to the effect that Thomas de Useflete had caused the bailiffs of Boston Fair to seize £400 worth of their goods at the Fair, on the ground that the Bardi ought to have supplied £400 worth of spices, etc., to the Wardrobe of Edward II for the like amount of money handed to them.   The company, claiming to have supplied £200 worth, appealed to Edward III, who appointed a day in Chancery for the hearing.[3]   Almost a year later, Thomas de Useflete was ordered to make restitution of certain goods "in consideration of good service done by the merchants to the King,"[4] and the aulnager, who had seized the goods, viz., six coloured cloths, ostensibly because they were not of standard length, etc., was ordered to return them and was informed of the defence of the merchants that they did not intend the goods for sale in this country, that they were bought in Flanders and intended for Brabant, and accidentally taken to Boston by their servants.[5]

The above appears to be fairly typical of the treatment of the merchants during the first ten years of Edward's reign. Local friction frequently occurred, but the Italians usually found a firm friend in the sovereign, and for the most part their appeals were answered in their favour.

On March 1st, 1327, protection and safe-conduct for a year under the privy seal was granted to Jacopo Niccolini, Dino Forzetti, Francesco Grandoni, Alessandro de' Bardi, Giovanni di Francesco, Pietro Rinieri, Pietro Bene, and Tano Cecco,

---

1. Appendix, pp. 133–4, below.
2. *C.C.R.* 1327–30, p. 120.   3. *Ib.*, p. 221.   4. *Ib.*, p. 305.
5. *Ib.*, p. 310.

merchants of the Society of the Bardi of Florence.[1] This was renewed for a year after it had only run for a little over three months, viz., on June 15th.[2] This is a typical entry constantly recurring throughout the period. A licence was granted by the King at the instance of Queen Isabella to the same merchants (the name of Alessandro de' Bardi alone being omitted) in May of the same year, allowing them to buy and export wools for one year without complying with the ordinances of the staple of wool, provided they paid the customs, etc., due thereon to the King.[3] Again, in August, the customers of Southampton were ordered to send to the King at once any money in hand of the customs of wool, hides and wool-fells, and of the new custom, any previous assignments notwithstanding, " except those to the merchants of the Society of the Bardi of Florence."[4]

These are all instances of privilege conferred on the Italian merchants, in defiance of statutes limiting the residence of foreign merchants in the realm and expressly forbidding the assignment of customs to their use.[5] Again, on 12 January, 1328, it was ordered that all monies received, or to be received, from the collection of the " twentieth" in the county of Kent, should be paid to the Bardi, to hold it for the King's use until further orders.[6] This exhibits the merchants acting as a " bank deposit" for the King. A month later they sold to the King certain " houses " they possessed in Lombard Street for the sum of £700.[7]

Evidence of the Crown's heavy indebtedness to the Bardi is afforded quite early in Edward's reign before the debts could have been of his own contracting.

On the 20th August, 1328, orders were issued to the collectors of the ' twentieth' in Southampton, London, and twenty-one counties (excluding Kent) to raise £4,435—to the collectors of the ' tenth ' of the clergy in twelve dioceses to raise

---

1. *C.P.R.* 1327–30, p. 23; see also Appendix below, for names of merchants.
2. *C.P.R.*, p. 124.   3. *Ib.*, p. 102.
4. *C.C.R.* 1327–30, p. 157.
5. 5 Edw. II, cap. 4 and cap. 8; also 17 Edw. II, Statute of the Exchequer.
6. *C.C.R.* 1327–30, p. 195; *cf.* also *C.C.R.* 1339–41, p. 225.
7. *Ib.*, pp. 259, 362, 378; *C.P.R.* 1327–30, p. 230. These houses were ultimately granted, in return for his great services to the King, to William de la Pole, merchant, on 27 September, 1339. (*C.P.R.* 1338–40, p. 394.)

£2,000—and to the 'customers' of the ports of Chichester, Southampton, and London to raise £1,565—in all £8,000. The amount to be raised by each collector is exactly specified, and it is required that the money be paid to the Bardi of Florence " in part payment of a great sum of money lent to the king."[1] The amount to be raised in the port of London is £1,390, but the whole of the revenue here is not available for the Bardi, owing to the claims of William and Richard de la Pole.   The latter share the customs revenue of London with the Bardi, and in addition receive by assignment all monies from the customs in Ipswich, Yarmouth, Lynn, Boston, Kingston-upon-Hull, Hartlepool, and Newcastle-upon-Tyne, because they have undertaken to provide the King with £20 daily for the maintenance of his household.[2] Assignments from the customs revenues, such as the above, are the security most often accorded to the merchants for repayment of loans.

The provision of money for the maintenance of the royal household had become one of the functions of the Bardi very shortly after the date of the writ just quoted.

The Exchequer was ordered on 20 August, 1329, to make speedy payment to the Bardi out of monies received " as much is owing to them,"[3] and as they had promised to find a certain sum (£20) daily for the expenses of the King's household for a certain time.[4]

This payment appears to have continued until All Saints' Day, 1331, and the day on which the payments commenced is elsewhere given as 17 August, 1329.[5]   Collectors of customs were ordered to make payments direct to the Bardi, and the Exchequer was to cause tallies at the receipt to be levied for the sums the " customers " paid to the Bardi in execution of the King's orders, " because they pay daily to the King's Wardrobe for the expenses of his household," and the tallies were to be delivered to the merchants, or their attorneys, for the discharge of the said collectors.[6]   This maintenance of the household for 807 days, involved a sum of £16,140, but the

---

1. *C.C.R.* 1327–30, p. 311.
2. *Ib.*, p. 353; *C.P.R.* 1327–30, pp. 333, 338.
3. *C.P.R.* 1330–4, p. 52.   4. *C.C.R.* 1327–30, p. 488.
5. *Ib.*, p. 507; *C.C.R.* 1330–3, p. 15, and especially p. 75.
6. *Ib.*, 1327–30, p. 507; also see *C.P.R.* 1327–30, p. 421, and *C.C.R.* 1330–33, p. 108.

merchants would be receiving repayment, more or less continuously, from the customs, etc., throughout the period.[1]

Under date 15 November, 1331, it is stated that the Bardi have agreed to find 1,000 marks per month for the royal household from 1 December to 1 October next, and an assignment was made in their favour " on the old custom of London, and on the old and new customs of Boston, Kingston-upon-Hull, Lynn, Newcastle-upon-Tyne and Hartlepool, also on a moiety of the old custom of Southampton (because with assent of the Bardi, the other moiety is assigned to certain merchants of Aquitaine)[2] and on all the new custom there to an amount not exceeding 500 marks yearly, with a further allocation of £1,000 out of the first issues paid by the Chamberlain of Wales, or from other monies of Wales, etc."[3]

The indenture drawn up at Windsor, containing the above details, concludes with an engagement " that the King will have regard to the Bardi for expenses of collecting, etc., in such manner as they shall consider themselves satisfied in reason."[4] The total liability of the Bardi under this obligation would be 11,000 marks.[5]

There is some evidence, particularly later, after the beginning of the French War, that repayments from assignments were not always satisfactorily made, but even at this period grants for losses sustained were being made to the Bardi, one of these, under date 16 December, 1332, was a gift of £1,000 promised for the ensuing Easter, on account of the merchants' losses, and " for furnishing the expenses of the household to Michaelmas last."[6]

After the first day of October, 1332, there follows a period of two years, to Michaelmas, 1334, during which the Bardi do not appear to be making the same regular contributions for the upkeep of the Royal Household which they had made for three years previously. They did make certain payments which are recorded, but with one exception, they were all in

1. *Cf.* pp. 101, 104 above.
2. *C.C.R.* 1330–3, p. 79; also p. 105.
3. *C.P.R.* 1330–4, p. 228; *C.C.R.* 1330–3, p. 388. 4. *Ib.*, p. 413.
5. The entry has been assumed to signify that the first payment of 1,000 marks was made on 1 December, 1331, and the last on 1 October, 1332 (eleven payments). This would cover the period from All Saints' Day, 1331, to 1 October, 1332, and would give continuity with the previous loans made by the Bardi for the household.
6. *C.P.R.* 1330–4, p. 380.

the last five weeks prior to Michaelmas, 1334. The entries relative to these transactions may be summed up as follows :— An acknowledgment of the King's indebtedness to the Bardi on 2 May, 1333, in £1,071 paid for the expenses of the household and other purposes, with an assignment on the customs of the port of London,[1] on 28 August, 1334, an order for repayment out of the customs of Southampton, and the custody to the merchants of one part of the " cocket " seal in that port, because they had lately paid 500 marks to Richard de Ferriby, keeper of the Wardrobe, for expenses of the household,[2]—on 12 September 1334, an order for payment from the old custom in the port of London, of £200, which had likewise been paid to Richard de Ferriby, as before,[3]—and lastly, under the privy seal as in the two former cases, an assignment out of the first issues of the coinage in the Stannary of Cornwall, because the Bardi had advanced two sums of money, one of which was 600 marks, paid to Richard de Ferriby for the household.[4] If the whole of the £1,071 mentioned above be included (although not entirely for the household) these payments amount to £2,004 6s. 8d. or 3,006½ marks, about sufficient, at the previous rate[5] to have maintained the household for three months. Certainly therefore, use must have been made of other sources of supply during the remaining twenty-one months of the period under consideration.

At the end of this two years the regular contributions of the merchants once more commenced. On 1 October, 1334, a grant from the old and new customs of London, Southampton, Boston, and Kingston-upon-Hull, saving certain other specified assignments,[6] was made to the Bardi, who were again supplying 1,000 marks monthly for the household for a year from Michaelmas last.[7] Their loans for this period (ending Michaelmas, 1335) would therefore be 12,000 marks. Again, on 12 December, 1335, a further assignment on the customs was made in favour of the Bardi, because they had arranged to find 500 marks per calendar month from 1 Novem-

1. *C.P.R.* 1330–4, p. 431.   2. *Ib.*, 1334–8, p. 6.
3. *C.C.R.* 1333–7, p. 250.   4. *C.P.R.* 1334–8, p. 23.
5. One thousand marks per month.
6. See below, pp. 109, 110 (Exceptions for John of Hainault, the Count of Jülich, and the Lord of Cuyk.)
7. *C.P.R.* 1334–8, p. 29; also see *C.C.R.* 1333–7, p. 345, where ' calendar ' month is expressly specified.

ber, 1335, until the ensuing Michaelmas.[1] This must have involved them in the payment of 6,000 marks. It is, however, hardly likely that the expenses of the household had been cut down by fifty per cent., hence it seems probable that a further 500 marks per month was being obtained elsewhere. Once more, on 2 October, 1336, the Bardi had undertaken to find 6,000 marks for the year ending Michaelmas, 1337.[2] It appears to be certain, therefore, from the foregoing, that this one company provided the household of the King with at least £41,477 13s. 4d. during the years from 17 August, 1329, to Michaelmas, 1337.[3]

Beyond one entry on 18 October, 1337, which orders the " customers" of Southampton to pay to the Bardi up to 2,000 marks everything—from the issues of the customs—from the subsidy of 20/- per sack on every sack of wool exported, granted to the King at Nottingham—and also from the loan of 20/- per sack of wool exported by foreign merchants— " because they (the Bardi) pay the expenses of the household "[4], the Patent and Close Rolls cease for the moment to afford evidence as to the contributions of the Bardi for household expenses. This may be due in part to the commencement of the French War and the King's frequent absence abroad, for the contributions of the merchants are usually designated from this time onwards as " for war requisites " in some form. The above entry, however, seems to indicate that the Society continued to assist in the maintenance of the household after Michaelmas, 1337, and there is definite evidence that they did so assist a year or two later. This will be again mentioned in due course.[5]

The King's immediate household was not, however, alone in its reliance and dependence upon the financial resources of the Bardi. Queen Philippa, Queen Isabella, and Edward,

---

1. *C.C.R.*, p. 456.
2. *Ib.* 1333–7, p. 615; *Ib.* 1337–9, p. 70.
3. *C.P.R.* 1330–4, p. 122, under date 21 May, 1331, acknowledges the King's indebtedness to the Bardi in £45 16s. 8d. paid through Richard de Bury for expenses of the household beyond sea. This was probably incurred during Edward's clandestine journey to France (4 to 20 April, 1331) on which he met Philip of Valois near Pont-Sainte-Maxence. (This £45 16s. 8d. is not included in the amounts given above.) See Murimuth, p. 63; Baker, *Chronicon,* p. 48; Déprez, *Les préliminaires de la Guerre de Cent-Ans,* pp. 74 to 76.
4. *C.C.R.* 1337–9, p. 195.   5. See pp. 118, 119, below.

Earl of Chester, required and received assistance. Queen Philippa received £400 for household expenses prior to 21 December, 1330,[1] and £2,268 15s. 0d. " paid at various times " for the same purpose by 4 February, 1333.[2] The Bardi are stated to have lent £4,535 11s. 11d. for the debts of Queen Philippa on 10 October, 1337,[3] and previously on 18 March, 1337, they had been ordered to pay £500 which they had received from the papal collector of the King's moiety of the clerical tenth, etc., " to John Darcy ' the nephew' as part payment of £1,000 which the King promised to pay to John for Queen Philippa, being part of a large sum the Queen owes John for the manor of Wark in Tyndale, which she has bought from him."[4]

£900 had been paid to Queen Isabella prior to 5 February, 1333,[5] and on 6 May, 1336, the King acknowledged his indebtedness to the Bardi for £7,200[6] paid to the Queen his mother. On 15 November of the same year the Society was ordered to lend £250 to Edward, Earl of Chester, the King's son, for expenses of his household, another equal sum being found otherwise.[7]

Very varied are some of the incidental necessities of the sovereign which the Bardi relieved—£100 for the funeral expenses of John of Eltham, the King's brother[8]—1,000 marks, part of which was for the expenses " of our sister Eleanor's passage beyond sea "[9]—1,635 marks on Eleanor's behalf[10] £1,000 being probably "her marriage portion" which was paid to Reginald,[11] Count of Gueldres—392½ marks paid to the King of Sicily[12]—£300 the King's gift to Queen Philippa[13]— £7 8s. 4d. to a London merchant for "spicery"[14]—£19 11s. 0d. for " couriers" on the King's business[15]—25 marks "to Colard Maloysel, yeoman of the Countess of Jülich, sister to Queen Philippa, for bringing news to the said Queen of the birth of a child to the Countess"[16]—£1,000 to Roger Mortimer, Earl

1. *C.C.R.* 1330–3, p. 86; *C.P.R.* 1330–4, pp. 32, 34.   2. *Ib.*, p. 399.
3. *Ib.* 1334–8, p. 534; *C.C.R.* 1337–9, p. 231.   4. *Ib.*, p. 41.
5. *C.P.R.* 1330–4, p. 398.
6. *Ib.* 1334–8, p. 261; *C.C.R.* 1337–9, p. 67.   7. *Ib.* 1333–7, p. 626.
8. Bond, " Extracts from the Liberate Rolls, etc.," in *Archæologia*, Vol. XXVIII, pp. 207 to 326, App, CLXXXVIII.
9. *Ib.*, CLXXII.   10. *Ib.*, CLXXIII.
11. *C.P.R.* 1330–4, p. 269.   12. Bond, App. CLXXVII.
13. *Ib.*, CLXXIX.   14. *Ib.*, CLXXXIV.   15. *Ib.*, CLXXXVI.
16. *C.P.R.* 1327–30, p. 523.

of March, in aid of the marriage of his daughter with the eldest son of Thomas de Brotherton, Earl of Norfolk, and Marshal of England, paid at the King's request[1]— £2,417 10s. 3d. for diverse jewels of gold and silver, delivered into the Wardrobe for the "solemnisation of the King's marriage"[2]—£22 for two cups bought for the King through Thomas West[3] —£863 7s. 8d. to Antonio 'Bache' for redemption of gold and silver jewels which the King had pawned to raise a loan[4]—£200 to Lapinus Roger, keeper of the table for the King's "exchange" at Dover[5] —4/8 to the King's smith in the Tower of London for his expenses in making tackle and an anchor for the "Christopher"[6]—40 marks to Raymond Spiawie of Bayonne, a poor, old, and faithful servant of the King and his father[7]—and even £27 8s. 10d.[8] and £97 17s. 11d. (arrears at 3/1 per day for nearly two years)[9] for the upkeep of the King's menagerie of lions and leopards in the Tower of London.

The above entries, chosen somewhat at random, will serve to indicate the universality of interests for which the resources of the merchants were requisitioned, but of course it was mainly as a result of hostilities that such assistance from them was necessary. The war, especially in its earlier stages, entailed a lavish expenditure in the form of "fees" or "pensions" to numerous dignitaries to retain them in Edward's service.[10] The case of John of Hainault will serve by way of illustration. On 7 February, 1327, the King assigned to him 1,000 marks annually, out of the customs of the Port of London, until the King should provide him with land to that amount in England.[11]   Dino Forzetti and his fellows of the Society of the Bardi of Florence were appointed by John, on 28 June, 1329, as his attorneys in London to receive this sum for him.[12]   It is stated on 16 June, 1329, that the Bardi have promised to pay to John of Hainault £7,406 6s. 9d. in full payment of a greater

1. *Ib.*, p. 502.   2. *Ib.*, p. 231.
3. *C.P.R.* 1330–4, p. 122.   4. Bond, App. CLXXV.
5. *C.C.R.* 1333–7, p. 518.   6. *Ib.*, 1337–9, p. 230.
7. *C.C.R.* 1333–7, p. 615.   8. Bond, App. CLXXXI.
9. *C.C.R.* 1337–9, p. 67.
10. Tout, p. 332; Murimuth, p. 84.
11. *Foed.*, II, ii, 686.
12. *Ib.*, 769; *C.C.R.* 1327–30, p. 557.

amount due to him from the King.[1] 10,000 marks from the King of Scotland was part of the assignment to them on this occasion, but they do not appear to have received it, although, apparently, it was paid to the King.[2] John's pension of 500 marks half-yearly was regularly paid by the merchants from Easter, 1329, to Michaelmas, 1336, and although after this date, with one or two exceptions[3] the pension does not appear to have been paid through the Bardi, John of Hainault is indicated as receiving it until Michaelmas, 1345,[4] that is to say, to within twelve months of the battle of Crécy, in which he was an adherent to the King of France, Philip of Valois. Like many another of Edward's German and Netherlandish allies he was probably more anxious to acquire his remuneration than to render any very effectual services.

Pope John xxii, by a bull dated 30 June, 1329, imposed a four-yearly tenth on the clergy of England, Ireland, and Wales, and also reserved the first-fruits of vacant benefices for the same period. This was done with the connivance of the King, to whom a moiety of the above was granted. The Papal Collector in England,[5] who would have to account with the King for the moiety due to the latter, was ordered to pay the King's share to the Bardi, for the whole of it was, in due course, part by part, made over to them as payment for services rendered to the King.[6]   When the papal agent fur-

1. *Ib.*, p. 470. The King was heavily indebted to John of Hainault, chiefly for military assistance. Baker, *Chronicon*, has this note, p. 214 :—
. . . . . . he appears to have received the following payments : 28 June, 1327, a warrant was issued in his favour for £700 (*Foed.*, II, 708) ; 20 August, 1327, the sum of £4,000 was ordered to be paid to him, the jewels in the Tower to be pledged, if needful (*Ib.*, p. 713) ; 6 March, 1328, the King undertook to pay him £14,406 6s. 9d. in two instalments, for twice coming to his assistance (*Ib.*, p. 733) ; and ordered part payment amounting to £7,000 on 28 June (*Ib.*, p. 745) ; the other £7,000 appears to have been paid in May 1329, with money advanced by the Bardi of Florence (*Ib.*, p. 764 ; *Archæologia*, XXVIII, 257).
2. *Foed.*, II, ii, 795, 804, 805 ; *C.C.R.* 1327-30, p. 490. See also as regards this payment to John of Hainault, etc., *Ib.*, pp. 463, 554 ; *C.P.R.* 1327-30, pp. 254, 395, 418 ; *Ib.*, 1330-4, p. 11 ; *C.C.R.* 1330-3, p. 109.
3. *Ib.* 1341-3, p. 2. When the King granted the customs of London to the merchants of Almain, an exception in favour of John of Hainault was made. See also p. 409, where John's attorneys, not specified, may, or may not, be the Bardi. (See p. 406).
4. *Ib.* 1343-6, pp. 161, 289, 309, 421, 518, 622 ; *Ib.* 1341-3, p. 406, states that the King still owes certain monies to John of Hainault.
5. Name given as Master Itherius de Concoreto.
6. *Ib.* 1330-3, pp. 60, 86 ; *C.P.R.* 1327-30, p. 549 ; *Ib.* 1330-4, pp. 11, 194, 212, 256, 273, 399 ; *Ib.* 1334-8, p. 391.

nished his statement as to the result of the first three years' collection, he gave particulars of the amounts received and in arrears, and of the sums paid over to the Bardi. These details are of some little interest. As regards the first-fruits of vacant benefices, over £10,312 is due, of which £8,135 has been collected. The King's share was therefore over £4,067, of which the collector had paid over already the sum of £3,627. Of this, however, the Bardi had only received a little under £648.

The clerical tenth of course was more productive. The amount due for the first three years was £57,075, at the rate of £19,025 per annum. The collector requested that £1,890 might be allowed to himself for expenses of collection and because of exemptions granted to certain cardinals beneficed in England. The balance due was then £55,185, of which the King's moiety was about £27,593. Four acquittances were produced by the collector shewing that he had paid £26,000 to the Bardi, and had advanced £1,000 for the King in Ireland.[1]

The death of Pope John xxii in December, 1334, is said to have interfered with the completion of the collection of the above tenth, and the King summoned the members of the Societies of the Bardi and Peruzzi and others to discuss the question. It is stated that the King considered that the advice of the merchants would be most opportune for the completion and happy disposition of this affair.[2]

The Calendars of Patent and Close Rolls contain very little of importance relative to the dealings of the merchants of the Society of the Peruzzi of Florence with Edward III prior to the year 1336. Though they were undoubtedly trading in the country, they do not appear to have been very closely associated with the affairs of the Court.

In 1330 they were acting in concert with the Bardi, as attorneys for the Count of Jülich, receiving for him the pension allowed him by Edward III.[3] In 1333, licence was granted to Neri Perini, Arrigo Accorsi, Giovanni Giuntini, and his companions of the Society of the Peruzzi dwelling in England, to take certain of their wools to the staples appointed,

---

1. *C.P.R.* 1330–4, pp. 453, 454. In stating the amounts above, shillings and pence have been neglected.

2. *C.C.R.* 1333–7, p. 485.   3. *C.C.R.* 1330–3, p. 73.

and to export them, after paying the customs, where they will, notwithstanding the ordinance of the staple directing that all wools shall be bought at the staples.[1]

Privileges of this kind, also accorded to the Bardi, may be taken as evidence that the Peruzzi were doing considerable private trade.   They dealt extensively in wool with the various religious houses[2]—as did the Bardi and others also—and they also cultivated business relations with the nobility. They were connected with the affairs of Hugh le Despenser the younger, and had to account to the King for certain properties, when the whole of his effects was forfeited to the Crown.[3] There is also a record of negotiations with the Prior of the Order of S. John of Jerusalem in England who pledged over 15,000 animals to the Bardi and the Peruzzi, together with 40 sacks of wool, and silver vessels worth 200 marks, in return for a loan of 2,681 marks.   The same prior also acknowledged his indebtedness to the societies in a sum of 34,000 marks, which he duly repaid.[4]

The Peruzzi family was of considerable importance in Florence, and during the days of the Republic produced ten "gonfalonieri" and fifty- four "priori."[5] The Head, or Director, of the Company during the period under consideration was Tommaso d'Arnoldo Peruzzi till 1331, then Giotti d'Arnoldo Peruzzi till 1336, then Bonifazio di Tommaso Peruzzi, who, compelled to leave Florence and visit London in 1339, when the affairs of the company became precarious, died there in 1340, "perchance," says Peruzzi, "from grief, foreseeing the impending catastrophe to his family, and to Florence."   He was succeeded as Director by his brother Pacino di Tommaso Peruzzi, who was a signatory to the "arrangement" of 6 September, 1347.[6]

The Society maintained agents in all important centres where they traded, their London representative being Giovanni di Tano Baroncelli, whose family, in common with those of

---

1. *C.P.R.* 1330–4, p. 434.
2. Peruzzi, pp. 71 to 79, gives a list of English and Scottish monasteries dealing with the Italian merchants.
3. *C.P.R.* 1334–8, pp. 277, 343; *C.C.R.* 1333–7, pp. 519, 599, 608; *Ib.* 1337–9, pp. 234, 235.
4. *Ib.* 1333–7, pp. 124, 126, 127.   5. Peruzzi, pp. 159, 260.
6. Ib., pp. 250, 251, 259, 475; see also App., p. 135, *infra.*

Giovanni Villani, the chronicler, Gherardo Gentili, Stefano Uguccioni, Baldo Orlandini, Francesco Forzetti, and others, had been connected with the company for over fifty years.[1]

In the year 1336 the Peruzzi advanced to the King sums amounting to £4,666 13s. 4d. for urgent matters and for the King's secret business beyond the sea, and were promised payment by fixed dates out of the tenth and fifteenth (in four counties) granted to the King by the commonalty of the realm and by the citizens and burgesses thereof.[2] This is all that is recorded for the year, but a very different state of activity is at once evident with the advent of the year 1337, in the first six months of which the company has provided the King with more than £18,000.[3] Moreover, it is fairly evident that the Patent and Close Rolls do not contain a record of the whole of the transactions with the company. For example, an entry, dated February, 1337, mentions that the Peruzzi have lent to the King £11,732 13s. 4d. for his war with Scotland and for the defence of the realm,[4] of which there is no definite account given, and further, in September, the King acknowledged his indebtedness to the Society, first for £28,000, then for £35,000, the former amount being included in the latter.[5] The Company, however, lent to the King £2,000 at the beginning of September,[6] so that, if we may assume that the £18,000 and £11,732 above mentioned, are independent amounts, which seems probable, there is evidence of debt to the extent of about £32,000. Further, the entry of 2 September, *re* the £35,000 which the King acknowledged, states that the Peruzzi have already lent the greater part of it, and are about to pay the rest.[7] Now the loans of the Company to the King were fairly continuous for some little time after this date, generally for purposes more or less connected with the war—as, for example, £100 for fitting out ships for the King's service,[8] £130 wages of mariners, conveying the King's envoys back to the realm,[9] £100 for building a galley at New Hythe, Kent,[10] 1,000 marks to the Earls of Salisbury and

1. Peruzzi, pp. 251, 252.
2. *C.P.R.* 1334–8, pp. 249, 312; *C.C.R.* 1333–7, p. 609.
3. *C.P.R.* 1334–8, pp. 388, 430, 466; *C.C.R.* 1337–9, pp. 3, 25, 36, 42, 56.
4. *Ib.*, pp. 9, 51, 228, 229.
5. *C.P.R.* 1334–8, pp. 515, 517; see also *C.C.R.* 1337–9, p. 206.
6. *C.P.R.* 1334–8, p. 515.   7. *Ib.*, p. 517.   8. *Ib.*, p. 515.
9. *C.C.R.* 1337–9, p. 85.   10. *Ib.*, p. 86.

Huntingdon, and to the Bishop of Lincoln[1], £200 for services rendered to Master Richard Bintworth, King's Clerk, [2] and (January, 1338) the sum of £7,139 16s. 8d. for specified purposes, of which £4,472 3s. 4d. was for Henry, Bishop of Lincoln, and the two Earls of Salisbury and Huntingdon, when sent as the King's envoys beyond the sea.[3]

In this connection, however, the most striking fact is, that there is an entry on the Liberate Rolls of the Exchequer, dated 15 October, 1337, which seems to prove that the huge sum of £35,000 was actually paid from the King's Exchequer to the Society of the Peruzzi on one writ alone.[4]

The making of gifts to the merchants by way of compensation for losses sustained through delay or failure on the part of the King to meet his obligations was a practice to which resort was frequently made. It was, no doubt, in some cases, a subterfuge by means of which interest on money lent could be paid to the merchants, without direct contravention of the laws against all usury. In some cases the King paid interest expressly as such [5] and he was frequently compelled to pledge articles of great value—even the crown of England,[6] two crowns of Queen Philippa,[7] or the jewels in the Tower, upon occasion—before he could obtain money at all. At other times the security took the form of the detention of some important dignitary of the realm, the Earl of Derby, for example, at the time of the crisis of 1340 and 1341. The Archbishop of Canterbury was also bound for the King's debts to certain men of Louvain, who would have imprisoned him without doubt, if they could have obtained possession of his person, but the Archbishop protected himself against both the King and the merchants, by wisely remaining within the precincts of his Cathedral of Canterbury.[8] Even the King himself was little better than a prisoner in Ghent, when in November, 1340, he dared not leave openly on account of his debts but was compelled to have recourse to clandestine departure.[9]

---

1. *Ib.*, p. 42.   2. *Ib.*, p. 157.
3. *C.C.R.* 1337–9, p. 232.
4. Bond, App. cxciii.   5. See pp. 101, 105, above.
6. *C.P.R.* 1338–40, p. 371, in connection with a loan of 111,000 florins of gold of Florence; see also *C.C.R.* 1339–41, pp. 597, 598; *Ib.* 1341–3, p. 448.
7. *Ib.* 1341–3, p. 565; cf. Bond, App. clxxv; also *C.P.R.* 1338–40, p. 391.
8. Tout, p. 350.   9. *Ib.*, p. 349; cf. Stubbs, II, 532.

A very definite example of the payment of interest by the King occurs in an indenture between the King and the Leopardi, where the former acknowledges that he owes to the latter (for non-payment of a sum of £9,897 6s. od. at the stipulated time) a further sum of £1,386, calculated at the rate of £346 10s. od. per month, for a period of four months. This amounts to 3½% per month, or 42% per annum approximately.[1] Again, in June, 1341, the King being in debt to certain men of Brussels, it is stated that he has paid to the Bardi 430 marks, which they, at the request of Henry of Lancaster, Earl of Derby, have paid for the King, ' in order to obtain respite for a time' from the payment of a sum of about 4,000 marks. This is about 10¾% of the total, but an exact computation is impossible in this instance as the time is not specified.[2] Further, in the same month as the preceding, the King, considering the services rendered to him by the Bardi and Peruzzi, and finding that they have not been able to obtain 1,800 sacks of wool granted for export with the ease that was presumed, now permits them to take 300 sacks, and allows them to have 2½ marks per sack (of the 40/- custom and subsidy) by way of rebate on the King's debts to them, provided that they pay the remaining half mark to certain merchants of "Almain" to whom the King has granted the customs, etc., in all ports of the realm.[3] This is not so definite and certain an example of interest, as those before given, as it depends upon whether the 300 sacks here mentioned are, or are not, part of the grant of 1,800 sacks. A careful collation of the several entries relating to these 1,800 sacks and stipulating the ports from which they are to be taken, has led to the conclusion that the 300 sacks are probably by way of compensation for delay in the acquisition of the larger grant.[4] It is perhaps almost impossible to arrive at certainty, as in the case of most of the larger grants of wool made to the Bardi and Peruzzi, the latter appear never to have been able within a reasonable time, or indeed at all, to acquire the total number of sacks allocated to them.

1. *C.C.R.* 1339–41, pp. 622, 623.
2. *C.P.R.* 1340–3, p. 276; cf. also p. 105, *supra*.
3. *C.C.R.* 1341–3, pp. 161, 162.
4. *Ib.* 1341–3, pp. 26, 36, 161, 167, 324, 330, 378, 410, 411, 417, 421; *C.P.R.* 1340–3, p. 145.

J

An example of the payment of interest covertly occurs at the very beginning of the reign.   In September, 1327, the King acknowledged a debt to the Bardi of £2,066 13s. 4d., of which £500 is described as "recompense for delay in repayment" of various sums of money by the King.[1]

Direct gifts to the merchants, particularly to the Bardi, are of somewhat frequent occurrence prior to the year 1339. After this date there is a marked scarcity of these awards, two or three alone being recorded.   Occasionally gifts were made to the wives or daughters of the merchants, probably as Bond suggests, with a view to securing the grant to some particular individual, and so preventing its absorption by the funds of the Company.   Five of these grants were made in June, 1339 —to the wives of Gherardo Boninsegni, Bartolommeo de' Bardi, and Dino Forzetti, of the Society of the Bardi, and to the wife of Tommaso d'Arnoldi Peruzzi, and the daughter of Bonifazio di Tommaso Peruzzi, to the last named on the occasion of her marriage.[2]   The Bardi were paid in July, 1340, there is no entry on the Liberate Rolls as regards the two grants to the Peruzzi.

By far the most remarkable of these grants are the two huge gifts of 28 June, 1339, £30,000 to the Bardi, and £20,000 to the Peruzzi, " in remembrance of time subsidies for the King's service, and their losses, labours, and expenses endured for him."[4]   It would be interesting to know whether these payments ever were really made, it seems to be almost impossible that they could have been made in one sum, and if it became a matter of assignment, there is grave doubt as to whether the greater part ever would be received by the merchants.   Besides the gifts specified above there are several other large awards, or promises of award, notably—one of £10,000,[5] one of £4,000,[6] one of 4,000 marks,[7] two of £2,000,[8]

1. *C.C.R.* 1327–30, p. 168.
2. *C.P.R.* 1338–40, p. 392.
3. Bond, App. cxcviii.
4. *C.P.R.* 1338–40, p. 388.
5. *C.C.R.* 1337–9, pp. 205, 206. This £10,000 was included in the greater sum of £62,000 for which the King had acknowledged indebtedness to the Bardi, *C.P.R.* 1334–8, p. 541. A later entry (*C.C.R.* 1337–9, p. 561) states that £50,000 of this was paid to the Bardi on 2 September, 1337. It is curious that this date is anterior by about six weeks to that of the entry acknowledging the debt of £62,000.
6. *C.P.R.* 1327–30, pp. 520, 521.   7. *Ib.* 1330–4, p. 269.
8. *Ib.* 1327–30, p. 395; *Ib.* 1330–4, p. 96.

one of 2,000 marks,[1] and five of £1,000,[2] to the Bardi, and
one of £9,000[3] to the Peruzzi.   Many of these were not
actual payments—promise to pay on a certain date was given,
or an assignment on some tax or on the customs, etc., was
stipulated.   Possibly also the gifts were sometimes made
with a view to inducing the merchants to negotiate further
advances; certainly several indentures drawn up between
themselves and the King refer quite pointedly to both assignments and further loans,[4] and it is occasionally stated that the
King has taken the merchants under his protection, on account
of the services they have rendered to him, "and more especially
because the merchants have granted that they will make a
further loan of the sums assigned to them, when they obtain
these."[5]   The King found it necessary to protect the merchants by letters patent with respect to the gifts he made to
them, stating expressly that the sums assigned by the King
and the late King to the merchants "have been pure gifts
made of mere liberality, and they are quit in respect of them."[6]
This was probably necessary to prevent various royal officials
from charging the gifts against the Companies. The King
also performed occasionally some act of favour at the request
of the merchants, as for example the conferring of a minor
office on some person preferred by them,[7] whilst on at least
one occasion, he appealed to the Doge and Community of
Venice for fair treatment of the Bardi in a dispute between
themselves and that city.[8]

It has already been remarked that the Bardi and Peruzzi
were apparently trading in concert shortly after the commencement of the year 1337.   In this year the dealings of
the Peruzzi with the Crown first become very prominent as
the King's necessities were greatly enhanced by the imminence
of war with France.   The Peruzzi appear at a first glance to
have been more generously treated in the way of repayments

1. *Ib.*, p. 463.
2. *Ib.* 1327–30, p. 231; *Ib.* 1330–4, pp. 29, 193, 380; *Ib.* 1340–3, p. 469.
3. *C.C.R.* 1337–9, p. 206. This is included in the £35,000 mentioned on
p. 114, above. There is again the same curious difficulty as to the dates of
the entries, part of the debt being acknowledged apparently after it had been
paid.
4. See *Ib.*, pp. 400 and 412.   5. *C.P.R.* 1340–3, p. 21.
6. *Ib.* 1330–4, p. 218; *Ib.* 1334–8, p. 29; *Ib.* 1338–40, p. 102.
7. *Ib.* 1330–4, pp. 192, 392.
8. *C.C.R.* 1330–3, p. 131.

by the King than were the Bardi who had really done more for him, but deeper investigation would be necessary for the absolute determination of this point.   The loans and assignments to the merchants afford evidence in many cases after a cursory examination that the share taken by the Bardi was to that of the Peruzzi in the ratio of three to two, in fact, that this was so, is once or twice expressly stated.[1]   The merchants were once again contributing to the upkeep of the royal household for a period of one year from 1 June, 1340.[2]   They were to find 2,000 marks per month of 28 days—in sterling when the King was in England and in current money for trade when he was abroad.[3]   The money was stated to be for the maintenance of the King's family, and for the wages of his servants, serjeants, etc., and it was to be paid monthly, as to 1,200 marks by the Bardi, and as to the remaining 800 marks by the Peruzzi,[4] according to agreement entered into between themselves and the King on 28 May, 1340.[5]   Assuming that this arrangement was observed it must have entailed an expenditure of 26,000 marks by the societies, and to enable them to meet it the King assigned to them all the subsidy of the ninth of sheaves, fleeces, and lambs, and the ninth of movables of the citizens and burgesses in the county of Gloucester of the first year.   The King emphasised the necessity of the strict observance of this grant to the merchants,[6] but it is very probable that they would experience the usual difficulty in obtaining repayments, especially after the conversion of the subsidy of the ninth, etc., into a subsidy of a definite number of sacks for the King in the Parliament of 1341, a procedure which would no doubt render their assignment invalid in its first form and would occasion application for some other allocation.[7]   Prior to this, a further grant had been made to the merchants towards household expenses.   An assignment of £2,650 for the Peruzzi and £3,600 for the Bardi was granted and apportioned to twenty-two ecclesiastical collectors to be paid to the merchants from the biennial tenth

1.   *C.C.R.* 1339–41, pp. 611, 612, 639, 640; *C.P.R.* 1340–3; p. 507.
2.   One entry—*Ib.*, p. 528—gives the date as 1 July, 1340, but all other entries agree as to 1 June.
3.   *C.C.R.* 1339–41, pp. 523, 528, 573, 593, 611, 612; *C.P.R.* 1340–3, p. 3; *C.C.R.* 1341–3, pp. 164, 165.
4.   *C.C.R.* 1339–41, pp. 611, 612.   5. *Ib.* 1341–3, pp. 164, 165.
6.   *Ib* 1339–41, pp. 611, 612.   7. Cf. *C.P.R.* 1340–3, p. 247.

granted by the clergy. It is stated that the Bardi complained that they had at the end of the year found £2,369 11s. 8d. more than they had received, and an order was made for this to be paid to them.[1] Since their share of the payment was 15,600 marks, this goes to prove that they obtained repayment to the extent of £8,030 8s. 4d.

Edward's only chance for the successful prosecution of the war lay in his ability with the assent and assistance of the merchants to manipulate the wool trade, as this provided the only real source of revenue on which he could rely for an extended period. In March, 1338,[2] it was agreed between the King and the Bardi and Peruzzi that the former should deliver to the latter all the wool (understood to be about 25,000 sacks[3]) granted to him in England, and that the merchants should sell them for as much as they could for the King's profit. The merchants were to have controllers to write down what they received and sold, and the King wished them to take the sacks as a rebate on that in which he was, or for which he would be, bound to them. Various assignments, dependent upon numerous stipulations, were then made to the merchants, and they undertook to advance £15,000 and to observe several conditions. The King further undertook to bring on his ships " to the sum of 2,000 sacks of the levies of the merchants," as quickly as possible, " at their cost and freightage, to sell them, if they can better supply the King's needs."[4] The custom on the wool was to be rebated to the merchants on that which the King owed to them at the rate of forty shillings per sack. No levies were to pass out of England except those of the Brabançons and the Germans until all the said levies had passed and were sold. Further, the King, realising that the merchants by undertaking these things were put in rebellion to the King of France, and would be in danger of losing what they had in his realm, promised to make amends to them for such losses. Finally, the merchants were to have every facility granted to them to enable

1. *C.C.R.* 1341–3, pp. 164, 165.
2. *C.C.R.* 1337–9, pp. 400, 412.
3. This figure is probably an over-estimate.
4. *I.e.*: the King will expedite the passage of the wool by taking it in his ships, and the merchants are to sell it, if by so doing, the King's needs can be the better supplied.

them to carry out their part of the undertaking whenever and wherever the same might be needed. This example may well serve to illustrate the manner in which the merchants were made serviceable to the King,—there was more involved than a mere loan and its repayment with or without interest—the merchants were to trade with the King's goods, they were, so to speak, to invest his wool in their business and account with him for the profit accruing on his " shares." There can be little doubt that the heavier customs and other dues, charged on the wool, would assist the merchants in efforts to buy more cheaply from the English producer, and the merchants would enhance the price as much as possible when selling in the Low Countries. This procedure in turn would be aided by Edward, if as promised, he prevented the export of all other wool until these particular wools were sold. The extreme slowness with which the King's wool was collected made the advances of the merchants still more necesssary to the monarch who required immediate supplies. During the autumn and winter of 1338–1339 a large fleet was held in readiness for transport at Harwich. The date of its departure is uncertain, but presumably it must have set sail before 24 March, 1339, since it does not appear to have been destroyed by the French, when, on that day, they sacked the town.[1] As time went on supplies of wool for the King became more and more difficult to secure, and in September, 1340, the Bardi were aiding him with their own wool " as he could not have the wool granted to him by Parliament, so readily as he believed at the time of the grant."[2]

In the section on Florentine affairs above,[3] an attempt was made to trace out certain influences at work in Florence, Naples, and France, which were contributing from 1339 onwards, and especially after 1343, to the ultimate downfall of the Florentine financiers. Similar forces were at work in England centring around the King's pecuniary necessities due to his wars with Scotland and France. The situation really became acute after the war with France became inevitable in 1337, and there was much native jealousy and irritation caused by the presence and operations of the merchants, and by the royal favour bestowed upon them. There may

1. Murimuth, p. 88; Baker, *Chronicon*, p. 63.
2. *C.C.R.* 1339–41, p. 534.   3. See pp. 93 to 98.

have been conspiracy on the part of English merchants against them, and the King may have been involved in it[1]—one thing is certain, that the storm seems to overwhelm them quite suddenly and without any very obvious cause. The Bardi and Peruzzi appear to have themselves requested an audit of their accounts and payment of what was owing to them. As a result of the audit we find the merchants in prison, seemingly convicted of malpractices, but with no specific charge against them except that they owe a large sum of money to the King, of which he demands payment by a fixed date under penalties, whilst admitting that his own debts to the merchants are greater than theirs to him.[2] The King graciously accorded his royal pardon to the merchants a little later,[3] but did not do anything further towards alleviating their distress. It remains, however, to examine events a little more closely.

There is notice of an audit of the accounts of the Bardi, taken with a view to the making of payment or assignment to them, as early as 1336,[4] it was therefore quite natural that they should ask for an audit at a later date, and perhaps, expect the same result. There seems to have been a tendency to desire the institution of a periodic audit of accounts, even of the royal accounts, about this time, on the part of the Commons, but no such result was obtained during the reign of Edward III.[5] Signs of aversion to the foreigners are early evident. John Molyns was entrusted with the arresting of all foreign merchants of Lombardy and elsewhere, except partners of the Bardi and Peruzzi,[6] in 1337, and in 1338 Edmund de la Beche, King's clerk, had a similar commission, and was not to be liable for impeachment or disturbance as a result of his appointment.[7] The King issued notice to the Exchequer in September of this year, not to pay any fees to the King's ministers by "writs of liberati" even though these writs be brought to them, nor cause any fees of the ministers to be allowed until they had received other mention by the King's writs. This action is defended on the ground that the King was incurring great expense for the defence of the realm,

1. Law, *English Nouveaux-Riches, etc., Trans. Royal Hist. Soc.*, IX, 61, 62.
2. *C.P.R.* 1343–5, pp. 468, 469; *C.C.R.* 1343–6, p. 673.
3. *C.P.R.* 1345–8, pp. 13, 14.   4. *C.C.R.* 1333–7, p. 565.
5. Stubbs, II, 566, 567.   6. *C.P.R.* 1334–8, p. 506,
7. *Ib.* 1338–40, p. 123.

and to recover the rights of his crown, and that, as all ought to assist in this, he had ordained, with the assent of the council, that the yearly fees of all ministers, as stated above, should cease, unless some of the ministers were so needy that they could not manage without this, and that the money should be applied in the meantime to the support of the said charges.[1] This order serves to show the trend which affairs were taking, and in the next year it was followed by another which affected the merchants more closely. On account of his necessity the King revoked on 6 May, 1339, all assignments, of money or other things, made by him or his ministers, before or after his passage beyond sea, " other than for defence of castles and towns in Scotland, and to the Bardi and Peruzzi," and of all respites of debts made since his last transfretation, and ordered that, until his return, no fees should be paid to any justices, barons of Exchequer, clerks promoted, or other ministers, who have other means of support.[2] This writ is exceedingly important, but it appears to indicate that exception was made in favour of the Bardi and Peruzzi, and this point of view also seems to be strengthened by subsequent entries in the Patent and Close Rolls.   On 18 May, 1339,[3] protection and safe-conduct were granted to the Peruzzi, who had made large subsidies for the King's service, since he went beyond seas and before, and had promised to pay large sums for him in England,—their goods were to be treated with the same care as if they were the King's goods; on 15 June, five weeks after the " revoking" order, £10,000 was assigned to the Bardi;[4] on the 26th of the same month an order for the payment of certain monies to individuals who had victualled the fleet expressly contained the words " in spite of assignment of this money to the Bardi, and assignment to them being excepted in recent order revoking all assignments made before this time;"[5] lastly, on 28 June, 1339, a writ was issued permitting William de la Pole to have his assignments, in spite of the " revoking" order (as he cannot otherwise continue to supply the King)—and this writ was to be obeyed " although the King lately revoked all assignments except those made to the Bardi and Peruzzi for the munition and defence of his

1. *C.C.R.* 1337–9, p. 467.
2. *C.P.R.* 1338–40, p. 255; *Foed.*, II, ii, 1080.
3. *C.P.R.* 1338–40, p. 272; see also *Ib.*, pp. 258, 260, 331, 357, 391.
4. *C.C.R.* 1339–41, p. 153.   5. *Ib.*, pp. 154, 155.

casfles and towns in Scotland."[1]   No doubt the order of 6 May, 1339, was sufficiently serious as indicating how little the merchants might ultimately expect from the King, and it was no doubt wise that the Director of the Society of the Peruzzi should come at once to London to attend to the affairs of his firm,[2] but the final breach with the English monarch had not yet occurred.

Edward promised, on 4 August, 1339, to protect and pay both the Bardi and Peruzzi, and enjoined his son to attend to the carrying out of this, if he should fall in the wars.   Seven witnesses vouched for the good faith of the King, and the writ referred to the sufferings of the two firms through their services to him, which had caused them to lose capital and credit, to undergo imprisonment, and to be called on suddenly for repayment through fears as to their solvency.[3]   A commission was appointed in July, 1340, possibly owing to the complaints of Parliament, to examine and audit the receipts and payments (from the time of the granting of the tenth for three years, and notwithstanding any acquittances or pardons made by the King) of the Bardi and Peruzzi and others, and the writ expressly states that the grants to the merchants had been made on the understanding that the King would do this.[4]

1. *Ib.*, p. 155. This entry seems to impose restriction as to the privilege reserved for the Bardi, but the other entries do not seem to do so, neither does the original "revoking" order of 6 May, 1339, appear to confine the excepted assignments of the Bardi and Peruzzi to those for Scottish affairs alone. Scottish assignments are separately mentioned.

Foed., V, 109, reads : "Nos attendentes, ..., 'Assignationibus, pro Munitione et Defensione Castrorum et Villarum nostrorum in Scotia, necnon Assignationibus, Dilectis nobis Mercatoribus de Societatibus Bardorum et Peruch', factis et concessis, dumtaxat exceptis,' ac etiam atterminationes seu installamenta et respectus debitorum nostrium post ultimam transfectationem nostram facta, ex causa necessitatis hujusmodi revocamus omnino. Teste me ipso : apud Antwerpen, vi die maii, anno regni nostri xiii."

The writer ventures the opinion that Peruzzi, pp. 471, 472, is not correct in stating that the above order revoked all assignments "including" those to the Bardi and Peruzzi.

2. The Director was Bonifazio di Tommaso Peruzzi. See pp. 112 and 135.

3. *C.P.R.* 1338–40, p. 391 ; also see *C.C.R.* 1341–3, pp. 542, 543, where, in an indenture of assignment to the merchants, dated 18 May, 1342, it is expressly stated, "this assignment the King and Council have agreed to keep, ..." which seems to indicate that the King's good faith was not beyond question.

4. Audit was ordered of the accounts, etc., of "William de la Pole; John Charnels; Paul de Monte Florum; the Bardi and Peruzzi; William de Northwell; William de Melchbourn; and others." The members of the investigating commission were John, Archbishop of Canterbury; Richard, Bishop of Durham; Roger, Bishop of Coventry and Lichfield; Henry, Earl of Derby; Richard, Earl of Arundel; William, Earl of Huntingdon; Thomas Wake, of Liddel; Ralph Basset, of Drayton; and Robert de Sadington. *Ib.* 1340–3, p. 87.

Nothing of importance appears to have resulted from the appointment of this commission, but it is very probable that the Bardi and Peruzzi were receiving very little repayment in comparison with the amounts owing to them from this time onwards, and we are informed in July, 1341, when a new assignment is being made to them, that it is "for relief of their estate, much depressed in these days by large payments made and undertaken on his (*i.e.* the King's) account."[1]

Under date 19 October, 1342, appears what seems to be the earliest notice of the appointment of the commission of "oyer and terminer," which was to examine all accounts of the Bardi and Peruzzi touching wool, jewels, money, and other things of the King received by them as well beyond seas as within, for which they should account.[2] This Committee probably did not sit immediately, and when it did meet, its deliberations seem to have been unduly prolonged.[3]   At first the commissioners numbered four, but in January, 1343, their total was brought up to nine.[4]   They were required to audit the accounts of the merchants from the beginning of the twentieth year of the reign of Edward the Second until a fixed date.   The treasurer and barons of the Exchequer were to search their files for all writs of allowance, warrants, etc., by which the merchants could have any allowance upon their accounts, and they were required to have the same transcribed, and sent under the Exchequer seal to the commissioners appointed to undertake the audit.[7] No doubt, the examination of these accounts was a long and tedious process, and it does not appear to have been completed before the end of 1343.[8] Robert de Wodehouse and his fellows had been ordered to do all that was just and reasonable, and to make all proper allowance to the mer-

---

1. *C.P.R.* 1340–3, p. 247.   2. *Ib.*, p. 558.
3. *C.C.R.* 1343–6, pp. 45, 106, 160, 199, 246, etc.
4. The first commissioners named are Robert de Wodehouse, Archdeacon of Richmond; John de Pulteney; William de Stowe; and William de Broklesby (*C.P.R.* 1340–3, p. 558); in January 1343 the names of Gervase de Wilford; William de Kirkeby; Ivo de Clinton; William de Northwell; and Robert de Pleseleye are added. (*Ib.*, p. 588, where audit is also ordered of the accounts of the Acciaiuoli and Albertini as well.)
5. *I.e.* from 8 July, 1326, a little before the time when Isabella and Mortimer aimed at supremacy in the Government. The loans of the Bardi to Queen Isabella have been mentioned.
6. Probably the end of 16 Edw. III, 24 January, 1343, *C.P.R.* 1340–3, p. 588.
7. *C.C.R.* 1343–6, pp. 45, 99.   8. *Ib.*, p. 199.

chants,[1] and further, if they came across anything doubtful, which had been claimed by the Bardi and Peruzzi, to put it by itself, so that when the matter came before the King and his council, they might declare as they thought fit.[2] There are several writs to the Commissioners, and to the Exchequer authorities, requiring them to make various allowances to the merchants, and the latter were apparently not at all satisfied with the statement which the Commissioners, as requested, submitted to the Exchequer authorities. This statement had to undergo examination in the Exchequer, and the treasurer and barons were urged to discharge the merchants of what was allowed to them in the accounts and proceed to a final issue in accordance with the law and custom of the Exchequer, always saving to the King and his council the discussion of any claims in the said accounts which the merchants had laid before the auditors.[3] As a further commission was appointed on 5 February, 1344, to examine carefully all the data furnished to the King and council, and to certify them in the matter, it seems probable that the merchants had appealed against the finding of the earlier commissioners and the Exchequer. There appears to be no further information about them until it is stated in the next month, March, 1344, that the King has issued a writ to the Sheriffs of London directing them to take certain of the Bardi and Peruzzi and all their fellows, and have them before the Chief Justice by a certain date, to satisfy the King for the trespasses and deceits whereof they were convicted before Robert Parvyng and his fellows.[5]

This order was superseded for a time but not countermanded, and affairs were by no means progressing favourably for the Italians. Giovanni di Portenari of Florence, and Antonio "Bache" were in the Fleet prison in March, 1343, for arrears of account,[6] and Ridolfo di Peruzzi was there in June,

---

1. *Ib.*, pp. 45, 160, etc.   2. *Ib.*, p. 160.
3. *C.C.R.* 1343–6, p. 199; see also pp. 246, 304, 324, 330, 372, 406, 407, 421, 422, 438, 500, 501, etc.
4. The members of this commission were the Archbishop of Canterbury; the Earls of Derby, Northampton, Huntingdon and Suffolk; John Darcy; Bartholomew de Burghersh; William de Cusancia; John Charnels; and William de Northwell. (*C.P.R.* 1343–5, p. 274.) Many of the orders, issued to the Exchequer, to make allowance to the merchants, as already mentioned on p. 124, may have been due to the deliberations of this committee. These orders are continued into the year 1345. (*C.C.R.* 1343–6, pp. 500, 501.)
5. *Ib.*, p. 360.   6. *Ib.*, p. 97.

1344, in company with two other of his associates.[1]   Safe conduct and protection for a year was granted in February, 1345, to the Bardi, who were going through various counties, collecting monies of an assignment which the King had made to them from the clerical tenth and from the tenth and fifteenth of the laity granted to the King in the last Parliament,[2] but in June and July the King was issuing orders to the Constable of the Tower to keep certain of the Peruzzi safely lodged there until further orders,[3] and to the Sheriff of London not to permit certain of the Bardi to be released from prison until they had satisfied the King for the debts in which they were bound to him. [4] The Bardi acknowledged in November of this same year that they owed the King £18,000 to be paid at Martinmas next, and the King granted that if £9,000 were paid at Martinmas, or before, the bond for £18,000 should be null, but otherwise the £18,000 should be rebated in the debt which the King clearly owed them, and if they failed in part in the payment, then the triple of what was lacking should be rebated in that debt. [5]

What the faults of the merchants were is not here stated,[6]

1. *C.P.R.* 1343–5, pp. 265, 269.
2. *C.C.R.* 1343–6, pp. 551, 552; *C.P.R.* 1343–5, p. 434.
3. *C.C.R.* 1343–6, p. 581.   4. *Ib.*, p. 638.   5. *Ib.*, p. 673.
6. There is, however, a hint of their fault in a later Calendar. The acknowledgment of a debt of £18,000 by the Bardi may possibly have been the price they paid for release from prison. The acknowledgments are dated 12 and 14 November, 1345. *C.P.R.* 1345–8, pp. 13 and 14, contains a statement of their "pardon" (by the King, who had ruined them by failure to meet his obligations), in words which seem worthy of record : " Although the King's lieges, especially those who have long done laudable service, sometimes by want of care or otherwise, offend him grievously, yet, by the example of Him, who in the midst of anger remembered mercy, he freely abates severity, willing to have mercy rather than vengeance—so, whereas he lately caused a great sum of money to be delivered to the Bardi as a loan to be paid for him at a certain time under heavy penalties, and they made default in the payment incurring the penalties, at which he has in truth been disturbed, especially because of the very damaging delay of important business caused by want of money; because those merchants coming humbly before him and offering various excuses have humbly submitted themselves to him herein, he, gratefully recalling their fruitful service at other times, and overcome by their prayers and humility, from his heart remits all the indignation, offence, and rancour conceived by him against them for this cause, admitting them to the grace of his former affection and familiarity." It is important to note that this pardon is dated 8 November, 1345, and that it was followed four days later by the acknowledgment of the Bardi that they owed £18,000 to the King. It would appear that the Bardi ultimately had offended the King by paying themselves somewhat instead of others with money he entrusted to them. No mention is made of the Peruzzi, but it is significant that they also went to prison, and they also became bankrupt. See also *C.C.R.* 1343–6, p. 670, where there is enrolled, under the same date, 8 November, 1345, a long indenture making a grant to various *English* merchants.

but it is conceivable that they might be such as might be con-
donable in the light of the conduct of the King, who appears
to have treated them with considerable injustice. Certain particulars given in April, 1345, deal almost exclusively with the
Bardi and fix their accounts with the King at £50,493 5s. 2½d.
for the period December, 1338, to July, 1340.

The amount is made up of £30,264 12s. 3½d. actual loans
in money to the King, £10,000 paid for the King and his
council, and £10,228 12s. 11d. granted as a gift for services
and losses. Certain sums are then mentioned as having been
received by the Bardi between December, 1342, and March,
1344, and it is stated that they are all accounted for by the
merchants in the return presented by Robert de Wodehouse
to the Exchequer, except a sum of £2,595 18s. 2d. still
required from the Bardi at the Exchequer. Finally the merchants are said to have been duly charged with all wools and
other things which they have received.[1] But this entry cannot
possibly be the completed return of Robert de Wodehouse
and his fellow commissioners, for it deals with a few years
only of the period under discussion, it gives receipts for one
period and loans for another, and it deals with the affairs of
one company alone.

The King promised in March, 1346, to pay the Bardi
£23,082 3s. 10½d. due in their account begun before Robert
de Wodehouse. This entry is followed by a number of others
mentioning debts of the Bardi to various individuals, and
these were always deducted from the above amount, the King
having undertaken to pay them. In this way the sum owing
to the Bardi was reduced apparently to £13,454 2s. 11½d. in
1348, after which date nothing further appears with regard to
it.[2] During this period, and indeed until 1360, the date of the
last Patent Roll available, protections and safe-conducts were
continuously issued for the Bardi, forbidding anyone to
attempt to obtain any payments from them, as they owed the
King a great sum, and might not be able to pay, if others
were allowed to sue them for debt, and " according to the
ancient prerogative of the Crown, the King ought to be pre-

---

1. *C.P.R.* 1343–5, pp. 467—469.
2. *Ib.* 1345–8, pp. 60, 80, 406, 441, 442, 443; *Ib.* 1348–50, pp. 10, 11.

ferred before others in the payment of debts."[1] The Calendars of the Close Rolls contain little of importance as to the Bardi and the Crown after 1345, but the merchants seem to have continued to trade in a very small way,[2] and a certain Gualtiero de' Bardi was master of the mint at the end of the reign of Edward III and at the beginning of that of Richard II.[3] The only payment they appear to have received towards the acknowledged debt of £50,493 5s. 2½d. was one of £150 in October, 1347 ![4] Many years later, in the reign of Richard II, under the date 10 November, 1391, occurs the following :—

" Pardon and discharge, for reasons agreed upon between the Great Council of the one part, and Gualtiero de' Bardi, merchant of the Society of the Bardi of Florence, their attorney, of the other part, and for the salvation and discharge of the souls of the late King, the King, his heirs and executors, as well as divers lords spiritual and temporal of the realm, their heirs and executors, to the said Gualtiero and merchants, their heirs, executors, and attorneys, of all actions, suits, and demands, sums of money, or other things the value of money, due to the King from them, or current in demand at the Exchequer or elsewhere in the King's places."[5]

Such then appears to be the end of the transactions between the English Crown and the Bardi.

There are but few facts recorded in the Calendars of the Patent and Close Rolls after 1345 as regards the Peruzzi. They were still in the Tower in March, 1346, but not closely confined there, being free to go and come as they chose.[6] The King's indebtedness to them in 1347 was given at £20,000, or rather, Walter de Chiriton and others, having assignments to the value of £40,000 were to satisfy the Peruzzi for the King[7] It is stated that Chiriton and his fellows had undertaken to pay £100,000 for the King's debts in Gascony and

---

1. *C.P.R.* 1345–8, pp. 87, 151, 197, 257 (Peruzzi), 281, 409, 410; *Ib.* 1348–50, pp. 6 (Peruzzi), 194, 418 (Bardi and Peruzzi), 573 (Bardi and Peruzzi); *Ib.* 1350–4, pp. 150 (Bardi and Peruzzi), 326, 501; *Ib.* 1354–8, pp. 103, 286, 439, 607; *Ib.* 1358–61, pp. 99, 274 (1 October, 1360).

2. See *C.C.R.* 1354–60, pp. 489, 490; *Ib.* 1364–8, p. 455; *Ib.* 1368–74, pp. 38, 121, 450.

3. *Ib.* 1360–4, pp. 296, 528; *Ib.* 1368–74, p. 1; *C.P.R.* 1377–81, p. 1.

4. See Bond, App. cciv.   5. *C.P.R.* 1391–6, p. 15.

6. *C.C.R.* 1346–9, pp. 53, 54.   7. *Ib.*, p. 204; see also p. 143.

£20,000 to the Peruzzi.[1] On the whole, however, the Peruzzi were, perhaps, somewhat more fortunate than the Bardi, for they appear to have received payments amounting to £6,375 in June, 1346,[2] and a further payment of £100 in August, 1352. [3] This is the last mention of the Society, perhaps they were among the Lombard merchants about whom the Commons complained as having left the country in that year.[4]

Villani gives certain particulars as to the affairs of the companies. He appears to have been himself financially interested to a small extent, first, in the Peruzzi,[5] with whom he had invested 2,000 lire,[6] and after 1308, in the Bonaccorsi. He is said to have been imprisoned for a short time on the failure of the Companies.[7] He notes the state of the accounts of the Societies in England at the time of the outbreak of war between that country and France, which was a serious misfortune to the Companies.[8] Villani puts the loans of the Bardi to Edward at 180,000 marks, those of the Peruzzi at 135,000 marks, and evaluates the total at 1,365,000 florins of gold,[9] " the worth," says he, " of a kingdom."[10]

The date of the failure is given as January, 1345,[11] and the indebtedness of the King of England is fixed at 900,000 florins to the Bardi, and 600,000 to the Peruzzi. The King of Naples had left debts of 100,000 florins to each company, therefore the grand total owing from the two Kings was 1,700,000 florins, or evaluating at the ratio used by Villani above, about £262,000 sterling. The debts of the merchants in Florence and elsewhere amounted to about 900,000 florins, or about £138,000. The Acciaiuoli, Bonaccorsi, Cocchi, Antellesi, Corsini, the Uzzani, Perendoli, many other small companies and private

1. *Ib.*, p. 260.   2. See Bond, App. cci and ccii.
3. *C.C.R.* 1349–54, p. 505.   4. Stubbs, p. 532, quoting *Rot. Parl.*, ii, 240.
5. Peruzzi, p. 253.
6. About £186 sterling, at that time, evaluating at an Exchange of lire 10.15.0 per £ sterling; see Peruzzi, pp. 276, 291.
7. Peruzzi, pp. 163, 462.
8. Peruzzi, p. 237, has the following from the accounts of the society of the Peruzzi :— .... " Per lo costo d'una barca armata che si mandò da Barletta a Rodi nel mese d'ottobre 1338 per far sapere ai nostri compagni le novità arrivateci per la guerra del re d'Inghilterra al re di Francia. . . . . . Lire 203.16." (About £19 sterling of the period.)
9. Villani, p. 820 (315,000 marks, £210,000.)
10. Ib. : " . . . . che valeano un Reame."
11. For this section see Villani, pp. 934, 935. Adopting Villani's ratio that 315,000 marks equals approximately 1,365,000 florins, the following are rough equivalents to the nearest £1,000 :—Debt of the King of England to the Bardi, £138,000; to the Peruzzi, £92,000. It is perhaps noteworthy that these amounts are still in the ratio 3 : 2, see p. 118, above.

individuals were all involved in the general destruction of the commercial importance of the city, which was bitterly lamented by the Chronicler, but ultimately attributed to the justice of God, in the punishment of the sins of the people.[1] The magistrates of Florence appealed on behalf of the Bardi to the King of England—" Regum Gloriosissime et Domine" —but apparently without effect,[2] the marked indifference of Edward and his Parliament being especially noted by Peruzzi.[3]   The King of France, instigated by the Duke of Athens, says Villani, made reprisals against the Florentines in his realm,[4] and before the end of 1345 several of the Bardi, being implicated in the introduction into the city of a number of coiners of false money from Siena,[5] were put to death in Florence.   The failure of the Florentines spread something very like panic throughout the trading communities of Europe, but an arrangement was ultimately arrived at and signed on 6 September, 1347, at a conference held in Florence under the auspices of the Commune.[6]   The names of the "syndics" appointed by the city to aid in the settlement of affairs between the societies and their creditors are given below, as are also those of the members of the companies at that period.[7]

The Bardi appear to have paid about six soldi per lira, or about 30%, whilst the Peruzzi paid four soldi per lira, or about 20%.[8]

To complete the account of the loans by Italians of this period to the sovereigns of England, it would be necessary to deal with numerous small companies and certain important individuals.   Such are the Acciaiuoli, Albertini, Leopardi,

---

1. Villani, p. 935: "O maladetta e bramosa Lupa piena del vizio dell' avarizia regnante ne' nostri ciechi e matti cittadini Fiorentini, che per cuvidigia di guadagnare da' Signori, mettono il loro e l'altrui pecunia, in loro potenza e signoria a perdere, e disolare d'ogni potenza la nostra Republica; . . . . . Ma non sanza cagione vengono a' Comuni, e a' cittadini gli occulti giudicj di Dio per punire i peccati commessi, siccome Cristo di sua bocca vangielizzando disse : 'In peccato vestro moriemini, etc.' "

2. Sir H. Ellis, *Original letters illustrative of English History*, 3rd ser., I, 39—43. The letter is from the *Cotton MS. Nero*, B, VII, folio 11, and is dated at Florence, 30th January, Xth Indiction.   It is addressed : "Serenissimo ac Gloriosissimo Principi et Domino, domino Heduardo Dei gratia Angliae et Francorum Regi," and is subscribed : "Devotissimi Majestatis vestrae (servitores), Priores Artium et Vexillani justitiae Populi et Communis Florentiae."

3. Peruzzi, p. 464.   4. Villani, p. 936.   5. Ib., p. 933.
6. Peruzzi, pp. 472, 473.   7. *Ib.*, pp. 474-476.   See p. 132, below.
8. Villani, p. 935.

and Bonaccorsi, certain merchants of Lucca, Siena, and Genoa, the Portenari, Antonio Pessagno, Antonio " Bache," and others, [1] some of whom made very important contributions to the royal needs, and no doubt were among the Lombard merchants who left the country in 1352,[2] that is, such of them as escaped the general " débâcle " of 1345.

Four great companies of Italian merchants had been ruined by dealings with English kings—the Riccardi of Lucca under Edward I,[3] the Frescobaldi of Florence under Edward II,[4] and the Bardi and Peruzzi under Edward III.

The two last mentioned Companies advanced £73,500[5] to the first Edward and his successor, and they appear to have found no less (if we include their contributions to the maintenance of the Household)[6] than £359,600 for Edward III.[7] This gives a total loan of not less than £433,000 to the English Crown between the years 1290 and 1345, by the merchants of the Societies of the Bardi and Peruzzi of Florence alone !

There is considerable ground then for the statement that as regards the repudiation of his obligations by Edward III of England " se non fu allora la sola causa per cui decadde la prosperità della repubblica di Firenze, ne fu certamente una delle maggiori."[8]

1. Perhaps also Matthew Dast, if the name is equivalent to Matteo d'Asti.
2. See p. 129, above.
3. See Rhodes, "Italian Bankers in England," &c., pp. 142, 156, 159.
4. Ib., pp. 145—152, 156, 161, 162.   5. Ib., pp. 163, 164.
6. See pp. 107, 118, above. These sums, £41,477 13s. 4d., and 26,000 marks, are probably not to any extent included in a sum of £300,757 12s. 10d., obtained by computation from the entries in the Calendars of the Patent and Close Rolls for the period.
7. The approximate total of the sums indicated in footnote 6. The amounts are given in the text to the nearest £100. More or less repayment was, of course, continuously being made throughout the period.
8. Peruzzi, p. 477.

E. RUSSELL.

K

APPENDIX.

Containing

(*a*) Lists of names of merchants of the Societies of the Bardi and Peruzzi of Florence, trading in England, during the reign of Edward III.   (Compiled from Calendars of Patent and Close Rolls.)

(*b*) Names of members of the Companies at the time of their failure, and names of the " Syndics" appointed by the Commune of Florence, to aid in effecting a settlement between the Companies and their Creditors.

Merchants of the Society of the Bardi of Florence trading in England
during the reign of Edward the Third.

Clavo Angelini	Bauchino Belchari
Alessandro de' Bardi	Pietro Bene
Bartolommeo de' Bardi	Francesco di Bocci, or Boschi N
Bartolommeo di (Sir) Rodolfo de'	Giovanni Boletti
Bardi.[1]	Gherardo Boninsegni
Bindo di Gianni de' Bardi [1]	Tano Cecco [2]
Filippo de' Bardi	Lottieri di Colino
Gualtiero di Filippo de' Bardi [1] [3]	Dino Forzetti
Pietro di (Sir) Rodolfo de' Bardi [1]	Giovanni di Francesco
(Sir) Rodolfo di Giovanni de'	Manetto Franzesi
Bardi [1] [4]	Andrea Gherardini
Taldo di (Sir) Rodolfo de' Bardi [1]	

1. These names appear towards the end of the period.

2. Given as Tane Jakes.

3. Honoured with a grant of " English citizenship " by Edward III ; see Peruzzi, p. 149.   A certain Walter de' Bardi was master of the mint in the Tower of London at the end of the reign of Edward III and the beginning of that of Richard II. See p. 128, *supra*.

N. This merchant appears to have traded also in the Kingdom of Naples for the Society ; see Yver, *op. cit.*, p. 403.

4. Head, or Director of the Company in 1345.

Merchants of the Society of the Bardi in England—continued.

Alessandro Gianni [3]
Filippo Gianni [3]
Lottieri Gianni [3]
Giotto di Giocchi [4] [5]
Giotto Ubertino di Giocchi [1] [5]
Francesco Grandoni
Roberto Infangati
Ubertino Infangati [1]
Francesco Lapi
Niccolò Marini [2]
Niccolò Marsi [2]

Pietro Maso
Perotto Mati [1]
Giovanni di Mevane
Cione Migliori [6]
Jacopo Niccolini
Pietro Rinieri
Rinuccio Rinucci [N]
Giotto Roberti [1]
Tommaso Tedaldi
Taldo Valori [7]

1. These names appear towards the end of the period.
2. Probably the same person.
3. Given as Loterinus Johan, Philip Johan, and Alexander Johan.
4. Given as Jonettus, or Chonettus, de Joky, or Joiky.
5. Possibly the same person.
6. Given as Chinus Meliory.
7. "A person of some political importance"; see Rhodes, p. 154; "Gonfaloniere in 1340."
N. See note, p. 132, above.

In 1345, at the time of the failure of the Bardi and Peruzzi, the Company of the Bardi under Sir Ridolfo di Bartolo Bardi was thus composed :—

Ridolfo di Bartolo Bardi
Filippo Bardi
Taldo Valori [1]

Gherardo Boninsegni
Lapo Niccoli
Angiolo di Gherardo Lanfredini

The above subscribéd the ' arrangement ' arrived at on 6 September 1347.

The following were the ' Syndics ' appointed by the Commune to assist the Creditors of the Bardi :—

Pegolotti Francesco Balducci
Piero di Lippo Aldobrandini
Silvestro di Rinieri Peruzzi
Naddo Bucelli
Giovanni Arnolfi

Silvestro di Manetto Issachi
Silvestro di Ricciardo Ricci
Paolo di Cecco Gianni
Jacopo di Piero Machiavelli

The above is taken from Peruzzi, pp. 474 to 476.

1. Litta states, see note, p. 101, above, that Taldo Valori died after the year 1344. The above excerpt from "Peruzzi," if correct, proves that his death must have been subsequent to 6 September, 1347. His name first appears in English affairs in 1313. See Rhodes, "Italian Bankers in England," p. 154

Merchants of the Society of the Peruzzi of Florence trading in England during the reign of Edward the Third

	Annual Salary in Lire.[1]
Arrigo Accorsi	145
Piero Aldobrandi [2]	
Tommaso d'Arnoldo de' Bagnesi (at one time representative of the Company in Genoa)	
Giovanni di Tano Baroncelli (Representative in London) ...	
Riccardo Baroncelli [2]	
Piero Bernardini [2][3]	
Piero di Bernardino Dini (priore) [3]	80
Guido Donati	200
Riccardo Fangni	217.10.0
Bonfantino di Vanni Fantini	
Jacopo di Gherardo Gentili (priore)	175
Jacopo Gherardi [2]	
Giovanni Giuntini	145
Baldo Orlandini N	
Piero di Simone di Giovanni Orlandini	100
Neri Perini [4]	290
Andrea di messer Amîdeo Peruzzi [5]	60
Bonifazio di Tommaso Peruzzi (priore; direttore, 1336-1340; died in London, 1340)	
Filippo di Tommaso Peruzzi	70
Jacopo di Filippo Peruzzi	60
Ridolfo di Tommaso Peruzzi	100
Dionigi di Giovanni di Giotto Peruzzi	75

1. Peruzzi, pp. 261—265. The figures are the annual salaries of such as were paid agents of the Company between 1335 and 1338. In an account of the period the English pound sterling was rated at lire 10.15.0 by the Company; see Peruzzi, pp. 276, 277, 291, 292. This enables the above salaries to be estimated in English money of that period.

2. Names not found in Peruzzi.

3. Probably the same person as above.

4. Given as Reyner, Nerus, and Nereus, Perini.

5. Given as Andrew Stramidey and Andrew Domini Amideni.

N. Probably also traded in the Kingdom of Naples; see Yver, *Le Commerce et les Marchands dans l'Italie méridionale, etc.*, p. 404.

Merchants of the Society of the Peruzzi in England—continued.

Roberto di Tommaso Peruzzi [4] [N] 120
Tommaso d'Arnoldo Peruzzi (priore, direttore, 1300-1331)
Zanobi di Tano Raugi (priore) [3] 40
Giovanni Ricoveri [5] ... ...
Piero Simone [2] ... ...
Angelo Soderini [2] ... ...
Giovanni Stefano [2] ... ...
Riccardo di Geri Stefano [6] 70
Stefano Uguccioni ... ...

Those merchants who held office in Florence at any time, or were 'Directors' of the Company have the office indicated in brackets after the name; see Peruzzi, pp. 250—265.

1. See note, p. 134, above.
2. See note, p. 134, above.
3. Given as Genobius Tani.
4. Given as Robert Thomays.
5. Given as Rechoneri, or Rekonery.
6. Given as Richard Digerii.
N. See note, p. 134, above.

Members of the Society of the Peruzzi from 1336 to the time of the failure, who subscribed the " arrangement " of 6 September, 1347. (Pacino di Tommaso Peruzzi was Head of the Company).

Bonifazio [1] and Pacino di Tommaso Peruzzi.
Niccolò, Ottaviano, Andrea, and Napoleone d'Amideo Peruzzi.
Pacino, Lepre, Sandro, and Giovanni di Guido Peruzzi.
Tommaso di Messer Filippo Peruzzi.
Berto di Messer Ridolfo Peruzzi.
Donato di Pacino Peruzzi.
Donato, and Bartolomeo di Giotto Peruzzi.
Gherardino, and Giovanni di Tano, and Gherardo di Michi Baroncelli.
Baldo di Gianni Orlandini.
Francesco Forzetti.
Ruggeri di Lottieri Silimanni.
Filippo Villani (brother of the Chronicler).
Stefano d'Uguccione Bencivenni.
Geri di Stefano Soderini.
Giovanni, and Guccio di Stefano Soderini.

1. Bonifazio di Tommaso Peruzzi was Head or Director of the Company from 1336 till his death in London in 1340. He had gone there on account of the Company's difficulties; see Peruzzi, pp. 251 and 259.

The following were the " Syndics " appointed by the Commune to assist the creditors of the Peruzzi :—

Sandro di Simone Quarata.   Braccino Feri.
Filippo di Giovanni Macchiavelli.   Vanni Rondinelli.
Zanobi di Ser Piero Ognano.   Manetto Filicaia.
Cambino Signorini.   Ugolino Vieri.

Taken from Peruzzi, pp. 474 to 476.

THE TAXATION OF WOOL. 1327–1348.

The constitutional importance of Edward III.'s reign has been thrown rather into obscurity by the dramatic events of the Hundred Years' War and the Black Death. Yet the long and bitter struggle Edward waged for Gascony and the French Crown had its counterpart and sequel in the protracted and spirited contest waged by the Commons against the king for the preservation of such control of the purse as they had gradually and with difficulty won from his predecessors. This struggle centres round the Taxation of Wool.

Edward III. inherited from his father two different incomes from wool :—the old custom of $\frac{1}{2}$ mark on the sack of wool or 300 woolfells, voted by Parliament and paid by all merchants, native and alien alike, and the new custom of 40d. on the sack of wool or 300 woolfells granted and paid by foreign merchants in return for increased protection and privilege. But, in addition to these sources of income which the nation recognised as lawful, Edward had had handed down to him the evil precedent of raising the custom rate without consulting the nation, i.e., of exacting a maletote.

Englishmen were apparently secured against extravagant or oppressive demands, for not only had Magna Carta forbidden an evil or unjust exaction,[1] but a statute of Edward I. had fixed the amount of the just and lawful tax.[2] Parliament had confirmed the King's ancient prerogative of levying customs at the ports, but had deprived it of its arbitrary and variable character. Later in the same reign a further advance had been made. The King had been bound by law in the Confirmation of the Charters 1297 not to raise, without the common consent of the Realm, any revenue from wool in addition to that which usage gave him.[3]

It would be rash to argue that this marks the establishment of the principle that no increase of the hereditary customs of the crown on any pretext whatever should be permissible with-

1. *Select Charters*, p. 301.   2. *Ib.*, p. 451.
3. *Ib.*, p. 495.

out the consent of Parliament. No specific way of ascertaining common assent was prescribed, although the Commons would doubtless regard themselves and would be regarded generally as the only organ capable of expressing such a decision. Consequently the King was left umpire in his own cause, and he could select at discretion that body which was likely to serve his interests best. Edward III. soon discovered that that body was not the Commons, and he availed himself of the loose wording of the law to consult the merchants so frequently and on such weighty matters that the Commons soon became alarmed for their privileges, and attempted further definitions of his rights.

With regard to the King's powers of raising imposts from aliens there was even greater laxity and uncertainty both in law and practice. Despite the burghers' refusal of 1303 and the temporary success of the Ordinances, Parliament had never effectively condemned the King's agreement with foreign merchants by which he gave greater protection in return for increased customs. Those dues which were fixed by Parliament in the case of native merchants had been, and could be in the case of alien merchants, enhanced by separate arrangement between the King and the merchants without the intervention of Parliament. The " new custom "[1] was the offspring of such an agreement, and the crown's immemorial right to impose restrictions upon foreign traders in the interests of the native community had not been limited by statute.

Thus the King undoubtedly had the right unquestioned in law and admitted in practice of increasing the new custom by arrangement with foreign merchants and arguing by analogy he might claim to increase the ancient custom in a similar way by agreement with native merchants. In addition he had the right to purveyance, which Parliament had never questioned nor attempted to annul, but the abuse of which it had frequently though vainly tried to moderate.

There was at the beginning of Edward III.'s reign considerable vagueness about the constitutional and legal position, and this uncertainty was increased by the fact that, although all the essential features of our constitutional govern-

1. *Foed.*, II, p. 747.

ment had emerged, without, it is true, attaining fixity, as yet there had been no precise differentiation of function amongst its component organs. The process of differentiation was hastened on by the financial crises of the reign. The action which Edward took under the stress of financial exigencies caused two definite issues to emerge quite clearly. (1) Could a great Council which differed from a Parliament not in the manner of its composition but merely in the form of its deliberations legally exercise Parliament's powers of taxation? (2) Was the consent of the merchants, *i.e.*, of the class who apparently paid the grant, all that the King required to authorise the raising of a subsidy from wool? These questions, which at the beginning of Edward III's reign possess no more than an academic interest, were soon converted by the King's actions into issues of vital and pressing practical importance. Edward found the prevailing uncertainty highly advantageous, since it very appreciably increased the number of alternative methods of raising funds and enabled him to play off one interest against another.

It is not surprising that the government's first attempt to raise additional supplies from wool should have been made under pressure of war. The first martial episode of the reign was the war with Scotland, and it was because of this war that many merchants, both denizen and alien, represented to the King that they could not with profit come to the Staple for the purchase and sale of wool as they had been ordered to do by an ordinance issued in May, 1327.[1] The King agreed to find a remedy during the said war, especially as the merchants undertook to pay a levy on exported wool as a loan for a certain time.[2] A council of magnates was called, and having regard to the need of encouraging alien merchants to visit the realm and to the "infinite treasure" the King would be compelled to expend in the war, granted that all merchants might freely buy wool till Christmas, without Staples as within, provided they paid beyond the custom due one mark on the sack or 300 woolfells and 20/- on the last of hides.[3] This levy was a loan, not a tax. The merchants paying it were to receive from the customers letters

1. *C.P.R.* 1327–30, p. 98. *C.C.R.* 1327–30, p. 116.
2. *C.P.R.* 1327–30, p. 169. *C.C.R.* 1327–30, pp. 236, 251.
3. *C.F.R.* 1327–37, p. 54.

patent, sealed with the cocket seal, acknowledging the receipt of the sums paid and binding the King to repay them at the stated term.

This loan on wool, for which of course Isabella and Mortimer were responsible, was raised as early as July, 1327[1] and as late as August 26th, 1329.[2] On previous occasions, though aliens had readily responded, native merchants, as in 1303, had refused to barter with the crown.[3] Now both natives and aliens united to secure a common advantage at a price which did not differentiate between them. The government's action in bargaining with English merchants was at least of doubtful legality, since the Confirmation of the Charters stipulated that common assent was necessary to raise the custom duties. In bargaining with foreign merchants it could plead Edward I.'s precedent of 1303 when the crown and foreign merchants arranged things to their mutual advantage without the assent of the nation, which did not seem to regard the agreement as a contravention of the Confirmation of the Charters. So too in this case the representatives of the nation made no protest in the Parliament which assembled in September. Possibly the Commons, recognising the necessity which spurred the government on and conscious that their protests could not obviate the need of a grant, and might, if effective, convert indirect into direct taxation, preferred to countenance the less onerous form, even when it was levied illegally.

A somewhat similar expedient was adopted in 1333. In that year Edward, requiring funds for another Scottish expedition, sought them where his guardian had done. He appealed to the merchants for a grant, and set up Home Staples in the hope of prevailing upon them to make one.[4] The merchants, however, excused themselves, but turned the King's request to good account by beating down the price of wool in the country to their own advantage and the people's loss. In the otherwise abortive Parliament at York in January 1333 the King claimed to have gained the sanction of the prelates and magnates for the subsidy he was demanding from the merchants of ½ mark on the sack of wool exported

---

1. *C.P.R.* 1327-30, p. 137.   2. *Ib.*, p. 421.
3. Stubbs, II, 552.   4. *C.F.R.* 1327-37, p. 342.

by denizens and 10/- on the sack exported by aliens.[1] It was to be levied on all the wool taken out of the country between February 2nd, 1332, and February 2nd, 1333, so that the order was in the main retrospective, and the collectors of the subsidy had to be supplied with lists of the merchants who had exported wool since February 2nd, 1332, and the amount they had exported.[2] As, however, it was complained that if the exaction were insisted upon wool would be sold in the country for a less price than it was wont, the King, with the consent of the Council and the merchants, on June 20th, 1333, recalled the order and issued instructions that the money which had been collected in the meantime should be restored to the merchants.[3] But before ordering the cessation of this levy Edward had induced the merchants to consent to another of 10/- on the sack, to be paid by denizens and aliens alike on all wool exported between May 14th, 1333, and May 14th, 1334.[4] This charge continued to be levied after the latter date,[5] but it was extremely unpopular among members of the merchant class, some of whom kept their wares in the kingdom to avoid payment,[6] whilst others flatly refused to pay.[7] Nor did it recommend itself to the nation. The Parliament which met at Westminster in September, 1334, shewed the King that the people were much damaged by the charge which the merchants had arranged to pay, and on September 21st it was recalled by royal ordinance.[8]

When war with France became imminent financial problems again commanded the King's attention. He had an army to equip and maintain, and numerous inefficient but costly allies to subsidise. It would have been quite impossible to have maintained the struggle with France on the old feudal revenues of the crown and the proceeds of the Customs, even had his exchequer not been drained by his troublesome friends, who were more intent on seeking pay than on fighting. Under the circumstances this could not be dreamt of. The King's extraordinary sources of income were limited in number and in productiveness. By Commissions of Array

1. *C.C.R.* 1330–3, p. 60. *C.F.R.* 1327–37, p. 342. 2. *Ib.*, p. 355.
3. *C.C.R.* 1330–3, p. 60. The levy had been very unpopular among the merchants, and they sought to evade payment. *C.F.R.* 1327–37, p. 354.
4. *Ib.* 1327–37, p. 365. *C.C.R.* 1330–3, p. 433. 5. *Ib.*, p. 277.
6. *C.F.R.* 1327–37, p. 404. 7. *Ib.*, p. 414.
8. *C.C.R.* 1333–7, p. 257.

and the exercise of his unpopular right of Pre-emption of Victuals, he might hope to raise and equip for a short period a fighting force of doubtful loyalty. By tallaging his demesne and borrowing from foreign bankers and even foreign princes and sometimes English merchants, he might scrape together sufficient money to silence his clamorous allies for a little while. But from none of these sources could he hope to maintain a protracted and costly war, not even from a combination of all. The endurance of the country was even more limited than its resources, and though a popular war might for a time induce the people to acquiesce in the King's arbitrary financial expedients, the most dazzling successes could not secure their consent throughout a lengthy period. Nor could the bankers of his day lend large sums for an indefinite period. Great as had been the advance in the power of credit, a much greater was needed before a King could sustain a protracted war on his success as a borrower.

From one source and one alone could the King hope to carry on the struggle. All wars are ultimately paid for by the products of the countries waging them. England at this time produced annually great quantities of wool of good quality, for which she found a ready market in parts beyond the sea. This was Edward's only spring of hope : to secure the goodwill of the merchants, and acting through their agency and on their advice to manipulate the wool trade in such a manner that it might subserve his financial interests and supplement his ordinary sources of revenue. From this date down to the Treaty of Calais these devices take a conspicuous place in the financial history of the country, and merchants consequently acquire unprecedented importance, and even seem likely at times to form a separate estate of the realm.

In 1336, when war was pending, Edward sought money and allies. A Parliament summoned to Westminster in March granted a $\frac{1}{10}$th and a $\frac{1}{15}$th.[1] But the King, fully alive to the fact that the magnitude of his schemes was out of all proportion to the supplies voted, endeavoured to supplement them from the most promising source—wool. He had frequent consultations with the merchants. Thus on May 8th

1. Stubbs, II, 397.

London and 21 other cities were ordered to elect 4 merchants each, to meet the King at Oxford on May 27th.[1] On June 1st 105 were summoned to Northampton for June 28th.[2] In August the export of wool was forbidden by royal letters, doubtless at the merchants' instigation,[3] and on September 1st 4 merchants of London and 37 others were directed to meet at Nottingham on September 23rd.[4]

What this assembly did, and what Parliament which, according to Stubbs, sat at the same time did, has long been uncertain. Stubbs says that Parliament granted a $\frac{1}{10}$th and a $\frac{1}{15}$th,[5] and that in addition it voted a subsidy of 40/- the sack from denizens and 60/- from aliens.[6] But the Rolls of Parliament make no mention of such grants, and the Calendar of Patent Rolls always refers to the $\frac{1}{10}$th and $\frac{1}{15}$th having been granted in the Great Council at Nottingham. Knighton[7] and the Scalacronica, however, support Stubbs' view of the grant of a subsidy from wool. The Scalacronica distinctly says that the duty was granted for a time, and that it was kept on afterwards. If a Parliament actually met at Nottingham this is quite possible.[8] The King certainly acted illegally in some way or other, for the Parliament of 1339 declared that he was levying a maletote which it had never sanctioned.[9] Either then he must have continued the subsidy after the expiration of the term of its grant by Parliament, as the Scalacronica alleges, or he must have levied it in the first instance without Parliamentary sanction. Sir James Ramsay declares that an assembly of merchants granted a war tax of 40/- from natives and 60/- from foreigners for $1\frac{1}{2}$ years, but the authorities he cites,—Knighton and the Scalacronica—do not support this view.[10] Neither mentions the time limit of $1\frac{1}{2}$ years, and both infer that Parliament, not the merchants, made the grant. There can be no doubt that the King asked the great Council or Parliament which met at Nottingham for a subsidy, since on May 28th he found it necessary to issue a proclamation to stifle a current rumour that he intended to take 20/- from every sack of wool,[11] and he encouraged the

1. *C.C.R.* 1333–7, p, 674. *Lords Report* p. 455.
2. *Ib.*, p. 458. *C.C.R.* 1333–7, p. 677. 3. *Foed.*, II, 943.
4. *Lords' Report*, IV, 147. *C.C.R.* 1333–7, p. 701.
5. Stubbs, II, 397. 6. *Ib.*, II, 399. 7. Knighton, c. 2568.
8. *Scalacronica*, p. 102. 9. *Rot. Parl.*, II, 104, 105.
10. Ramsay, I, 246. 11. *C.C.R.* 1333–7, p. 681.

Commons to make such a grant by fixing minimum prices below which no wool could be bought. Parliament may in return for this concession have granted a 40/- subsidy for a limited time, as the chroniclers assert, but the Patent and Close Rolls contain no reference to it. Nor do they make any mention of the levy of a grant of 40/- the sack from natives and 60/- the sack from aliens made according to Sir James Ramsay by some assembly or other on Nov. 12th, 1337.[1] They prove conclusively, however, that the merchants assembled at Nottingham granted the King a subsidy of 20/- the sack,[2] and it would seem as if in addition to the gift of the subsidy the merchants promised to make the King a loan of 20/- on the sack if his necessity required it.[3] The subsidy was being collected as early as Sept. 26th, 1336,[4] and as late as March 8th, 1338,[5] in which year the 20/- rate was increased to 40/-.[6] The loan of 20/-, after being occasionally exacted from alien merchants during the summer of 1337 was demanded by an order issued on Oct. 15th, 1337 of all such merchants.[7]

The yield of the 20/- subsidy by the merchants in the Great Council of Nottingham, coupled with the grant of a $\frac{1}{10}$th and a $\frac{1}{15}$th, did not satisfy the King, and in the summer of 1337 he laid hands on all the wool in the kingdom by an arrangement with the merchants.[8] The King arrogated to himself the sole right of buying wool in the kingdom and of exporting it out of the kingdom, hoping apparently to use his monopoly to force up prices. The profits of the export trade in wool, which had hitherto made the fortunes of families like the Poles, were to provide the English King with funds for war. The purchase and the sale of the wool, however, was to be effected by those who were experienced in the business. At the King's command a number of merchants were assembled.

1. Ramsay, p. 89. Such an order issued Nov. 12th, 1338. *C.F.R.* 1337–47, p. 105.
2. *C.C.R.* 1337–9, pp. 97, 195, &c. *C.P.R.* 1334–38, p. 332. *C.F.R.* 1337–47, p. 557.
3. *C.C.R.* 1337–9, p. 217. *Ib.* 1337–9, pp. 226, 296, &c.
4. *C.P.R.* 1334–8, pp. 322, 327.   5. *C.C.R.* 1337–9, pp. 313, 323.
6. Apparently the King agreed with the Bardi and Peruzzi on March 11th, 1338, to raise the subsidy to 40/- the sack, and probably an assembly of merchants which met on March 16th authorised this rate. But exportation was forbidden until August 1st.
7. *C.F.R.* 1337–47, p. 50.
8. Murimuth, p. 80. Knighton, II, 1. *C.P.R.* 1327–30, p. 480.

The wool of the different counties was priced, and in each case a group of merchants was told off to make the purchase, the whole body making themselves responsible for the sale and for the payment to the King of £200,000 in instalments as the wool was sold. [1]

The order for the purchase of wool seems, despite exceptions in favour of the King's merchants of the society of Bardi and Peruzzi, to have been executed with great strictness. [2] Exemptions were also granted to the Chancellor and Justiciar of Ireland. [3] The Chancellor turned his privilege to good account by sheltering the wool of others who were less fortunate; but the offence was soon detected and punished. [4] Even the affection of the King towards the Count of Hainault by reason of which he granted permission to the count's merchants to buy up all manner of goods in the realm was not strong enough to induce him to include wool amongst them. [5] The King was keenly alive to the dangers of evasion. Collectors of wool were commissioned to seize as forfeit to the King all the wool of "those who, not regarding the safety of the realm, have removed or concealed their wool." They were enjoined to certify the King from time to time the names of those who had so removed or concealed their wool, and these he would cause to be punished as they deserved. [6] Sheriffs were ordered to make proclamation directing people to show their wool without dissimulation on pain of forfeiture, and to allow purchase to be made. [7] In addition special commissioners were appointed to scrutinise all wool sent abroad, to confiscate, sell and give to the King the proceeds of all wool so found, not the King's, and to arrest the offenders. [8]

The wool, estimated at 30,000 sacks, was to be sent in charge of Henry Burghersh, Bishop of Lincoln, and the Earls of Northampton and Suffolk with many men at arms, archers, and Welshmen into Brabant. [9] Men and ships were com-

1. *C.C.R.* 1337–9. p. 148. Longman, I, 89, 117, follows Knighton, II, 1, in saying that the price of wool in each county was 9 marks a sack. This was the price of Leicester wool, and Knighton evidently assumes that the price of wool in other counties was identical with that of his native shire.
2. *C.P.R.* 1334–8, pp. 543, 554, 580, &c. *Foed.*, II, ii, 971.
3. *Ib.*, p. 478. 4. *C.C.R.* 1337–9, p. 184.
5. *C.P.R.* 1334–8, p. 536. 6. *Ib.*, p. 480.
7. *C.C.R.* 1337–9, p. 282. 8. *C.P.R.* 1334–8, pp. 509 and 577.
9. Murimuth, p. 80.

mandeered for its transport.   Throughout the summer and autumn they lay idle in the Thames and in ports of the South east, to the dislocation of trade and the detriment of the country.[1] The fleet sailed about the Feast of All Saints (Nov. 1), but not with the full complement of wool.[2] The total amount of the country's wool would probably amount to 40,000 sacks ;[3] the fleet carried only 10,000.[4]

The purveyance of wool in 1337 was followed by a legal grant of wool in 1338.   The King's departure had now been decided on, and was only delayed by financial considerations. A Parliament held at Westminster in February granted him half the wool of the kingdom, amounting to 20,000 sacks, to be raised in the following summer from clergy and laity alike, notwithstanding that the clergy had not been summoned, and were only represented by a few prelates, who according to Murimuth, were unwilling to defend the interests of their order.[5] Arguing that there should be no taxation without representation, the clergy refused to supply the wool voted in their absence.   For this reason Convocation was summoned to meet at London.   It assembled there on October 1, and granted a $\frac{1}{10}$th for a third year beyond the $\frac{2}{10}$ths originally promised, and agreed to pay the $\frac{1}{10}$th for the ensuing year sooner than had been arranged.   This aid was accepted by the King as a substitute for wool.[6]. Nevertheless, collectors continued to take wool from clergy, and the King had to issue frequent orders to them to de-arrest such wool.[7].

The clergy were not the only people whose wool escaped confiscation.   Numerous licenses were granted chiefly to foreign merchants to export wool bought previous to the grant of Parliament.   Thus the merchants of Almain, the houses of Bardi and Peruzzi, the Duke of Brabant's bankers, the Pope and Cardinals were granted exemptions.[8]   Political and diplomatic reasons explain these exceptions to the general order.   The Duke of Brabant was Edward's ally : the Pope and Cardinals were mediators between him and the King of

---

1. Murimuth, p. 80.   2. Knighton, II, 2.
3. 20,000 sacks is referred to in *C.P.R.* and *C.C.R.* as moiety of the wool of the country.
4. Knighton, II, 2.   5. Murimuth, p. 82.
6. Baker, *Chronicon*, p. 62. Murimuth, p. 85. Knighton, II, 5.
7. *C.C.R.* 1337–9, pp. 538, 539, 607–9, &c.
8. *C.P.R.* 1338–40, pp. 27, 43, 51, 86, 129, &c.

France, besides commanding respect and immunity by reason of their exalted station; while the Bardi and the Peruzzi had paid large sums of money at the King's request to his confederates beyond the sea, in default of wool not sent at the proper time. Charitable motives also induced the King to make exception in the case of slenderly endowed hospitals.[1]

It was not the intention of Parliament to make the King a free gift of 20,000 sacks of wool in addition to the $\frac{1}{10}$th and $\frac{1}{15}$th they had already voted him in the autumn of 1337. The grant was an alternative, not an additional, method of taxation, a device for enabling the King to receive the benefit of taxes before they had been actually raised. Owing to the stoppage of trade and the drain of taxation in the preceding years there was plenty of wool but little money in the kingdom.[2] Ordinarily, taxes took a considerable time to realise. The disturbed nature of the time would increase the delay. Mainly to meet the King's urgent necessity, which could brook no delay, partly perhaps to relieve the country of wool which was rapidly deteriorating, an arrangement was improvised which would, without involving the country in extra taxation, provide the King with funds before the taxes voted had been collected. The wool was not to be a tax paid by the entire nation, but a loan to the King made solely by the wool-growing classes.

All who had more than one sack of wool were to keep half for themselves and lend on good security the other half of the previous year to the King up to 30,000 sacks. In the meantime they were to be free from all other exactions. These conditions were not observed. Wool was taken from men who had less than one sack. It was taken from the present as well as from the previous year's portion, and collectors did not confine their demands to owners of wool. They compelled those who had no wool to purchase it from those who had and to hand over a quantity which not only supplied the King's requirements but provided in addition a convenient portion for themselves.[2]

The temper of the country was inflamed by the extortions of the collectors: it was further exasperated by an order issued by the King on March 10th for-

1. *Ib.*, p. 112. *C.C.R.* 1337–9, pp. 502, 594.   2. Murimuth, p. 86.

L

bidding the exportation of wool.   On that date all sheriffs
were ordered to make proclamation in all places they thought
fit " that no merchant, native or foreign, through himself or
another, buy wool on any pretext whatever henceforth or take
it to foreign parts or cause it to be taken there openly or
secretly without special warrant until all our wools are collected."   Anyone acting contrary to this proclamation without such warrant was to incur forfeiture, and sheriffs were
ordered to send from time to time in chancery the names of
merchants thus buying wool, who they were, and the quantity
thus forfeited.[1]   This restriction was keenly resented by the
nation.   The King had left the people half their wool, but
this was of little avail when they could neither sell nor export
it.   Moreover, it was a flagrant violation of the original compact made between the King and the people's representatives.
They had granted him half the wool of the kingdom on the
express understanding that they could do as they liked with
the other half.[2]   Yet within a month of giving this undertaking the King, finding the free sale and export of wool
would interfere with the collection of his grant, withdrew it
without apparently consulting the other parties to the transaction.

Under the circumstances, it is not surprising that the
collection of wool proved a difficult business.   The country
was in an ugly temper on account of the previous year's arbitrary exactions and little disposed to endure a repetition.
Evasions were more frequent,[3] and detection more resented.
Merchants, in defiance of the King's orders, exported wool in
butter-tubs and cheese-boxes.[4]   Concealment was more widespread, and its discovery sometimes led to disorder, as at
Beverley, where the sheriff of York, when he tried to make
inquisition concerning the concealment of wool, was assaulted
and prevented.[5]   Thus it is not surprising that on the King's
departure, in spite of his urgent orders, only 3,000 sacks out
of the 20,000 voted had been collected.   Edward, who was
staying at the manor of Walton, within easy reach of the port
of embarkation, chafing at his enforced idleness, occupied his
leisure in drafting a comprehensive list of ordinances.   These,

1. *Foed*, II, ii, 1022.   *C.C.R.* 1337–9, p. 393.
2. *Foed.*, II, ii, 1022.   3. *C.C.R.* 1337–9, p. 601.
4. *C.P.R.* 1338–40, pp. 175, 187.   5. *Ib.*, p. 146.

headed by a command that he should use all possible expedition in the collection of the wool, he forwarded to the Chancellor on July 12th, ordering him to read them before the council and secure their observance. Among them were many useful provisions such as the creation of machinery for the payment of royal debts, the withdrawal of all exemptions from the payment of custom dues, $\frac{1}{10}$ths and $\frac{1}{15}$ths, &c., the establishment of an annual term of office for sheriffs, the appointment of customers by the people of the town, and of controllers by the full county court. But none of them was calculated to facilitate appreciably the collection of the wool, for in none of them was there any trace of an attempt to set up more efficient machinery of collection.[1]

Edward sailed for France on the 16th of July, and the task of expediting the collection devolved upon the regent, Edward's eight year old son, the Duke of Cornwall, and his council. On the day of his departure the King issued an urgent command to each sheriff to cause four of the most discreet and richest merchants of his bailiwick, within liberty or without, to be at Northampton on August 3rd, in order to treat with the guardian of the realm, the Chancellor and others of the Council on matters most closely touching the affairs of the King and kingdom.[2] In the meantime an ordinance was issued by the warden of the realm and the Council on July 27th ordering that all wool in the ports of London, Sandwich, Ipswich, Lynn, Boston, Kingston-upon-Hull and Newcastle on Tyne should be brought to the port of Great Yarmouth before August 25, or at the latest by August 25, from whence it was to be dispatched to foreign parts. For this purpose the sheriffs and collectors of customs in each of the aforesaid ports were ordered to arrest as many ships as should be needed to take all the wool in port first to Great Yarmouth and then to parts beyond the sea. To man the ships they were to choose enough discreet and honest men.[3] The ordinance contains the first documentary evidence of a recognition on the part of the central authority that special officials were needed to cope with this special affair. Robert Howell and Robert Watford were appointed to supervise all wool in each port, to

---

1. *Foed.*, II, ii, 1049.   2. *Ib.*, 1051. *C.C.R.* 1337-9, p. 517.
3. *Foed.*, II, ii, p. 1051.

hasten the collection and the shipping of the wool, and for this purpose were empowered to commandeer the necessary ships and to impress the necessary men.   They were accorded full powers to choose whomsoever they would to assist them or to act as their deputies provided they retained all responsibility, as well as to commit to prison during royal pleasure all who hindered them.   All sheriffs, admirals, ministers, lords, masters and mariners of ships were strictly charged to assist them and their deputies and assistants in all things as far as in them lay, by counsel and help whenever and however they were requested by order of the council or by the above executors. [1]

But the King, who was now spending money with a lavish hand in sumptuous entertainments to dazzle his allies, and compromising himself for the future by equally lavish promises, to retain them, was not content to entrust the council at home with such urgent business as the replenishing of his depleted treasury.   On August 7 he sent a missive[2] to John Waweyn, William of Kingstown and Thomas of Baddeby, declaring that putting his trust in the grant of wool, he had made promises of payment to his allies.   The wool had not come in quickly, but at the urgent request of the prelates and magnates he had crossed the sea hoping to find it at Antwerp on his arrival there.   Only 2,500 sacks were, however, awaiting him, which were not sufficient either to satisfy his allies or to meet his immediate necessities.   Unless the residue came quickly he would be in great peril.   But he had confidence in the fidelity and foresight of the merchants, and to them he entrusted the task of collecting the wool in the counties and especially the residue of the amount of wool granted.   They were thus allotted the double task of collecting the outstanding portion of the loan, and at the same time of buying up the supply of wool still remaining in the counties.   Indentures were to be made, containing the amount of wool taken, the price to be paid, and the names of the persons from whom it was taken, and sent to chancery. Letters obligatory containing the amount to be paid were to be given to all those from whom wool was taken.   The wool so collected was

---

1. *Foed.*, II, ii, p. 1051.
2. *Ib.*, p. 1054. *C.P.R.* 1338–40, p. 189.

to be sent to Antwerp with all speed. Sheriffs were ordered
to provide carriage for the wool at the ports as well as canvas
for sacks from the exits of the shire and the collectors of customs were to pay the mariners engaged in the transport of
wool out of the customs of the ports.[1]

This common and necessary measure, the appointment of
collectors directly responsible to the central authority, the
King and his Council each supplemented by other measures,
the Council concerning itself with raising the remainder of
the Parliamentary grant, the King with the seizure of all the
additional wool that could be found in the country.[2]   On
August 1 the Council at Northampton ordained that the
17,500 sacks of wool remaining to be levied of the 20,000
granted by Parliament should be collected after the rate of
a $\frac{1}{15}$th " to wit from every 20/- of the said $\frac{1}{15}$th[3] 10 stones of
wool, each stone being 14lbs. and from more or less in propor-
tion." Those who had no wool might pay in money. Thus
London acquitted itself of wool by paying 1,000 marks and
York by the payment of £108.[4]

This regulation was a belated attempt to systematise a
levy, the unsystematic character[5] of which had previously
excited great annoyance and caused considerable oppression
because of the scope it afforded for extortion on the part of the
collectors, and as such it would be welcomed by those wool
owners who had not yet handed over half their wool. But
it marks the abandonment of the King's original intention and
the partial failure of the scheme for drawing upon the nation's
taxes before they had been collected.   By his original plan
the King had hoped to accomplish two things : to obtain (1)
a much needed supply of ready money a considerable time
before the taxes on which he was absolutely dependent had
been collected, (2) monopoly profits.   The first of these objects had not been realised, though the terms of the King's
bargain with the Bardi and the Peruzzi, who were to dispose

1. *Foed.*, II, ii, p. 1054. *C.P.R.* 1338–40, pp. 189, 190.
2. Order executed. *C.C.R.* 1337–9, pp. 453, 570, 582, &c.
3. *Ib.*, p. 457.
4. *C.P.R.* 1338–40, p. 244. *C.C.R.* 1337–9, p. 584. Knighton, II, 4.
5. The arrangement was still unsatisfactory because it fixed a uniform price
of 52/- a sack for wool all over the country, whereas the value of wool
varied greatly in the different counties.

of the wool, saved him from complete disappointment.[1]   The second object remained for him to achieve.   The first step to its accomplishment was the prohibition of exportation which was taken on March 10th.[2]   Apparently the King hoped that all his wool would be collected by August 1st, for early in 1338 he contemplated allowing exportation of wool left in the merchants' hands after his own portion had been received, between that date and September 29th.[3]   But all such exportation was to be subject to a payment of 40/⸳ subsidy beyond the ancient custom.   Thus a considerable margin of profit was still secured to the King even when the prohibition of exportation was removed.   Merchants were anxious to export even at this rate, and because of their urgent request the King granted that on declaring the goods to be their own and promising to take them to lands in the King's friendship, they might after October 1st export woolfells and lasts of hides on payment of the custom and subsidy.[4]   It was not until March, 1339, that they were allowed, for a similar payment and on promising to take their merchandise to the staple at Antwerp, to export sacks of wool.[5]

The King, as we have seen, made arrangements for the purchase of all the wool that could be found in the country. It is evident that the conviction of the inadequacy of Parliament's liberal grant, strictly collected, for his increasing needs was already growing upon the King when in direct contravention of the spirit and the letter of that grant[6] he determined to supplement it by exercising his royal right of purveyance to seize what additional wool might be found in the counties. True in decreeing that the price fixed by Parliament should be the indenture price,[7] he showed some deference to Parliamentary authority, but the undoubted object of this move was to disguise the real nature of his act and to identify the purveyance with the grant.   In all probability the price arranged was of slight significance.   The letters obligatory given to the owners of wool would probably be as valueless as the order that the collectors of custom should pay the mariners' wages.

1. *C.C.R.* 1337–9, pp. 400, 412.
2. *Foed.*, II, ii, 1022.   *C.C.R.* 1337–9, p. 393.
3. *C.C.R.* 1337–9, p. 424. See article on "Estate of Merchants," pp. 195, 196.
4. *C.C.R.* 1337–9, pp. 503, 571.   5. *Ib.*, p. 42.
6. Murimuth, p. 86. *Foed.*, II, ii, 1022.   7. *Ib.*, 1054.

With the chief source of customs revenue ceasing to yield, owing to the King's embargo, and with practically the whole native trading fleet commandeered for royal purposes, trading operations could be neither extensive nor productive of much custom revenue. Certainly they could not have borne so heavy a charge as to pay for the transport of the whole annual supply of wool, probably about 40,000 sacks, from the various ports to a common centre and from that centre to a depôt abroad.

But there was little likelihood of the customers being requested to meet so heavy a demand. Whether through the opposition and evasion of the owners of wool or through the remissness of officials or the inadequacy of the machinery of collection or through a combination of all these circumstances, certain it is that the collection of wool made very slow progress. The King's repeated injunctions to officials and his frequent appointment of officers to supervise those he had set to watch over others indicate that he was not convinced of the unimpeachable integrity of his officials or of their zeal and devotion. Thus, on August 20th he wrote to Robert Chigwell, his chosen clerk, appointing him to accelerate the collection of wool and to stimulate John of Waweyn, William of Kingstown and Thomas of Baddeby, whom he had but a fortnight before appointed to stimulate others.[1] The accompanying order that if the 20,000 sacks were not yet collected Robert should take all wool wherever he found it, within liberty or without, from clergy as from laymen, sparing none, suggests that the King was driven to desperation by his financial difficulties, and that he was not prepared to respect the rights of property where his interests were concerned. He probably calculated that so drastic a measure would coerce the recalcitrant and expedite the collection.

The collection of the wool continued throughout the winter 1338–9. A great fleet was gathered at Harwich for its transport. Contrary winds delayed its departure, and after the winds a fear of the galleys which prompted those in charge to await the arrival of more ships that they might cross in safety.[2] The date of the sailing cannot be fixed with certainty,

1. *Foed.*, II, ii, 1057. *C.P.R.* 1338–40, p. 190.
2. Murimuth, p. 88.

but there can be no doubt that the fleet had left port before March 24th, 1339, on which day the French attacked Harwich, burning the town.[1] Had the wool so laboriously collected been seized or destroyed some notice of such a catastrophe would certainly have appeared in the chronicles. Nor is it probable that any descent would be made on the town in the presence of such a great fleet as had been collected for the transport of the wool.

The delay experienced in the collection of the wool, while it embarrassed the King was still more embarrassing to the merchants of the societies of the Bardi and the Peruzzi. As early as March 11, 1338, *i.e.*, shortly after the grant in the February Parliament, the King had bargained with them concerning the distribution of the 20,000 sacks voted,[2] and this arrangement was ratified on May 7th with slight modification.[3] The whole of it, however, was thrown out of gear by the difficulties of collection. Nevertheless, in spite of his failure to carry out the terms of the agreement, the King achieved the result he had in view in striking the bargain. He obtained a supply of ready money for his passage, and unscrupulously threw all the burden of the loss which the delay in collection occasioned on other shoulders. The merchants contracted to lend the King £15,000[4] for his passage, and on the passage of the first levies of the wool a further £20,000. Thus, instead of being compelled to delay his departure until the wool had been collected and sold, the arrangement enabled Edward to sail long before the wool had been gathered. The proceeds of the sale of the wool were to be employed not in meeting the King's necessities but in paying past debts, and thus encouraging his creditors to advance further sums to meet his future needs. As additional security Edward granted the merchants £30,000 of the second year of the $\frac{1}{10}$th and $\frac{1}{15}$th voted by the clergy and laity for 3 years. To safeguard the King's interest one or two controllers were to check the amounts of wool received by the Bardi and the Peruzzi.[5]

While Edward was thus attempting to meet old debts he was rapidly incurring fresh ones. He exhausted his

1. *Ib.*, p. 88. Baker, *Chronicon*, p. 63.
2. *C.C.R.*, 1337–9, p. 400.
3. *Ib.*, p. 412. See article on "The Bardi and the Peruzzi," p. 119.
4. *C.C.R.* 1337–9, p. 420.   5. *Ib.*, p. 412.

resources in maintaining an army in idleness, in subsidising numerous costly allies, in splendid entertainments in Brabant and in the pompous pageantry of Coblenz.[1] It was again necessary to summon Parliament and to solicit an aid.

In October, 1339, Parliament met at Westminster in a determined but not unsympathetic spirit. It readily conceded the necessity of a grant, but showed a disposition to insist on conditions. The Lords agreed to pay a $\frac{1}{10}$th for 2 years, but expressed a wish that the maletote might be entirely abated and only the old custom taken, and that an Act of Parliament might be passed forbidding the raising of such an aid in the future.[2] The Commons adopted a similar attitude. They admitted the King required a liberal aid, but declared that without the consent of their constituents they could not venture to make one. They petitioned that two knights from each shire be summoned to the next Parliament to represent the Commons, and that no sheriff nor royal officer should be eligible. Like the magnates they prayed for the removal of the maletote, and added a number of other points on which they required redress.[3] Their demand for a new election was conceded, and a new Parliament met on Jan. 20th, 1340.

Again the Commons showed little disposition to make a grant. After deliberating for a month they offered the King 30,000 sacks of wool conditional on his granting the petitions they presented,[4] and it was only under considerable pressure from the magnates and after long negotiation that they decided to raise immediately 2,500 sacks as part of the 30,000 in case their demands were granted or as a free gift in case they were refused.[5] These demands were regarded as so important as to require the King's personal consideration. He returned to England on Feb. 21st, met a new Parliament on March 29th, and received a grant. The prelates, barons and knights of the shire voted a tax in kind of the ninth sheaf, fleece, and lamb, the towns and boroughs a $\frac{1}{9}$th of their goods, and the rest of the nation a $\frac{1}{15}$th.[6] There was no mention of the conditional offer of the Commons in the previous Parliament of 30,000 sacks of wool.

In return for this grant the King accepted the petitions of

1. Tout, p. 335.   2. *Rot. Parl.*, II, 104.   3. *Ib.*, 105.
4. *Ib.*, 107.   5. *Ib.*, 108.   6. *Ib.*, 112.

the Commons, and a Committee of judges, barons, prelates and 12 knights and 6 citizens and burgesses chosen by the Commons was appointed to review them and to turn into statute form such as were to become law. This committee drafted four important statutes covering a wide range. Two of these were of first rate importance in the history of wool taxation.

The Commons had petitioned that the King would bind himself by law never to take more than ½ mark customs on the sack of wool or 300 woolfells. But the King " prayed the Prelates, Earls, Barons and all the Commonalty for the great business he had on hand that they would grant him some aid upon wool, woolfells and other merchandise to endure for a small season," and in response to this request Parliament voted him a subsidy of 40/- to be taken on every sack of wool or 300 woolfells exported between Easter, 1340, and Pentecost, 1341. To procure this temporary grant of a subsidy the King had to renounce his right ever to take more than the customary ½ mark on the sack without the consent of Parliament. Two statutes were enacted, both of which established that for the future " the King nòr his heirs shall not demand, assess, nor take nor suffer to be taken more custom of a sack of wool of any Englishman but ½ mark only." " And the King hath promised in the presence of the Prelates, Earls, Barons, and others in his Parliament no more to charge, set or assess upon the Commons but in the manner as afore is said."[2] " In the same manner the Prelates, Earls and Barons have promised lawfully, as much as in them is, that they shall procure the King as much as they may to hold the same and that they shall in no wise assent to the contrary if it be not by the assent of the Prelates, Earls, Barons and Commons of the realm and that in full Parliament."[3]

But not only did the King abandon the special power he had been claiming and exercising of taxing wool without Parliament's consent so far as it affected Englishmen.[4] He surrendered any general right he might possess to impose any

1. 14 Edward III, St. 1, c. 21. *Rot. Parl.,* II, 112.
2. 14 Edward III, St. 1, c. 21. 14 Edward III, St. 2, c. 4.
3. 14 Edward III, St. 1, c. 21.
4. Apparently the King still retained the right, which had led to the establishment of the new customs, of raising the custom rate to aliens without consulting Parliament.

form of taxation save that sanctioned by Parliament. The second of the statutes of 1340 enacted that henceforth no charge nor aid was to be made but by the common assent of the prelates, earls, barons and other great men and commons of the realm and that in Parliament. To give greater security to the statute and " to cause all to eschew counsel to the contrary " the prelates promised to give sentence upon all who offended against it.[1]

The Commons had won a great victory. They had vindicated their right to be consulted in the raising of supplies, whether by direct or indirect taxation. Assemblies of merchants were henceforth to be deprived of their great and growing importance by the stipulation that assent to taxation was to be given in full Parliament. These statutes thus cleared up the vagueness of the Confirmation of the Charters on this all important point, for since that great statute had not defined how common assent to taxation was to be given, it had been possible for the King to argue that in fixing taxation in consultation with the merchants he was acting not merely within but according to law. Such methods would in future be frankly illegal. The King was no longer left to judge how common assent to taxation could best be obtained. Nevertheless, the Commons were at the beginning rather than at the end of their struggle. The law, it is true, had been explicitly and unmistakably placed on their side by the statutes of 1340, but the King still possessed an inexhaustible treasury of evasion upon which he drew liberally, as the history of the next decade shows.

Before many months had elapsed the financial arrangements made by the March Parliament had had to be modified because of the King's urgent necessity. In July another Parliament was considering the vending of the $\frac{1}{9}$th when its deliberations were interrupted by the Earls of Arundel and Gloucester and William Trussel, messengers from the King, bearing letters mentioning his recent victory, and making plain his dire need unless he were speedily supplied with ready money[2] It was recognised that the $\frac{1}{9}$th was inadequate to meet the requirements of the situation, and after the various alternatives had been canvassed it was decided that a number

1. 14 Edward III, St. 2, c. 1.
2. *Rot. Parl.*, II, 118.

of sacks of wool must immediately be secured and sold to merchants who would be prepared to advance loans upon them.   The lords who were present offered their wool, and also decided to commandeer the wool of those who were absent.[1]   Finally it was agreed that 20,000 sacks of wool should be raised in the kingdom at a price formerly arranged at Nottingham and sold at a mark less than the Nottingham price to merchants, who were to export it, paying custom and subsidy and the price of their contingent to the King in parts beyond the sea.

The conditions of the Commons leave no doubt as to their intention in making the grant of wool.   It was not to be an additional but an alternative form of taxation.   The ninths for two years granted in the previous Parliament were both to be collected, but only the ninth of the first year was to be paid direct into the royal treasury.   The yield of the ninth of the second year was to be reserved as a fund for the payment of those who had sold wool to the merchants for the King's use, and no portion of it was to reach the treasury until all obligations had been discharged.[2]

It is hardly surprising that this arrangement broke down. Some of the wool was levied and paid for out of the ninth of the second year, but a large portion was never raised.[3]   The country opposed the levy, as at Boston, where the people refused to sell wool, although they had a great quantity and locked it up in houses,[4] and at Nottingham, where a number of people, after selling their wool, plundered the houses in which it had been lodged and carried it off.   The merchants, too, failed to live up to their contracts.   They delayed making the stipulated payments,[6] and discharged their obligations so perfunctorily[7] that in April, 1341, the King, finding the greater part of the 20,000 sacks still unlevied, remodelled the arrangement, substituting open trade for the monopoly venture.[8]

The failure of the 1340 arrangement is apparent in the King's speech to the Parliament which met in April, 1341.

---

1. *Rot. Parl.*, II, 122.
2. *Ib.*, 119. *C.P.R.* 1340-3, p. 30.
3. *Ib.* 1340-43, pp. 148, 222, 239, 348, &c.   4. *Ib.*, p. 211.
5. *Ib.*, p. 110.   6. *Ib.*, p. 103.   7. *Ib.*, p. 258.
8. See below, p. 164.

In it he complained that the supplies voted him by the Commons had been badly spent by his ministers, and that he had not profited by them as fully as he ought. He requested the members to consider how he could most rapidly and profitably be aided by the ninth of the first and second years which had been voted but not yet fully collected.[1] In return for the establishment of a number of statutes and on certain stated conditions Parliament granted that instead of the ninth of the second year the King might raise 30,000 sacks of wool from the country, 20,000 in 1341 and 10,000 in 1342.[2] The grant was a substitute for the ninth of the second year which now ceased to be raised.[3] ·But it was supplementary, not alternative, to the grant of 20,000 sacks[4] in the previous year, for it was decided to allow the King to pass across the sea before September 29th what remained of the 20,000 sacks, until which date all other exportation of new wool was forbidden under heavy penalties. Old wool, however, could be exported on the payment of a 40/- subsidy.[5]

The two grants, of 20,000 sacks in 1340 and 30,000 sacks in 1341, were thus entirely different in character. The 20,000 sacks voted in 1340 were a loan to the King for which the lenders were to be paid from the nation's taxes, and the Parliament of 1341 insisted as a condition of a further grant that all such payments should be duly made.[6] But the grant of the 30,000 sacks in 1341 was a tax in wool. The Bishop of Chester, the Lord of Wake and Robert de Sadyngton, aided by men who had intimate knowledge of the different counties, apportioned their varying contributions according to their assessment for the ninth or fifteenth.[7] All who were liable for the ninth were now ordered to pay the assessment of wool under penalty of a heavy fine.[8] The Patent and Close Rolls contain many interesting records of the assessments. The difficulty of collecting 20,000 sacks of wool becomes intelligible when the small amount of many of the individual contributions is noted. The following are summaries of a few of the recorded assessments. A group of twelve people in Cumber-

---

1. *Rot. Parl.*, II, 127.   2. *Ib.*, 131. *C.C.R.* 1341–3, p. 255.
3. *Rot. Parl.*, II, 133. *C.P.R.* 1340–3, p. 261, &c.
4. The 20,000 sacks were to be paid for out of the 30,000. *C.C.R.* 1341–3, p. 209.
5. *Rot. Parl.*, II, 131.   6. *Ib.*, 133.   7. *Ib.*, 131.
8. *Ib.*, 133.

land, among them the Prior of Carlisle and the Prior of Weder-
hale, were assessed at amounts varying from 1 sack, paid by 5
people, to 5 stones paid by 2.   The total assessment of the
dozen amounted to 5 sacks and 82 stones, valued at
£25 16s. 1½d.[1]   A group of Oxford wool growers had much
lower assessments.   Twenty-two people were called upon to
furnish together 26 stones 16lbs. of wool, valued at £5 17s. 8d.,
the highest individual amount demanded being 6 stones 7lbs.
and the lowest 4lbs.   Eleven of the 22 paid less than 1 stone.[2]
Very similar was the assessment of 27 other people of the
same county, who were together required to provide 1 sack
23 stones 11lbs. of wool, valued at £11 9s. 4d.   In this case
5 stones was the highest and 7lbs. the lowest individual assessment.[3]   Much higher assessments are recorded for the
County of Salop.   Here out of 42 people, among them the
Earl of Arundel, who was assessed at 1 sack, 14 people paid
1 sack or more, 20 paid ½ sack or more, whilst of the other
assessments the highest was 5 sacks 1½ quarters 32lbs., and
the lowest 2½ stones.[4]

Parliament, which had made arrangements for these assessments, also made arrangements for their collection.   It commanded all who had wool to sell in order to make possible
the raising of the grant, and decreed that collectors of wool
should be worthy men of the same county chosen in Parliament and not to be changed by any order.[5]   Further, it fixed
the weight of a sack of wool at 26 stones, each stone to
contain 14lbs., and stipulated that in every county 2 persons
should be appointed to hear and decide the suits of those who
complained of the conduct of the collectors[6] and receivers,
while to assist the collectors of the tax the exportation of new
wool was forbidden between May 20th and Sept. 29th,[7] after
which date exportation was to be free on payment of the old
custom.   The machinery for disposing of the wool was
similar to that employed in 1340.

This Parliamentary grant of 30,000 sacks of wool was
meant to serve a double purpose.   With it the King not only
hoped to raise supplies for future campaigns but to pay debts

1. *C.P.R.* 1340–3, p. 410.
2. *C.C.R.* 1341–3, p. 334.
3. *C.C.R.* 1341–3, p. 334.   4. *C.P.R.* 1340–3, p. 498.
5. *Rot. Parl.*, II, 133.   6. *Ib.*, II, 133.   7. *C.C.R.* 1341–3, p. 142.

contracted in the past. He was deeply involved with his Flemish allies, so deeply that he could only obtain their consent to his departure to meet Parliament in February, 1340, by pledging himself to return before Michaelmas day and by leaving as hostages his queen, his two sons and two earls.[1] Later in the year, when, after his return to Flanders and the conclusion of the treaty of Esplechin, he wished to cross to England to wreak vengeance on the officials on whose remissness he blamed the non-appearance of the wool, he was reduced to the undignified expedient of running away.[2] He sought to appease the wrath of his allies on account of his disappearance and his debts by assigning them wool according to the magnitude of their claims. To the "good men of the town of Ypres," with whom Edward was involved to the extent of £7,000, he sent 700 sacks of wool, declaring each sack to be worth £10.[3] To the Duke of Gelderland he assigned 1,030 sacks,[4] to the Duke of Brabant 3,300.[5] Even the King's captains had to engage in commercial transactions before they could draw their pay. Thus Sir Walter Manny was assigned 200 sacks in lieu of wages, and[6] Edward Montague 12 sacks for wages amounting to £76 for maintaining 20 men at arms, 12 armati, and 12 archers with himself as banneret for 40 days.[7]

But it was easier to procure the assignment than the wool. The country was by this time becoming expert in all the arts of evasion and deceit. Despite the King's compliance with Parliament's petition for the appointment of two trustworthy men in every shire to settle disputes that might arise,[8] disorder and disaffection everywhere characterised the collection. The grant of the Duke of Gelderland was openly refused.[9] That this evasion was no local phenomenon is illustrated by the case of the Duke of Brabant's grant. In July, 1341, he was assigned 3,300 sacks to be collected from the counties Warwick, Nottingham, Suffolk, Norfolk and Kent. In October not a single sack had been raised.[10] The King's authority was set at nought : his agents were defied. In Worcester inferior wool was foisted on the collectors, who found they could not obtain

1. Tout, p. 344.   2. Ib., p. 349.   3. C.P.R. 1340–3, pp. 257, &c.
4. Ib., p. 284.   5. Ib., pp. 259, 290.   6. Ib., pp. 258, 264–5.
7. Ib., p. 260.
8. C.P.R., 1340–3, p. 314.   9. Ib., p. 284.   10. Ib., p. 290.

for it the price covenanted with the King.[1]   In Norfolk and Lincoln there was open violence.   In the latter county the wool was locked up in houses that were eventually stormed :[2] in the former the arrest of wool granted to the King's allies in return for a £30,000 debt was broken.[3]   In Norfolk, Suffolk, Warwick, Nottingham and many other counties serjeants at arms were appointed.[4]   Smuggling flourished on a grand scale, despite the frequent appointment of commissions to suppress it and the institution of special officials to patrol the coast both at home and abroad.   Threats of confiscation and liberal offers to share the spoil with diligent officials alike failed to check it.[5]

The complaints were not all on one side.   In many counties the temper of the people was sorely tried by the unscrupulous methods of the collectors.   In their own interests they often tampered with the weights both during and after collection.   Frauds were detected and the offenders displaced, as in the county of Sussex, where the collectors were found abstracting two cloves from each sack after collection,[6] and in Salop, where the collectors used a fraudulent weight.[7]   The King soon realised that the collectors were more intent on their own interests than on his.   On July 1st he issued a sharp reprimand to all takers and purveyors of wool.   In it he declared his belief that they were lukewarm and negligent in the business, and commanded them on pain of forfeiture of all they possessed to lay aside everything else and to attend to the collection of the wool.   They were empowered to appoint deputies and to arrest and imprison anyone who was remiss, to seize their lands and retain them until the King gave other orders.[8]

Notwithstanding this sharp rebuke, the King deemed it necessary later in the year to appoint assistants to safeguard his interests in the counties of Oxford, Hereford, Essex, Sussex, Somerset, Dorset, Suffolk, Norfolk and Kent.[9]

But the King's actions were not calculated to pacify the country.   He violated the solemn pledges given to the Commons, and with the consent of the merchants carried

1. *C.P.R.* 1340–3, p. 386.   2. *Ib.*, p. 211.   3. *Ib.*, pp. 324, 345.
4. *Ib.*, pp. 291, &c.   5. *Ib.*, pp. 213, 216, 218, 290, &c.
6. *Ib.*, p. 326.
7. *C.P.R.* 1340–3, p. 388.   8. *Ib.*, p. 248.   9. *Ib.*, p. 274.

through measures which were only legal when confirmed by Parliament. The conflict between Parliament and the merchants, which we have seen foreshadowed on a previous occasion, now seriously began. The party which we may call the constitutional party, though Parliament did not always voice its views, opposed and tried to beat down the party of the prerogative backed by the merchants.

The Parliament of 1340 had granted the King a subsidy of 40/- on each sack of wool exported, to run from April 16th, 1340, to June 4th, 1341.[1] This grant the King, alleging the consent of certain merchants and others, extended in two ways. (1) Before the expiration of the term of its legal grant he raised the rate of the subsidy from 40/- to 20/-. (2) After the expiration of the term of its legal grant he made arrangements for collecting a maletote in place of the subsidy.

(1) The first exaction was accompanied by an apparent concession—the partial withdrawal of the monopoly scheme and the resumption of open trade. The King's monopoly schemes had all the same disadvantage that they diminished considerably the yield of the customs, one of his most profitable sources of income. The characteristic feature of Edward's interference with the wool trade was the control of half the trade by the King and the entire suspension of the other half during the period of royal control. Even supposing that Edward had gathered the full complement of his wool, which he never did, this would have involved the loss of half the customs revenue. With the failure of the monopoly schemes the loss was much greater. Now the failure of the 1340 scheme was complete. The two merchants who alone kept their contracts with the King and made the stipulated payments only managed to lay hands on 35 sacks of wool out of 600 sacks sold to them.

When the failure of the monopoly scheme became apparent the King began to devise other means for making the subsidy profitable. He hit on three different expedients. One device was to authorise the exportation of feeble wool, twice shorn wool and " other wool called peltewolle, cobblewolle and wool of malemort," on condition that no wool of the better sort was mixed with it, that it was taken to lands in the King's

---

1. 14 Edward III, St. 1, c. 21. *Rot. Parl.*, II, 112.

M

friendship, and that 40/- was paid on each sack for custom and subsidy.[1] A second device was to drive hard bargains with his creditors. He granted them permission to export new wool on condition that they deducted for each sack exported 80/- in some cases, 70/- in others, from the amounts he owed them.[2] His third device was to generalise this practice —to grant permission to export wool, up to 20,000 sacks, to all merchants instead of to a privileged few and to demand of them for the privilege 80/- instead of the legal subsidy of 40/-. This step the King, alleging the consent of certain merchants and others, took on April 1st, 1341. Exportation was to be made from one of the five ports, London, Southampton, Boston, Kingston upon Hull, Newcastle on Tyne; and the other wool ports were for the time closed down.[3]

This scheme, which was to supply the Flemish weavers with much needed wool and the English King with much needed money, did not prosper. The merchants, regarding the £4 subsidy as excessive and mindful that 40/- of it would automatically expire at Whitsuntide, delayed exportation in the hope that by waiting a couple of months they would be able to save £2 a sack on the shipment of their wool. The King early detected their plan, and on April 8th he sternly commanded all merchants and others who had wool to export it or sell it before Ascension next so that he might receive the custom and subsidy on every sack. All wool found in the hands of merchants or others after that date would be forfeit.[4]

Although the Rolls of Parliament contain no record of it, it is probable that the Parliament which met on April 26th, 1341, protested against this disingenuous scheme for raising the customs rate without its consent, for on May 4th, *i.e.,* while Parliament was actually sitting, the scheme suffered further modification. The ports which had been closed to the wool trade by the King's order of April 1st were now opened and the customs rate was dropped, not to the 40/- level which Parliament had authorised in 1340, but to 50/-[5]

(2) But in addition to exacting a larger subsidy than Parliament had granted the King continued to demand the payment of the subsidy when according to his agreement with

1. *C.C.R.* 1341–3, pp. 22, 27, 28, 38, &c.
2. *Ib.,* pp. 29, 33, &c.   3. *Ib.,* p. 52.
4. *Ib.,* p. 54.   5. *Ib.,* p. 70.

Parliament he should only have taken the customary $\frac{1}{2}$ mark. The term of the legal grant of the subsidy expired on June 4th, 1341.[1] Meanwhile on May 20th, 1341,[2] the exportation of wool had again been forbidden, to facilitate the raising of the 30,000 sacks granted by Parliament, 20,000 of which were to be collected that year. The merchants contracting to sell this wool, which was to be gathered and exported during the summer, *i.e.*, after the expiration of the term for which the 40/- subsidy had been granted, were only, it is true, to pay $\frac{1}{2}$ mark for customs, but the high prices they undertook to pay for the wool included the subsidy which was not paid separately through the customs.[3]

There were two other forms of exportation during 1341–2 in addition to that of the monopoly scheme—licensed exportation and the exportation of 100 sacks of wool which the King in his bargain with the merchants had reserved his right to pass from each of the 15 wool ports. Hugh de Ulseby, Henry Goldbeter and Walter Prest, who were authorised to export 1,220 of these 1,500 sacks, had to pay a maletote of 43/4 a sack in addition to the custom of $\frac{1}{2}$ mark,[4] while one of the King's creditors, John Beaumont, who exported 200 sacks, paid $\frac{1}{2}$ mark customs on each sack and deducted 43/4, from the amount the King owed him, for each sack exported.[5]

In the exportation which the King licensed he was able to make his own bargain with the merchants, and sums of varying amounts, free will offerings, as the King called them,[6] were exacted. Sometimes these " free will offerings " amounted to 50/-, sometimes to 40/-.[7] Sometimes they were paid wholly or in part at the Exchequer,[8] sometimes to the customers, but in one way or another and at one rate or another the King continued to exact a maletote down to the meeting of the merchant assembly on July 8th, 1342, when the proceeding was, after a fashion, regularised.

The " community of merchants," which met the Council at Westminster on that date, agreed that all merchants,

---

1. 14 Edward III, St. 1, c. 21.
2. *C.C.R.* 1341–3, p. 142. *Rot. Parl.*, II, p. 131.
3. *C.C.R.* 1341–3, p. 255.
4. *Ib.*, pp. 190, 204, &c. *C.P.R.* 1340–3, p. 277.
5. *C.C.R.* 1341–3, pp. 189, 234, &c. *C.P.R.* 1340–3, p. 254.
6. *C.C.R.*, 1341–3, p. 238. 7. *Ib.*, pp. 193, 390, &c.
8. *Ib.*, pp. 321, 331, &c.

denizen and alien, and all others might freely buy wool in the kingdom, by arrangement with vendors but not below the Nottingham price, and take it to the Staple in Flanders, paying 40/- subsidy on the sack or 300 woolfells beyond the custom till Midsummer (June 24th), 1343. Anyone exporting without paying custom and subsidy was to be expelled from the community of merchants, and no merchant, denizen or alien, was to communicate with him even though he made redemption by forfeiture or obtained remission or pardon.[1]

The Parliament of 1343 asked for the abrogation of this grant, which was a flagrant violation of the statutes of 1340. The Commons petitioned that the custom of wool be taken at ½ mark as it used to be in former times. They pointed to the maletote's mischievous effects upon the Commonalty, and declared it to be " beyond reason that the Commons should be charged in their goods by the merchants."[2] Edward replied that it was not his intention to charge the Commons with the subsidy which the merchants had granted, and that it could not be understood to be a charge upon the Commons since the price of wool was fixed in the different counties, and he willed that the price should stand, and that no wools should be bought below it on pain of forfeiture.[3] A compromise was ultimately arranged : the Commons agreeing to make the grant of a subsidy at the rate of the previous maletote and the King to re-establish the prices for wool in all the counties.[4] The Commons made this grant strictly conditional. Provided that no wool was bought below the price ordained in Parliament and that all wool exported paid the full custom and subsidy and that the King pledged himself not to grant exemption to anyone whatsover, either to buy wool below the legal price or to export it without payment of the custom and subsidy, the Commons consented to grant a subsidy of 40/- a sack in addition to the custom to be collected from midsummer to Michaelmas, 1343, and until the end of 3 years next following.[5]

Parliament also fixed the prices below which no wool was

---

1. *C.C.R.* 1341-3, pp. 553, 640. *C.P.R.* 1340-3, p. 415. See article on The Estate of Merchants," pp. 213-14 below.
2. *Rot. Parl.*, II, 140.
3. *Ib.*, II, 140.   4. *Ib.*, p. 138. *Foed.*, II, ii, 1225.
5. *Rot. Parl.*, II, 138. Murimuth, p. 146.

to be sold and the penalties for non-observance of the regulation.[1] These the King embodied in an ordinance which he issued from Westminster on May 20th, 1343, to all sheriffs in England, to provide for their execution. The ordinance, after reciting Parliament's sanction and arrangements, strictly charged the sheriff to make public proclamation, both in the cities, boroughs, markets and ports as well as in other places in his bailiwick, within liberty or without, wherever he thought fit, that no native or alien should buy wool below the price ordained for that county from June 24th until Sept. 29th and for 3 years following under penalty of the forfeiture of all wool so bought. The last two clauses of the ordinance are important. Buyers, not sellers, were to incur the penalty, and the statutory price, though it was to be a minimum, was not to be a maximum. Anyone could sell wool at a higher price than that fixed by law according to agreement with the merchant who wished to buy.[2]

Parliament had increased the King's hereditary custom revenue by a direct grant: it strove also to safeguard the increase by improving the system of collection. The Commons declared against the practice of customers and controllers who held their offices in fee or on a term of years or for life, letting out their posts to farm at the petition of the great men, whereby owing to the negligence of such farmers the King lost heavily in custom revenue. All such officials were to be removed, notwithstanding that their offices might have been granted for a term of years or for life, and the practice discontinued.[3]

In this same year the Truce of Malestroit was concluded.[4] Freed from the immediate necessity of raising supplies for a campaign, Edward found himself able to abandon some of the measures by which he had sought to supplement his ordinary resources. While the maletote, now a subsidy, was to be retained as a valuable addition to his customary revenue enabling him to pay off an infinitesimal part of the debts he had incurred, the prohibition of the exportation of wool, which was a necessary precaution for the collection of a grant of wool, could be annulled now that the occasioning cause was

1. *Rot. Parl.*, II, 138.   2. *Foed.*, II, ii, 1225.
3. *Rot. Parl.*, II, 139.   4. Murimuth, p. 129.

removed. In 1344 the prohibition was recalled by statute.[1]
The Commons of that year petitioned that the ordinance fixing
the price of wool in every county might be abrogated; that any
one might buy wool according to agreement with the seller;
that no one might be vexed because of purchases contrary to
the regulation, and that the sea might be open to all manner
of merchants to pass merchandise. The King graciously
heard the petition of his faithful Commons; the ordinance
fixing the price of wool was wholly annulled and the sea
thrown open to all merchants.[2]

The term of the grant of the subsidy expired in Sept. 1346,
the month in which Parliament reassembled. The merchants
had, in view of the King's necessities, already consented along
with the prelates to continue the grant for two years more.
But the Commons reminded the King of the compact made
with them three years ago binding him to cease the levy of the
40/- subsidy now and to take only half a mark henceforward.
The King, however, determined to continue the subsidy, and
in defence of his action pleaded an arrangement with the merchants to whom in the previous year he had let out the customs
to farm.[3] The Commons' protests were vain. Their constituents protested in a more effective manner by smuggling
their wool out of the country uncustomed and uncoketed. The
universal prevalence of this method of evasion is proved by
the universal appointment of special officials, deputies and
commissioners of arrest.

Edward had equipped his famous Crécy expedition by
exacting heavy fines from foreign clergy in English benefices
and by using his right of purveyance to buy up corn, bacon,
meat, wine, horses and munitions of war. But the victorious
issue of the campaign did not dissipate his financial difficulties.[4] The $\frac{2}{15}$ths voted by the laity and the tenth voted by
the clergy in the Parliament of September, 1346, did not
suffice to wipe out his heavy accumulation of debt, and he had
to plunge into further financial experiments.

1. 18 Edward III, St. 2, c. 3.
2. *Rot Parl.*, II, 148, 149, 150. The merchants had petitioned against
the ordinance in 1343, saying Nottingham prices were not fixed for all time,
and asking that they might be allowed to buy freely as other merchants
by agreement between buyer and seller. *Ib.*, p. 143.
3. *Ib.*, p. 161. See article on "Estate of Merchants," pp. 216-7, below.
4. Knighton, II, 32.

A great Council held by Lionel of Antwerp, Guardian of the Realm, on March 3rd, 1347, adopted two expedients for raising supplies. (1) It negotiated, without the consent of Parliament, what has been called a loan of 20,000 sacks of wool,[1] and (2) it levied a duty of 2/- upon each sack of wool exported and on each tun of wine imported, and of 6d. on every pound of merchandise imported or exported. between then and September 29th.[2] It is probable also that this Council made arrangements for a great merchant assembly which was summoned to meet on April 21st by writs issued on March 20th, in the hope, which was not disappointed, of constraining the merchants to make a series of individual loans. Many of the merchants agreed to advance different amounts;[3] others more dauntless flatly refused,[4] while some equally reluctant but more timid consented in haste and repented at leisure. Edward himself took over the task of coercing the recalcitrant. Those who would advance no money were ordered to meet him at Calais before May 18th, 27 of them, 4 in the county of Lincoln, 3 in Northampton, 7 in Gloucester, 1 in Huntingdon, 3 in Nottingham, 2 in Norfolk, 1 in Leicester, 4 in Yorkshire, and 2 in London failed to put in an appearance. So on May 28th Edward ordered the sheriffs of their shires to attach them.[5] Determined that none should defy his authority with impunity Edward dealt no less sternly with those who, overborne by the regent and his council, had consented to make a loan but had neglected to do so. On the same day on which he dealt with their more resolute comrades, he issued an ordinance commanding them under penalty of forfeiture of all they possessed to make the contracted loan before June 20th.[6]

The levy of wool likewise occasioned trouble. The 20,000 sacks were sold to the farmers of the custom, John de Wesenham, Walter de Chiriton and his fellow merchants of England, at 23/4 less per sack than the Nottingham price, each sack to contain 26 stone, each stone being 14lb. In return the merchants were to pay the King £40,000 between April 2nd and July 9th, £10,000 between Aug. 1st and Sept. 29th, and £16,666 13s. 4d. between Sept. 29th and Christmas. The

1. *C.P.R.* 1345–8, pp. 362, 438.
2. *Rot. Parl.*, II, 166. *C.P.R.* 1345–8, p. 264.
3. Knighton, II, 53.　　4. *C.C.R.* 1346–9, p. 282.
5. *Foed.*, III, i, 122.　　6. *Foed.*, III, i, 121.

residue was to be paid on Feb. 2nd.   Meanwhile no wool was to pass out of the realm until Easter following save by their consent.   Edward was to provide ships for its transport, but the merchants were to bear the expense.   He also agreed to sustain any loss incurred through tempest, accident, or any circumstance other than negligence, as well as the costs in-curred in the transport of the lost portion on adequate proof of the loss and the costs being given.   It was provided that if the merchants were not entirely served with the wool before Easter following, all the customs and subsidies, both petty and great, were to remain in their hands, after Walter de Chiriton and Gilbert de Wendlingburgh had been paid the 40,000 marks which they had lent the King in Flanders and for which they had assignments upon the same customs and subsidies, until they were requited for what was lacking of the 20,000 sacks.   All the ports of the realm, within franchises as without, were to be closed and all wool taken out of the realm in contravention of this order was to be forfeited to the King.[1]

All counties were to be allowed to compound in silver or gold for their portion of the wool.   The merchants were given full power to choose whomsoever they wished to act as their deputies and agents, and the chancellor and treasurer were ordered to make out the writs, necessary for collecting and receiving, free of charge.[2]

The prohibition of exportation which had been backed up by an order issued on June 24th[3] was universally misunder-stood.   People were afraid either to sell, buy, or gather wool. The weaving industry was at a standstill and the nation threatened with grievous loss.   On July 23rd Edward issued a remedial ordinance in which he declared his intention of allowing anyone whatsoever to sell, buy or gather wool to turn it into cloth, as they wished, provided no wool was taken out of the kingdom before he was served with his wool.   To remove all doubt on the matter sheriffs were ordered to pub-lish the ordinance in all parts of their bailiwick.[4]

It has generally been assumed that the 20,000 sacks were to be raised as a loan to the King, as was the case, for example, in 1340.   But the proceedings in 1340 and 1347 were entirely

1. *C.C.R.* 1346–9, pp. 290–1.
2. *Ib.* 1346–9, pp. 290–1.   3. *Ib.*, p. 282.
4. *Foed.*, III, i, 126. *C.C.R.* 1346–9, p. 357.

different in character. In 1340 merchants buying wool were to give vendors letters obligatory promising repayment at a stated term, and a definite fund was set aside to meet such payments. In 1347 no security for repayment was given and no fund was allocated for that purpose. Payment of wool was enforced as a tax at the rate of a $\frac{1}{15}$th,[1] as had happened previously in 1341 and 1342, but with this difference, that whereas in 1341 the 20,000 sacks were to be levied in lieu of the $\frac{1}{9}$th of that year, in 1347 they were levied in addition to the current $\frac{1}{15}$th which Parliament had voted in 1346.

The funds provided by these arbitrary measures were inadequate to meet the King's necessities, and he supplemented them by numerous requests to clergy of all ranks for grants of wool,[2] and by the imposition of duties on all cloth exported from the realm.[3]

To each county he sent, on April 8th, 1347, a faithful messenger bearing letters to all bishops, abbots, priors, deans and chapters, setting forth his dire needs and the promises of aid received in the Great Council, and requesting that they should follow the magnates' example and grant an aid in wool. They were to communicate to the bearer, in whom they could repose absolute confidence, what aid they were willing to give, the King promising to repay them at an appointed time.[4] By August 20th the mild request of April had grown into a stern demand, notwithstanding the clergy's response. On that day the King issued two sets of letters, one demanding money[5] and the other wool.[6] The tone of both documents was similar, though the latter was less peremptory. In the former Edward after declaring that whilst the war could not be maintained on his ordinary income plus the subsidies granted, yet if it were abandoned the English tongue would be blotted out and the Kingdom subverted, commanded that a loan of a certain amount contained in the letter be given him in wool or money at a time and place also fixed in the letter, whereupon letters obligatory for the pay-

1. *Ib.*, pp. 333–4.
2. *Foed.*, III, i, 131. Knighton, II, 47, 52.
3. *Rot. Parl.*, II, 168. For this see Dowell, I, 135. Cf. *C.P.R.* 1345–8, p. 276.
4. *Foed.*, III, i, 116. *C.C.R.* 1346–9, pp. 262—270.
5. *Foed.*, III, i, 130. *C.C.R.* 1346–9, pp. 382–4.
6. *Foed.*, III, i, 131.

ment of that amount at some future date would be given. The latter recited the King's previous appeals and conveyed his thanks for the grant which it had evoked.   But his need and the danger threatening him, the Realm and the English Church, had become more serious.   The war could not be sustained without additional supplies, as the discreet clergy well knew, so in his necessity which was subject to no law, he asks for a number of sacks of wool, in gold or silver, according to the sort of the county, and since in so short a time they could not be sent to the appointed place, the price of them, along with that of those previously promised, must be paid at London to the treasurer before a fixed date, when letters obligatory for the amount would be given.   This document, like that demanding money, ended with an assertion that no excuse would be accepted.

This form of letter was sent to a far greater number of clergy than the form demanding a stipulated money payment.   The latter was sent to 2 bishops, 13 abbots, 11 priors, 2 archdeacons, 10 chapters, and 16 others of the clergy.[1] The former, sent to 2 bishops, 37 abbots and 15 priors, who had previously promised 122 sacks, produced another 112 to be delivered before Sept. 15th; while similar letters sent to 3 bishops, 24 abbots, 5 abbesses, 26 priors, 1 prioress, and 4 others who had not yet contributed, fixed that they should furnish 208 sacks by the same date.   In the same way 1 bishop, 19 abbots and 6 priors, who had previously arranged to provide 50 sacks, were asked for another 65 to be ready for Sept. 30, and the Archbishop of York, 3 bishops, 15 abbots, 1 abbess, 21 priors, 1 archdeacon and 2 others of the clergy who had paid nothing as yet were to provide 143 sacks by the same date.[2]   By this means Edward hoped to raise, in addition to the $\frac{1}{15}$th granted in 1346, a total of over 700 sacks of wool or their equivalent, roughly about £3,500, an average of over £19 per each individual.[3]

The high-handed action of the Great Council, followed by the equally arbitrary proceedings of the King in subjecting the nation to charges unsanctioned by its representatives, in flagrant contravention of statutes rendering such assent essen-

1. *Foed.*, III, i, 131–133.
2. *Ib.*
3. Calculated from average annual prices. Rogers, I, 390, et seq.

tial to the legality of the imposition, produced an outburst in Parliament. The glorious termination of the war did not restore confidence or blind the nation to the gross breach of trust which had been perpetrated. There was deep distrust and growing apprehension, and this acting upon the minds and dispositions of the Commons made them more eager to play the part of barristers summoning the King before the tribunal of his own laws than of counsellors advising him in his extremity.

A Parliament summoned by the King in January, 1348, in the hope of obtaining a considerable grant, presented 64 petitions for redress of grievances.[1] These included protests against exactions which were legal but obnoxious, as well as petitions against palpably illegal impositions. The Commons petitioned against the levy of the subsidy which had been granted for 2 years in 1346, as well as against the new duties imposed by the Great Council in 1347 on wool, wine, cloth and general merchandise,[2] the tyrannous exercise of the right of purveyance,[3] and the conduct of the collectors of wool.[4] They declared that the King was taking more than he ought, and asked that henceforth wool might be exported freely on payment of the old custom only. The King replied that according to the term of its grant the subsidy had still some time to run, but he promised during that time to take the advice of his Council as to what was best to be done for the profit of his people.[5] Further the Commons petitioned against the imposition on cloth on the ground that it was ruining the labourer, the producer and the merchant, but Edward argued that it was reasonable he should have the same profit from cloth as from wool, and retained it.[6] However, he told his faithful Commons who begged him to take pity on them and not to impoverish them when they were annually bearing the great burden of $\frac{1}{15}$ths, $\frac{1}{10}$ths and grants of wool, that he would make no imposition save when driven by great necessity and then only with the assent of the Prelates, Earls, Barons and other magnates, along with the Commons. With regard to purveyance, right was to be done on all who

1. *Rot. Parl.*, II, 165 et seq.   2. *Ib.*, 166.   3. *Ib.*, 166, 169, 171.
4. *Ib.*, 169.   5. *Ib.*, 168.
6. *Ib.*, II, 168.

took it saving the King's prerogative.[1]   The promise of
moderation in taxation was worthless.   It was vitiated by the
saving clause concerning great necessity—for the King alone
was judge of such necessity—as well as by the King's immediate embarrassments.   So also was the promise regarding
purveyance, for the prerogative which was saved was the
source of all the trouble, and until the King consented to or
the Commons insisted on its definite limitation   abuses
would   continue.   But the recognition of the Commons'
consent to taxation was, in view of recent violations, an
important re-assertion of the most valuable principle of the
Confirmation of the Charters tantamount to an acknowledgment on the King's part of the illegality of his previous
actions.

Despite this success, the multifarious complaints of the
Commons of January, 1348, were for the most part unavailing.
But in one other particular which concerns our subject, they
gained their point, nominally at least.   The merchants to
whom the customs had been farmed in 1345 had been oppressive and extortionate in the exercise of their functions.   The
Commons quoted one flagrant example of illegality, and
hinted darkly at others.   The merchants, they declared, had
levied an additional impost of 2 marks a sack in addition to
the custom and subsidy, to the great damage of the realm and
the lowering of the price of wool.[2]   Edward granted the Commons' request that they might be apprehended and made to
reply in Parliament.   But other complaints were brought
against them.   If they had been oppressive and fraudulent, as
farmers of the custom, they had been none the less so as purveyors of wool.   Instead of the legal stone of 14 lbs. they
had extorted 16lbs. and 18 lbs. and had demanded further
payment before they would give a town acquittance.[3]   Further, it was stated that by confederacy amongst them they had
bargained with the King to his own great loss and the
impoverishment of his people.[4]   There is no need to suppose
the Commons guilty of exaggeration.   Such conduct was but
the natural and inevitable consequence of entrusting private
individuals with important public duties uncontrolled save by
an absentee King who was only keen on securing the full

1. *Rot. Parl.*, II, 166.   2. *Ib.*, II, 169.   3. *Ib.*, 171.   4. *Ib.*, 170.

discharge of the merchants' obligations to himself. The Commons laid their iniquities before Edward, and prayed for a remedy " for the love of God." The King graciously heard their petition, and appointed some of his council to inquire into the truth of the charges, promising if the complaints were substantiated to hand over the offenders to the justices of peace and the justices appointed to inquire into false money, to do right. Satisfaction was not made, however, for the complaints were renewed in the March parliament, when further allegations were made against the merchants. They were now accused of using false weights, and it was said that although they had raised much more than the full amount from the Commons the King had not had a third of the profit of the 20,000 sacks.[1]

It was found on investigation that those who had exhibited the petition in Parliament had had no knowledge of the nature of the contracts made between the King and the merchants for the sale of wool. Moreover, the merchants won the King to their side by their frank offer to answer before him or any of his council he should depute concerning all their dealings with him, and to satisfy him of everything wherein they had been delinquent. Assured that his interests had not suffered along with the nation's, Edward repudiated his promise to the Commons, and gave the merchants a comprehensive pledge of security. He guaranteed that they should be in no wise impeached or molested by reason of the Commons' petition or compelled to answer before his justices or ministers touching anything relating to the matter of the wool in question or to other contracts made with him in the past.[2]

The Commons were more successful in dealing with abuses connected with another exaction. The avowed object of this imposition was not to raise revenue but to defray the expenses of protecting trade. In spite of the armistice which had been arranged after the capture of Calais, commercial operations were still attended with considerable danger to person and property. The spheres of trading operations had been the centres of the late warfare, and though peace nominally reigned all the lawlessness and disturbance which accompany

1. *Ib.*, 201.
2. *C.P.R.*, 1345–8, p. 104.

war still prevailed.   Not only French privateers, sore at their defeats, but Flemish creditors, sore on account of debts, were ready to pounce down upon the unoffending merchant and to revenge themselves on him for the iniquities of his master.[1] To protect them against these disturbers of the peace and to conduct the merchants safely to the staple, men at arms, archers and others had been engaged, and a charge of 12d. a sack exacted to maintain them.   Through official remissness or corruption the 12d. had been scrupulously levied but the corresponding protection had been withheld, with the result, said the Commons, that many merchants had been killed and £20,000 worth of goods lost.   Such culpable negligence could not be glossed over, and the King appointed persons and places for hearing offenders.[2]

The Parliament of March, 1348, followed the example of that of January, 1348.   It stated its complaints boldly and distinctly.   These were chiefly financial—the aid for knighting the King's son, taken without the assent of the Commons, contrary to the statute of 1340, and at double the customary rate, the petty oppressions by which the agents of the collectors of wool beat down the price to the sellers and enhanced it to the buyers, the subsidy on wool, and the 20,000 sacks borrowed.   The Commons declared that the subsidy produced £60,000 annually, which came out of the pockets of the landowners, because in consequence of the subsidy merchants simply paid so much less for every sack.   [3]" It was a land tax not a tax on merchants."   Eventually they included these points in a numerous list of conditions to which they demanded the King's assent before making a grant.   If he would undertake amongst other things that the subsidy on wool should cease at the end of the term of its 3 years' grant and not be again granted by the merchants, who did not bear the burden of it since they gave so much less for the sack of wool; that the 20,000 sacks should be restored and no impost, tallage or charge laid upon the Commons by the Privy Council with their assent, they would grant a $\frac{1}{15}$th and a $\frac{1}{10}$th for three years.[4]

1. Cunningham, I, 300–303.
2. *Rot. Parl.*, II, 171, 172.   *C.P.R.* 1345–8, pp. 76 and 77.
3. *Rot. Parl.*, II, 200, 201.
4. *Ib.*, 201.

The King accorded most of the petitions in order to secure the grant, but no new statute was issued embodying them, nor was any needed, for they were all explicitly and completely covered by existing law. What was required was not the King's sanction for a new legislative pronouncement, but his observance of an old one. In the face of his frequent and flagrant defiance of the statutes of 1340 the Commons' only resource was to take their stand firmly by those laws and steadfastly to refuse to countenance the King's infractions of them. This they did with great pertinacity. The struggle was long but it was decisive. The Commons, after wresting from the King repeated confirmations of the 1340 statutes, made only to be broken, succeeded in reasserting in law, both in 1362 and 1371, the principle for which they had contended throughout the reign, and also in extending its application to alien merchants.

The results were momentous, not in what was achieved but in what was averted. The work of the Commons was not initiation but preservation, conservation. By asserting their right to control the then only important form of indirect taxation as well as all direct taxation, they established a precedent and laid the foundation for the successful claims of the Commons of the future to control all indirect as well as all direct taxation.

By excluding the merchants from most important direct political influence the Commons made it impossible for the King, by allying himself with the merchants, to tax the body of the nation at his discretion, and finally bound him to abide, both in the letter and in the spirit, by the terms of the Confirmation of the Charters. By the end of the reign the process of differentiation and definition of function had been carried a stage further. The Statute Book now gave clear and unequivocal answers to the two questions which the King's action had raised early on in the reign. His attempts to organise a quasi-Parliamentary body, as powerful as Parliament to work his ends, less powerful than Parliament to resist them, had been defeated and the Commons had filled in that lacuna in their powers which we noticed at the beginning of the reign.

F. R. BARNES.

THE ESTATE OF MERCHANTS, 1336—1365.

I.

A COUPLE of pages in Stubbs' *Constitutional History*, and half-a-dozen references and footnotes in the same authority, contain all that was until quite lately known about the estate of merchants.

A chapter in Professor Tout's recent book on "The Place of the Reign of Edward II in English History,"[1] has cast a flood of new light on the subject, and has shown conclusively that the assemblies of merchants which were a marked feature of the policy of Edward III from 1336 to 1354, had their main antecedents, not in the reign of his grandfather, but in that of his father. The history of the estate of merchants under Edward III is briefly summarised by Stubbs[2] as follows :—

"Although in that king's reign the wool was made a sort of circulating medium in which supplies were granted, and the merchants were constantly summoned in large numbers to attend in council and parliament, they wisely chose to throw in their lot with the commons, and sought in union with them an escape from the oppression to which their stock and staple made them especially liable."

There is no reason to question the substantial accuracy of this account, but there are several questions of considerable importance for constitutional and economic history which it leaves unanswered. From what class or classes of traders were the assemblies of merchants drawn? Was their character in this respect uniform throughout the critical period of Edward III's reign, and if it varied, how far were the variations connected with observable changes of policy? If we can obtain answers to these questions we may proceed to inquire what were the likeliest motives of class interest that operated positively or negatively, continuously or alternately,

1. Manchester, 1914.   2. Stubbs, II, 202.

N

in unison, in concordance, or in conflict through the assemblies of merchants? And, finally, we may ask, though here, perhaps, we ought not to look for more than tentative answers, what were the relations between this organisation, under state auspices, of sectional or class interests and the growing articulation of a more national interest in parliament?

Fortunately, we possess full lists of the merchants who were summoned to most of the assemblies from 1336 to 1356. There are more than a score of these lists, the longest containing nearly two hundred names, the shortest less than a dozen.[1] Some names are those of "merchant princes" like William de la Pole of Hull, the leading English financier; John Pulteney, who died of the plague in 1348, leaving a ruby ring to the Bishop of London, and a diamond ring to the Earl of Huntingdon, that they might see to the fulfilment of his religious bequests[2]; and Henry Picard,[3] whose wealth was great enough to give substance to the legend that he entertained four kings at one feast, "and after kept his hall for all comers, that were willing to play at dice and hazard." Many other names, though less illustrious, are those of men whose business affairs are known to us through numerous entries in the national records; whilst the very obscurity of the remainder —for the most part small traders in country towns—lends significance to their inclusion in the longer lists. Only one list—that of the assembly that preceded the establishment of Home Staples in 1353—includes aliens: Lombards, Germans and Genoese.

As each of the special studies contained in this volume casts some new light on our present subject, it ought not to be impossible, by a comparative study of the lists and by bringing them into connection with what we already know of the constitutional, social and economic history of the period, to come to a better understanding of what is involved in the phrase "estate of merchants."

At the outset of such a study it will be helpful to indicate the central importance of the lists of merchants who constituted the assembly of February 1338, the membership of which is

1. *Lords' Report*, IV, 46.
2. *Cal. Wills*, I, 609.
3. Stow, I, 106, 240. The legendary character of this story is shown in Prof. Tait's *Chronica Johannis de Reading, etc.* (Manchester 1914), p. 312.

identical with that of the Staple Company of 1337. The previous assemblies of 1336 and 1337 can be best explained when they are regarded as stages in the formation of the Company which, in August 1337, undertook to operate a monopoly in the exportation of wool and to advance an immense sum to the King on the proceeds; and though the history of this arrangement was brief and disastrous, its after effects were of an enduring character and furnish the central clue to the subsequent arrangements down to 1348.

Let us therefore endeavour to place the assemblies of 1336 and 1337 with their culmination in the Staple Company of July 1337 and the assembly of February 1338 in an intelligible relation to the social and constitutional history of these two years. First of all, it may be noted that in these two years the "budget" of Edward III reaches high-water mark almost at a bound. In the year 1330–1 the total revenue, according to Sir Jas. Ramsay, was £37,597, in 1331–2 £72,620, in 1335–6 £179,641, in 1337–8 £272,833.[1] The ordinary revenue of the Crown for this period, apart from Parliamentary grants, is estimated by Sir James Ramsay at £30,000, and the normal Parliamentary grant of direct taxation brought in £38,000.[2] Whilst, therefore, the total of 1330–1 represents little more than the ordinary revenue, and that of 1331–2 the ordinary revenue supplemented by a normal Parliamentary grant, the total of 1335–6 is equivalent to a four-fold grant, and that of 1337–8 to a six-fold grant of direct taxes in addition to ordinary revenue.

Now, it is scarcely necessary to say that neither Edward III nor any other English king in the Middle Ages ever induced a Parliament to make a six-fold or even a four-fold grant of direct taxation to cover the expenses of a single year. When a three-fold grant was made in later years it was intended to meet three years' expenditure; and the collection was spread over three years. The grants obtained by Edward in 1336–7 were on the same basis. He got three grants in two years, but it was intended that the collection, if not the expenditure, should cover a third year. Yet, even so, the result secured was unprecedented, and extraordinary efforts

1. Ramsay, II, 101.   2. *Ib.*, II, 85.

had to be made to obtain it. To meet the expense of his actual war with Scotland, and of preparation for a threatened war with France, Edward had persuaded Parliament to follow up the grant made in the spring of 1336 with another in the autumn. But that this was meant to be an anticipation of next year's taxation is shown by the fact that no further grant was made in the spring session of 1337. When the King began to contemplate an appeal in the autumn of 1337 for a third grant, in anticipation of 1338, it is clear that he expected stout opposition to his demands. Professor Willard has described the extraordinary measures employed by the King to forestall this opposition—the summoning of assemblies in each county, the appointment of commissioners to lay the King's case before them, and the final renunciation of the grant already obtained, when the pressure thus exercised on Parliament had induced it to vote supplies in a more constitutional way.[1]

In view of these facts it seems unlikely that the same Parliament that was reluctantly making unprecedented grants of direct taxation can have consented freely to the imposition of new forms of indirect taxation that were equivalent in one year to at least a three-fold direct subsidy.

A successful resistance to precisely similar methods of taxation in 1297 had been the most memorable achievement of the English Parliament : and a renewal of these devices on a smaller scale had been defeated as recently as 1334. The statement, therefore, of the chronicler that the Parliament which, in the autumn of 1336, made a second grant of direct taxation, also authorised a subsidy of 40/- on wool, would require strong support to make it credible, especially as Parliament itself always subsequently denounced the wool tax as an illegal imposition. And the evidence of the records as reviewed by Mr. Barnes shows clearly that the tax was sanctioned, not by Parliament, but by an assembly of merchants in conjunction with the council, that it took the form at first of a tax of 20/-, with a loan of 20/- in addition, that the 40/- tax was not imposed till 1338, and that it was not sanctioned by Parliament till 1340.[2]

1. Willard. " Negociations for a grant in 1337," *Eng. Hist. Rev.*, XXI, 727.
2. See article on " The Taxation of Wool," pp. 143 *et seq.*, above.

During the year 1336-7, the King, whilst, on the one hand, straining the machinery of the Constitution to secure the maximum of direct taxation, was, on the other hand, making continual use of the assemblies of merchants to obtain a maximum of indirect and unconstitutional taxation. It now remains for us to study more closely the working of the assemblies of merchants in this connection.

There were three distinct councils of merchants summoned in the course of 1336. On May 8th, about the time of the King's departure for his campaign in Scotland, the municipal authorities of London, and of twenty-one other cities and boroughs were required to send four each of their more sufficient and discreet merchants to meet the King or his council at Oxford on May 27th.[1] We have no record of the doings of this assembly. It is quite likely that the boroughs did not send representatives in sufficient numbers to transact the business proposed. But the character of the agenda is revealed by a mandate addressed to the Sheriff of York from Woodstock, on the day after that fixed for the assembly. Certain merchants of the realm and their accomplices, with a view to diminishing the price of wool, had been spreading the news that the King intended to levy an extra export tax of twenty shillings per sack. The Sheriff was directed to issue a proclamation forbidding such statements, to imprison those who persisted in making them, and to send in their names to the Council.[2]

As the consent of the merchants to this extra tax on wool was the main result of a later assembly, it is fairly certain that it must have been already in contemplation, and it is also extremely probable, either that the intended council at Oxford never met, or that the negotiations with the merchants proved a failure. One or other of these conclusions seems justified by the fact that on June 1st a new writ was issued from Woodstock summoning another council of merchants to meet at Northampton at midsummer.[3] This time there was no scope left to the inertia or resistance of the municipalities. The King issued separate writs to a hundred and five individuals. Thirty-three of these were citizens of London of the aldermanic class, and the rest were merchants from the chief centres of the wool trade. Of the whole number thus summoned only

1. *Lords Report*, IV, 457.
2. *C.C.R.*, 1333-7, p. 681.   3. *Lords' Report*, IV, 458.

seventeen were amongst those who ultimately took part in the great bargain of the following year. But most of the seventeen were leading merchants who played a dominant part in the subsequent arrangement. London, Yorkshire and Southampton each sent three of the principal later contractors, whilst Lincoln, Northampton, Nottingham, Ipswich, Gloucester and Salop were each represented by one. The county groups led by these men undertook, in 1337, two-thirds of the great contract for 30,000 sacks. At the Northampton assembly, therefore, of 1336 it is possible that preliminary arrangements were made of an informal or secret character by which the Government was to levy a super-tax on wool and the merchants were to enjoy a monopoly of the exportation. The presence at the assembly of the whole body of London aldermen suggests the further possibility that negotiations were then opened for the restoration of those trading privileges of the capital which had been lost by the " free trade " legislation of 1335 and which were restored in the spring of 1337.

Our inferences about this June assembly, like those about the earlier gathering in May, must remain largely conjectural. What is certain is that the main object for which they were summoned was first realised in a third [1] assembly convened a week before Michaelmas at Nottingham, whither a Parliament, or, as the official documents always style it, a Great Council, had been simultaneously summoned to discuss foreign affairs with the King on his return from Scotland and to meet his urgent demand for more supplies. The unprecedented grant made by this Great Council of a second levy of direct taxation within a single year was far from adequate to the King's needs. The grant would at best bring in less than £40,000; and the King had, early in July, authorised his financial agents to raise loans to the extent of £200,000.[2] For such loans security would be required, and the only available resource was heavy taxation on wool, or a monopoly in the exportation, or both combined. The King obtained a grant of a twenty shilling subsidy and a twenty shilling loan on each sack, in addition to the ordinary customs, but the official documents make it perfectly clear that this grant, though

1. *Lords' Report*, IV, 464.   2. *Foed.*, II, 942. *C.P.R.* 1334–6, p. 260.

made *at* the Great Council at Nottingham, was made *by* an assembly of merchants. It is interesting to compare the membership of this assembly with that of the earlier gatherings. It was a much smaller body than either of the others, numbering only forty-one. Fifteen of these were to be among the contractors of the following year, and ten of the fifteen appear for the first time at this assembly. It would certainly seem as if the consent of this body of merchants to the new taxation was closely connected with negotiations for securing a monopoly of exportation. And it was doubtless to reassure the minds of wool growers in this respect that a list of minimum prices for the wool of the various counties was promulgated at this meeting—" the Nottingham prices " frequently referred to in later Parliamentary debates.

But whatever the King's plans for raising money out of the wool trade may have been, they were not destined to be speedily realised. Eighteen most eventful months were to elapse before any considerable amount of English wool was to appear in the markets of the Netherlands, and in the meantime the constitutional and fiscal situation above described was to be complicated by continually changing military and diplomatic factors. The wool supply was not only the main support of Edward's war finance, it was also the main resource of his diplomacy. In the alliance which he desired with Brabant and Flanders the establishment of wool staples at Antwerp and Bruges was the strongest inducement he could offer. But, just as in order to gain his financial purpose he must restrain the exportation of wool till he had acquired fixed control of it, so to achieve his diplomatic object he must withhold the staple till he had bargained for an equivalent.

In the meantime it was the natural aim of the French King to hinder the realisation of Edward's policy in either of its branches. For some weeks before the Nottingham assembly met, the depredations of Norman and Scottish privateers had rendered the narrow seas unsafe to peaceful shipping, and it had scarcely concluded its sittings before the Count of Flanders, at the instigation of Philip, caused the arrest of all the English merchants in Bruges, and thus cut the connection between the English wool supply and its principal market. Soon afterwards the Francophil nobles of Flanders, by occupying the island of Cadsand, stopped the approaches of English shipping, not only to Bruges, but also to Antwerp. For more than a year, English trade with Flanders was absolutely at a standstill, and direct intercourse with Brabant was likewise suspended. It was to Dordrecht that the English ambassadors repaired in April 1337 under the protection of a powerful fleet to discuss the question of the staple, and at the end of the year Dordrecht was still the only safe destination for the King's wool when at last it began to be shipped.[1]

There can be no doubt that both England and Flanders suffered greatly from this complete stoppage of one of the main channels of the economic life of each country. Froissart and later historians have naturally laid most stress on the sufferings of Flanders, and perhaps these were the greater, but even Froissart sufficiently indicates the other side of the matter when he makes the Count of Flanders assure his subjects that the English people are in open conflict with their King and cannot hold out long without a market for their wool.[2] It is noteworthy that the receipts of customs for 1336 reach a much lower level than those for any year since 1321, in spite of the large additional grant made at Nottingham. They were only one-half the amount hitherto raised in a normal year of peace, and only one-tenth of the amount produced two years later, when the war tax on wool was in actual operation.[3]

The entire arrest of foreign trade, the doubling of direct taxation, and the continual summoning of unconstitutional assemblies, made the year that followed the autumn of 1336 one of great unrest. The Mayor of London and special commissioners were busy arresting suspected persons.[4] There was all the economic pressure and social ferment of war time without any of the counterbalancing absorption in military achievement. It is unfortunate that the legislation of this disturbed and abnormal period should have been so widely accepted as representing permanent aims of royal or parliamentary policy. At a time like the present, when titled ladies are forming national societies to repress the extravagance of servants, we can readily understand the Great Council of

1. *Foed.*, II, 948.
2. Kervyn de Lettenlove. *Œuvres de Froissart, Chroniques*, II, 41.
3. Ramsay, II, 101.   4. *C.P.R.* 1334–8, pp. 365, 367, 375.

Nottingham, which had just sanctioned the equivalent of a double income tax proceeding to enact " that no man shall cause himself to be served with more than two courses, and each mess of two sorts of victuals at the most, on the grounds that the King's subjects are not able to aid themselves or their liege lord in time of need, and that many other evils have happened to their bodies and souls." [1] We have no need to attribute this ordinance to the adoption by Edward III of the conclusions of McCulloch or Nassau Senior.

Still less are we justified in assuming that the Act of 1337 prohibiting the exportation of wool and the importation of foreign cloth indicates a far-sighted policy of fostering native industry. At that moment a whole year's wool supply was rapidly accumulating in the ports. The King's war plan entirely depended upon this wool paying a high export duty, and securing a monopoly price in a foreign market. But negotiations were still proceeding with Brabant and Flanders for such a disposal of the wool as would secure a maximum of diplomatic and fiscal result. It was necessary to persuade the nation to acquiesce in a continued stoppage of the wool trade. The Act of 1337 was intended to combine both these objects. It set the embargo laid upon exportation in a two-fold patriotic light. It proposed to penalise the chief branch of the enemy's foreign trade, and at the same time to foster native industries. Foreign cloth makers were invited to settle in England, and no foreign cloth was to be imported after the following Michaelmas.[2] This time limit was a diplomatic weapon placed in the hands of the plenipotentiaries who were then on the point of embarking for the Netherlands.[3] It was doubtless hoped that before Michaelmas a treaty would have been made by which the Act would be largely superseded, and, as far as Brabant was concerned, these hopes were realised. The Brabançons were licensed to buy wool in England on May 24th, 1337, and had acquired 2,200 sacks before Michaelmas. A preliminary treaty was drawn on July 13th, and later on the importation of cloth from Brabant was freely resumed.[4]

As the settlement of the foreign staple seemed approaching, it became necessary to bring to a head the negotiations with

1. 10 Edw. III, pt. 2.   2. 11 Edw. III, c. 1.
3. *C.P.R.* 1334–7, p. 428.
4. *Foed.*, II, 221. *C.C.R.* 1337–9, p. 318.

the English merchants for securing a monopoly profit on the exportation. This was done by means of three special assemblies, which met in rapid succession during June and July. A brief consideration of the lists of these assemblies, and of their obvious relation to one another will enable us to follow the course of the negotiations. The first, the smallest, and probably the most important of these assemblies, met at Stamford on June 16th, and consisted of only twenty-four persons. With one exception, all those who were summoned took a leading part in the subsequent contract. Amongst them were four of the six Yorkshire contractors, headed by William de la Pole, all the four Lincolnshire men, and the chief men of the Northampton, Leicester, Warwick, Huntingdon, Nottingham, and Derby groups of contractors. As these counties furnished the greater part of the English wool supply, and as the writs summoning the assembly had been issued from Stamford, where the meeting was to be held, it seems not unlikely that the general scope of the plan had been agreed upon among the principal contractors, and that the assembly met to confirm its adoption and to make arrangements for forming similar groups in the less important southern and western counties.[1] After a week's consultation writs were issued at Stamford for another assembly to meet at Westminster on July 9th. The thirty-five merchants individually summoned were less unanimously prepared to take part in the contract. Twenty-five of them, however, ultimately did so, and these comprised the whole of the London group, and of the Wiltshire group three of the six Southampton contractors, two leading representatives of the Salop group, two of the Hertford and Essex group, two from Chester and Flint, and one each from Hereford, Worcester, and Gloucester. Writs had been simultaneously issued from Stamford to the Sheriffs of Essex, Kent, Surrey, Sussex, Cornwall and Devon for the election of two merchants apiece to the Westminster assembly, but if any merchants came in response to these writs they took no effective part in the scheme prepared.[2]

If we include the twenty members of the Stamford

---

1. *Lords' Report*, IV, 474. Since writing the above I find my conjecture fully confirmed by Archbishop Stratford's statement in 1341. See *Anglia Sacra*, I, 30.
2. *Lords' Report*, IV, 477.

assembly, fifty-five merchants had now been individually summoned, and forty-four were prepared to take part in the contract. This was less than half of the total number of contractors, who were ultimately to number ninety-seven, but it included all the leading capitalists. The Yorkshire, Lincolnshire and London groups, which were to undertake between them half the amount of the contract, were already formed. Of the seventeen other groups ultimately formed, each containing three to eight members and representing a county or a group of counties, the three groups representing the Northern Counties were not called to any of this year's assemblies, but dealt with separately. In regard to all the remaining fourteen groups save one, a nucleus had been formed of two or three members who were doubtless prepared to negotiate on behalf of the others in their several districts.

The details of the arrangements must have been settled during the fortnight that followed July 9th by an assembly of some fifty merchants, most of whom were personally concerned in the bargain. But on July 13th a large additional body of a hundred and ten merchants was summoned to assemble at Westminster on July 25th. Eighty-two of these received separate writs, and twenty-eight were to be sent by the seven towns of Bristol, Gloucester, Leicester, Northampton, Coventry, Chichester and Wenlock.[1] As the contract was completed and agreed on July 26th, these newcomers cannot have played any decisive part in determining its character. Two reasons may be assigned for summoning them, one fairly certain, and the other at least probable. They were certainly needed to complete the groups of contractors; fifteen of these eighty-two summoned by name are found later amongst the various groups. They were probably also summoned to swell the numbers on the day of the final decision and to give an appearance of consent to a wholly unconstitutional proceeding.

The character of the arrangement made by the body of contracting merchants through their two elected representatives, William de la Pole of Hull, and Reginald de Conduit of London, with the King has been often misunderstood, and a clear understanding of it is an absolutely essential preliminary

---

1. *Lords' Report*, IV, 478-9.

to any fruitful study of the constitutional and economic developments of the next ten years. The merchants were to buy 30,000 sacks of wool for the King's use, *i.e.* they were armed with the prerogative of preemption. The prices of the best wool in each county were fixed, but inferior wool was to be bargained for freely. Those who sold the wool were to give six months' credit for half the amount, and twelve months' credit for the other half, but this credit was to be conceded, not to the King, as has sometimes been supposed, but to the merchants, who were to give promissory notes to the sellers. The average price to be given was about £5 a sack, and the cost of the 30,000 sacks in England was to be a little over £150,000. By the exercise of a stringent monopoly of exportation, it was hoped that a high profit would be realised, and of this the King was to take half. Custom and subsidy on the wool would amount—if the subsidy were twenty shillings a sack—to another £40,000. On the security of these prospective gains, the merchants were to make advances to the King by instalments, as fast as they disposed of the wool, to the total amount of £200,000, and they were to secure the remainder of the custom until this was repaid. The wool growers were to lend their wool to the merchants: the merchants were to lend the proceeds to the King.[1]

The question which at once suggests itself is—what was the expected amount of profit—and on this point we have no certain information. The statement of Knighton that £20 per sack could be obtained in Brabant when the price was £6 a sack in England, thus yielding a profit of over 200 per cent., seems at first sight the natural exaggeration of a chronicler;[2] but two considerations make it possible that this estimate may not be very greatly in excess of the one actually entertained. The first of these is to be found in the prices which in 1341 the groups of merchants undertook to pay in Flanders to the King, and which, therefore, contain only the King's share of the prospective profit. These prices were from 75 per cent. to 100 per cent. higher than the "Nottingham Prices," at which the wool was to be bought. The second reason for assuming a high prospective rate of profit is that

1. *C.P.R.* 1334–8, pp. 480, 505. *C.C.R.* 1343–4, p. 423.
2. Knighton, II.

without it the merchants could not have undertaken to advance so large a sum as £200,000.

To another question of more vital importance we may hope to give an approximate answer. In what relation did this syndicate of merchants stand to the whole body of traders interested in the wool trade throughout the kingdom? The documents arising out of the breakdown of the arrangements shed some light on this matter. In May 1338, after 11,497 sacks had been exported, the King seized all the wool at Dordrecht and gave the owners acknowledgments of the amount due to each, which they were to recover by remissions of subsidy on future exportations.[1] In this list of the King's creditors we can distinguish at least three classes, two of which were within the syndicate and one outside. About half the members of the syndicate do not appear to have taken any appreciable share in the enterprise. Of the other half, a dozen were large capitalists whose shares in the transactions were upwards of a £1,000, the highest amount being £4,430, whilst another forty had exported wool for amounts between three hundred pounds and a thousand. But a third body of merchants, numbering about two hundred, to whom the King acknowledged indebtedness from sums varying from ten pounds to more than three hundred pounds, were not members of the syndicate. Some of these had sold their wool to the wealthier members of the company. We find the four chief Lincolnshire contractors, who had between them exported wool to the value of £12,056, handing over the greater part of the King's acknowledgment of debt to sixty-three lesser merchants, who would appear, by virtue of some arrangement with the syndicate, to have exported wool on their own account. Forty such merchants in London exported on the average thirty sacks each, twenty-five merchants in the Lincolnshire towns about twenty sacks each, twenty-three in Beverley about twenty sacks each, twenty in Newcastle about a dozen sacks each, and there were lesser bodies of small exporters in the principal towns of Leicestershire, Warwickshire, Salop, Norfolk, and Durham.

The general result of these somewhat rough calculations shows a striking resemblance to the more accurate statistics

1. *C.C.R.* 1336–8, p. 424.

that have been compiled from the records of the wool export of the year 1273. In that year, of 32,743 sacks exported, 11,415 were exported by 284 English merchants, with an average of forty sacks apiece[1] : the largest amount exported by one merchant being one hundred and sixty sacks.

Two important changes are, however, revealed by the statistics of 1337. One of these lies in the larger amounts exported by the chief English capitalists, and the other in the rise from comparative insignificance to a position of predominant importance of the wool trade and the wool merchants of Lincolnshire and Yorkshire.

But the two hundred and fifty exporters—fifty of them in the syndicate and two hundred outside it—thus accounted for, by no means represent the whole body of wool dealers in the England of Edward III. The forty sacks, each weighing 364 lbs., taken out by the average exporter, must have been collected as a rule from ten or a dozen villages, and bargained for by a score of small traders in the nearest market town. We shall not, I think, be overstepping the mark in assuming behind each of our two hundred and fifty exporters, the activity of at least ten of these lesser agents—the gild merchants of a hundred boroughs and market towns.

It is not difficult to realise the strong objections of the wool growers and of the local wool merchants to the King's scheme of monopoly. At that moment they were being urged in county assemblies, and were soon to consent in Parliament, to make a third grant of direct taxation within two years. The chief source from which they were to pay these unprecedented taxes was their wool. A year's growth was awaiting a market; and the demand was forcing up prices. They were asked to dispose of all their supply at a fixed low price on credit to a small body of merchants, who were to share the high profits with the King, and to postpone full payment for a twelve-month. No wonder they withheld their wool wherever possible, and sought for any other available market. Nor were offers wanting. It is probable that two-thirds of the wool supply was exported still by aliens, as it had been in 1273, when the Italian merchants exported 8,000 sacks, the

1. A. Schaube. "Die Wollausfuhr Englands, vom Jahre 1273," in *Vierteljahrschrift für Social und Wirthschaftsgeschichte*, 1908, 2 Heft, 68.

merchants of Brabant 3,678 sacks, and the German merchants
1,440 sacks. In 1337 also, the Germans, the Brabançons, and
the Italians were buying wool throughout England in competition with the syndicate and under the special protection of the
King. The men of Brabant were the King's allies, and the
Italian bankers were just then making heavy loans; and we
find him intervening on several occasions to rescue the wool of
both from the hands of his own purveyors. The purveyors
themselves would realise far higher gains on smuggled wool
than on that which had to pay half profits to the King, and
at least one sack in every six sent by them at this period was
smuggled. For these reasons it was found quite impossible
to collect, in accordance with the contract, 30,000 for the
King's use. Indeed, the 10,000 sacks actually received was a
larger amount than was ever afterwards obtained at one time
by way of purveyance. By the first of November it was ready
for exportation. Throughout the summer a fleet had been
gradually requisitioned to transport it, and under cover of a
successful attack made simultaneously by Sir Walter Manny
on the Island of Cadsand, the wool arrived safely at Dordrecht,
where it remained unsold till the following May. There is no
reason to think that the merchants were to blame for this delay,
or that they would have withheld the wool from the market if
the King had decreed it to be sold. Political and diplomatic
motives were alone adequate to account for the prolonged
restraint of trade. Economic pressure was at length produc-
ing its effects on the Flemish cities, and the rising at Ghent
under Van Artevelde in Christmas 1337 against the French
policy of the Count, followed by negotiations for a supply of
wool from Dordrecht, the rising of Bruges, and the alliance
between the Flemish cities in April, leading up to a series of
commercial treaties with Edward in July [1]—this rapid succession of events, with the disturbed economic and diplomatic
conditions that accompanied it, sufficiently explains the
suspension of the staple question. The King's seizure of the
whole of the syndicate's wool at Dordrecht in May, when the
settlement was in sight, gave him complete control of his chief
diplomatic resource and enabled him to secure the whole profit
immediately, instead of the half profit to which he would have

1. W. J. Ashley. *James and Philip van Artevelde*, pp. 81-110.

been entitled in due course. It is true that he was thus blindly sacrificing his future credit to gain a momentary advantage; but the records of his reign furnish no evidence of the honesty or foresight that would have prevented such action.

But was not Edward renouncing also the immediate aid of the syndicate in collecting the rest of the 30,000 sacks? The answer is that he had already abandoned the syndicate as a broken reed, and was seeking to procure the wool in other ways. The new and important phase in the history of the Estate of Merchants which had opened with the completion of the contract of July 26th, 1337, had come to an end in March 1338. Whether during that interval the merchants had ever realised their corporate autonomy by assembling, as they were authorised to do, to discuss their own and the King's affairs, at Northampton, we do not know. They had, however, been summoned by the King on two occasions— November 30th, 1337, and March 16th, 1338,—to meet at Westminster; and the little we know of the intermediate Parliament of February 3rd, 1338, depends for its interpretation on its connection with these two assemblies of merchants. The summons to the first, which had been issued on October 20th, before the sailing of the 10,000 sacks, was repeated on November 20th, and accompanied by an urgent demand that the rest of the 30,000 sacks should be forthwith collected.[1] But the merchants had already advanced in customs, subsidy, and loan upwards of £25,000 to the King, and had pledged their credit for another £65,000 to the growers, who were destined in most cases to receive only a small percentage of the debt; and the assembly that met on November 30th must have given little hope that more wool could be raised without Parliamentary consent. Of the Parliament that was subsequently summoned on December 30th, 1337, and met on February 3rd, 1338, we know little more than that it consented in some form or other to the King's purveyance of half the wool in the kingdom, on the distinct condition, however, that his subjects should be free to dispose of the other half to their own best advantage.

There is no record in the Parliament Rolls of this grant.

1. *C.C.R.* 1337–9, p. 276.

Its terms are only incidentally noted in a Royal writ,[1] and the sole evidence of its constitutional character lies in the fact that it was not formally repudiated by later Parliaments. But under whatever forms it was made, it clearly represents a bargain. The King renounced his claim to one-half the wool and acquired some show of Parliamentary authority for the preemption of the other half, which had the further advantage of applying to the wool of a new year.

It might be supposed that the most natural instrument for the exercise of this monopoly would be the syndicate of English merchants already organised (especially as, according to their contract of the previous year, they had still to export an amount of wool nearly equivalent to the new Parliamentary grant); and it is possible that the summons to all its members on February 24th to assemble in Council on March 16th [2] may have been issued with a view to re-arranging the terms of the existing bargain, or of negotiating a new one. It is, however, certain that no such negotiations actually took place. Five days before the assembly of merchants met, a fresh contract had been made on the basis of the new grant with the two great firms of Italian bankers—the Bardi and the Peruzzi— who were the King's leading creditors. This arrangement was soon to prove futile, but in the meantime it nullified the bargain made with the English syndicate as regards that portion of the 30,000 sacks which had not yet been exported. We can only surmise the topics discussed in the assembly of March 16th to have been the disposal of the wool that had already crossed the sea, and that was awaiting a market at Dordrecht, and the assistance that might be rendered by the English merchants in collecting the rest of the King's wool for the Italians. [3]

The King probably came to the conclusion that any further immediate aid he could expect from the syndicate in England was small compared with the immediate gain he would derive from the seizure of their wool at Dordrecht. Accordingly he directed the two leaders of the company on May 8th to take possession of it, and to hand it over to the King's agents. The merchants were repaid in money, what appears to have

1. *Foed.*, II, 2, 1022.   2. *Lords' Report*, IV, 491.
3. It is not unlikely that the King obtained from this assembly an authorisation to raise the subsidy on wool to 40/- per sack.

O

been the amount they had advanced as customs, subsidy, and loan—a sum of £25,000, and for the wool itself they received paper acknowledgments of debt to the amount of £65,000,[1] two-thirds of which was still undischarged five years later, and much of it still unpaid in 1348.   The seizure made a painful and lasting impression on public opinion, and seriously impaired two of the chief sources of credit.   It affected three distinct interests, each in a different way.   The growers or lesser dealers to whom the merchants were indebted for the wool were not allowed to sue their debtors till the King had discharged his obligations.   The merchants, whether within or without the syndicate, tended to fall into two groups, according as they were or were not in a position to make use of the King's paper.   The only serious asset of the royal debtor lay in the wool subsidy, and the obligations mainly took the form of exemption from subsidy.   But as the exportation of wool continued except for long intervals till 1353 to be in the hands of different bodies of monopolists, only those capitalists who kept in touch with the King's fiscal operations could continue from time to time to realise something upon the obligation.   The great majority of the merchants who had exported wool in 1337, whether inside or outside the syndicate, found themselves, after many years of fruitless waiting, driven to get rid of the King's paper at a ruinous discount.   In the meantime, as their one hope of repayment lay in gaining exemption from a heavy export tax paid by others, they were led to support the continuance of the tax, both in Parliament and in their special assemblies.   Since, however, the subsidy on wool was almost the sole basis on which the King could raise fresh loans, he had no desire to lose any more than he could help in paying old debts, and was continually adopting new devices for eluding the exemptions he had granted. Special arrangements were made with alien and native capitalists for this purpose, and one such scheme frequently displaced or overlaid another.   There was thus a broad division between the larger capitalists, native or alien, who were serving the King's more immediate necessities and the general body of merchants who were pressing for a liquidation of former debts.   From time to time, however, as a concession

1. S. Terry. *The Financing of the Hundred Years' War*, p. 21.

to the discontent of the merchants, or as an appeal for a larger measure of their support, proposals were put forward by the larger capitalists with the approval of the King, which claimed the merit of reconciling the opposing interests. It is the gradual divergence of these interests, their conflicts and the recurrent attempts at reconciliation that lend significance to the history of the Estate of Merchants after the spring assembly of 1338.

Before that assembly met its membership had ceased to be identical with that of the syndicate controlling the export of wool; and the monopoly which it had exercised had passed into the hands of the Bardi and the Peruzzi.[1] Although the King had promised that his subjects should be free to sell half their wool, he had afterwards issued a proclamation that no one was to buy or export any till the twenty thousand sacks granted to him had been taken out of the country by the Italians.[2] Now the wool was never intended as a free gift. Only the profit and the customs were to go to the King. The growers were to be paid by the King's collectors, and after the previous year's experience they were not content to be paid with empty promises. The only source from which they could receive payment was the proceeds of the three-fold grant of direct taxation confirmed by the autumn Parliament in 1337, the second and third levy of which still remained to be collected in 1338 and 1339.

But during the spring and summer of 1338 the King was pressing forward the collection of these taxes, and offering easy terms to those boroughs and townships that would compound for the second and third years in advance.[3] The whole of the three-fold levy would not more than pay for twenty thousand sacks of wool, and the greater part of it was being rapidly collected and spent in other ways. The growers, therefore, refused to deliver their wool without solid guarantees of payment. By the middle of July, when the King crossed to the Continent, only 2,500 sacks had reached Antwerp, and the monopoly of exportation conferred upon the Italians was to expire on August 1st.[4] On that day the licences granted

1. *C.C.R.* 1337–9, pp. 400, 412.
2. *Ib.*, p. 393 (March 9, 1338).
3. *C.P.R.* 1338–40, pp. 32, 100, 122, 123, 132, etc.
4. *C.C.R.* 1337–9, p. 424.

to the merchants whose wool had been seized at Dordrecht would come into operation.   From August 1st to Michaelmas they would be free to export wool on payment of half the subsidy of forty shillings.   After Michaelmas they were to be entirely free from subsidy till the whole debt was recovered. Unless, therefore, some steps were taken to prolong the restriction of export, the greater part of the year's wool would pass out under licenses, and the King would gain little immediate advantage from the staple which he was just about to establish by treaty at Antwerp.

These circumstances sufficiently explain the proceedings of the Great Council, and of the Assembly of Merchants which met at Northampton between July 27th and August 14th, 1338.   The two bodies did not meet simultaneously, and the order of events deserves to be carefully noted.   A select number of councillors were summoned for July 23rd.   The main body of the Great Council or Parliament did not meet till July 27th.   William de la Pole was required to be present on July 31st.[1]   On August 2nd writs were issued for payment of some of the members which seems to imply that the session was already over.[2]   The assembly of merchants did not meet till August 3rd.

The business to be done was of a two-fold character—to provide such security for the payment of the growers as would facilitate the collection of the King's wool, and to authorise the continuance of restrictions on exportation in connection with the new staple at Antwerp.   The Great Council, as representing the growers, was alone competent to deal with the first of these matters, and it ordained that all wool delivered to the King's collectors should be counterbalanced by a remission of direct taxes or paid for out of the proceeds of direct taxation.[3]   As to the business in regard to which the King consulted the assembly of merchants we may doubtless infer its nature from the terms of the proclamation issued after its close on August 14th.   Henceforward all wool hides and

1. *Lords' Report*, IV, 492–51.   2. *C.C.R.* 1337–9, p. 516.

3. *Ib.*, p. 457.   This ordinance was issued on Aug. 1 before the meeting of the merchants.   The rest of the 20,000 sacks was to be collected and levied according to the portion of the fifteenth, touching all persons of whatever estate; to wit, ten stones of wool for every twenty shillings of the fifteenth.

fells exported were to be taken to the staple which the King had ordained at Antwerp; but for the present all private exportation was to be suspended till the rest of the 20,000 sacks had been collected and despatched for the King's use. We are not told whether the assembly of merchants consented to these measures, but it is fairly certain that its consent was sought, and, since the main point lay in the indefinite suspension of the licences recently granted to the members of the syndicate, it would have been of no purpose to consult the assembly of 1337 with whose gradual development we have hitherto been mainly concerned. The assembly of August 1338 was accordingly a new body summoned through the sheriffs, who were each to send four merchants to consult with the Keeper of the Realm, the Chancellor and others of the Council at Northampton. The intentions must have been to seek another body of mercantile interests, apart from the late syndicate and its agents, that would be willing to assist in the operation of a prolonged monopoly.

The attempt cannot have been very successful, since towards the end of the year we find the King recurring to the method of the individual summons in a more violent form with a view to securing financial support from the merchants. During November, writs were issued to eighty-four individuals who had refused to obey a previous summons, and the sheriffs in their several counties were simultaneously ordered to arrest them in case of further refusal. The first meeting had been fixed for November 11th, but it was subsequently postponed till November 19th, November 26th, and, finally, till December 22nd. Only a small proportion of those summoned had been actual members of the 1337 syndicate, but others had shared in the exportation of that year, and most of their names were those of wealthy wool merchants.[2] The purpose of the summons may be inferred from the extensive loans which the King was receiving from the English merchants in November and December 1338,[3] frequently in the form of payment in advance at a reduced rate of subsidy on the exportation of wool licensed by the King.

1. *C.C.R.* 1337–9, p. 516.
2. *Ib.*, pp. 578, 614, 621.
3. *Ib.*, pp. 575, 606. *Ib.* 1334–41, p. 7.

By far the greatest of these loans were those made by
William de la Pole,[1] who from this time to the crisis of 1340
became the leading creditor of the King, advancing him
even greater sums than the Italian bankers. He was also
one of the King's chief officials. He had been made mayor
of the new staple in August 1338, and remained at Antwerp
for more than a year assisting the King in his negotiations.
In October 1339 he was appointed second Baron of the
Exchequer. Twelve royal manors in Nottinghamshire and
Yorkshire were made over to him entirely, and eight others
placed in his keeping for ten years. The King also undertook
to find wealthy husbands for all his daughters, and was
profuse in other promises for the future. By midsummer 1339
he had advanced money to the amount of £76,180, and the
campaign of that year was entirely dependent on de la Pole's
financial aid. But as the head of the syndicate of 1337, de la
Pole was responsible to the merchants as well as to the King,
and both merchants and wool growers in Parliament held him
accountable for the seizure of the wool at Dordrecht. He was
therefore driven, by considerations of his own safety and
interest, to provide some satisfaction for the claims of the
lesser creditors of the King. In January 1339, when he was
authorised to receive all the customs and subsidy in the leading
ports in repayment of his loans, it was with the explicit
reservation that the Dordrecht creditors should enjoy the
partial exemption from subsidy which had been promised and
again withdrawn.[2] The export licenses were accordingly now
issued. At first exemption was granted for the whole of the
subsidy,[3] but from the end of February only half the subsidy[4]
(20/-) was allowed. As the amount to be recovered from the
King was upwards of £60,000, this method of repayment
would have occupied more than two years, even if the
Dordrecht creditors could have secured the whole of the wool
supply. In point of fact they received exemption during the
next four years on only about 20,000 sacks, *i.e.* on an average
of about 5,000 sacks a year.

Since the ordinance of the Great Council in August 1338
the collection of the King's 20,000 sacks had proceeded more

1. *D.N.B.* Article on William de la Pole.
2. *C.C.R.* 1339–41, p. 41.   3. *Ib.*, p. 20   4. *Ib.*, pp. 15–18.

smoothly. In March 1339 a shipment of over 13,000 sacks was made,[1] and the collection continued throughout the summer. Some of the wool was taken in substitution for direct taxes, but for the greater part the growers received promissory notes that were little likely to be honoured. The most fortunate of the growers were those who managed to dispose of their wool to the German merchants, who exported some 4,000 sacks during the year, and to other aliens. The whole amount exported must have been greater than for many years past. The customs, which had produced £32,249 in 1338, amounted to £69,868 in 1339.[2]

But heavy as taxation had become, the King's needs and obligations far outran his new sources of supply. His magnificent and costly progress up the Rhine, the subsidies paid or promised to his numerous allies, and the campaign of 1339 had involved him in debts amounting to £300,000. In October 1339 Edward sent de la Pole over from Antwerp to ask Parliament for a further grant of direct taxation,[3] and at this point the record of the great constitutional conflict of the reign begins. For the previous three years the Commons had been groaning under a three-fold burden of taxation. They had authorised an annual levy of tenths and fifteenths. A heavy export tax authorised by the merchants had lowered the price of that portion of their wool for which they were fortunate enough to be paid in cash, and the rest, as well as a large quantity of military stores, had been taken by the King's purveyors and paid for in rapidly depreciating paper. They were willing, in view of the King's urgent needs, to renew taxation in one form as long as it was not simultaneously levied in the other two forms. In the Parliament of October 1339 the magnates offered a grant of direct taxation, and asked that the maletote on wool export should cease, whilst the Commons asked that they might consult their constituents before making even this concession.[4] The maletote, however, had become the most productive part of the royal revenue, and, moreover, its abolition would destroy the value of the exemptions held by the Dordrecht creditors. An assembly

1. *C.C.R.* 1339-41, pp. 5-35.   2. Ramsay, II, 101.
3. *Rot. Parl.*, II, 104.
4. *Ib.*, p. 103.

of forty-five merchants, which included all the leading capitalists of the 1337 syndicate, was therefore summoned to meet simultaneously with the new Parliament on January 20th, 1340,[1] doubtless in order that they might be consulted upon any proposals that might be made by the Commons. When Parliament met, the Commons were requested, in case they were dissatisfied with the methods of raising money hitherto employed, to suggest a mode of taxation that would combine a minimum of chargeableness to themselves, and a maximum of assistance to the King. They took four weeks to deliberate, and came to the conclusion that a grant of 30,000 sacks of wool would best meet the case, if they could secure safeguards against abuses in the purveyance of it, and guarantees against illegal taxation for the future. The ministers felt unable to give the requisite assurances in the absence of the King. Accordingly Parliament was adjourned till March 29th, and, at the explicit request of the Commons, writs were to be issued to all the great merchants of the realm to meet the King in person on March 27th.[2] This is the first instance of a summoning of an assembly of merchants by the authority of Parliament, and its significance deserves to be carefully considered. The terms of the Commons' resolution imply some degree of estrangement between them and the merchants who are warned that by the neglect of the summons they will incur the grave indignation of the King. It would seem either that the earlier assembly had not met yet, or, what is more likely, that it had not been found amenable to the proposals of the Commons. This impression is strengthened by the subsequent events of the year.

The list of the merchants summoned for March 27th is more than three times as numerous as that of the earlier summons. It includes nearly all the members of the 1337 syndicate, and over forty other wool merchants from London, Yarmouth, Newcastle, Lincoln, York, Beverley, and Norwich —in all one hundred and fifty-four.[3] If the assembly met, its deliberations did not encourage the Commons to repeat their offer of 30,000 sacks. Instead of that they granted the King the ninth sheaf, fleece, and lamb, and legalised the super-tax

1. *Lords' Report,* IV, 510.
2. *Rot. Parl.,* II, 107–8, pars. 6–10.
3. *Lords' Report,* IV, 512.

on wool for a year, on condition that it should afterwards cease. They appointed committees to inquire into the accounts of the Dordrecht seizure and the other abuses of purveyance.[1] And they required that all the merchants who had been summoned for March 29th should be once more required to assemble on May 26th.[2]

Whatever the purpose of this renewed summons, it is interesting to find the same Parliament that had protested strongly against the unconstitutional use of the assembly of merchants by the King, preparing to recognise its activities in some subordinate capacity.

It is extremely probable that the merchants were summoned in order that they might make bids for the proceeds of the ninth which had just been granted. During May a large part of these proceeds was assigned in advance to various companies of foreign bankers, who made loans to the amount of £52,000 [3]; and the City of London received an assignment on the taxation of Kent as security for a loan of £5,000.[2] In the course of June about forty English merchants, individually and in groups, offered similar advances amounting altogether to £8,724, but the majority of them had not been amongst those summoned to the assembly of May 26th.[4] These loans, or offers of loans, had much more than covered the whole produce of the tax for one year, even if all were duly collected. But the collection was encountering much evasion and opposition, and Parliament, which had re-assembled on July 9th, was discussing these difficulties when the news of the victory of Sluys, and the King's urgent demand for immediate supplies, led to a grant of 20,000 sacks of wool, which it was thought would be raised by purveyance much more quickly than by any tax. This wool was to be paid for out of the next year's taxation, but in the meantime the owners would have to lend it, and the merchants who purveyed it would have to advance the value of the wool to the King, and to pay the subsidy. The success of the scheme depended entirely on the existence of a double fund of credit, and the unscrupulous action of the King in relation to the

1. *Rot. Parl.*, II, 113–14.
2. *Ib.*, p. 115, par. 38.
3. *C.P.R.* 1338–40, pp. 532–4.
4. *Ib.*, pp. 414–423.

similar scheme of 1337 had seriously impaired both sources of this fund.

The crisis in the autumn of 1340 is a repetition in a graver form of that of the autumn of 1337. The growers were still less willing to lend their wool, the merchants still more reluctant to advance their money on the chance of getting the wool. There were the same universal attempts to evade the King's collectors, and to sell the wool to aliens, the same riots in London, the same measures of repression.[1]

On the rising of Parliament five groups of English merchants were induced to offer loans, payable at Bruges, on terms which would be extremely favourable to themselves, if the wool with which they were to be repaid were really forthcoming. But, bad as these terms were for the Government, the loans only covered about one-fifth of the wool granted by Parliament.[2]

In the hope of attracting more offers the ministry had recourse to another merchant assembly, which, if it ever came together, was the largest body of the kind on record, and differed entirely in its composition from the earlier assemblies of this year. The sheriffs of each county were to send from two to six merchants to represent each of the chief towns, and from two to eight to represent the county. Yorkshire would thus have twenty members, Lincolnshire eighteen, London twelve, and the total number was to be two hundred and eighty-four.[3] This assembly was summoned on July 27th to meet on August 21st, but it certainly did not do much to solve the financial problems of the Government, and on September 15th the fifth, and final, assembly of the year was summoned to meet on October 1st, composed of sixteen of the leading wool merchants summoned individually, and sixty to be sent by the fifteen chief ports.[4] Amongst the sixteen were three who had already taken part in the wool contracts of this summer; and that is the only practical connection that can be traced between the assemblies and the contracts.

During the months of August and September half-a-dozen fresh groups or partnerships had been formed to take over about 4,000 sacks. These, with about 1,000 bargained for

1. *C.C.R.* 1339–41, pp. 616, 621.   2 *Rot. Parl.*, II, 20.
3. *Lords' Report*, IV, 524–5.   4. *C.P.R.* 1340–3, p. 258.

by William de la Pole, and 2,000 assigned to a foreign firm of financiers, the Leopardi,[1] and the 4,300 sacks taken by the five groups already referred to, make up little more than half the 20,000 sacks granted by Parliament.

But this deficiency affords no adequate measure of the reluctance of the merchants, and of the failure of the scheme. The sole purpose of the grant of wool was to secure an immediate supply of money in Flanders, and every other consideration was sacrificed to this object. So far from sharing in the profits the King was actually to receive a mark a sack less for the wool through his merchants in Flanders than he engaged through his agents in England to pay next year to the growers. But even at this price he was not to receive the full value of the wool. Most of the contractors were already the King's creditors, and they naturally bargained that part of the value of the wool should be allowed to them for past debts.[2] The King would thus receive very little for the wool, but the vital part of the bargain was that he should immediately receive a considerable advance on account of that little to support his campaign in France. Yet only one small advance of two hundred marks arrived in time to be of any use. This was not the fault of the contractors. Most of their loans were not due till Michaelmas, and the campaign was ended by the truce of Esplechin on September 25th. Moreover, the terms they had made, though ruinous to the King, were not necessarily advantageous to themselves. There was no certainty—not even a strong probability—that they would receive wool enough to cover advances. As a matter of fact we find that some of them got little or no wool, so that any advances they had made became a part of a rapidly depreciating war loan.

II.

This leads to another aspect of these transactions which invites careful study. The piecemeal allocation of a wool monopoly amongst a number of groups or partnerships which remained the dominant method of crown finance from the summer of 1340 to the summer of 1342, and which had been

1. *C.C.R.* 1339–41, pp. 514, 518, 519, 538, 548.
2. *Rot. Parl.*, II, 120.

coming gradually into use since the summer of 1338, after the breakdown of the second scheme of concentrated monopoly, had important effects on the development of opposing interests within the Estate of Merchants. Many of those who individually, or in partnership, took part in the contracts of 1340 and 1341 had been involved in the financial operations of 1338 and 1339, and one of their chief motives for entering into the later transactions must have been a desire to recover their earlier advances to the King. Some of them, it is true, had been amongst the leaders of the syndicate of 1337, and might be supposed to have a common interest with the less wealthy members in securing repayment for the wool seized at Dordrecht in 1338. But they had to a considerable extent transferred this debt to the smaller merchants who had acted as their agents, by handing over to these agents the King's licences of exemption from future customs. Having thus lightened their earlier burdens they were enabled to make further loans, as other large merchants were doing, in the course of 1338 and 1339.

Since the later loans were made upon the same security as the earlier—that of future customs—it might be supposed that they had an inferior claim to repayment. But the King's financial rectitude never amounted to more than a lively sense of benefits to come. The debt owed to the large body of Dordrecht creditors was much greater, and their power of lending was relatively exhausted. If their licences of exemption were allowed to operate the wool customs would, for several years, almost cease to be either a source of revenue or a valid security for further loans. The larger capitalists, on the other hand, if the repayment of their later and lesser loans were provided for in the bargain, might be induced to postpone their share in the Dordrecht claim and to make further advances as part of a fresh scheme of monopoly.

These considerations furnish the main clue to the new contracts made with the merchants by the King in 1341,[1] after Parliament, in return for his concessions had authorised him to make purveyance of 20,000 sacks. Somewhat less than

1. The great constitutional crisis of 1340–1 is here entirely passed over, as it is fully dealt with in article on "The Taxation of Wool," pp. 155–65 above. Cf. also Mr. Lapsley's articles in *English Hist. Rev.* on " Archbishop Stratford and the Parliamentary Crisis of 1341."

half of this wool (8,631 sacks) was covered by twenty-three contracts made in July 1341 with native merchants, seven of them with individuals and sixteen with small partnerships.[1]

1. It would be possible to trace the earlier and subsequent history of most of the contractors in some detail; but it will perhaps be sufficient for our purpose to follow the previous fortunes of a dozen Yorkshire merchants who played a leading part in half the contracts.

Only two of them—Henry Goldbeter and Walter Kelsterne—had actually been members of the syndicate of 1337, but three others—John and William Lutrington and John Randman—had shared with them in the exportation to Dordrecht, and the King's total debt to these five merchants on that account amounted to 2,104 marks. (*C.C.R.* 1339–41, p. 501.)

In the spring of 1339 another group of fourteen Yorkshire merchants who had made a loan were authorised to collect and export 1,000 sacks; and at the end of the year the customs of York were granted to the five leading members of this group—William de Shirebourn, Thomas Gra, William de Acastre, John Goldbeter and Thomas de Lyndsey—until they had recovered advances made to the King beyond seas. In May 1340 the King took away from this group, whilst still in their debt, the customs of York and handed them over to a company of Hanseatic merchants as security for another loan. (*C.C.R.* 1339–41, p. 417.)

In the meantime Henry Goldbeter and his four partners had come to the conclusion that they could only hope to recover their Dordrecht debt by undertaking more Government business. Accordingly, in July 1340 they offered to advance an additional sum of 2,104 marks on the security of the ninth sheaf, fleece and lamb about to be collected in Lincolnshire if they might be allowed the 2,104 marks of Dordrecht debt from the same source. At the same moment ministers were anxiously seeking for advances on account of the 20,000 sacks of wool which Parliament had granted on hearing the news of Sluys and were being obliged to accept very low offers. (*C.C.R.* 1339–41, p. 501.)

This seemed a favourable moment to both the Yorkshire groups, and, in order to take advantage of it, they united their forces. A new partnership, consisting of two members of the Dordrecht group—Henry Goldbeter and John Lutrington—and two members of the other group—Thomas Gra and William Acastre—offered a loan on account of 1,500 sacks of wool, on condition that the £1,000 still owing by the King to the second group should be deducted from the total amount at which the wool was valued. (*Rot. Parl.*, II, 120.)

But the hopes of the Yorkshire merchants that their new operations would make good the loans upon the old were soon to be disappointed. The Dordrecht group had advanced another 2,104 marks, but at the beginning of 1341 only 200 marks of the 4,208 had been recovered from the ninth. The new partnership had made a fresh loan of £1,500, but the wool which was to cover this amount, and also the £1,000 already owed by the King, was only to be had in small and quite inadequate quantities.

This was the situation in July 1341 when the new contracts were made. The ten Yorkshire merchants who composed the two groups are found participating in no less than eight of the twenty-three contracts. The five Dordrecht creditors, headed by Henry Goldbeter, contracted for 565 sacks of Lincolnshire wool. The members of the other group, distributed in three partnerships, contracted for 822 sacks of the North-East Riding wool and 156 sacks of the West Riding. In all a total of 2,365 sacks was contracted for entirely by the Yorkshiremen, whilst Henry Goldbeter took part in another large contract for 1,177 sacks. (*C.C.R.* 1341–3, p. 255.)

The rest of the contractors in 1341 belonged in about the same proportions to the two classes represented by the Yorkshiremen, *i.e.* about one-third of them were amongst the Dordrecht creditors of the King, whilst the other two-thirds had not shared in the operations of the syndicate of 1337. But almost all had advanced money or goods to the King since 1337 which they hoped to recover through the contracts of 1341.

There are three points to be specially noted in regard to these contracts. The first is the emergence of individual capitalists as contractors with the King, and of two in particular—Walter de Chiriton and John de Wesenham—who were to play a prominent part in the finance of later years. The second is that all the contracts with native merchants did not nearly cover one-half of the wool granted to the King, nor much more than a quarter of the normal output of the kingdom. The rest of the grant was assigned to foreign merchants or to the King's allies, or used directly to meet military needs; and beyond the total grant of 20,000 sacks there must have been a great quantity of wool seeking a market. This fact lends significance to the third point. The prices at which the merchants contracted to pay for the wool were remarkably high. In August 1340 the Government had been obliged to accept offers from the merchants at one mark per sack less than the " Nottingham prices " which the merchants paid to the growers. In July 1341 many of the prices agreed to by the merchants were 100 per cent. higher than the Nottingham prices. It is true that the 1341 prices included the subsidy of fifty shillings per sack, which was not paid separately, and also covered the cost of insurance against risks of transit which the King undertook to meet; but even when these allowances are made the net amount of the King's monopoly profit must have been above 50 per cent. Now, it is clear that so large a profit could not be realised on part of the nation's wool unless the exportation of the rest were restricted whilst the chief markets were being held; and this restriction involved a loss of subsidy which had to be set off against the gains of monopoly.

The very serious difficulties encountered in the collection of the 20,000 sacks granted for 1341 and of the 10,000 sacks granted for 1342 have been elsewhere described.[1] At one time all the merchants were under arrest for delay in payment, at another time the collectors were suspended for fraud and oppression; but in the end a considerable proportion of the grant seems to have been got in. In the spring of 1342, as this source of revenue was approaching exhaustion, whilst the King was contemplating a renewal of the war by intervention

1. See article on " The Taxation of Wool," pp. 161 *et seq.* above.

in Brittany, the problem of finding an equivalent source became pressing. It would have been vain to expect another grant of any kind from Parliament, even if the memory of Edward's shameless repudiation of the concessions by which he obtained the last had not still been fresh. The exercise of preemption had been found extremely difficult even when authorised by Parliament. Without that authorisation it would have been certain to have failed more completely in 1342 than in 1337 and 1338.

A maletote, on the other hand, might be a very productive source of revenue if the consent of a sufficient number of exporting merchants were secured. Now any such body must be composed very largely of Dordrecht creditors who might be willing to consent to the maletote as long as their own licenses of exemption were allowed to operate. As this, however, would very seriously impair the revenue to be derived from the tax, some other inducement must be found. To discover such an inducement was the object of the Assembly of Merchants summoned in June 1342, which, after that of 1337–8, is certainly the most interesting of the series.

Its membership is practically identical with that of a later assembly, which met on the day before the opening of the Parliament of 1343. Neither of these two assemblies can be understood without reference to the other, and the proceedings of Parliament need interpreting in the light of both. The majority of the one hundred and forty-two merchants summoned in June 1342 was composed of the King's Dordrecht creditors, whether within or without the syndicate of 1337, but along with these were many large merchants who had not taken part in the purveyance of 1337, though most had exported wool in subsequent years.[1] The assembly was no doubt intended to be representative of the whole body of native exporters so that any export tax to which it consented would have a fair prospect of being collected. But what motives could the Government furnish for such a consent? The answer must be sought in the agreement made between the King and the merchants at the close of the conference and communicated officially to all the sheriffs of England. Apart from the business contract made with the syndicate in 1337,

1. *Lords' Report*, IV, 540.

this is the first explicit record of the results of an assembly of merchants. The essential points are only two. The first is, that " all merchants, denizen and alien, and all others, may buy wool in the realm as they can settle with the vendors, but not at a price below that ordained at Nottingham, and may take the wool, etc., to Flanders to the staple, paying 40/- a sack, etc., beyond the custom due thereon till midsummer next "; and the second is, " that if anyone be convicted of taking wool, hides or fells out of the realm without paying the custom and subsidy, and elsewhere than to the staple, he shall, besides the forfeiture, be expelled from the communion of the merchants in the realm, so that no merchant, whether denizen or alien, shall communicate with him."[1]

The nature of the King's main concession to the community of merchants is sufficiently clear. It consists in a promise of free and open trade and the withdrawal of the system of monopoly which, in one form or another, had dominated the wool trade, except for brief intervals, since 1337. But how are we to interpret the second clause in the agreement—the enforcement by " boycott " of the restriction of the wool export to the Bruges staple ? Can we regard it as having been adopted partly in the interests of the community of merchants, or was it merely a concession to the diplomatic and fiscal interests of the King ? In order to get light on this point we need to recall the history of the Staple in the immediate past.[2]

During the revolution with which the reign opened the foreign staple established in 1312 had been abolished at the demand both of wool growers and merchants, and the home staples, by which the earlier system was then displaced, were themselves abandoned two years later. The re-establishment of the home staples in 1333 was part of a scheme for raising an unconstitutional tax on wool. A revival of the foreign staple in its most stringent form was the essential feature of the monopoly arrangements of 1337, but the syndicate broke down before the locality of the staple had been determined.

The establishment of a staple at Antwerp in 1338 was, as we have seen, probably authorised by an assembly

---

1. *C.C.R.* 1341–3, p. 553.
2. A full account of the earlier history of the Staple is given in Prof. Tout's *The Place of the Reign of Edward II in English History,* pp. 241–66.

of merchants quite distinct in composition from the 1337 syndicate, and elected through the sheriffs *ad hoc*; but there is no reason for regarding this body as constituting a company of staplers.[1] In 1340, on Wednesday after mid-Lent, the King made a formal promise to his Flemish allies that " with the assent of the present Parliament at Westminster," he would establish a staple at Bruges.[2] It is therefore certain that the exceptionally large Assembly of Merchants which had been summoned at the request of Parliament and was sitting coincidentally with it was consulted on this matter, and it is highly probable that the three later assemblies of 1340 were concerned to some extent with the problem of organising a staple.[3] The purveyance contracts of the autumn of 1340 imply a *de facto* staple at Bruges, since they provide for the delivery of all the King's wool there; but the breakdown of the contracts, and the crisis that ensued, delayed its formal establishment till August 1341, when the monopoly contracts for that year had been drawn up and the export of the King's wool might be expected to commence. A charter was then issued, " on the mature advice of expert councillors and at the urgent request of the merchants of the realm," placing the government of the staple in the hands of the mayor and constables, nominated, in the first place, by the King, but removable on just cause by the merchants who received power to elect future officials. All pre-existing liberties and charters of the staple merchants were confirmed, and they were authorised to hold their courts of law merchant to punish offenders, to share with the King forfeitures for breach of staple, to assemble once a year in England, and to lay reasonable impositions or tolls on all merchandise carried to the staple.

Who were the staplers invested with these powers, and what was the significance of their new charter? The record of the working of the staple, which we can follow almost day by day for six months afterwards, justifies us in assuming that the company of staplers was practically identical with the forty-three merchants who, as individuals or in partnerships, had undertaken the twenty-three contracts in July 1341. One

1. *Cf. ante*, p. 199. 2. *C.P.R.* 1338–40, p. 511.
3. *Cf. ante*, p. 202.

P

of their number, Hugh de Ulseby, was mayor of the staple. The significance of the charter depends upon the fact that, seven weeks after it was granted, if the King kept his plighted word, the monopoly of exportation would cease for that year, and the trade would be open to all on payment of the ordinary custom of half a mark per sack. But as the collection of the King's wool was by no means completed the contractors would be ruined if the trade were opened at Michaelmas, whilst the King on his part was probably not minded in any case to relinquish the forty shilling tax which, since 1338, had been one of the main sources of his revenue.

There can be little doubt therefore that the machinery of the staple was deliberately devised to prevent the resumption of open trade, especially as, by one of the clauses of the charter, a tax of sixty shillings per sack could be imposed upon any exporter seeking to evade the staple. After Michaelmas, in spite of the King's promises, the forty shillings per sack continued to be exacted, though it was paid, not through the customs, but through the Exchequer, and nominally perhaps as a free-will offering. This form of exportation went on side by side with the collection of the King's wool during the first half of 1342, and as the latter source of revenue began to get exhausted it became important to secure a broader basis of consent for the former. Hence the Assembly of Merchants and the treaty of June 1342. The King conceded an open trade; the merchants on their part authorised the forty shilling tax. They also engaged to enforce the staple at Bruges. Was this a further concession on their part, or did they stand to gain by it? The answer is, apparently, that by virtue of the agreement they themselves became the company of staplers, and the enforcement of the staple would be of value to them in so far as the staple machinery enabled them to confine the export trade within their enlarged, but still limited, circle.

The new arrangement therefore displaced a strict and narrow monopoly in the hands of forty-three merchants by an attenuated quasi-monopoly in the hands of a hundred and forty-two merchants. It mitigated the grievances of the lesser exporters against the greater exporters, but it left comparatively untouched the grievances of the growers, of the home traders, and of those exporters who were still excluded, against those men included in the staple. And it made no provision for paying off the Dordrecht debt.

All these defects in the settlement came clearly to light at the next meeting of the assembly in April 1343. The King called the merchants together on the day before the opening of Parliament so that he might confront the Commons, who had come to petition against the maletote with the renewed consent of the assembly. But in order to secure that consent he had to consider the grievances of the merchants and to make further concessions. It would seem from their petitions that the majority of the merchants, whatever their views may have been at the previous assembly, did not now desire the continuance of the staple at Bruges. The experience of the past year had shown them that the manufacturers who controlled the Flemish cities were not prepared to allow foreign buyers, or even the smaller Flemish towns, a free access to the wool market. Moreover, the exemptions from staple restrictions granted by the King for fiscal reasons and the dislocation of the foreign exchanges owing to the recent debasement of the coinage made it difficult for the English trader to export at a profit. Worst of all was the increasing mass of the unliquidated royal debt. Two-thirds of the Dordrecht wool and a considerable part of that more recently seized by the King's collectors from growers and traders and handed over to companies of contractors was still unpaid for. If a substantial exemption from the payment of subsidy were granted to the King's creditors who formed at least two-thirds of the assembly of merchants, they were prepared to confirm its continuance at the rate of forty shillings per sack. They would prefer to have the staple established in England, as that would give the majority of English merchants the freest access to foreign buyers and would relieve them of the technical difficulties of the foreign exchange. But if, for diplomatic reasons, it must remain at Bruges, they requested that the sea ought to be open to all—to foreigners as well as to natives—to private traders as well as to the King's merchants.[1]

A committee of twelve was empowered by the Assembly of Merchants to negotiate with the King and come speedily to an agreement. In return for their confirmation of his

1. *Rot. Parl.*, II, 143.

subsidy of forty shillings, the King would allow his creditors an exemption of twenty shillings per sack for the first year and of half a mark for the second and third years in part payment of his debts. The staple was to remain at Bruges, and was to be organised in the form now known as a cartel. " They will take it [the wool] to the staple, and there be at the orders of the mayor and company of merchants, saving to each one his freedom, so that all those who pass wool are of one condition and agreement to keep the wool at a high price and receive such payment as shall be agreed by the King and his council and by the said merchants." The " community of merchants " was to have a third part of the forfeitures of ships and wool which were found evading the staple, and, as a safeguard against the renewal of purveyance monopolies, the King grants " that if any one by his grant has permission to buy wool within the said time in any county then the community of merchants shall be of as free condition in such buying."[1]

On the strength of this agreement with the Assembly of Merchants the King was enabled to effect a compromise with the wool growers in the Commons. Rather than have the tax imposed as an unconstitutional maletote, they gave an unwilling consent to its imposition for three years as a subsidy on condition that the minimum prices fixed at Nottingham shall be revised in accordance with the subsequent depreciation of the currency.[2]

The constitutional problem was for the time being solved, but a difficult fiscal problem remained. As between the King and the community of merchants the matter could not rest where it was. A simple promise of exemption from subsidy was no adequate guarantee to the Dordrecht creditors. During the past five years the customs had been transferred with bewildering rapidity from one of the King's creditors to another, and at that moment three-quarters of the wool taxation was in the hands of Italian and German merchants. The King might be glad enough of an excuse to resume the most productive branch of his revenue and yet be quite unwilling to see the greater part of it absorbed in the repayment of still older debts. The customs must be entrusted to some inter-

1. *C.C.R.* 1343–6, p. 217.
2. *Rot. Parl.*, II, 17, 138.

mediary who would undertake to satisfy the demands of both claimants. Such an intermediary was found in a body of thirty-four capitalists chosen out of the Assembly of Merchants who contracted, on July 8th, 1343, to furnish the King, out of the customs and the wool subsidy, with a monthly revenue of a thousand marks, and to account for the balance quarterly after allowing for the promised exemptions to the Dordrecht creditors.[1]

The significance of the new arrangement is, however, mainly revealed in two other clauses of the contract. Over and above the amount of the customs the syndicate engaged to pay the King 10,000 marks a year; and they were empowered to buy up and use any licenses of exemption held by Dordrecht creditors who could not take part in exportation. The first of these clauses exhibits the monopolist character of the new staple, since from no other source than monopoly profits could the additional 10,000 marks be derived; and the second clause shows that the minority, into whose hands the control of the staple had passed, would have the power of discounting the Dordrecht paper of the majority at a profit to themselves.

Under these circumstances the unity of mercantile interests aimed at in the staple of June 1342, and still nominally maintained in the agreement of April 1343, could not be expected to last. A division of interests between the syndicate of capitalists and the other members—numbering about a hundred—of the Assembly of Merchants was certain to arise, and as the over-large syndicate narrowed, the division widened. In March 1344 only thirteen of the thirty-four members appear to have remained in active exercise of their functions as King's merchants.[2] It is not surprising, therefore, that complaints should be heard of the evasion of the staple, nor that the Parliament, which met in June 1344, should renew its demands for freedom of trade in wool at home and abroad. The King, on his part, was ready to sell concessions. The resources of the staple syndicate were beginning to dry up. The main part of the wool revenue was secured by parliamentary grant for two more years, and by yielding for the moment to the

1. *C.C.R.* 1343–6, p. 266.
2. *C.P.R.* 1343–45, p. 225.

demand for an open trade, he was able to obtain an additional grant of direct taxation for two years.[1]

The arrangement of 1342–3 thus practically came to an end. The syndicate could no longer either fulfil the contract or profess to represent the Assembly of Merchants. Two-thirds of its members formally withdrew from the contract, and the dozen who remained under the leadership of Thomas and William Melchbourn, of Lynn, could only attempt to carry it on with the support of the leading firm of foreign bankers. For another year they held together under the style of the Associated Merchants of England till the renewal of the war and the stoppage of the wool trade forced them into bankruptcy. The King released them from the third year of their contract, while holding them accountable for the farm of the two years that had elapsed. Before this he had made an attempt to revive the syndicate in its larger form and to bargain with it on the basis of a renewal of the staple monopoly. In July 1345 he had summoned not only the surviving thirteen of the Melchbourn company, but the twenty-one who had retired in the previous year and a score of other prominent members of the earlier assembly, and it was only after the refusal of this larger body to appear[2] or to negotiate that he handed over the farm of the customs and of the once more re-established wool monopoly to a private firm of English financiers headed by John de Wesenham.[3]

From this time onwards through the constitutional and fiscal crisis aoccasioned by the Crécy campaign and the siege of Calais, these two departments of public finance which had come to be connected in the staple passed through the hands of a rapid succession of private firms. The Wesenham Brothers were partially displaced in their farm of the customs by Henry Picard & Co.[4] in January 1346, and displaced entirely in April 1346 by Chiriton and Swanland.[5] In February 1347 the King negotiated a new loan upon the security of the customs with the new firm of Chiriton and Wendlingburgh,[6] and in the following April he handed over the purveyance of 20,000 sacks of wool granted by a council of magnates to Wesenham and Chiriton, who undertook to pay 100,000 marks.[7]

1. *Rot. Parl.*, 8–12, 116–51, 148, 149–56.
2. *Lords' Report*, IV, 555.   3. *C.C.R.* 1343–6, p. 648.
4. *C.C.R.* 1346–9, p. 40.   5. *Ib.*, p. 72.   6. *Ib.*, pp. 204, 249, 260.
7. *Ib.*, p. 196.

The men who played the leading part in this rapid series of reconstructions—which clearly point to an extreme instability in the royal finances—were the wealthiest members of the class of purveyors to the King's armies and navies.[1] But they were not able to carry out the contracts they undertook without the support of Italian and German financiers; and a leading feature in each of the successive arrangements—one of the many sources of their prospective profits—was the power vested in them of discounting the Dordrecht promissory notes : of buying up the King's bad debts at the expense of the lesser merchants, whose wool had been seized in 1338.

In the year 1347 the fiscal and constitutional history of the reign reached a climax. Under strong pressure in 1346 Parliament had made a new grant of direct taxation and had protested in vain against the renewal of the forty shillings subsidy on wool, which it did not regard as having been constitutionally granted in 1343. On the top of this two-fold taxation, a council, which met on March 3, 1347, authorised the simultaneous requisition of a loan of 20,000 sacks of wool, and imposed other taxes on the export and import trade in aid of the fleet. It has been generally supposed, on the basis of a conjecture in a footnote by Stubbs,[2] that an Assembly of Merchants consented to these impositions. Strong evidence would be required to prove this. The Assembly of Merchants had never presumed to make a loan of the nation's wool. The King had, in the first instance, claimed to levy the wool by the prerogative of purveyance; and later on he had obtained the sanction of Parliament. Even the forty shillings subsidy which the merchants themselves had to pay, was only granted by them under the influence of special motives, and those motives had ceased to operate since the collapse of the staple arrangement of 1342-3.

There is, however, no evidence that the merchants as a

1. The varied activities of Thomas de Melchbourn are typical of this class. He was one of the collectors of customs at Bishops Lynn and deputy butler there, purveyor of King's victuals, one of the takers of the moiety of the wool, receiver of wool, purveyor of hemp, iron and other necessaries for making anchors and cables for the King's use, purveyor of necessaries for building a galley and barge for him, and arrayer of men, mariners and arms for the said men, appointed to arrest all victuals passing to Norway and Sweden, and deputy of admirals of the fleets in the county of Norfolk." (*C.P.R.* 1342, p. 383.)
2. Stubbs, II, 416, note 3.

body consented to the loan of wool or even to the other taxes. Ten leading merchants—five of whom belonged to firms of financiers holding contracts—were summoned for the 12th February; and on February 18th the council which actually authorised the loan, and which is once referred to later on as " the community of the realm," was summoned for March 3rd. It was composed of six bishops, twenty-five abbots and priors, eight earls, six other lay magnates, and two merchants—John Pulteney and William de la Pole.   At any rate, William de la Pole was summoned by a separate writ carried by two special messengers, who were to inform him confidentially of the business to be transacted.[1]

It is almost certain that the additional taxes imposed on foreign trade for the benefit of the navy were authorised by this council, as they were announced on March 15th,[2] and the first real Assembly of Merchants for this year was not summoned till March 20th, and did not meet till April 21st.

The method of summoning the assembly was significant. Seventy-nine of the leading wool merchants of thirteen counties received separate writs, but the sheriff of each county was simultaneously instructed to see that these merchants attended the council, and to choose four or six other merchants to accompany them.   It is clear from subsequent events that the primary object, not only of these summonses but of those issued on May 28th, on June 30th, and on August 20th, was not consultation upon policy but the raising of a loan.   Of those summoned by name to the first assembly one-third refused the loan outright, another third made promises in the council chamber and withdrew them on their return home, and it is probable that a great many of the rest did not answer the summons.   From Lincolnshire, as the chief wool-producing county, no less than twenty merchants had been summoned by name.   Eight of these promised loans amounting to a total of £286.   On May 28th writs were issued for the arrest of these eight for having broken their promise, and of another four who had refused,[3] whilst six others who had apparently not answered the first call, were summoned, along with four new merchants from Lincolnshire, to a second

1. *Lords' Report*, IV, 562–3.   2. *C.P.R.* 1345–8, p. 264.   3. *Foed.*, III, 121.

assembly of seventy-one merchants to be held on June 20th.[1]
Four of the six who had thus been twice summoned still failed
to appear.[2]

On June 30th a hundred and eighty writs were issued to
individual merchants and others, who were required to come
before the council in July, on half a dozen different days and
therefore not for the purpose of a general meeting.[3] The last
of these efforts was made on August 20th, when a hundred
and twenty-six persons were summoned for eleven different
dates in August and September, whilst ninety-nine writs were
issued for the arrest of earlier defaulters.[4]

There is undoubtedly one object of policy apart from the
mere levy of a forced loan which it might seem natural to
connect with the writs of summons issued on August 20th.
Calais had fallen into English hands on August 3rd, and on
August 12th a proclamation had been issued offering grants
of houses and lands to merchants and others who were willing
to settle there. The staple of cloth, tin, lead and feathers,
which was set up at Calais in the following April, may have
been already in contemplation,[5] and in view of the uncertain
political relations with Flanders it it not improbable that the
Government was considering the desirability of removing the
wool staple also to Calais. But there is no ground for
believing that such a project was discussed with any representative assembly of merchants, though it is quite likely
that those who were called up in groups during August and
September were pressed to take grants of allotments in Calais
in return for loans. The list of grants made on October 8th,
1347, reveals no connection between the general body of the
settlers and the general body of any assembly of merchants.
On the other hand, the list does contain the names of almost
all the greater capitalists who had been concerned in the farm
of the customs and of the wool monopoly since 1344, *i.e.* the
two Melchbourns, Cheriton, Swanland, Wendlingburgh and
Picard.[6]

The Estate of Merchants, whether regarded as representa-

---

1. *Lords' Report*, IV, 566.   2. *C.C.R.* 1346–9, p. 375.
3. *Lords' Report*, IV, 567.   4. *C.C.R.* 1346–9, pp. 375–80.
5. See article on "Calais under Edward III," p. 321, below.
6. *C.P.R.* 1345–8, pp. 563–5.

tive of class interests or as an instrument of royal policy, had been in process of disintegration since 1343. The events of 1347 exhibit it in a condition of complete collapse. The records of the Parliament of 1348, especially when compared with those of the Parliament of 1343, explain and illustrate more fully both the disintegration and the collapse. In 1343 the petitions of the merchants represent a separate body of interests consulted before the rest of the Commons; and a treaty with that body, in which the greater and the lesser exporters were combined, was used as a means of extracting concessions from Parliament. In 1348 the petitions emanating from the merchants and representing a variety of different interests, are mingled with those of the Commons and the many petitions of the Commons express to a large extent the grievances of the merchants. It is the Commons who now complain of the restrictions of the Bruges staple, both upon supply and upon demand, and of the dislocation of the exchanges due to the debasement of coinage.[1] It is the Commons who declare that "certain merchants" who hold the farm of the customs and subsidy claim, and have also contracted to purchase the King's wool, and will not suffer any other merchant to export wool unless he pays an extra levy of two marks a sack.[2] Most striking of all is the fact that the Commons, who in 1343, specially intervened in the discussion of the currency problem with the request that the merchants should be obliged to deposit two marks of silver plate before exporting each sack of wool,[3] are found in 1348 petitioning that this regulation should be no longer maintained as the merchants cannot comply with it and dare not buy wool while it is in force.[4]

The counterpart of this new solidarity of the general body of merchants with the Commons is to be found in the incurable division of interest that has arisen between the handful of capitalists who now manage the royal finances and the great majority of those who once composed the Estate of Merchants. This is fully explained by the petition in which the latter demand once more the long deferred payment for the wool seized at Dordrecht. "The King," they say, "with the

1. *Rot. Parl.*, II, 110–65.   2. *Ib.*, 138–69.   3. *Ib.*, 116–38.
4. *Ib.*, 115–202.

common assent of Parliament granted allowance for this debt in exemptions from the wool subsidy of twenty shillings per sack. And a great part of the rich merchants have availed themselves of this mode of recovery, but the poor merchants are still unsatisfied because the rich merchants have acquired from the King the sole right of buying the debts of the poor merchants and pay for them whatever price they think fit."[1]

Looking back over the dozen years whose records have been traversed, we can distinguish primarily between two types of merchant assemblies. One of these was summoned by writs to the mayors of cities and boroughs, or to sheriffs; and the other by writs to individual merchants. The first of these methods was the one originally employed in 1336, but it failed, and the assembly, which was identical with the syndicate of 1337-8, was built up mainly by the method of individual writs. The active members of this syndicate, together with their agents and clients form the greater part of most of the assemblies which were subsequently summoned by individual writs, and this element of continuity will perhaps justify the application to those assemblies of the term Estate of Merchants. It was from the assemblies of this kind that the King in 1336-7 and in 1342-3 obtained authorisation of the subsidy on wool, and it was with them or with representatives chosen by them that he attempted, in 1337, and again in 1343, an arrangement of his customs revenue which, if it had proved successful, would have supplied a new starting-point for English fiscal and constitutional history. The inherent causes of the instability and disintegration of this Estate of Merchants were two-fold—the existence of a wider body of mercantile interests outside the estate which found expression through the House of Commons or in the assemblies summoned through the mayors and sheriffs,—and the formation of smaller groups of financiers within or without the estate who were more fitted to handle the highly speculative operations of royal finance.

III.

The history of the Estate of Merchants during the seven years that intervened between the crisis of 1347 and the

1. *Rot. Parl.*, II, 39-169.

enactment of the Statute of Staples in 1354 may be briefly outlined in the light of the above interpretation of the preceding development. By the spring of 1348 the resources of the small group of English financiers who now furnished the King's supplies were rapidly becoming exhausted, and Edward was obliged to meet a Parliament in which, as we have seen, the wool growers and the merchants were united in their opposition to the restraints on the wool trade and to the continuance of the maletote. A grant of direct taxation for three years was only to be obtained by a promise that the illegal indirect taxation on wool should cease. Whether under normal circumstances the King would have fulfilled his purpose is a point that is perhaps hardly worth discussion. But the circumstances were very far from being normal. The Black Death, which began its ravages in the autumn of 1348, must have greatly diminished the produce of direct taxation, whilst it gave the King a good reason for not meeting Parliament until 1351. That Edward therefore should, in spite of his pledge, seek to retain his hold upon the maletote is readily intelligible. The main obstacle to success in this direction lay in the impending bankruptcy of the firm of Chiriton, Swanland and Wendlingburgh, which had been financing the maletote and the purveyance of wool since 1346.[1] As a means of staving off this eventuality the King, in March 1349, attempted to resuscitate an Estate of Merchants on the lines of that of 1343, except that it was to consist of only half the number of members. He summoned to his counsels at Easter[2] an assembly of seventy-six merchants in the hope, apparently, that by authorising some of their number to take over the farm of the subsidy, they would not only save the financial situation but would confer a quasi-legality on the maletote and provide some guarantee of its efficient collection. If this was the King's scheme it failed. A body of thirty-two merchants was indeed got together who undertook to be guarantors for Chiriton & Co., but only four or five of them had been amongst those summoned to the assembly, nor do they appear to have possessed any other claim to a representative character. A year later they were involved in the ruin and disgrace which, sooner or later, overtook all the King's

1. *C.C.R.* 1349–54, p. 61.   2. *Ib.*, p. 64. *Lords' Report*, IV, 586.

creditors,[1] and the King himself, especially as the truce with France was expiring, was again compelled to seek parliamentary sanction for his finance.

The importance of these middle years of the fourteenth century in the history of Parliament can scarcely be exaggerated. During the first half of the reign of Edward III all the main features of our parliamentary constitution had emerged, but none of them had attained fixity. The exclusive right of a properly constituted parliament, as distinguished from a Great Council however summoned, to authorise taxation, and its claim to initiate and determine legislation had been repeatedly asserted by the Commons and clearly acknowledged by the King. But Great Councils in consultation with irregular assemblies of merchants had continued to levy new taxation; the petitions of the Commons, even when fully granted, had remained without statutory effect, and the representative basis of the Commons, as determined by writs of summons, had changed its character from one Parliament to another. The conflict on all these connected issues had been clearly approaching a climax in the January and March sessions of 1348; but the pestilence of the autumn had enabled the King once more to repudiate his concessions and to reassume control over finance and legislation.

In view of what had happened, the parliament of 1351 could hardly be expected to make a new grant of direct taxation in the simple faith that the King would cease to impose the wool tax. Since the renewal of war necessitated further taxation it was safer to authorise for a limited period the subsidy which the King was certain to exact, and to extort in return as many concessions and safeguards as possible.

This was the origin of the "free trade" enactments of 1351,[2] which, so far from embodying, as has been generally supposed, a policy of plenty conceived and inaugurated by the King[3] represent the protests made by the Commons against the King's fiscal expedients in the past and the safeguards adopted by the Commons against the repetition of those expedients in the future. The Commons pray that, " as the tax of forty shillings on the sack of wool which the merchants

1. *C.C.R.* 1349–54, p. 197.
2. 25 Edw. III, c. 2.   3. Cunningham, I, par. 98.

have granted to the King falls in no wise on the merchant, but on the people, that it may please the King for the relief of his people that the said forty shillings be not henceforth demanded or levied, and that commission be not made for such special grants except in full Parliament, and that if any such grant be made outside Parliament it may be held as of no effect.   And that all manner of merchants, poor as well as rich, aliens as well as the King's subjects, the King's enemies only excepted, may be free to pass with their merchandise without being restrained by those who call themselves the King's merchants or by any other individual as long as they pay the King what is due.   And in case it please the King in this his great necessity to have the aforesaid subsidy of forty shillings for half a year or a year longer, may it please him to show his will to the Peers and Commons of the land for their comfort.[1]"

The grant of the subsidy for two more years which the Lords and Commons were ultimately induced to make was, it is clear, the price paid for the King's consent to the Statute in which their demands for freedom of trade were fully conceded.   There were, however, three serious elements of instability in the settlement thus attempted in 1351.   In the first place, the new statute, in empowering all merchants, native or foreign, to buy and sell freely in all parts of the realm, set aside, not merely the monopoly of a small group of financiers, but the gild privileges enjoyed by a considerable number of that middle section of the trading class from which the Estate of Merchants had been mainly drawn.   In the second place, the King was not likely to accept as final a settlement which would not only deprive him in two years time of his main fiscal resource, but would, in the meantime, if strictly observed, prevent him from offering special terms to any body of merchants in return for an advance on the subsidy.   And in the third place, whilst free trade in wool was nominally established, the staple at Bruges, in which that trade had for ten years been concentrated, was still in operation and possessed all the advantages of a highly organised market.

It was this last condition that gave force to the other two, as it enabled the King to negotiate once more with the

1. *Rot. Parl.*, II, 229.

exporting merchants. In the autumn of 1351 he obtained £5,000 in advances upon the security of future subsidy from over a hundred exporters. In half a dozen cases the loans were made by boroughs in their corporate capacities, including Norwich, Lynn, and Coventry. As early as April the aldermen and certain leading commoners of London, on behalf of the city, had given their consent to a much larger loan of 20,000 marks on the same security, but the main body of the commoners had repudiated the action of their representatives, and even brought two of them for trial at the Guildhall. Similar opposition to the assessment of the loan was manifested at Coventry[3] and York.[4] Without entering more fully into the wider social and economic significance of these municipal conflicts we may, I think, take it for granted that the negotiations of the loans with the mercantile oligarchies of the towns involved a deliberate infraction of the conditions upon which the Commons had agreed to continue the subsidy. It foreboded in fact a renewal of the attempt to displace Parliament by an Estate of Merchants; and it is this attempt and its failure that afford the main clues to the constitutional development of 1352–4, as recorded in the Rolls of Parliament.

The issues raised in the Parliament of January 1352 and the Great Council of July 1352 have not been overlooked by historians, but their bearing and importance become clearer in the light of the previous history of the Estate of Merchants and of the subsequent events of 1353–4. In opening the January Parliament on behalf of the King, Chief Justice Shareshill proposed that the Commons should delegate twenty-four or thirty of their number to negotiate with the great men of the Council. This, it will be remembered, had been the course adopted with the Assembly of Merchants in 1343, and the result had been to separate the interests of the delegates from those of the main body of merchants. The Commons refused to derogate from their responsibility as an assembly, and insisted on continuing to deliberate as a whole. The other issue was the vital one of their legislative capacity. Again and again since the beginning of the war the King

1. *C.C.R.* 1349–54, p. 342.　　2. *Bk. F.*, p. 235; *C.C.R.* 1349–54, p. 392.
3. *C.P.R.* 1349–54, p. 201.　　4. *C.C.R.* 1349–54, p. 336.
5. Stubbs, II 428, 617; Ramsay, I, 376.

had purchased supplies by granting the petitions of the Commons, but no effective way had been found of giving statutory force to those concessions or of preventing subsequent evasion of his promises by the King. In 1348 the Commons had requested that their petitions might be heard by a committee of prelates, lords and judges in the presence of four or six of their own members so that they might be reasonably answered in the present Parliament and when they were answered in full the answers might remain in force without being changed.[1] In 1351 the full text of the principal statutes enacted in that year, including the Statute of Labourers and the statute in which the "free trade" demands of the Commons were embodied, was appended to the Roll of Parliament. As a precedent these steps were of great consequence; but, measured by the standards of solid constitutional achievement, they were no more than tentative beginnings—the expressions of a tendency that might easily be frustrated.

From this point of view the procedure of the January Parliament of 1352 is of great interest. In making his appeal to the whole Commons for a further grant of supply, after their tacit refusal to negotiate through delegates, Chief Justice Shareshill encouraged them to present to Parliament petitions either for redress of grievances or for amendment of the law. The Commons, after long consultations with their constituents on the one hand, and with members of the King's Council on the other hand, upon the two inseparable questions of supply and the legislative redress of grievances, appeared again before the King to present a roll in which a grant of two tenths and fifteenths was made conditional upon a speedy and favourable reply to a long list of forty-three petitions attached to the offer. It is true that according to the literal sense of the roll the only absolute condition was the grant of the first petition, *i.e.* that the fines levied for breach of the Statute of Labourers should go to the diminution of the taxes, but there can be no doubt that the favourable replies attached to the great majority of the other petitions, including the full text of the new Statute

1. Stubbs, II, 603–9. *Cf.* J. Redlich, *The Procedure of the House of Commons* (trans. A. E. Steinthal), I, 14.
2. *Rot. Parl.*, II, 231–5.

of Treasons, were clearly intended as part of the bargain and recorded as such upon the Roll.[1]

The solution of his financial problems which the King thus achieved was but a temporary one. Experience had shown that the expense of the war which had now recommenced required the simultaneous imposition of the wool subsidy along with direct taxation. Parliament had now made a grant of direct taxation, whilst the wool subsidy previously authorised had still a year to run, but the price of this concession was the acknowledgment of its control over taxation in future, and it was not at all likely to authorise the simultaneous renewal of both forms of revenue. At this point there was added to the problem a further complication. The foreign staple at Bruges which, through the organisation of a restricted market, had rendered it possible for the King to secure not only a high export tax on wool but also monopoly profits in addition, was ceasing in the summer of 1352 to be practicable owing to the growing hostility of the Flemings.[2] If the large revenue hitherto derived from the wool trade was to be maintained some new arrangement must be made. Staple restrictions were not absolutely essential to the imposition of a high subsidy, though they made its collection easier, but they were essential to any scheme of monopoly, and the prospect of sharing in monopoly profits had been the chief motive that had induced successive assemblies of merchants to authorise the subsidy, and to make advances on the security of it. The great majority of the native traders had found that prospect to be illusory, and in recent parliaments their denunciations of the staple at Bruges and the forms of monopoly associated with it had been blended in a common protest with the wool growers' denunciations of the subsidy. The abandonment of the Bruges staple which was becoming a political and fiscal necessity might be represented as a valuable concession with which the King might expect to purchase some kind of parliamentary authorisation of the continuance of the subsidy. But such a bargain would be most likely to be successfully accomplished in an assembly dominated by the native traders, since their objections to the foreign staple

1. *Rot. Parl.*, II, 237–42.
2. *C.C.R.* 1349–54, pp. 454–5. 506, 508.

Q

were stronger and their objections to the subsidy were weaker than those of the wool growers.   Moreover, the separate interest of the native traders, more especially those of the home staple towns, would afford the most convenient basis for a new arrangement for collecting the subsidy and for negotiating loans.

Some such considerations as these would at any rate serve to explain the character and the sequence of the assemblies called together in 1352–3, the Great Council of August 1352, the Assembly of Merchants of July 1353, and the Great Council of September 1353.   It was in the last of these assemblies that the Ordinance of the Staple was enacted, but the question had very probably been under discussion in all three.   The development of their representative character is therefore worth noting.   Eleven boroughs and the Cinque Ports were represented in the first, twenty-three in the second, and forty-three (including the Cinque Ports) in the third.   In the first and second assemblies the towns represented were, with two or three exceptions, ports or previously recognised " home staples," whilst in the final assembly over a dozen of the chief inland centres of the wool trade were added.[1]

From the constitutional point of view, however, the character of these assemblies is determined not so much by the narrower or wider representation of the mercantile element as by the due subordination of that element to the larger social interests that had come to find normal expression in parliament.   The Great Council of July 1352, with its thirty-seven knights and fourteen borough members, was a miniature parliament not much larger than the committee which the Commons had been invited to appoint in the spring.   It would doubtless have been a dangerous precedent for such a body to have assumed the power of discussing the future basis of taxation, but as the county members summoned were in a considerable majority over the borough members, they would be scarcely likely to sacrifice the interests of the wool growers to those of the merchants.   The Great Council was probably summoned to deal administratively with the threatened stoppage of the Bruges staple; and as the re-establishment of the home staples would, apart from the question of the subsidy,

1.   *Lords' Report*, IV, 595–601.

be a popular measure, the King may have mooted the proposal at this assembly, especially as all the boroughs represented, but one, were included in the subsequent scheme. But from the King's point of view the "home staples" proposal was a valuable concession to be sold to the highest bidder, and he would not be likely therefore to begin serious negotiations about it except with an assembly that would find it worth while to offer a high price, *i.e.* with an assembly composed mainly of merchants.

In those negotiations two main stages are clearly indicated by the calling of two quite distinct assemblies in July and September 1353, but it is only the second of these bodies—the Great Council—by which the ordinances of the staple were fully discussed and finally approved that has left us any account of its deliberations. We may be quite sure that the earlier assembly was called to consider the staple question, but in what form this was done and what relation the proposals laid before it or emanating from it bore to the later ordinances must be entirely a matter for inference or conjecture. In its composition and the form of its summonses the assembly did not differ from the bodies with which in 1337 and 1343 the King had concluded his contracts of monopoly except that it contained, along with seventy-one native wool merchants, thirteen of the King's Italian and German creditors.[1] The possibility, therefore, that some project of monopoly was considered and rejected by the assembly cannot be altogether excluded. On the other hand, it is to be noted that the merchants summoned were not, as in the case of earlier assemblies, largely from inland wool-producing districts, but, with two exceptions, were all from staple towns or from the ports, a fact which makes it extremely probable that they were consulted in the drafting of the ordinances that established the home staples. It is indeed not impossible that the scheme in its main features was drawn up by this purely mercantile body and was afterwards submitted to the more parliamentary assembly of September, partly in order to secure a greater degree of sanction, but still more as a valuable concession by which a continuance of the wool subsidy might be purchased.

1. *Lords' Report*, IV, 596–8.

Of the assembly that met at Westminster on September 23, 1353, Stubbs says: "This body acted very much as a parliament . . . . it was in fact a 'magnum concilium,' including a representation of the Commons: except the beneficed clergy . . . . it contained all the elements which were necessary to a perfect parliament, but these elements were combined in different proportions."[1]   And Sir James Ramsay says: "It was in fact an expanded merchant assembly summoned to sanction a change of mercantile policy."[2]   Each of these descriptions is true; but the whole truth is best expressed by a combination of both.   In summoning eighty-two burghers from forty-three towns specially selected for their interest in the wool trade, and only a single belted knight from each of thirty-seven shires, the King undoubtedly intended to give such a preponderance to the mercantile element as would facilitate his bargain about the subsidy and the staple; and it is equally certain that by including the knights and the other elements of a perfect parliament he hoped to secure parliamentary sanction for any bargain that was struck.   He was successful in both these immediate aims, but if he hoped to establish a precedent he was disappointed.   The Great Council, it is true, "acted very much as a parliament"; it authorised a three years' continuance of the wool subsidy and it enacted the Ordinances of the Staple.   But whilst consenting to exercise temporarily the powers of a parliament, it showed in two important respects an effective desire to safeguard the rights of a properly constituted House of Commons.   Its own attitude and procedure were those of a parliament, and not those of an assembly of merchants; and it insisted that its legislative action should be confirmed and recorded by a parliament summoned on strictly constitutional lines.[3]

The procedure adopted in regard to the enactment of the Ordinances of the Staple constitutes perhaps the first formal acknowledgment of the legislative power of Parliament.   The ordinance as first presented to the representatives of the Commons took the form, not of an administrative measure framed primarily in the King's fiscal interests, but of a remedy devised against a popular grievance—the admitted

1. Stubbs, II, 429.   2. Ramsay, I, 378.
3. *Rot. Parl.*, II, 242–53.

monopoly of the King's financiers in the foreign staple. It had been drawn up by the prelates and great men of the King's Council without the advice of the Commons, but now that their assent was sought they were requested to put in writing any amendment to the ordinance which seemed to them desirable. " And upon that the Commons demanded a copy of the said points; which copy was delivered to them, this is to say, one copy to the knights of the shires and another to the citizens and burgesses. And they, after great deliberation, had between them showed to the Council their opinion in writing; which writing, having been read and debated by the magnates, the Ordinances of the Staple were made in the following form : ' Edward by the grace of God, etc. . . . Inasmuch as after good deliberation with prelates, dukes, earls, barons, knights of shires, and commons of cities and boroughs, we have, by the counsel and common assent of the said prelates, dukes, earls, barons, knights and commons aforesaid, ordained and established.' "[1]

From this it is clear that the Commons took an active part in framing the ordinances. From the actual provisions of the ordinances, from the demands that they should receive statutory form, from the later petitions of the Commons that they should be thoroughly enforced, and from the indignation of the Commons when they were set aside, it is equally clear that they represented in the main a body of concessions made by the King to his people at large. This aspect of the matter is somewhat obscured by the fact that the primary object of the ordinances was the organisation of the home staples, and this seems to be a fiscal concern of the King's. Even on this side, however, the purpose of the ordinances was to displace an unconstitutional and monopolistic organisation of foreign trade by an organisation which, whilst duly providing for the collection of the revenue, would leave to buyer and to seller the greatest possible amount of freedom. Viewed as a whole the ordinances of 1353 and the statute of 1354 may be regarded as a re-enactment of the " free trade " statute of 1351 with the addition of elaborate machinery intended to secure the practical realisation of the policy demanded by the Commons. Wool and hides, lead and tin must be taken

1. *Ib.*, 242–6.

before exportation to the staples that they might be duly cocketed and customed, but they might be bargained for freely by native or foreign merchants in any part of the country, and similar freedom was conferred upon the import trade in wine, victuals and other commodities.[1]

To this general demand for free trade there was a remarkable exception which has been a stumbling-block to most commentators, but which is seen on closer examination to be an exception that proves the rule. Native merchants were entirely prohibited from exporting staple produce,[2] and a similar though not quite so complete a restriction was placed on the native importation of Gascon wines. As the King gained by the higher rate of custom paid by aliens on staple produce, it is possible to regard this clause of the Ordinance entirely as a concession to his fiscal interests. But those who have followed the history of the wool trade as it has been recorded will probably find no difficulty in believing that the exclusion of the native exporter was supported, not only by the wool growers, but by the majority of native traders as a necessary safeguard on the freedom of trade. In the incurable division of interest which this implies, and which was destined to endure for a generation to come, the Statute of Staples may be considered as marking the final collapse of the Estate of Merchants as a dangerous rival to the House of Commons.[3]

IV.

So far we have been considering those larger common interests of the people as producers, consumers and taxpayers, the convergence of which, in conjunction with the fiscal interest of the King, produced the legislation of 1353–4. If we wish to understand the forces that made for the instability and led to the reversal of that policy we must turn to those divergent lesser interests which also found expression in Parliament and with which it was equally possible for the King to make terms. In following the history of the Estate of Merchants we have been led to distinguish broadly between

1. *Rot. Parl.*, II, 246–52.
2. *Ib.*, II, 247.
3. Another assembly of merchants (apparently the last recorded) was summoned by individual writs in June 1357. (*C.C.R.* 1354–60, p. 314; *Lords' Report*, IV, p. 609.

four classes interested in the wool trade—the score of financiers, tax farmers and army contractors at the top, the couple of hundred merchants of staple towns who formed the remainder of the merchant assemblies; the lesser traders. perhaps a couple of thousand, who were members of " gilds merchant " in the burghs; and finally the more numerous body of still smaller traders outside all these categories.

It was the gradual isolation of the wealthiest of these four classes by the King's monopolist devices that had led the other three classes to join the wool growers in demanding a return to a system of Home Staples; and that system as established by the Ordinances of 1353 involved the recognition to a certain extent of the special privileges of the second class—that of the staple merchants. The gild merchants of non-staple towns, on the other hand, though they stood to gain greatly along with other traders by the increased access of foreign merchants and the improvement of internal intercourse, suffered by the free trade enactments of 1351 and 1353–4 a relative loss of status and privilege which was certain to cause discontent and friction. A brief consideration of the relations between the gild merchants and the classes below and above them, *i.e.*—the country traders, the fellow townsmen who were not members of their gild, and the merchants of the staple towns, will be the best introduction to the study of the somewhat complicated class conflicts of the fourteenth century.

The gild merchants of Derby, when their privileges were challenged by the law officers of the Crown in 1330, were accused of oppressing the people coming to their town with goods to sell by charging them double tolls, by forbidding any outside merchant to buy from any other outsider or to sell except by wholesale to one of their number, " and if anyone brings into the town, cowhides, wool or sheepskins for sale and one of the gild puts his foot on the wares and offers a price for it . . . . the owner will not dare to sell it except to one of the gild nor for a greater price than was first offered." The profits that thus accrued to the gild members were not shared by the burgesses at large who could not join the gild except by paying a heavy entrance fee. As a result of the enquiry the merchants of Derby, in consideration of the payment of a sum of forty marks to the King, were left in possession of their privileges with the exhortation not to charge excessive tolls or to oppress the people.[1]

Another case will serve to illustrate more fully the effect of gild privileges on restricting trade. The port of King's Lynn was, throughout the middle ages, one of the most important centres of the English grain trade. It was practically the sole outlet by which the rich surplus of the corn-growing districts of Huntingdon, Cambridge and Bedford and West Suffolk supplied the needs of London and the foreign consumers.[2] River-craft, large and small, freighted or owned by traders not only from towns like Peterborough or Ely, but from many of the villages that bordered the Nen and the Ouse, carried down the corn, the beer, the wool and the hides of that flourishing region and returned laden with the fish, the salt, the wine and the other foreign and native wares for which Lynn afforded an excellent market.[3] It was clearly in the best interests of the national economy that such a trade should be free to expand in as many hands as possible. Yet in 1335—just before the enactment of the first of the free trade statutes—the good people of the town of Ely and other places in the county of Cambridge complained to Parliament that whereas they and their ancestors had sold beer and all manner of other victuals and also merces and merchandise in the town of Lynn as well retail as in gross and as well to merchants and to strangers as to the town, the Mayor and Bailiffs of Lynn would not now suffer them to sell . . . except to the people of Lynn and that in gross.[4]

The merchants of Lynn had a twofold advantage over the traders of Cambridgeshire. They were organised in a powerful gild, and though their town was not an authorised staple, it was by virtue of geographical position the natural staple of the corn trade of the east midlands.

In the case of Winchester and Southampton the conflicting interests were on a more equal footing. The gild merchant

1. Gross. *The Gild Merchant*, II, 51–3.
2. N. S. B. Gras. *The Evolution of the English Corn Market*, pp. 72–6.
3. *Cartularum Monasterii de Ramseia* (Rolls Series), III, 141–157.
4. *Rot. Parl.*, II, p. 93.
5. Gross. *The Gild Merchant*, II, 151.

of Winchester was traditionally the oldest,[1] as that of Southampton was commercially one of the most influential in the Kingdom.   The ancient capital and its port had the strongest interest in each other's prosperity, and they had shown an enlightenment rare in the middle ages in recognising that mutual interest by a treaty of reciprocity for the remission of tolls.[2]   This friendly relationship was disturbed by the establishment of a staple at Winchester in 1332, which caused a serious shrinkage in the customs duties of Southampton;[3] and it was apparently by way of retaliation for this that the gild merchants of Southampton began in 1333-4 to prohibit those of Winchester as well as those of Salisbury from dealing directly with the foreigners who called at the port.[4]   It was no doubt with a view to preventing the recurrence of this conflict that when the Home Staples were again established in 1353, Southampton received the official status of port to the Winchester staple.

Of the strife engendered by gild privileges between the gild members and their fellow townsmen the case of Newcastle on Tyne affords perhaps the best example.   Newcastle was not only the staple for the wool export of the four northern counties: it became also in the fourteenth century and remained till the nineteenth century the one English staple of the coal trade.   In the tendency to draw a sharp line between the members of the gild merchant and the members of the craft gilds and to exclude the latter from all share in foreign trade the constitution of Newcastle resembled that of the Scottish burghs.   The opposition to this policy was first brought to a head in a struggle over the election of the mayor in 1342, which occasioned such a disturbance of trade and stoppage of customs as to call for royal intervention.   The settlement arrived at involved a change in the municipal constitution of the kind to which the historians of continental cities apply the term 'gild-revolution.'   The twelve chief misteries were to elect the mayor and to share in the control of municipal finance. There was to be an equal law for rich and poor and every burgess whether poor or rich was to have the liberty of going on board the ships of foreigners or

1. Gross. *The Gild Merchant*, II, 252.   2. *Ibid.*, II, 256.
3. *C.P.R.* 1334, p. 435.   4. *Rot. Parl.*, II, 87.

natives and of buying merchandise for himself and family.[1]
The struggle between the gild oligarchy and the rest of the
burgesses was only one factor in the situation. During this
period Newcastle was endeavouring to suppress or to control
the rivalry of Tynemouth and Gateshead in the development
of the mining resources of the district.[2]

That these various causes of friction did not work in
isolation from each other is strikingly exemplified in the case
of Yarmouth, which presents a combination of all the factors
already considered with several others in addition. Like
Newcastle, Yarmouth had its long standing quarrel between
rich and poor burgesses about the exercise of gild privileges;[3]
and what Tynemouth and Gateshead were to Newcastle,
Gorleston and Lowestoft were to Yarmouth.[4] The relation
of the port of Southampton to the staple of Winchester had
an exact parallel in the relation of Yarmouth to Norwich,
which led to a similar conflict in 1333–5,[5] and for which the
same solution was attempted by the inclusion of Yarmouth
in the Home Staple arrangements of 1353. And just as the
merchants of Lynn tried to monopolise the function of middleman in the export trade of Cambridgeshire in corn, so those
of Yarmouth endeavoured to restrict the share of the same
hinterland in the import trade in herrings. The additional
factors in the complicated situation at Yarmouth were at least
as important as those already enumerated. The herring
market was older than the town; and the men of the Cinque
Ports who had been accustomed from time immemorial to
land and sell their fish there claimed to share the jurisdiction
over the annual fair with the townsmen on equal terms. At
the beginning of the war, disputes arising out of this claim
had to be settled by arbitration before the English navy could
put to sea. The relations between Yarmouth and London
were no less vital. In the middle of the 14th century the
Fishmongers were the most numerous, wealthy and powerful

1. Gross. *The Gild Merchant*, II, 185. Brand. *Hist. of Newcastle*, II,
155–6. This settlement was upset three years later by a counter revolution,
restored in 1371, upset again in 1377, and restored in 1378 (*C.P.R.* 1343–5,
p. 540). The intervening period was one of fierce party conflict, causing now
and then unrest and bloodshed (*C.P.R.* 1364–7, pp. 18, 20, 47).
2. *C.P.R.* 1354–8, pp. 547; 1364–7, pp. 16, 31, 90, 410.
3. *Rot. Parl.*, II, 353.
4. Manship and Palmer. *Hist. of Yarmouth*, II, 67, 334.
5. *C.P.R.* 1354–7, p. 598.

gild in London.[1]   Amongst them were found the leading
shipowners of the country, and they probably freighted more
ships than they owned.   They imported fish from the
Baltic and exported it to Gascony.[2]   They rode in company
down to Yarmouth at the time of the Fair, and many of them
had depôts and drying places there.   From the supplies thus
brought to London they met the increasing demands of the
metropolis and of the surrounding counties.   Opposition to
their monopoly in this supply was one of the leading factors
in London municipal politics.   But the London monopolists
were free traders at Yarmouth, whilst the Yarmouth
monopolists were free traders in London.   The London
Fishmongers resisted the attempts of the Yarmouth merchants
to make themselves the sole channels of the foreign supply at
Yarmouth and to suppress or control the rival trade of
Lowestoft in Kirkley Road.   On the other hand it was the
competition of the Yarmouth merchants (some of whom had
probable depôts in Southwark) that prevented the complete
domination of the metropolitan consumer by the Londoners.[3]

In the middle of the fourteenth century London was as
yet very far from that preeminence amongst cities which it
had attained by the close of the seventeenth century.   In 1685
London claimed not only to be the largest city in Europe but
to have a population seventeen times as great as Bristol or
Norwich.   In the year 1377 it was but a small city as compared with Paris, Florence or Ghent, and its population of
some 40,000 was only three times that of York, less than
four times that of Bristol, five times that of Coventry, or six
times that of Norwich.[4]   The capital was no doubt at this
period growing more rapidly than any other city of the
kingdom.   It is probable that in spite of repeated visitations
of the pestilence, its population may have doubled during the
reign of Edward III.

In the almost continuous conflict on mercantile policy
that characterised the parliaments of Richard the Second, the

1. Unwin. *Gilds and Companies of London*, pp. 38–42.
2. *Calendars of Letters from the Mayor and Corporation of the City of
London, circa* 1350–1370 (ed. R. R. Sharpe), pp. 94, 97, 126, 143.
3. *C.P.R.* 1354–60, pp. 49, 231, 357, 423, 425; *Ib.* 1357, pp. 598, 654;
S.R., I, 369–70; *Rot. Parl.*, II, 253, No. 117.
4. Oman. *The Great Revolt of 1381*, App. II, p. 164.

lead on both sides appears to have been taken by Londoners. What was the nature of the economic interests whose expansion is thus indicated, and what relation did they bear to similar interests in other trading centres?

The commerce of London was mainly distinguished from that of the lesser ports by the increasing degree of specialisation which separated its merchants into mercers, pepperers, vintners, fishmongers, skinners and drapers. As a rule each of the lesser ports was interested mainly in one branch of trade. The merchants of Lynn were chiefly concerned in the export of corn, those of Yarmouth in the import of herrings, those of Newcastle in the coal trade. But this did not assist specialisation—it hindered it. The other branches of trade were each too small to support a special calling. The merchants of these ports were general merchants, though in each case with a different predominant interest in one class of trade. The gild organisation of commerce outside London was of a corresponding character. On the official and legal side it was represented in each borough by a single Gild Merchant. On the religious and social side it was embodied as a rule in a single fraternity of Corpus Christi or Holy Trinity. New fraternities were rapidly springing up amongst all classes in town and country during the reign, and some of these, it is very probable, represented a struggle between different groups of traders in the same town for the control of the gild merchant. But there is little evidence of specialisation and the conflict generally ended by the absorption or displacement of one rival fraternity of merchants by the other.[1]

In the case of London on the other hand, the extent and variety of the import trade had produced some degree of specialisation in very early times. There is no evidence that at any time the commerce of London was controlled by a single Gild Merchant, and the origin of the gilds representing separate branches of trade can be traced back to the twelfth century. But it is not till the middle of the fourteenth

---

1. M. D. Harris, *Life in an Old English Town*. M. Bateson, *Records of Leicester*, II, Intro. lvi–lxiv. J. M. Lambert, *Two Thousand Years of Gild Life*, pp. 106–31. M. Sellers, *A Short Account of the Mystery of Merchants and Company of Adventurers of York*, 1913. *C.P.R.* 1364–7, pp. 20, 74, 97.

century that their actual records begin.[1] At that period their social and economic organisation, in most cases, makes a fresh start; in all cases it acquires a new significance both for the municipal history of London and for the commercial history of England.

The privileges or " liberties " of the London merchants, which had been suspended by the free trade enactment of 1335 admitting foreigners to wholesale or retail trade in the city on equal terms with citizens, were presumably restored at the outbreak of the war in 1337 as part of the King's bargain with the native capitalists. In the period of monopoly that followed we find the greater gilds of London aiming at political or economic power by new or revised forms of social organisation. When parliament in 1351 by re-enacting free trade again withdrew the privileges of the gildmen, London replied by calling upon its thirteen leading gilds to elect its Common Council[2] and by petitioning the King for the restoration of its liberties. But the Parliament of 1354, which authorised the Home Staples, restricted those liberties still further. It declared that the notorious misgovernment of London by mayors, aldermen, and sheriffs who were interested in gild monopolies was greatly raising prices and setting a bad example to other cities and boroughs, and it withdrew the ultimate correction of these abuses from the hands of the civic authorities and placed it in those of an Inquest representing the counties of Kent, Essex, Sussex, Hertfordshire, Buckinghamshire and Berkshire.

From this humiliating position an escape was offered by the renewal of the war in 1355. The King was soon in need of native capitalists, and amongst these Londoners now took a much more decisive lead. In a large assembly of merchants summoned by the King in June, 1356, nearly half were citizens of London.[4] Still more striking evidence of the growing predominance of the capital in national finance is to be found in the petition of the Londoners for a restoration of their franchises in which they recapitulated their former services to the King. " They had," they claimed, " been

1. Unwin, *Gilds and Companies of London*, pp. 45–60, 103–9.
2. *Bk. F.*, p. 237; *Bk. G.*, pp. 3, 15, 23.   3. *Rot. Parl.*, II, 259.
4. *Ib.*, II, 456.

at greater charges than others of the Commons in respect of the King's expeditions to Scotland, Gascony, Brabant, Flanders, Brittany, and France, as well as at the siege of Calais and against the Spaniards in providing men at arms, archers and ships in aid of the war." . . . " They had lent for the King's use when before Calais and elsewhere the sum of £40,000, ... and at divers other times more than £30,000 which had not been repaid." But the most remarkable claim is the one that figures first in their petition,—" they had lent the King at Dordrecht more than £60,000." From the full account already given of the forced loan of wool taken at Dordrecht in 1338 it will be seen that a total of £65,861 covers the debts acknowledged by the King to over three hundred merchants of England, of whom the Londoners formed but a small minority. In the ten years that followed these debts frequently changed hands. The heavy discounting of the King's promissory notes by the wealthier merchants was one of the main subjects of complaint in the Parliament of 1343–8. The claim of the Londoners that they were the holders of the Dordrecht loan has no meaning unless it implies that London capitalists had, in the intervening period, taken over the King's debt from his other creditors, and this, if true, indicates that London was becoming the centre of national credit.

Numerous facts in support of this inference are to be found in the correspondence between the city of London and other municipalities during the period 1350–1370. The wealthier members of the London gilds are found advancing capital in various ways to the tradesmen in most of the leading cities and boroughs. Grocers and vintners, skinners and fishmongers of London have given credit for goods supplied to dealers in Colchester, Bristol, Chichester, Oxford, Norwich, and Winchelsea for amounts varying between £20 and 100 marks. A London woolstapler has placed £40 in the hands of a Canterbury barber for the purchase of wool.[2] A London chandler has invested capital as a sleeping partner in the vessel and stock in trade of a Faversham merchant.[3] A London fishmonger has a depôt in

1. *Bk. G.*, p. 85–6.
2. *Calendar of Letters from the City of London* (ed. Sharpe), p. 31.
3. *Ib.*, p. 82.

Worcester, where he claims to carry on a daily retail trade. Another Londoner entrusts through an agent a tun of oil to a Southampton retailer who is to sell it on his behalf.[1] It is in great part the resistance of the other towns to the penetration of London capital and enterprise that has preserved a record of these cases; and that resistance showed itself in the almost universal attempt to restrict London merchants by the imposition of local dues.   During the years 1352–66 London addressed sixteen protests to thirteen towns on this subject.[2]

These examples may serve—though very inadequately—to represent the variety, the complexity and the mutual hostility of the economic interests which were from time to time seeking the support or the sanction of King or Parliament.   It was out of such heterogeneous material that the King during the first period of the French war attempted to form an Estate of Merchants, by whose aid he might levy taxes without recourse to parliament and at the same time secure loans in advance of the taxes.   The gradual breakdown of this alliance in the years 1344–8 was due in the main to the incurable dishonesty of the King; but also in part to a natural divergence of interest within the estate of merchants. On the one hand there was the continually shrinking group of capitalists into whose hands the King's financial necessities threw the monopoly of the chief branch of foreign trade; on the other hand there was the great majority of lesser merchants chiefly engaged as acting middlemen between Englishmen and foreigners who came to realise that they too, like the general body of producers and consumers, would benefit by the free access of foreign merchants to the kingdom and who therefore fell away from alliance with the King and entered into a temporary alliance with the country party of which the Statute of Staples was the fruit.

From the constitutional point of view indeed, the alliance had permanent results.   In spite of one more serious effort on the part of the King to detach the merchants, their absorption from this time onwards in the Commons may be regarded as accomplished.   But this was because they realised that a House of Commons in which the enormous over-representation of the boroughs gave them frequently a majority of

1. *Ib.*, p. 126.   2. *Ib. passim.*

voices was a much more effective guardian of their interests than an unconstitutional Assembly of Merchants. For that very reason, however, they were not likely to be long satisfied with the policy formulated in the Statute of Staples. That statute entirely excluded native merchants from the export trade in staple articles on pain of death; it greatly restricted their share of the import trade in wine; and it struck a serious blow at their local gild monopolies of the function of middle-man between foreigners and Englishmen. The King, who had for the moment exhausted the resources of the native capitalists, and who received a higher rate of custom from alien merchants, acquiesced in the arrangement, and may even have prompted it; but if, when the native merchants were once more in a position to help him, they were willing to pay the increased rate of custom, he would be quite ready to form a new alliance with them on that basis.

This new alliance was actually in process of formation during the period of renewed warfare in the years 1355–61. In June, 1356, an assembly of a hundred and sixty-nine merchants representing thirty-six cities and boroughs, and including over seventy citizens of London, was summoned by individual writs to Westminster.[1] We have no record of its proceedings, but there can be little doubt that the matter under discussion was the reopening of the staple trade to native merchants on condition of their paying the alien rate of custom and of agreeing to the continuance of the high subsidy which was about to expire. Whether or not this bargain was struck with the merchants, the enthusiasm aroused by the victory of Poitiers and the capture of the French king in August, 1356, strengthened Edward in demanding similar concessions from the Parliament of 1357. The continuance of the subsidy was granted for six years; but the wool trade was only to be open to native exporters for six months, and the precautions taken against the lowering of prices paid to producers show that the Commons feared a revival of the monopoly syndicates.[2]

Their fears proved to be well grounded. When the six months expired, the native merchants continued to export

1. *Lords' Report,* IV, 609; *Rot. Parl.,* II, 456.
2. *S.R.,* I, 348–51; *Bk. G.,* p. 87.

wool in defiance of Parliament under license from the King; and in 1359 a still more decisive step was taken towards the re-establishment of the foreign staple system. The Company of English Merchants at Bruges whose existence had been suspended by the Statute of Staples, was restored by the authority of the King. The privileges of self-government and the power of controlling the trade of its members bestowed by the Duke of Brabant in 1296,[1] and later as regards his dominions by the Count of Flanders and confirmed by the King of England, were the machinery by which earlier schemes of fiscal monopoly had been worked, and the revival of the company was ominous in spite of the assurances of the King that no harm was intended to " free trade " and the Home Staples.[2] In the stress of the campaign of 1359–60 these omens began to be fulfilled. Direct taxation was levied unconstitutionally as in 1337 through local assemblies, and new indirect taxes were imposed on commerce with the consent of an assembly of merchants towards the end of 1359.[3] The speedy close of the war and the indemnity exacted from France enabled the King to dispense with both these irregular forms of taxation, and the Parliament of 1361, in return perhaps for this concession, consented to relieve the native exporters from the danger of impeachment which they had incurred by ignoring the authority of its statutes.[4]

A new epoch in the fiscal history of the reign was opened by the Treaty of Bretigni in 1360. For a quarter of a century the nation had been reluctantly bearing war burdens of an unprecedented kind in the form of direct and indirect taxation. It now expected, not unnaturally, to be relieved of both. The heavy subsidy on wool imposed continuously since 1337 had been admittedly a war-tax, and should cease on the conclusion of peace. Even the more normal and constitutional grants of direct taxation in the form of tenths and fifteenths had been usually made to meet the extraordinary needs of wartime, and could not be reasonably demanded from a nation which had

1. H. Obreen, "Une charte Brabançonne inédite de 1296," in tome lxxx of *Bulletin de la Commission Royale d'Histoire de Belgique*, 1911. Cf. review in *Eng. Hist. Rev.*, XXVII, 810–11.
2. Cunningham, *Growth of English Industry and Commerce in the Early and Middle Ages*, App. C, 4.
3. *Foed.*, III, 459, 480, 503.   4. *C.P.R.* 1358–61, p. 564.

R

levied on its defeated foe a king's ransom equivalent to a ten years' grant of direct taxation from laity and clergy. Accordingly during the whole of the following decade no grant of direct taxation was made, and though Parliament was induced in 1362 to continue the wool subsidy at half the war rate, this was only on condition that it should thereafter entirely cease.[1] But natural as these views of the Commons were, it was hardly to be expected that the King would share them. Even though Edward's abandonment of his French ambitions had been final and the payment of the ransom of John absolutely certain, it is extremely unlikely that he would have acquiesced in the extinction of the wool tax which had furnished for twenty-five years the most substantial portion of his revenue. In his view no doubt the wool tax had been finally secured in 1353 by a bargain. The Commons had received an equivalent in the abolition of the foreign staple and in the "free trade" enactments of 1353-4. As they now proposed gradually to withdraw the wool tax, there was nothing left for him but to withdraw the equivalent and to re-establish his hold upon indirect taxation by a system of monopolies such as had been in existence before the Statute of Staples was passed.

That this was a main motive for the institution of the Calais Staple in 1363 is scarcely open to question. Diplomatic and dynastic motives also, in this episode as in that of the earlier staple at Bruges, played a considerable part. Early in 1362 negotiations were already on foot for a marriage between Edmund, Earl of Cambridge, and Margaret of Flanders,[2] which was intended to cement a new alliance between Flanders and England, on the strength of which Flanders might secure a dominant position in the Netherlands.[3] The proposed cession to the Earl of Cambridge of Ponthieu, Guines and Calais with a new staple was a strong bid for the support of the Flemings to the marriage and the alliance. These negotiations were destined to go through many vicissitudes before their final failure in 1369, when the marriage of Margaret to a rival suitor, Philip of Burgundy, opened a new and important chapter in dynastic history.

1. *Rot. Parl.*, II, 273.
2. *C.P.R.* 1361-4, p. 167.
3. H. Pirenne, *Histoire de Belgique*, II, 187-8.

As the diplomatic motives for the Staple disappeared, the fiscal motives were strengthened. Calais, as an English port on French soil was free from some of the objections raised against a Flemish Staple whilst it offered even better securities for fiscal control and monopoly.

Moreover as the headquarters of the army, Calais was in continual need of supplies of food, drink and clothing. Most of these supplies would come from the surrounding country, but they might be got cheaper if the surplus produce of England were forced into the Calais market. In either case supplies would be more readily brought in and more easily paid for if Calais were made a great market for English wool and for foreign wares at which profitable return cargoes could be secured. But an army would need pay as well as supplies. To export money for this purpose from England would be to sin against a leading principle of mediæval economics. If all the export trade of England were compelled to pass through Calais the principle of cash payment might perhaps be even more strictly insisted upon than it had been in the Home Staples. The greater part of the proceeds would flow back into England, but, incidentally, enough would be available to meet the expenses of the garrison and to furnish timely loans to the government.

These reasons account for an attempt to set up a Staple in Calais in 1347–8 which the opposition of the Commons, the plague and the renewal of hostilities combined to render unsuccessful. The peace of 1360 afforded a more auspicious opportunity. In May, 1361, an assembly consisting of forty-five merchants representing all the Home Staples, together with six merchants from Calais, was summoned to Westminster to discuss the project.[1] It would seem that there were considerable differences of opinion amongst the merchants, but that the King found enough support to induce him to seek the consent of Parliament in 1362. The lords were friendly to the project, but the knights of the shires, when examined before the lords, said that they had spoken to several merchants about the matter, some of whom thought the staple would be good for Calais, others the reverse. " And therefore they prayed to be excused from saying one or the other since

1. *C.C.R.* 1360–4, p. 267.

knowledge of that matter lay with merchants more than with any other, and so this article remains pending the opinion of and agreement with merchants and others."[1]

This was the Parliament whose historic achievement lay in the enactment "that no subsidy or other charge shall be granted on wool by merchants or any other without the consent of Parliament." It might therefore have been expected to pronounce more clearly against a revival under any form of the foreign staple which had always been associated with unconstitutional taxation through merchant assemblies. The whole method of its consultation and its willingness to throw the responsibility for a decision upon the mercantile section shows that the absorption of that section into the main body of the Commons, though in process of accomplishment was still far from complete. That the Commons were anxious to maintain their newly won unity by reasonable concessions to the merchants is clearly shown by their removing this year the ban which had been placed on the native exports by the Statute of Staples. And since native merchants were to be free to export English wool it might have been thought that the question as to the desirability of a depôt at Calais was one for them to decide. But that Parliament had no intention of delegating powers of taxation or monopoly to the merchants is sufficiently clear.

In both these respects the Staple set up at Calais by royal ordinance in March, 1363, was a breach of the King's frequent and solemn engagements with Parliament. It placed practically all the export trade of the country under the control of a corporation of merchants chosen by the King from the ruling class in the chief trading centres which displaced the municipality of Calais and received power to levy a new tax on wool. The immediate protest of the Commons expressed the views not only of the knights of the shires,[2] but also of many of the borough members, and the dissensions that arose between the mercantile interests in Calais itself necessitated complete reconstruction of the Staple within a year of its establishment.[3] Under these circumstances the

1. *Rot. Parl.*, II, 269.
2. *Ib.*, II, 690. It included half-a-dozen aldermen of London, the ex-Mayor of Newcastle, an M.P. for Hereford and leading men of York, Bristol, Norwich, Lynn, Boston, Coventry, Leicester, Shrewsbury, Canterbury and Lewes.
3. *Rot. Parl.*, II, 276.   4. *Foed.*, II, 719, 723.

abandonment of the scheme at the demand of Parliament in January, 1365, might at first sight seem to be the natural end of an episode closely resembling earlier conflicts between King and Parliament. But the actual situation is more complicated and more interesting. The Parliament of 1365, at the very moment when it was denouncing the policy embodied in the Calais Staple, was itself formulating measures on which a similar policy could be based. In their anxiety to check the rising prices due mainly to the recent pestilence, the Commons petitioned the King to forbid the exportation of corn and other victuals without licence, and requested that every merchant and every craftsman should henceforth be limited to one branch of trade.[1] The King readily assented to both these petitions. The desire of the first he hastened to fulfil, whilst Parliament was still sitting, by issuing a writ to the sheriffs prohibiting the exportation without license not only of corn, malt, beer and herring, but with certain exceptions, of cloth also.[2] Soon after this, licences began to be issued for the export of cloth, corn and beer, and much of the foreign trade of 1364 was carried on under this form of exemption.[3] The second petition was answered by a clause in that remarkable code of social reconstruction which constituted the main work of the session. That ordinance carefully prescribed the dress of all ranks except the nobility and higher clergy; it forbade all carters, swineherds, labourers in husbandry or others with less than forty shillings in goods or chattels to indulge their unruly desires for meat and drink; and it required every merchant and craftsman to choose a particular branch of trade before next Candlemas and to follow no other.[4] On the pretext of enforcing this last clause, the King began in the summer of 1364 to issue charters to various wealthy bodies of merchants, to the Vintners of England, to the Fishmongers and the Drapers of London authorising them to regulate and monopolise their several callings.[5] Edward was thus enabled, as the staple began to prove ineffectual, to find support for his fiscal devices in the most recent enactments of Parliament; and

1. *Rot. Parl.*, II, 17–23, 277.   2. *Foed.*, II, 710.
3. *C.C.R.* 1360–4, p. 492. A large number of East coast traders were licensed to export money to buy salt.
4. *Rot. Parl.*, II, 280–2.   5. *C.P.R.* 1364–7, pp. 4–6.

Parliament in attacking the policy of the King was driven to a sweeping repeal of its own legislation[1]   In this transitory situation the germs of a new development may be detected. For a moment, by virtue of its associations with parliamentary authority, the King's fiscal opportunism takes on the guise of a national policy. We are here in touch, as Dr. Cunningham has acutely observed, with the origins of mercantilism.[2]

If, however, we are to understand this much-discussed piece of legislation we must distinguish carefully not only between the use to which it was put by the King and the intentions of Parliament, but also between the quite distinct and even opposite bodies of intention which may have supported its passage through the Commons.

The main and indeed the only avowed intention is clear enough.   The statute aims at the suppression of what is now called " profiteering," by merchants called Grossers, who engross all manner of vendible merchandise, who suddenly buy up the whole supply and fix the prices by a secret agreement amongst themselves called Fraternity or Gild Merchant; and by a similar mutual arrangement hold back part of their stock till dearness or scarcity arise in the land.[3]   The intention here implied is identical with that which underlies all the free trade legislation of Edwardian parliaments. It is the intention of the main body of consumers and of rural producers as represented by the knights of the shires.   But the real significance of any piece of legislation is to be sought quite as much in the character of the remedy applied as in the nature of the evil for which a remedy is sought.   And the remedy in this case bears so little practical relation to the evil that it immediately suggests another body of intention.   The knights of the shires though they represented a majority of the nation did not constitute a majority in the Commons.   Parliament might indeed be said to have established its claim to be the constitutional exponent of the national will; and the Estate of Merchants had now voluntarily merged itself in the larger and more authentic voice of the Commons.   But the danger

1. *Rot. Parl.*, II., 286.
2. Cunningham, *Growth of English Industry and Commerce in the Early and Middle Ages*, par. 116.
3. *Rot. Parl.*, II, 277–83.

lest the general interest should be overborne by particular interests was not less real because it had become less obvious.

The borough members were a majority of the Commons, and, though their mere numbers were doubtless overborne on most occasions by the greater prestige of the knights of the shires, they would scarcely fail to have some effect when mercantile matters were under consideration. In voting for one man one trade the county members may have thought they were providing a sound remedy for the confusion of an evil time by a return to the generally recognised principles of natural right; but that does not exclude the possibility that some of the borough members had private axes to grind. " One man one trade " expressed in a broad way the basic principle of craft gild organisation, and during the second and the third quarters of the fourteenth century that form of organisation had been spreading more rapidly throughout Europe than at any time before or since. But the different crafts represented many widely divergent social and economic interests, and the cry ' one man one trade ' had entirely different meanings in the mouths of opposing parties. At first sight it might seem to be a popular protest against the encroachments of capitalism in industry and commerce, but the facts show that this was not invariably —perhaps not even generally— the case. It is true for example that the members of the one or other of the textile crafts—the weavers, fullers, dyers, etc.—frequently invoked this principle against some wealthy member of another of the crafts who was superintending two or more branches of the manufacture under one roof.[1] But after this function of superintendence had become the basis of a separate calling, as happened in London about the middle of the fourteenth century, the drapers who exercised that calling and who included in their ranks some of the leading citizens, invoked the principle of one man one trade against the independence of the several handicrafts. The " making of cloth " was now to be a separate trade confined to the draper. The weaver, the fuller or the dyer was not to go beyond the limits of his own craft. He must not make or sell cloth on his own

1. Unwin, *Industrial Organisation in the Sixteenth and Seventeenth Centuries*, pp. 28–37. Cf. A. H. Johnson, *History of the Drapers' Company*, I.

account. He must work for the draper, and find his sole access to a wider market through the agency of the draper as a middleman. Such, briefly stated, was the purport of the charter granted in July, 1364, to the Drapers' Company of London which was professedly based on the statute of 1363.[1]

The story of the wine trade, which has been told with an instructive wealth of detail in another chapter of this book, although it covers very different ground, has a similar bearing. In the thirteenth century all classes, lay and clergy, noble and simple, from the King and the Archbishops down to the cobbler dealt in wine, which was indeed almost a form of currency. The King and his nobles imported much wine for themselves, but the rest of the nation were mainly dependent on the supply brought by Gascons, Spaniards, and Germans, and the main concern of Parliament was that the free access of thes · foreigners to the consumers in the country should not be hindered by the privileges of English traders in the chief ports or in the boroughs with gild merchant. Down to the outbreak of the French war the separate calling of the vintner had no greater footing in England than the separate calling of the manufacturing draper. Specialisation would have occurred in any case, but the form it actually took was undoubtedly the product, to a large extent of war conditions. It is very significant that the leading members of both the new callings, *e.g.* John Pulteney the draper and Henry Picard the vintner, were amongst the chief native financiers of the King. The supply of the King's armies with wine and cloth, with corn, herrings and other victuals was no doubt the most lucrative branch of these various trades as long as the King paid his debts; and in order to secure payment the army contractor must also be a financier and politician. Under these circumstances the concentration of capital and the growth of monopoly were inevitable, and they gave a sinister turn to what might otherwise been the free and healthy development of specialised professions.

The importance of a free import trade in wine cannot be understood by those who have not realised that the expansion of a nation's commerce depends mainly upon the multiplication of small unrecorded spontaneous forms of enterprise.

1. *C.P.R.* 1364–7, pp. 4–5.

During the fourteenth and fifteenth centuries the bulk of English trade was increased not by the operations of the tax farming Stapler which underwent a steady decline, but by the bold ventures of the petty tradesmen in the smaller ports who carried over little cargoes of corn, ale or cloth to Zealand or to France, and who made their profit on a return cargo of salt and wine. Most of the general merchants in the ports had shares in one or more vessels and dealt in wine; and it is difficult to accept the statement of the Vintners' charter that wine was made dearer by this widespread form of enterprise. The new Vintners' Company were on more solid ground when they argued that a trade dispersed in so many hands was difficult to regulate and that the larger ships which their syndicate employed were more available for the navy. In war time, when big ships were needed and public regulation of prices was loudly demanded, these reasons no doubt carried weight. But whether they were or were not sufficient to justify monopoly, it is equally clear that the application of " one man one trade " to the wine business meant the displacement of the small dealer by the larger capitalist.

The charter granted to the Vintners of England embodied a curious and inconsistent combination of trading privileges. The English trader was not to be allowed to compete with the English vintners in Gascony lest by absorbing all the available supply he should prevent the Gascon vintner coming to compete with the English vintner in England. And the Gascon vintner when he arrived in England was not to be allowed to sell his wines except by wholesale to the nobility and to the English vintner. The Vintners' Company was further empowered by charter to regulate the trade of the retailing taverner who was frequntly the agent of the vintner in a " tied house." Whilst the vintner was thus to enjoy in his own trade a wholesale monopoly against native competitors, he was to be allowed to encroach on the export trade in cloth and herrings in order that he might carry goods and not money out to Gascony to pay for the wine. But the effect of this concession would be to bestow a monopoly of the export trade to Gascony in herrings and cloth upon the vintners as other merchants would be precluded from obtaining a return cargo in wine. Such were the practical results of the application of the principle ' one man one trade ' in the case of the Vintners.[1]

The Fishmongers' charter was less anomalous, but in view of the greater importance of the fish trade, more oppressive to the consumer.   In this case the source of supply was not merely or mainly to be found in foreign ports but at the Herring Fair of Yarmouth.   The charter was conferred upon fishmongers not of England but of London, and these could scarcely be invested with a monopoly of the wholesale trade to the exclusion of the fishmongers of the East Coast and of the Cinque Ports.   In the London market, however, they were granted a complete monopoly of the retail trade.   All other importers must dispose of their cargoes to the London fishmongers or sell it wholesale under their inspection to the consumer.[2]

The effect of the legislation of 1363 and of the royal charters based upon it was to sow violent dissension in the urban communities.   The prohibition of all foreign commerce except under licence, the limitation of each man to one branch of trade, the restrictions as to the dress and food of the middle and labouring classes roused universal discontent.   In several cities and townships, the authorities were forbidden by the inhabitants on pain of death to promulgate the statute.[3] This opposition was repressed in 1363, but in the summer of the following year after the grant of the monopoly charters it was renewed in greater force.   Fierce election contests took place in London,[4] York,[5] Newcastle,[6] and Coventry.[5]   The conflicting interests of the gildsmen in different trades and sometimes in different sections of the same trade led to sanguinary riots.

We know more about London than any other town, and in London, though the range of class interests is wider than elsewhere and the situation more complicated, the main issues are fairly intelligible.   A list of the various sums contributed to a present made by the city to the King in 1363 enables us to classify the gilds at this time.[7]   The six leading gilds of

1. *C.P.R.* 1364–7, pp. 6–7.   2. *Ib.*, pp. 5–6.
3. *Chronica Johannis de Reading et Anonymi Cantuariensis* 1346–1367 (ed. Prof. Tait), p. 158.
4. *Ib.*, p. 161.   5. *C.P.R.* 1364–7, p. 208.
6. *Ib.*, pp. 18, 23, 71, 74.
7. *Bk. G.*, pp. 171–3.

wealthy merchants each contributed over £30; it was from these that the aldermen, mayors and sheriffs of the city were selected. Another dozen gilds which contributed sums of from £5 to £23 constituted the commonalty—the middle class of citizens represented in the Common Council. This class was composed of well to do victuallers, Butchers, Brewers, Poulterers and Chandlers, and of manufacturers—Goldsmiths, Tailors, Girdlers, Saddlers, Pewterers, Ironmongers, etc., who gave out work to suburban small masters and who sought a market for their products in the fairs, boroughs and market towns. A third class of fifteen gilds representing the more prosperous craftsmen made smaller contributions either collectively or through their wealthier members, but there were probably at least a dozen organised crafts of lesser social status which made no contribution at all.

It was the middle class or Commonalty who voiced the discontent of London in the autumn of 1364. Their grievances when formulated at the request of the aldermen face in two opposite directions. On the one hand they demand the abolition of the new restrictions on the wholesale trade. Every freeman of London " ought to buy and sell wholesale within the city and without any manner of merchandise on which he can make a profit." But they desire on the other hand to have the restriction on retail trading confirmed and to strengthen the monopoly of each organised trade by strictly limiting the entrance of new freemen to the gilds and by giving the gilds fuller control over the trades. The minimum entrance fee was fixed at sixty shillings; " for it were better," the commonalty explained, " that those unable to pay this sum should continue to serve either as apprentices or as hired servants than that the number of masters should be unduly increased. Also the Commons make it known that they suggest these articles for God's glory and for the general profit of the city and in order to restore the good old franchises and usages to their ancient force and perfection; but in this they are hindered by the excessive privileges accorded by the King to foreigners who are the source of all the evils that have occurred to the City."[1]

These restrictions, though enacted at the moment, were

1. *Bk. G.*, p. 179–80.

not maintained.   In less than two years it was found that
they were causing the withdrawal of prospective citizens, and
as the population of London had recently been greatly
diminished by the plague a more liberal policy in regard to
the admission of freemen was adopted.[1]   At the same time
the threatened development of a rigid and exclusive gild
system was prevented by an ordinance allowing every freeman
who had served an apprenticeship in one trade to transfer
his capital and enterprise to any other.   By these later
measures which made its subsequent expansion possible,
London constituted itself a remarkable exception to the general
trend of urban development[2] as exhibited in the demands of
its middle classes in 1364, in which we seem to hear the civic
economy of the middle ages pronouncing sentence of death
upon itself.   The arrest and decay of most mediæval cities
after the close of the fourteenth century has been rightly
attributed to the exclusiveness of their municipal and gild
policy, but the close connection of this with fiscal conditions
has hardly been sufficiently recognised.   "The aids levied for
the ransom" [of King John II], says M. Delachenal. .   " have
an extreme importance for the financial history of France.
They were the first attempt at regular and permanent taxation.
They were also. . . the origin of the *octrois* granted to a
great number of towns in France."[3]   The heavy debts and the
system of excise imposed on the cities of the Netherlands
by the war finance of their Burgundian rulers checked the
growth of their population, raised the cost of living and
occasioned a demand for protection against the industrial
competition both of the neighbouring villages and of foreign
countries.[4]   The same causes were operative in England.   In
a very instructive passage Dr. Cunningham has pointed out
the amounts levied on the trading classes by the poll tax of
1379 "are as large as those taken from the nobility, if the
Dukes of Lancaster and Bretagne, and the Archbishop of
Canterbury, who were each to contribute £6 13s. 4d., are
left out of account.   The Lord Mayor of London was to pay

1. *Bk. G.*, pp. 203–4, 211–12.
2. In the case of London as in that of other capital cities there were of
course other exceptional causes of expansion.
3. Delachenal, *Histoire de Charles V*, II, 329–30.
4. P. J. Blok, *Geschiedenis eenen Hollandsche stad*, II, chap. vi.
A. Meerkamp van Embden, *Stadsrekeningen van Leiden*.

£4, like an Earl, Bishop or Mitred Abbot; the London Aldermen and the Mayors of larger towns £2 each, like barons or abbeys with a rental of £200 a year. The mayors and jurators of other towns and the great merchants were to give £1 each, like knights or abbeys with a rental of over £60. The substantial merchants and mayors of small towns were to pay 13s. 4d., 10s., or 6s. 8d., according to their estate, like the landed esquires and lesser abbeys; and smaller merchants and artificers were to give 6s. 8d., 3s. 4d., 2s. 1s., or 6d. All seems to show that the trading classes had come to form a very important section of the community for fiscal purposes." And again Richard II " seems to have borrowed chiefly, though not by any means exclusively from corporate bodies : on one occasion he pledged his jewels with the city of London and obtained £9,000; but all the mercantile and manufacturing centres had to contribute large sums on various occasions." To the loan raised in 1397 seventy cities and boroughs contributed a total of nearly £12,000, and £6,666 13s. 4d. of this was raised by London alone.[1] In these facts we may find an adequate explanation of the mercantilist policy of the parliaments of Richard II and of those restrictions on foreign traders enacted in 1393 by which the " free trade " ideals of Edwardian parliaments were deliberately set aside.[2]

1. *Growth of English Industry and Commerce in the Early and Middle Ages*, I, par. 116.
2. Ashley, *An Introduction to English Economic History and Theory*, Part II, 14.

G. Unwin.

THE WINE TRADE WITH GASCONY.

During no period of the English rule in France were the ties which united England and Gascony more numerous or more powerful than in the reign of Edward III. For nearly two centuries their intercourse had been developed by subjection to a common ruler, and the opening of the Hundred Years' War greatly contributed to the same end by necessitating the residence of increasing numbers of English officers in the Duchy, by making it a base for hostilities and a depôt for supplies. The connection between the two countries was moreover not merely political, it was also economic, and it was for this reason[1] chiefly that the Gascons valued the union with the English Crown.

The basis of this economic attachment was the trade in wine—a commodity which was in more general demand in mediæval than in modern England. The frequency with which fines[2] were then paid and security given in wine is evidence of this, while the still existing custom of estimating shipping by tonnage ('wine tuns')[3] indicates the primary importance of wine as an article of foreign trade. Wine was not, however, England's sole import from Gascony. Salt[4] and armour[5] regularly formed part of the cargoes of ships coming from the Duchy. The salt pits of Bordeaux,[6] Poitou,[7] and Soulac[8] provided England with her best supplies of salt, while throughout Southern France the salt of Bordeaux was highly regarded and even preferred to that of

---

1. *I.S.Gironde*, E. Suppl., p. 3, § 2,165; *cf. A.M.Bord.*, I, 224, 228 233, 321.
2. Riley, *Mem.* 158; also *Bk. G.*, p. 53.
3. *Bk. G.*, pp. 41, 51.   4. *C.C.R.* 1339–41, p. 289.
5. *C.P.R.* 1327–30, p. 80.
6. *C.P.R.* 1340–3, p. 419; *C.P.R.* 1232–47, p. 44.
7. *Foed.*, III, pt. i, 190.   8. *I.S.Gironde*, G. Suppl., p. 90.

257

Languedoc. So general was the importation of salt and armour into England that there is scarcely a single inventory[1] of the goods of any ship returning from Gascony which does not make mention of both.

The trade with Gascony moreover was not at this period confined to imports, or it would have been less lucrative than it was. English ships on the outward journey, and those of Gascons returning carried great quantites of corn, wool, cloth, and fish. At times even bullion was carried. In the reign of Edward III the exportation of corn to Gascony was incessant and increasing. The amount of corn grown in the Duchy was quite inadequate to meet the needs of the inhabitants, as was often the case in Toulouse if not in Saintonge,[2] Périgord, and the Haut Pays. In Toulouse scarcity of corn was very frequent, and could only be remedied by obtaining[3] freedom to seek it in all parts. Corn was therefore brought to Bordeaux by sea and conveyed thence by river. Bordeaux itself seems to have been very dependent at this period upon supplies from England and the corn-growing parts of the interior, and the latter means of supply was often utilised to the full, as in 1401, when it was required[4] of inland dealers in parts which were rebellious that they should bring with the wines they conveyed to Bordeaux a very large proportion of corn. It has indeed been stated that Bordeaux possessed more vineyards in the fourteenth century than at any other period, and that at that time[5] there were many who complained that it was dangerous to sacrifice the cultivation of corn to that of the vine as the city ran the risk of starvation amid its riches. It was no doubt because of this scarcity of corn in Gascony that English nobles and officers visiting those parts in the royal service usually purveyed[6] corn in England to supply their needs in Gascony, the Black Prince reserving[7] two manors for this purpose. In time of war the amount of corn exported was exceptionally great, but such exportation can usually be distinguished not only by the circumstances under which it occurred but also by the fact that on such

---

1. *E.g. C.C.R.* 1337–9, pp. 455–6.
2. *I.S., Lot. E.*, p. 4.
3. *I.S.Toul.*, A.A., p. 134.
4. *A.M.Bord.*, I, 303.
5. Jullian, *Hist. de Bordeaux*, ch. xiv.
6. *C.P.R.* 1350–4, p. 382.
7. *C.C.R.* 1354–8, p. 482.

occasions it was consigned to some official, the Seneschal of Aquitaine, the Mayor of Bordeaux, òr the Receiver of the King's Victuals in Aquitaine. Moreover, in these circumstances wool also was usually sent for the purpose of maintaining the King's armies. Innumerable instances, however, exist of the grant of licences for the export of corn at times when there was no military or political reason for unusual numbers of English subjects to be in the Duchy. It was a daily occurrence for licences to be given for the exportation of corn to Gascony ' to trade[1] with ' or ' to make profit of.' The King knew no better way of rewarding the men of St.- Sever and Bayonne than to grant[2] them a quantity of corn. The need of Gascony was made the ground[3] for granting pardon to many who exported corn to the Duchy contrary to general prohibition; and usually, when prohibition was made against all exportation, exception[4] was allowed in the case of Gascony. In the latter years of the reign a larger normal exportation was necessitated by the devastation of Gascony by the French, the Count of Armagnac, and the English themselves, but the exportation of corn had always been profitable, and in periods of famine very extensive, as in 1334, when seven merchants received licence[5] to export 52,000 quarters, and in 1347 when ships bound to Gascony with corn were ordered[6] back to London owing to a scarcity having arisen in the city. French[7] merchants carried on a considerable trade in victualling the Duchy, while English merchants constantly sought to increase their gains by taking out corn[8] in the same ships in which they hoped to bring back wine.

Besides corn Gascony received from England large quantities of herrings and of the dried fish of Cornwall and Devon. As in the case of corn, exporters of these were required to give security that they would not be taken to hostile ports. This trade was in danger of being destroyed in 1364 by the policy of restricting merchants to one trade

---

1. *C.P.R.* 1330–4, pp. 514, 544.   2. *C.C.R.* 1337–9, p. 372.
3. *C.P.R.* 1350–4, p. 313.
4. *Ib.* 1343–5, p. 186; *C.C.R.* 1346–9, p. 281.
5. *C.P.R.* 1330–4, p. 539.   6. *C.C.R.* 1346–9, p. 307.
7. *Ib.*, 1327–30, p. 186.   8. *C.P.R.* 1345–8, p. 291.
9. *Ib.*, 1361–4, p. 496.

S

only. It was however preserved by exception [1] being made in the case of the merchant vintners of Gascony who in the words of the charter were allowed ' to meddle in the craft of the fishmongers ' so that they might bring herring and take it to their own country, the exportation of money being thus avoided.

Wool, cloth, and hides [2] as well as victuals were constantly exported to Gascony. In the early part of the reign of Edward III there was a good market for wool in the Duchy, and it was often sent by the King to finance [3] his affairs in those parts. Complaint was on one occasion made that the whole of Aquitaine was in danger of subjection to an alien power through delay in sending wool.[4] Such wool was usually '' the King's wool ''[5] and free from custom and subsidy. At one time there existed in the Duchy a cloth making industry, and records survive of a grant [6] made in 1236 by Henry III to Bonafusus de Sancta Columba, citizen of Bordeaux, of a monopoly of cloth making in that city. In the reign of Edward III this industry nearly died out, and by 1360 the exportation of wool was largely superseded by that of cloth. This branch of trade suffered however from unfortunate hindrances. In 1373 there arose a dispute [7] between English cloth merchants and the customs officials of Gascony concerning the true standard of measure. The location of the staple at Calais in 1363 was also a serious if temporary hindrance. It necessitated either the taking of wool or cloth first to Calais by the seller and thence by the purchaser to Gascony, or else the procuring of special license to take it direct. To the merchants of Ireland and the West of England this was ruinous as not only demanding an unnecessary and lengthy voyage to Calais but exposing them to great peril in the Channel, where piracy was rife in an age of almost continuous warfare. In 1364 the merchants of Drogheda and Waterford

1. *C.C.R.* 1364–8, pp. 74–5.   2. *Ib.* 1343–6, p. 22.
3. *Ib.* 1339–41, pp. 34, 68.   4. *Ib.* 1339–41, p. 63.
5. *Ib.*, p. 69.   6. *C.P.R.* 1232–47, p. 138.
7. *A.M.Bord.*, I, 374.

complained[1] that they were obliged to take their wool to Calais although there were in that place no commodities which they wished to bring to their own country. They were therefore obliged to take a cargo thence to Gascony, thus paying double freights for their imports. Exception was made in their case,[1] as also in that of the Gascons,[2] who received permission to export herrings and woollen cloth direct to the value of the wines they imported. As in 1348, the year succeeding the first location of the Staple in Calais, so in 1364, the year succeeding the second location the records contain a great number of special[3] licenses for the exportation of wool and cloth direct to Gascony from the ports of Cornwall, Devon, Essex, Suffolk, and Yorkshire. In the same year the general licence which had been accorded to Hull [4] in 1363 was extended to Bristol[5] for one year, it being expressly stipulated that wine should be imported to the value of the wool, cloth, and other merchandise thus exported. The number of such licences and the great quantity of cloth which they exempted from the application of the ordinances of the Staple are themselves evidence of the magnitude of the normal trade with Gascony both as regards wool, cloth, and wine.

A branch of trade so profitable as that between England and Gascony naturally engaged the attention of traders of many different types and nationalities. English, Gascon, French, Flemish, and Spanish merchants as well as Italians of Asti, Piacenza, and Chieri, and the merchants of Italian banking societies like the Bardi, Peruzzi, and Frescobaldi, found in it profitable occupation.[6] The English Kings moreover interested themselves in the trade, perhaps more deeply than all these, and indeed utilised their services in their own behalf. The demands of the royal household and retinue for wine were large in normal times, but the needs of the Crown were enormously augmented by war, and in this reign war was almost incessant. In the satisfaction of the royal demand officials and merchants of many different types were

---

1. *Foed.*, R. III, pt. ii, 732; *C.C.R.* 1364–8, p. 8.
2. *Ib.* 1360–4, p. 542.
3. *C.P.R.* 1348–50, pp. 135, 193, etc.; *Ib.* 1361–4, p. 496, et seq.
4. *C.C.R.* 1360–4, p. 475.   5. *C.P.R.*, 1361–4, 485.
6. *Ib.* 1338–40, p. 19; *Ib.*, 1334–8, pp. 47, 349.

employed, but of these the one most fully devoted to the work was the King's Butler, known previous to 1319 as the King's Chamberlain or Taker of Wines. It was essential to the person holding this office not only that he should be a man of marked business capacity and knowledge of the wine trade but that he should be in a position to allow the King considerable credit. Hence the office was held not infrequently by wealthy vintners. Thus in the reign of Edward I Gregory de Rokesle, who was King's Butler, and eight times Mayor of London, if not a vintner at least dealt[1] in wines, while William Trente [2] and Arnold Micol,[3] who held the same office later were merchant vintners of Gascony, the former a native and burgess of Puyguilhem, the latter a native of Bazas and burgess of Bordeaux. In the reign of Edward III Henry[4] Picard, who was the King's Butler, and John Stodeye, his deputy, were both active and influential vintners, and great creditors of the King. Although the King obtained large quantities of wine by the right of prisage, no small amount was obtained by the purchases of the Butler at home and in Gascony. In the early years of the reign the royal credit, though as a whole poor, with Gascon merchants was fairly good as a consequence of the repayment,[5] during the Regency, of debts contracted by Edward I and his successor with the communities and merchants of Bourg, Blaye, St.-Sever, St.-Quitterie, Bordeaux and other Gascon towns. Moreover during these years the new purchases were paid for and accordingly were made with facility. Very shortly however after the young King assumed personal control, financial difficulties supervened, the royal credit declined, and the Butler's duties became more difficult. Immediate payment for purchases of wines at once became less frequent, and there arose instead the practice of making assignments upon the issues of customs in various ports. The outbreak of war and the consequent increase in the liabilities of the Crown rendered this mode of payment even less satisfactory than before, great as its disadvantages then were. Assignments were made upon issues already assigned, and merchants were often compelled to wait[6] long periods before they could even begin to

1. *Bk. A.*, pp. 39, 82.　　　　2. *Ib.*, p. 128.
3. *C.P.R.* 1340–3, p. 173.　　4. *Ib.* 1358–66, pp. 231, 272.
5. *C.C.R.* 1330–3, p. 78.　　　6. *C.P.R.* 1343–5, p. 383

realise on the grants they had received. Frequently they were 'amoved' from the customs after receiving only part satisfaction for their debts, and the issues were assigned to more pressing creditors. In 1345, for example, a debt of £750. 6s. 10¾d., which the King had incurred by purchases of wine from certain Gascons was duly acknowledged. Payment was promised, together with £100 'beyond the sum due,' 'in consideration of the loss and damage sustained in the long prosecution of payment.' The whole sum was to be paid by an assignment upon the issues of the custom of two shillings per tun due to the Crown upon wines imported by aliens, it being granted that £360 was to be raised in the port of London. More than three years later no[1] payment had been made, and in 1352 there was still wanting[2] to the sum appointed to be collected in London £51 17s. od. The case of these merchants is little worse than that of the majority of Gascons who sold to the King after the earliest years of the reign, and sufficiently illustrates the difficulty of realizing on an assignment. Another, and somewhat satisfactory means of satisfying the King's Gascon creditors, was the practice of making grants[3] of wool or cloth, with or without the obligation to take it to Calais or the Flemish Staple before exporting to Gascony. Unable to obtain wine by just purchase, the Butler had in 1339 made unjust prisage, with the result that Gascons began to absent themselves from the country and the royal intervention[4] was required. The effect of this treatment of the Gascon merchants was to bring to an early close their dealings with the King and his ministers in England. The increased demands occasioned by the war received no response in this quarter, and there is evidence of very few purchases made by the King's Butler from Gascons in England after 1345.

Whenever he wished to supplement the supplies obtained by prisage the Butler was compelled to make purchases at the source of supplies in Gascony usually out of his own

1. *C.C.R.* 1346–9, p. 464.   2. *Ib.* 1349–54, p. 329.
3. *Ib.* 1343–6, p. 22.   4. *Ib.* 1339–40, p. 290.

resources.   This was also the means adopted by Picard[1] in 1356, while Arnold Micol[2] and John de Wesenham,[3] when holding this office, exported great quantities of corn for the purchase of wine for the King.   Necessity compelled them to have recourse to this method so frequently that the Butlers had deputies[4] in the Duchy who were often Gascons and who procured wine on their own[5] or the Butler's credit.

Beside the Butler and his deputies there were also officials of a much more exalted rank who rendered valuable service to the King in this respect.   These were the Seneschal of Gascony and the Constable of Bordeaux.   Thus Anthony de Pessaigne,[6] Seneschal of Gascony under Edward II, was his creditor to the extent of £5,288, 22d. for the purveyance of corn and wine and for other expenses incurred at the time of the war with Scotland.   The Constable[7] of Bordeaux regularly purchased wine in Gascony, paying for both the wine and its carriage from the issues of the Duchy, from which source the purveyances of the Butler also were largely financed.   As these officials in Gascony were able to make extensive purchases, without the intervention of a middleman, and as such wine was free[8] of all customs, this became the usual means of procuring wine for the King when required in large quantities, as in the time of war and for the coronation feast.[9]

Private merchants were also engaged in the work of supplying the King's demand for wine and their professional knowledge was utilised by their being sent to Gascony for this purpose.   Sometimes their engagement was very temporary, but often their connection with the King's service was closer, and they appear in the records under the title of King's merchants, and many of these were Gascons.   They were not mere ship-masters, but merchants, and often employed foreign[10]ships in their affairs.   While serving the King they frequently entered into transactions for themselves,

1. *C.P.R.* 1354-8, p. 384.   2. *Ib.* 1330-4, Aug. 20 1333.
3. *Ib.*, 1345-8, p. 376; *Ib.*, 1348-50, p. 469.
4. *Bk. D.*, pp. 49, 227.
5. *C.P.R.* 1340-3, pp. 173, 274; *Bk. C.*, p. 153; *Bk. D.*, p. 236.
6. *C.P.R.* Oct. 16 1331.
7. *C.C.R.* 1333-7, p. 287; *C.P.R.* 1330-4, p. 23.
8. Michel, *Hist. Bordeaux*, I, 171-2.   9. *Foed*, II, 7.
10. *C.C.R.* 1341-3, p. 154.

part of the ship's freight being the King's, part their own.[1]
Like the Butler they were often the King's creditors,[2] paying
for his wine as well as their own, and recovering their outlay
with an additional sum upon or after the delivery of their
cargo. Moreover at need they advanced[3] money to the King
so that debts due to other merchants might be paid off. The
activities of King's merchants in the wine trade seem to have
ceased after the early years of the reign, and the King became
almost wholly dependent for his supply of wine upon the
Butler and his deputies and officials of the Crown who were
engaged in the work of administration in Aquitaine.

In securing a supply of salt[4] and in its sale the King had
also an interest. The salt pit of La Bay in Poitou was his,
and the entire sale of salt in that district was in 1349 strictly
reserved.[5] as a Crown monopoly under the administration of
the Earl of Lancaster, who was then " the King's captain " in
those parts. The salt pit of Bordeaux, which had been in the
possession of the Crown in the time of Henry III[6] was given[7]
in 1342 to John de Grailly, an influential Gascon nobleman, a
gift expressly designed to retain for the Crown his services in
the wars. So important were these pits as the sources of the
best supplies of this commodity that the conditions under
which they were regulated were constantly proclaimed in the
city of London.

Other noblemen in like manner received valuable trading
privileges. Thus Bernard Ezii[8], the Lord of Albret, and the
Earl of Lancaster[9] himself received on occasion preferential
treatment at the hands of the customs officials, the former
receiving exemption from the custom of two shillings per tun
on the wines of aliens, the latter from the subsidy of forty
pence per tun. Privileges however were scarcely needed to
induce the nobility, both Gascon and English, to engage in
the wine trade. Self-interest commended it to those of
Gascony whose estates produced wine in excess of their needs,
and they are frequently mentioned as dealing in company with

1. *C.P.R.* 1327–30, p. 212.
2. *Ib.* 1340–3, p. 274.
3. *C.C.R.* 1341–3, p. 190.
4. *C.P.R.* 1327–30, p. 212.
5. *Foed.*, III, pt. i, 190.
6. *C.P.R.* 1232–47, p. 44.
7. *Ib.* 1340–3, p. 419.
8. *Ib.* 1350–4, p. 241..
9. *C.C.R.* 1349–54, p. 288.

merchants[1] of Bordeaux.   English nobles upon whom lay the maintenance of a large household and retinue were also moved to commercial activity by reasons of economy.   These could not afford any more than the King to depend for their regular supplies on the merchant vintners and taverners of England, and though they frequently purchased from Gascon importers,[2] they had their own merchants, and their butlers visited Gascony with a view to procuring supplies cheaply. Thus Roger Mortimer,[3] Earl of March, had in his service several merchants, while early in the reign the King's uncle, the Earl of Kent,[4] sought supplies of salt and wine in company with the King, exporting goods for their purchase in the ships of Thomas de Binedon, King's merchant.   In 1348 the men and merchants of Queen Philippa at Galway[5] received protection for two years with license to trade in Gascony and other parts of the King's dominions.

The trade between England and Gascony moreover was not confined to the laity.   Gascon ecclesiastics found the English market for wines highly convenient for disposing of the surplus produce of the estates of the Church.   Thus the Archbishop of Bordeaux,[6] the Bishop of Agen, and the Bishop of Saintes[7] all made sales of wines to English merchants, while in the reign of Edward I the Archdeacon of Aunis,[8] in the bishopric of Saintes, maintained a merchant trading in his behalf in England.   So extensively did ecclesiastics trade that it is no surprise to learn that in Gascony wines coming from the estates of the Church enjoyed special exemptions,[9] though the same scarcely appears to have been true of the wine of individual[10] clergy.   As regards salt, the Archbishop of Bordeaux and the Prior of Soulac had a joint[11] interest in the salt pans of Soulac and sold to English merchants.   The Chancellor of St. Patrick's, Dublin,[12] took out corn to Gascony for commercial purposes, while papal nuncios[13] are known to have availed themselves of their stay in England in the business of the papacy in obtaining

1. *Ib.* 1279–88, p. 127.
2. *Bk. C.*, p. 189; *C.P.R.* 1258–66, p. 258.
3. *Ib.* 1327–30, p. 513.
4. *Ib.*, p. 212.
5. *Ib.* 1348–50, p. 150.
6. *I.S. Gironde*, G. Suppl., p. 122.
7. *C.C.R.* 1360–4, p. 408.
8. *Bk. A.*, p. 176.
9. *I.S.Gironde*, G. Suppl., p. 1,561.
10. *A.M.Bord.*, I, 152.
11. *I.S.Gironde*, G. Suppl., p. 90.
12. *C.P.R.* 1345–8, p. 403.
1.3 *Ib.* 1334–8, p. 568.

royal licence to send servants to the Duchy for wine. The activities of the clergy did not end, however, with the satisfaction of their wants or with the wholesale tradè. In Bordeaux the Archbishop and clergy of St. André and St. Seurin sought and obtained [1a]from the Earl of Lancaster permission to sell in tavern wines obtained from their own domains in that diocese.

From these facts it is clear that the wine trade was carried on to a surprising extent by officials, nobles, and ecclesiastics. Especially was this the case in the thirteenth century and among Englishmen, for the free merchants class emerged but slowly until the latter half of the reign of Edward I. Occasional instances of English merchants trading in Gascony are indeed to be found, as the men of Winchelsea and Shoreham [1] in 1265, but for the most part such activity was limited to men who also had a public character, as Rokesle the Chamberlain and Henry le Waleys,[2] who was Mayor of London and of Bordeaux in consecutive years (A.D. 1274, 1275). Of those whose activities were purely commercial the first to trade extensively were the Gascons, as is abundantly proved by the large number of recognisances for sums owed by Londoners to Gascons in the early part of the reign of Edward I, while there is very little contemporary mention of the English dealing except as taverners. The presence of Gascons of Bordeaux, Bayonne, Bazas, Langon, and Libourne was one of the most marked features of thirteenth century London, while the merchants of La Réole frequented one district so greatly as to earn for it the name [3] of their own town. One Gascon at least, William Trente, a native of Bergerac, received the office of Gauger of Wines in England and Ireland for life, and rose to eminence as the King's Chamberlain, Taker of Wines and Coroner in the City, alderman and member of Parliament.[4] In other parts of the kingdom also Gascons were· to be found. Thus there was Pierre la Gride, merchant of Bordeaux, who was a burgess of Melton, John Frembaud, citizen of Bordeaux, and townsman of Carnarvon, and John de London, of Bordeaux, who held the freedom of Southampton.[5] They did not, however, receive

1a. *A.M.Bord.*, I, 289.   2. *Ib.*, p. 519.
1. *C.P.R.* 1258–66, p. 477.   3. *Cal. Wills*, I, 153n.
4. *C.P.R.* 1307–13, pp. 16, 109; *Bk. B.*, p. 190; *Bk. E.*, p. 54.
5. Michel, *op. cit.*, I, 187; and *C.P.R.* 1292–1301, pp. 156, 398.

admission to the citizenship of London in the reign of Edward I, though it is clear from the difficulty with which they were brought to submit to the restricted liberties of alien traders that they had enjoyed some of its privileges.

The wine brought by the Gascon merchants was sold in large quantities and to a variety of persons, goldsmiths, butchers, woolmongers, dealers in iron, as well as taverners and vintners being recorded as purchasers. In London aliens traded under severe restrictions which the City maintained to have been prescribed by the Great Charter. The Gascons, however, as dealers in a favoured commodity, appear to have evaded them very largely. Thus although they were forbidden to retail or sell to other aliens,[1] the Gascons in 1292 resisted the attempts of the City to enforce these restrictions, and claimed[2] freedom of sale as a right, having enjoyed it, in practice at least, since the suspension of the City's franchise in 1285. Aliens were also under the obligation not to remain in England more than forty days, at the end of which time they must dispose of such wine as remained unsold, since wine could not be exported from England without the King's special licence. It is certain that the Gascons evaded this obligation also, for the action taken against them by the City in 1292 gave rise to a struggle upon this issue which continued with little cessation for thirty years, often, if not generally, in the Gascons' favour. By means of extending their stay beyond the limit of forty days, and by disposing of the wine which they were unable to sell to natives or to other of their countrymen in England, the Gascons escaped the necessity of selling at a reduced rate the wine they imported. With the same object they gave some perpetuity to their visits by trading as partners,[3] visiting England in turn and appointing one another as attorneys,[4] to represent them during their absence from the country, while the services of such attorneys were also very useful in the recovery of debts.

Such was the nature of the dealings of the Gascons in London during the earlier portion of the reign of Edward I. As yet the English vintners, who in later days were to be their competitors, were both few and feeble. They were indeed rarely distinct from the taverners, both names being frequently applied interchangeably to the same person.[5] With

1. *Bk. E.*, p. 45.   2. *Rot. Parl.*, I, 87a.
3. *Bk. A.*, pp. 38, 40; *Bk. B.*, pp. 32, 68, 137, 172. etc.
4. *Bk. A.*, p. 6; *Bk. B.*, pp. 68, 179, 192.   5. *Bk B.*, pp. 20, 22, 49.

the exception of Rokesle and Waleys, who, as has been seen, united in one person the characters of merchant and official, they were men of no wealth, as is proved by the modesty of their bequests and the small scale[1] of their transactions. The sphere in which their activities as yet lay is shown in a quarrel which arose in 1285 between the City and the Gascons with regard to the fee for brokerage of wines. Rokesle and Waleys, the former of whom was then Mayor of the City, appear to have been almost alone in supporting the Gascons in their demand for the lower fee. The quarrel ended with a compromise, the rate being fixed at threepence per tun, but it illustrates the exceptional nature of the position of these two and how small as yet was the number of English merchants who imported. This was not, however, the only occasion on which Rokesle and Waleys supported the importer. In 1301, and on this occasion with the support of native merchants as well as Gascons, they obtained[2] from the Crown a decision against the barons of the Cinque Ports and the mariners of Yarmouth awarding to merchants compensation from the shipmaster in cases of loss by jettison. The fact that on this occasion they were supported by native merchants indicates some development of the interests of these in over-sea trade. By the middle of the reign, however, little advance had been made in this respect and native vintners confined their efforts to enforcing the traditional restrictions upon the activities of aliens after their arrival in this country. In this they could depend upon the support of Waleys and Rokesle, since these, if as importers they had interests with the Gascon aliens, as native merchants had interests in common with those of the home vintner in opposing the liberties of the alien in England.

In 1288 an attack was made[3] by the city upon the liberties of stay and of sale enjoyed by Gascons both in London and without. But despite the representations[4] of Waleys and William de Hereford in 1292 the Gascons next year obtained a recognition[5] from the Crown of the liberties they claimed, and the quarrel was not again renewed until the year 1300. The motives with which the city was now

1. *Bk. A.*, p. 115; *Bk. B.*, pp. 40, 49, 172, 222.
2. *Bk. C.*, p. 86.
3. *Bk. A.*, p. 122.
4. *Rot. Parl.*, I, 87a.
5. *Ib.*, I, 99a.

actuated may be gathered from the fact that in the meantime it had attacked the liberties of Winchelsea while in the year 1300 it extended its opposition to the Teutonic and Portuguese merchants as well as the Gascons.   In 1298 during the mayoralty of Waleys, it was declared by the mayor and aldermen of London that merchants of Sandwich[1] should not trade with foreigners, while at the same time the right of selling wine in London was restricted[2] to freemen of the city.   The barons of the Cinque Ports, thus deprived of their chief source of wealth, found a strong supporter of their rights in Archbishop Winchelsey, who condemned the city's action as contrary to the Great Charter, confirmed the preceding year, and threatened Waleys with excommunication, declaring that it was unworthy of the Mayor's dignity to injure others in order to gain popular favour.   Two years after this event, in April, 1300, the freemen of London, intensely dissatisfied that since 1293 the Gascons in virtue of their possession of the King's permission, had enjoyed the same privileges of residence and of sale as themselves, determined to enforce their claims of their own accord.   In that month a number of aliens of influence who kept hostels received notice to quit and were informed that henceforth they were to lodge with freemen and that for a period of not more than forty days within which they must dispose of their wines.   The petition of the Gascons for permission to reside in cellars in which they kept their wines was also promptly refused.[3] Among the aliens thus expelled were many of great influence and favour with the King, as the Portuguese merchant Gerard Dorgoyl, and William Trente, the vintner of Bergerac, who in the following year became the King's Chamberlain, Taker of Wines, and Coroner in the City. This success of the City was, however, merely temporary. In August, 1302, Edward made a "Convention"[4] with the merchant vintners of Guienne the terms of which six months later were to form the basis of the more general agreement with alien merchants known as the Carta Mercatoria (Feb. 1st, 1303).   By this "convention" or "charter," which had no parliamentary sanction, the Gascons, in return for an

---

1. *Bk. B.*, p. 216.
2. *Bk. C.*, p. 31.
3. *Ib.*, pp. 65, 75, 80.

4. *C.C.R.* 1300–26, pp. 29–31.
5. *Liber Custumarum*, 1, 211.

agreement to pay increased customs, received a promise that no unjust prises of their goods should be made, and were accorded freedom to sell in gross to natives or aliens, and to lodge where they wished and for as long as was the pleasure of those into whose inns or houses they were received. Thus after two years' enjoyment of the exclusive rights it had asserted the City found the alien admitted to the same liberties of trade as were enjoyed by natives with the single exception of the right to retail, and this condition of affairs it held to be contrary to Magna Carta and the Charter of the City, and as having been produced by the illegal collusion of the King and the aliens. The dissatisfaction of the Londoners remained without effective expression until the reign of Edward II. It was then maintained,[1] probably with truth, that the increased customs with which the aliens had purchased these privileges enhanced prices, and the King, in consequence of the need he then felt of conciliating opinion with the unauthorised return of Gaveston, suspended (Aug. 20, 1309) the exactions for twelve months with the alleged motive of observing their effects on prices. It was during this period that the hostility of native and Gascon in London was fiercest. In March, 1310, regulations were issued for brokers of wine, the most important of which forbade brokers to act as hosts to merchant strangers and prohibited them from bringing strangers together for purposes of trade. In May, in reply to a writ from the King, brought forward by the Gascons, the City strongly maintained that the immunity of aliens from murage and portage enjoyed by virtue of their payment of the new custom ceased with its suspension. Thus with the suspension of the additional customs the aliens lost the liberties they had held. The protests of the Gascons led to outrages committed against them, and these were followed by the arrest of many citizens at the King's command, and a confirmation[2] of the grant of royal protection to Gascons coming to trade. The crisis did not pass until the Gascons purchased[3] a confirmation of the Carta Mercatoria at the price of £600 advanced by five vintners of the Duchy who afterwards received the King's permission to recover the sum by a levy upon wines imported.

---

1. *C.C.R.* 1307–13, p. 170.   2. *Bk. D.*, pp. 219, 225, 228, 232.
3. *C.P.R.* 1307–13, p. 284.

The new Customs, together with the privileges of aliens, were therefore renewed in August, 1310, the King alleging that the suspension of these dues had been of no effect in reducing prices.

Thus the City failed for the time to break down the agreement by which the Gascons, in return for increased customs, had received from the King the full liberties of trade enjoyed by natives, with the single exception of the right to retail. This branch of trade, commonly regarded as the rightful monopoly of the native, the Gascons, with few exceptions, appear to have been content to leave for the exploitation of their less wealthy rivals. The liberty to stay at will, and the freedom to sell in gross, to aliens as well as to natives relieved the Gascon of the obligation to dispose of his wines at a less rate at the end of forty days. These privileges, which he purchased by payment of the New Customs, together with the advantages he possessed in his own country, rendered him at least equal as a competitor with the native for the wholesale trade. As a result the merchants of London, and even the consumers, believing that it was at their expense that the King and the aliens enriched themselves, gave support to the active opposition to the Crown which now began, and for the rest of the reign the economic status of alien and native varied with the fortunes of the King and those who opposed him.

The triumph of the King's opponents resulted in the ordinances of 1311, and these included provisions which closely affected the wine trade, and are the more important as they remained in force until 1322. It was ordained in 1311 that the charters should be observed, and the new custom abolished.[1] With the abolition of these customs the liberties of aliens, which they had received by the Carta Mercatoria, were revoked. The old restrictions as to length of stay and freedom to sell to other aliens were strictly enjoined,[2] and the Gascon importer was exploited by the native dealer. The opposition to the alien was not conducted merely as it had been before. New measures were taken which reveal at once both the power which native interests had now acquired and the identity which was believed to exist between their

1. 5 Edw. II, c. 11.   2. *Bk. D.,* p. 282; *Bk. E.,* pp. 42, 45.

cause and that of the City and the ordinances. New taxation was devised, which was imposed upon resident aliens, while with a view to better regulation citizens were compelled,[1a] under penalty of fines, to reside within the City. The opposition extended beyond this. The instability which had characterised the conditions under which in recent years the Gascons had traded had caused many to seek enfranchisement as the only way of securing lasting economic liberty. Dorgoyl[1] and Trente[2] had been among the earliest of these and had kept hostel by right of citizenship. The severity of the conditions by which this right was obtained indicate at the same time its value and the disadvantages under which the Gascons had often pursued their activities. It is also significant that citizenship was sought most during the abeyance of the Carta Mercatoria. In October, 1309, Peter Caban, a Gascon merchant, had obtained[3] the citizenship but only upon payment of the sum of one hundred shillings, while in Lent, 1310, Elyas Peres, who had been deputy butler in Gascony to the King, was only admitted[4] upon payment of 22/6 and the security of Walter Waldeshef, the King's butler, and William Trente. So intense was the hostility to the Gascons that in March, 1312, even this narrow way to economic equality was virtually closed by a petition[5] of the Commonalty of the City, who urged that aliens should not be admitted to the citizenship except with their consent in full husting. As reason for their action they declared that enfranchised aliens avowed[6] the goods of others. It was for this reason, as well as for selling to other aliens the wine he had thus harboured, that Dorgoyl was deprived[7] of the citizenship he had acquired, it being frankly admitted that by this means the alien obtained a higher price. Thus the ordinances may be seen to have had a deep effect on the economic life of London, but the disturbances they produced were not without a parallel elsewhere. At Ravenser[8] in Yorkshire complaint was made in 1313 that the burgesses

1a. *Bk. D.*, pp. 58, 61, 75, 86.
1. *Bk. E.*, p. 14; *C.P.R.* 1307–13, p. 229.
2. *C.C.R.* 1313–8, pp. 87, 513; *Bk. D.*, p. 49
3. *Bk. D.*, p. 36.   4. *Ib.*, p. 49.
5. *Bk. D.*, p. 283; *Bk. E.*, p. 13.   6. *Ib.*, p. 281.
7. *Bk. E.*, p. 14.   8. *C.P.R.* 1313–7, p. 63.

made ordinances "against the King and his State" in consequence of which foreign merchants coming to the town were not permitted to sell their goods at their true value, while at Bawtry, in the same year, disturbances resulted in the death of a Gascon merchant.

So successful was the opposition to the Gascons and so great the disgrace which overwhelmed the King in 1314 that nothing was heard of the liberties of aliens for some years. It is strange that they should then be revived as an indirect result of the war with the Scots which in 1314 had contributed to keep them in abeyance. Like other military enterprises of the middle ages the siege of Berwick in 1319 occasioned a demand for wine which now seems surprising. The King, already heavily burdened with debts[1] owing to Gascon vintners for wine, had great difficulty to procure supplies. He was assisted by grants and purveyances in Gascony, but was helped most by an agreement with the Gascons of London and Bristol. In June of that year the mayors and sheriffs of London and Bristol received mandates from the King[2] "upon petition of the Gascons" to permit them to take their wines to the King in the north for the "hosting" of the war with Scotland. At the same time the King took the part of the Gascons in a dispute that had arisen respecting their liberties, and granted[3] that until next parliament they should have freedom to sell in gross to whomsoever they wished, native or alien, since a "greater abundance" would be made by freedom of sale, and this it behoved him to encourage at a time when he was at war with the Scots. These concessions were won for the Gascons by their proctor Arnold de Ispannia, who afterwards received[4] permission to recover from those who benefited the sum of eighty pounds expended in the prosecution of this business. In December 1320 these liberties were confirmed[5] with the omission of all restriction as to the period of their operation, and the Gascons received also liberty of export conditional upon their not taking wool to Brabant, Flanders or Artois contrary to the laws of the Staple. Thus, in consequence of their ability to assist the royal cause which for the moment was not distinct from that of the nation, the Gascons, not indeed without the oppositon[6] of London

1. *C.C.R.* 1313–18, p. 551.
2. *C.P.R.* 1317–21, p. 355.
3. *C.C.R.* 1318–23, p. 144.
4. *C.P.R.* 1317–21, pp. 377, 379.
5. *Ib.*, p. 533.
6. *C.C.R.* 1318–23, p. 144.

but with the royal consent, recovered the more important of the liberties they desired by a temporary grant which was afterwards confirmed without restriction.

This success was the signal for the reopening of the whole contest, which for some time was carried on with more advantage to the Gascons than formerly. With the fall of the Ordainers in 1322 and the resumed exaction of the new customs the Gascons successfully claimed the old liberty of stay. It was the period of the triumph of the Despensers and the Court party, and they appear to have favoured the demand of the aliens.

In April 1323 the Gascons in England received authority [1] to levy contributions on their fellow-countrymen importing wine in order to defray expenses, amounting to two hundred marks, incurred "in the prosecution of affairs of common utility." The nature of the liberties they then received is probably revealed in a petition [2] of the first parliament of Edward III, when it was urged that foreign merchants should be restricted to a stay of forty days within which they must dispose of their goods. It was complained that the liberty they had of late possessed had been granted to them by the evil counsellors of the late king without the consent of prelates and nobles, and that it had resulted in making goods "outrageously more dear." It is not difficult to see what interests prompted this petition. The fiscal interests of the Crown and the economic interests of the City merchants had brought the two into rapidly increasing antagonism. In consequence of this the King had in 1322 suspended the City mayoralty, but as a result of the rebellion of Isabella and Mortimer and the proclamation of the Regency in October 1326 he was compelled to restore [3] it in December. At the same time the City seized the opportunity to carry a demand which fully reveals the exclusiveness of their designs. All foreigners who had obtained the freedom of the City, it was ordained,[4] should be deprived excepting only the merchants of Amiens, Corbie and Nesle, and henceforth no foreigner should be admitted to enfranchisement excepting in full husting, with consent of the Commonalty,

1. *C.P.R.* 1321-4, p. 283.
2. *Rot. Parl.*, II, 9.
3. *C.P.R.* 1324-7, p. 337.
4. *Bk. E.*, p. 214.

T

and on the security of six reputable men of his trade.   The violence to which the City was moved was exhibited in the murder of the reforming bishop Stapledon, who during the rule of the Despensers had served the King as Treasurer and Chancellor of the Exchequer.   That the exclusiveness of the City was not in agreement with the real interests of the Crown is evident from the temporising reply[1] made in the first parliament of Edward III to the demand for the enforcement of the forty days' restriction, and it is still more evident in the confirmation of the Carta Mercatoria in the following year (1328).

From this time until 1335 no general change took place in the relative standing of the two interests competing for mastery in the wine trade, which during this period was carried[2] on under the conditions restored by the reconfirmation of the Carta Mercatoria in 1328.   The relations existing between the two were however by no means amicable, and the old hostility of the native broke[3] out in 1334 in Bristol and London in acts of violence of which the Gascon traders were the victims.   The avowed cause of these outrages was the privileges which aliens enjoyed by the restoration of the charter of Edward I.   The general withdrawal of the Gascons from the country which followed inconvenienced all, and not least the King, who at all times had an interest in maintaining in England a good market for wine.   It was largely in consequence of these disturbances, and partly from an appreciation on the part of the Crown of the increase of customs that would accrue from this course, that in the Parliament of York (1335) freedom of trade was conferred upon aliens by statute.   What was the precise extent of the liberties the aliens then received it is impossible to state.   No mention was explicitly made of any right of retail, though this was conferred by a similar enactment[5] of 1351.   It is, however, certain that the liberties conferred by the Carta Mercatoria, and more especially the right of aliens to sell to

1. *Rot. Parl.*, II, 9.   2. *C.C.R.* 1330–3, pp. 142, 382, 556, 578.
3. *Rot. Parl.*, II, 74a. During the same period (1327—1335) the City was hostile to the freedom of other English traders; *e.g.* case of Oxford, *Bk. E.*, pp. 252, 253. They were not permitted to sell to each other, and were obliged to live with a host; *e.g. Ib.*, p. 262. Their position was much that of aliens.
4. 9 Edw. III, St. 1.   5. 25 Edw. III, St. 3.

aliens, then received parliamentary sanction. The importance of the statute of 1335 lies in this that the liberties accorded to aliens by charter were now established by statute so that it was no longer possible for natives to regard them as only existing by a doubtful exercise of the royal prerogative. No measures appear to have roused greater opposition in London than the statutes of 1335 and 1351, and in March, 1337, the citizens recovered[1] what they claimed to be the full exercise of their franchise, though the liberties of aliens in other parts of the country were not withdrawn.

It remains to observe what causes produced this sudden reversal of policy in regard to the wine trade in 1337. The hostility aroused by the act of 1335 played a considerable part, but the fiscal situation created by the French declaration of war in 1336 contributed most to the result. Immense funds were needed, and it was imperative that they should be raised without delay. The recognised sources were exploited to the full, including repeated grants on moveables made by the towns, but they were inadequate and yielded too slowly. The means adopted by Edward I in 1297 were therefore applied, and the Crown secured a monopoly of the wool crop as well as loans from Italian, Hanseatic, and English merchants. The towns therefore acquired a new importance to the Crown, especially London, where the capitalists of the City, among whom many vintners were now conspicuous, took a great part in financing[1] the King. It was natural in these circumstances that they should recover their ancient privileges.

During the period of the struggle of Gascon and native in London (1288–1337) the native vintners had made great advances in status both as individuals and as a class. At the beginning of the period, as has been seen, lack of capital had confined them, with two exceptions, almost entirely to the retail trade. In the first decade of the new century, however, indications of growth became visible, and fairly large dealers were to be found among their number. The record of debts is evidence of this. In 1302 Ralph of Honey Lane owed a sum of two hundred marks to a Gascon merchant, in 1306 sixty pounds to John de Wengrave, in 1307 nineteen pounds to a

---

1. *C.P.R.* 1334–8, p. 460; *Bk. F.*, pp. 14, 15.

' corder,' and at death five hundred[1] marks to a goldsmith. Ralph Hardel was an alderman of the City and the owner of several tenements[2] in the Vintry and elsewhere.   The reign of Edward II, as might be imagined from the success with which the native opposed the united efforts of the Crown and the alien, witnessed a remarkable rise in the wealth and influence of the native vintner.   It was in this reign that Reginald atte Conduit, John de Oxenford and Richard de Rothyng, capitalist vintners, rose to prominence as financiers, and their rise was accompanied with that of many others. Whereas the name of no vintner was to be found in the highest class of tax-payer in 1319, the names of four occurred[3] in 1332.   Such a comparison, however, does not indicate the real greatness of their wealth or the extent of their activities.   This can only be realised by an examination of the debts due to them, and from these it appears that the wealthy were frequently creditors in sums of £1,000 and upwards.   The dealings of Oxenford involved an extraordinary amount of capital, and though his activities were frequently those of the financier he was doubtless the greatest vintner of his time.   His transactions were frequently carried on in partnership with Rothyng, who can perhaps be ranked next as respects the extent of his commercial and financial undertakings.   Conduit, though always a vintner, assumed more and more the character of an official, and devoted most of his energy to the service of his mistery, the City, and the Crown.   All three occupied high civic office, serving the City as sheriff, alderman, and representative in parliament. Both Rothyng and Conduit attended the famous parliament of York in 1322, while the latter was also present at those equally important in 1327 and 1335.   Conduit and Oxenford held the Mayoralty of the City, the former in 1335, the latter in 1342, while Conduit received knighthood in the same year in which he was mayor.   The names of all three are prominent in the records of the doings of the vintners' mistery, and appear first among those of the thirteen elected for its government in 1328, while Oxenford and Rothyng so far identified themselves with its interests as to join the

---

1. *Bk. C.*, pp. 189, 246, 247; *Bk. E.*, p. 45.
2. *Cal. Wills*, I, 180; *Bk. C.*, p. 198.   3. See page 58 above.

taverners in closing their taverns and refusing to sell when general dissatisfaction prevailed among them in consequence of the assize of wine in 1331. The financial assistance of such men was earnestly sought by the Crown at the outbreak of war in 1337, and was given in many ways. Conduit and Oxenford were among the most important of those to whom was entrusted the provision of revenue for the Crown by the seizure of wool in 1337.

In 1336, the year which intervened between the enactment of the Statute of York and the reconfirmation of the liberties of London, the merchants of the City made gifts to the King. These included 1200/- each from Oxenford and Rothyng, 40/- from John Fynche and 20/- each from Michael Mynot and Nicholas Ponge, as well as smaller sums from other vintners.[1] In 1340 the King after seeking in vain to raise £20,000 in the City, received a grant[2] of £5,000 for which the Mayor was assessed at £100, Oxenford at £300, Rothyng at £200, Conduit at £60, Mynot at £40, Fynche at £10 and Ponge at £5. The grants of the vintners thus enumerated were but a part of the total financial assistance afforded at this time by the City. It was this rise of the City as a factor in the successful prosecution of the war which won it fourteen years' unbroken enjoyment of the liberties for which it had so long struggled, while in the provinces the alien enjoyed the privileges he had acquired by the Carta Mercatoria which had received confirmation by statute in 1335.

While the vintners of London thus strengthened themselves against aliens they also attained high place among the misteries of the City. They regularly made scrutiny[3] of wines, thus acquiring some powers of supervision over their sale, and in 1321, along with the fishmongers, petitioned[4] to be allowed to govern their mistery and 'redress faults therein according to ancient usage.' Their petition was granted, and in 1328 they elected[5] thirteen members of the government of their mistery. Their increasing influence as a body is also shown by the decree by which in June, 1331, the burgesses of Oxford lost[6] their liberty to sell by retail in

1. *Bk. F.*, p. 5.
2. *Ib.*, p. 46–9.
3. *Bk. E.*, p. 109.
4. *Ib.* p. 143.
5. *Ib.*, p. 232.
6. *Ib.*, p. 252.

the City, and were forbidden to make wholesale purchase of wine in London from merchant strangers if intended for resale.

As the interest of the vintners had brought them into opposition to aliens and provincials they too now found opposition within the City. In 1311 complaint [1] was made of the growing dearness of wine. Retail prices were therefore regulated at five pence per gallon for wines of the best quality, fourpence for those of the next, and threepence for those of least value. At the same time it was also ordained ' that no merchant, an engrosser of wines keep a tavern himself, neither privily by any other person nor yet openly,' nor should any taverner be an engrosser, but for long this ordinance was not strictly enforced. Thus in 1319 Thomas Drynkewatre entered into an agrement to keep tavern for James Beauflur, vintner, whose wines he was to sell. It is also certain [2] that in 1311 Oxenford, Rothyng, and other vintners of influence had taverns in Vintry, while even later [3] no clear distinction can be made between the two classes of dealers. Along with these attempts to define by legislation the activities of those engaged in the trade, the regulation of prices and conditions of sale became gradually more frequent, and to the taverners more oppressive. In 1321 petition was made [4] to the King and Council against the assize of wine. In 1330 it was enacted [5] that assize of wines should be made twice yearly at Easter and Michaelmas, and in other towns as well as in London. In 1331, at a time when, it is important to remark, Pulteney, [6] a wealthy draper, was mayor, and mercers, pelterers, and members of kindred misteries had great influence as aldermen, the assize proved so little satisfactory that a large number of taverners of Vintry and Cheap closed [7] their taverns rather than sell at the price ordained. Despite minor difficulties of this nature, however, the vintners of London, in possession of the great advantages secured in 1337, continued to prosper until by the middle of the century they had won for themselves such a position as made them the object of the greatest jealousy

1. Riley, *Mem.* 81.
2. *Ib.*, 1;1; *Bk. E.*, p. 38.
3. *Bk. F.*, p. 19; *Bk. G.*, p. 35.
7. *Bk. F.*, p. 9; *C.C.R.* 1330–3, pp. 410, 545, 557.
4. *Bk. E.*, p. 141.
5. 4 Edw. III, c. 12.
6. Riley, *Mem.*, 180.

and aroused general opposition on the ground that they used their power to ' corner ' the supply of wine and thus raise prices by artifice.

From this time (1337) until the year 1351 no event affecting the vintners as a body is recorded, and interest passes from their struggles for status to changes in customs, duties and conditions of navigation produced by the war. These, which constituted to a large extent, the most vital conditions of trade, affected native merchants more closely than before, as by this time they too were actively engaged in the work of importation. The exigencies of war directed the attention of the Crown to the customs as an important source of revenue, and a means of exerting political influence. At the same time their manipulation closely affected traders in wine since this was the chief article of common consumption imported from abroad, and therefore the chief subject of prise and purveyance. The customs on wine varied according as the importers were freemen of favoured towns such as London, York, and the Cinque Ports, natives of other English towns and districts, or alien merchants. Among the last named were the Gascons, as is made clear by the Carta [1] Mercatoria, while further evidence of the same fact may be found in the temporary [2] exemptions of the Bayonnese in 1341 from a levy of threepence in the pound on merchandise imported by aliens, as also in the refusal [3] in 1356 to exempt Gascons from the custom of 21d. levied upon ' every whole cloth of assize ' exported by alien merchants. Only in the ordinances of the staples were they ever regarded [4] as other than aliens, and the exceptional nature of their position there was expressly recognised in the statutes.

The customs levied upon the goods of aliens in the years immediately succeeding the grant of the Carta Mercatoria were higher than those to which the goods of native traders were subject. It was only to be expected that the Crown in granting to aliens liberties which aroused the greatest opposition among natives should demand higher customs from those on whom it thus conferred benefits. That this was the nature of the new customs, as these levies upon aliens were called, is clear; but this inequality, at least as regards the

1. *Foed.*, II, pt. ii, 747.
2. *C.P.R.* 1340–3, p. 279; made permanent, *C.C.R.* 1374–7, p. 397.
3. *C.C.R.* 1354–60, p. 287.   4. *C.P.R.* 1327–30, pp. 98–9.

customs on wine tended to disappear as the century advanced. As the value of wines increased from year to year the butler's takings by prisage acquired greater value, while butlerage, as the custom of two shillings per tun levied on the wines of aliens was called, remained the same. It was partly for this reason that in the reign of Edward III the struggle regarding the customs, so persistent in the reign of Edward II, no longer existed, while for the same reason the King, who benefited more from natives than formerly, was the more willing to restore to the Londoners their old liberties of trade.

The chief exaction to which the wine of native importers was subject was the Recta [1] Prisa by which the King's Butler or his deputy took two tuns for the King's use from each ship bearing twenty tuns or more, and one tun from those bearing ten tuns and less than twenty, a sum of twenty[2] shillings being paid by the Crown as freight for every tun thus prised. From this custom, however, the 'barons' of the Cinque [3] Ports were exempt as early at least as 1278, while the citizens of London [4] acquired the same immunity in the first year of the reign of Edward III, and those of York [5] in 1376. The merchants of Bordeaux also had long enjoyed virtual exemption from the same custom, for in 1254, by a charter which they purchased for two thousand marks, they became exempt[6] from all Crown customs except the Recta Prisa, while it was agreed that for the wine thus taken they should receive the price. In 1302 the Gascons as a whole obtained exemption [7] from this custom as well as from levies for murage, pontage, and pannage in the City of London,[8] but agreed to pay instead the " New Custom" of two shillings on every tun brought to port and landed for sale.[9] It was this agreement which was extended to other aliens next year, thus becoming part of the Carta Mercatoria. In addition to these customs natives and aliens alike paid the 'ancient customs',[10] which consisted of a small money due 'levied at the ports, not only by the Crown as of its prerogative but

1. *Liber Albus, trans.* Riley, 217.
2. *C.P.R.* 1307–13, p. 358; *C.C.R.* 1358–61, p. 124.
3. Atton and Holland, *The King's Customs*, p. 8.   Cf. *C.P.R.* 1272–9, p. 22; *C.C.R.* 1337–9, p. 512; *Ib.* 1339–41, p. 216.
4. Atton and Holland, p. 20.   5. *C.C.R.* 1374–7, p. 316.
6. *C.P.R.* 1247–58, p. 294.   7. *A.M.Bord.*, I, 160.
8. *Bk. D.*, p. 225; *cf. C.P.R.* 1258–66, p. 519.
9. *C.C.R.* 1302–7, p. 127; *cf. C.P.R.* 1247–58, pp. 278, 294.
10. Atton and Holland, p. 5; Hall, *Customs*, I, 65–96; 25 Edw. III, St. 5.

also by certain franchises as a port or harbour toll, while they were also subject to purveyance or ' pre-emption ' 'ad opus regis,' though for wine thus seized the King's Butler was supposed to recompense the owners. Only one other due levied upon imported wine remains to be mentioned. This was the gauger's fee, which in London in 1356 was at the rate[1] of a penny per tun, half being paid by the buyer, half by the seller. On other goods imported the Gascons paid poundage, though in some cases, as in that of the Bayonnese, this was not always exacted. On exports, chiefly of wool and cloth, they paid the higher rates to which the goods of aliens were subject.

In addition to these customs which were regularly exacted throughout the reign of Edward III there were also special subsidies which were frequently levied during the same period to defray the expenses of the armed[2] convoys which in consequence of the increased piracy that accompanied the Hundred Years' War, were often needed to escort the annual wine fleet in its voyage to and from Bordeaux. They were sometimes levied only on wine actually convoyed,[3] but not infrequently they were exacted on all that was brought to England and sometimes on all that left Bordeaux, whatever the port to which it was consigned, so that Gascons and other aliens were obliged to contribute equally with the English towards protection from which they clearly derived less benefit. Heavy as the subsidies were, however, they at first occasioned little complaint either among English or Gascon merchants, as the convoys rendered important and necessary services, and the levies usually ceased ' promptly whenever a truce was made. Thus when a levy of twelve pence on every sack of wool and sixpence on each tun of wine was imposed in 1340, to repel pirates and safely convoy ships crossing with merchandise,' the order[4] for its cessation was made within a fortnight after the conclusion of hostilities by the truce of Esplechin. It is also noteworthy that in this case protection was accorded to ' ships of the realm' while the levy was ' granted ' by alien merchants. In 1347, during the guardianship of the Kingdom by Lionel of Antwerp, the

1. *Bk. G.*, p. 56.
2. *Rot. Scot.*, I, 467, 468.
3. *E.g.*, in 1372.
4. *C.C.R.* 1339–41, p. 643.

Council of magnates, lay and clerical, imposed[1] a tax of two shillings per tun on wine and sixpence in the pound on merchandise for the protection of merchant shipping. These levies were repealed 'in Michaelmas of that year, but in 1350 a new levy of two shillings on the sack of wool, twelve pence on the tun of wine, and sixpence in the pound on merchandise was imposed.[2]   In this year the subsidies were unusually heavy, for the levy of twelve pence per tun on wine had only been repealed[3] in June, when in October an exaction of fortypence[4] per tun was imposed upon all wine leaving Gascony to defray expenses that were expected to arise for the protection of commerce from the depredations[5] of the Spaniards.   On this occasion though the tax was collected, no protection was given, and the Commons in the next parliament petitioned[6] for the return of the money received.   A convoy was again necessitated by the hostilities which took place during the period which elapsed between the Treaty of London (1359) and the Treaty of Bretigni (1360).   On this occasion, however, no new levy was made, but a subsidy of sixpence in the pound on imported wine which was already being taken was replaced[7] by one of two shillings per tun—an exaction of somewhat similar rate but easier to collect and greater in yield.   This levy also was promptly abolished[8] when peace was made, but was reimposed in 1371[9] and the following year.   On the latter occasion it was exacted only on wine actually convoyed, and it was provided[10] that should the convoy during the voyage take any goods from enemy ships at sea or make any profit from freightage of wine or by trading, such profit should be deducted from the tax for convoy.   It was believed that convoys engaged in other activities than those for which they nominally existed and there now arose among the Commons a growing dissatisfaction with the levies for their support.

1.   See article on the Estate of Merchants, p. 217.
2.   *Bk. F.*, pp. 203, 204; also *C.P.R.* 1348–50, p. 481.
3.   *C.C.R.* 1349–54, p. 241.
4.   *Ib.* 1349–54, p. 288; *Foed.*, R. III, pt. i, 206.
5.   *Foed.*, R. III, pt. i, 202, 206.
6.   *Rot. Parl.*, II, 229; *C.C.R.* 1369–74, p. 263.
7.   *Foed.*, R. III, pt. i, 468.
8.   *Foed.*, R. III, pt. i, 500; *C.C.R.* 1360–4, p. 49.
9.   *Rot. Parl.*, II, 310; *C.P.R.* 1370–4, p. 204.
10.   *Ib.*, p. 204.

This is evident in a petition which they presented in 1373 on again granting the two shilling subsidy for a period of two years in which they also asked that the money should be spent on the war and on that only. From this time the two shilling subsidy on wine, or tunnage, 'became[1] with some variations of rate a regular parliamentary grant.'

In addition to the customs taken in England wine was also subjected to numerous dues as it was brought to port down the rivers of Gascony, in the City itself, and in earlier times as it passed to the sea down the estuary of the Gironde. Scarcely a castle did it pass whose lord had not some claim[2] to a levy upon it, and in the proceeds of these the King had usually an interest,[3] while Gascon ecclesiastics, as the Archbishop of Bordeaux,[4] the Archprior of Perrefitte,[5] and the Chapter[6] of Agen enjoyed rights to highly remunerative river dues. In the time of Edward III, moreover, the number of levies made in Gascony was increased[7] in no small degree for the purpose of defraying the cost of fortifications and their repair. Bordeaux exacted a custom for municipal purposes upon wine descending from the inland towns, while not even corn[8] was allowed to pass to the interior duty free. The customs levied in Bordeaux were exceptionally high.[9] In

---

1. Stubbs, *Const. Hist.*, II, 446, 557; *Rot. Parl.*, II, 317.
2. Often nominally for repair of roads, *e.g. C.P.R.* 1232-47, p. 7. The Crown had often to prohibit illegal exactions of this type, *A.M.Bord.*, I, 188, A.D. 1343, where Edw. III forbade barons to exact "unum scutum auri vel circiter pro quolibet dolio sic traducto." Such extortion was resumed later, *cf. A.M.Bord.*, I, 191, 214.
3. *C.P.R.* 1345-8, p. 560. Castle of Rochefort on the Charente. Its lord to have 6d. per tun on wine brought within the district of the castle, "whereof one moiety shall be for his own use, and the other moiety for the King." See also *C.P.R.* 1361-4, p. 18; also *I.S.Gironde*, E. Suppl., p. 359, § 3,105; for earlier times see *C.P.R.* 1232-47, pp. 7, 382, from which it also appears that the customs of Bordeaux were the King's exclusively.
4. See Miss Lodge, *Estates of Arch. of Bord.*, pp. 20, 123. At end of the twelfth century he had all trading dues on the river between Mortagne and Langon; *A.M.Bord.*, I, 416.
5. *A.M.Bord.*, I, 422 (100 livres annually for the poor).
6. Michel, I, 225.
7. *A.M.Bord.*, I, 142.
8. *I.S.Gironde*, E. Suppl., 3,105, p. 359.
9. Neighbouring towns suffered keenly. Thus *I.S.Gironde*, E. Suppl., p. 56, 1 July 1401, declaration du roi d'Angleterre touchant certains privilèges accordés par lui à Bordeaux; il n'entend prejudicier à Bourg, Libourne, et St-Emilion. Also Série G. (921-3156), p. 98, Seigneurie de St-Seurin, "Lettre du prince de Galles portant que les habitants de Bruges, Eysines, et St-Médard ne pourront pas être soumis aux tailles de la ville de Bordeaux."

their passage (avalage)[1] through the city three distinct local
customs were taken on wines in addition to the " Great
Custom " and dues for keelage,[2] the gauge,[3] and the " cypress[4]
branch." They were known as the customs of Royan,
Mortagne, and Montendre. Of these the most important
was the custom of Royan. It is held[5] to have been levied
for protection afforded to shipping at the mouth of
the Gironde where it was at one time exacted, but its collection
was transferred later to Bordeaux and taken along with the
Great Custom. In 1287 definite regulation[6] was made of the
greater customs. The Great Custom of Bordeaux, the issues
of which were exclusively the King's, and which was levied
upon wine exported from Gascony, was then fixed at 5 sols.
4 deniers tournois or 6 sols. 5 deniers 1 obole in Bordeaux
money per tun, and that of Royan at two deniers 1 obole
tournois, one pipe out of twenty tuns being allowed free from
all customs. The citizens of Bordeaux moreover by a charter
of John were exempt[7] from all customs both in the City and
on the Gironde upon wine obtained from their own estates,
exception[8] being made only in the case of the wine purchased
by them from the Gascons. On these the usual levy was at
the rate of 13 sous 4 deniers per tun, though it was temporarily
raised by Edward III to 20 sous, only to be reduced to its old
rate in 1369. Edward III was not so favourable as his predecessors to the fiscal immunities and advantages of the
Gascons, and after first confirming the charter of John to the
citizens of Bordeaux he reduced[9] the number of those to
whom its advantages were conferred. The customs paid in
Bordeaux alone on the wine carried by the English wine
fleet of 1380 amounted[10] in the sum to nearly one-third of a

1. Avalage in Bordeaux put to farm to the City in 1238 for five years for
3,000 pounds of Bordeaux (*C.P.R.* 1232-47, p. 187).
2. Jullian, *Hist. de Bord.*, ch. xiv; also Michel, I, ch. 8.
3. *A.M.Bord.*, I, p. 157.
4. Michel, I, ch. 8; Jullian, ch. xiv. Given to the master of the ship and
for which he paid a due.
5. Michel, I, ch. 8. Moreover, in the *Arch. de Bord. Livre des Bouillons*,
p. 416, is a complaint made in 1275 that the custom of Royan was levied
twice—at Royan and at Bordeaux.
6. *I.S.Haute Garonne*, A.A., p. 31, § 179.
7. *Liv. des Bouillons*, 156, 416.
8. Michel, I, ch. 8.
9. Michel, with ref. to *Rot. Vasc.*, 10 Edw. III, m. 5.
10. Simon. *Hist. of English Wine Trade*, p. 122.

pound Bordeaux money per tun. It is therefore not incredible that wine nearly doubled [1] its value as it passed from the Gascon cultivator to the English consumer.

Unhappily for trade, the customs of wine in Gascony, apart from those collected in Bordeaux, were conspicuously variable throughout the reign of Edward III. The King, it is true, was not without an eye to commercial advantage when this was consistent with his political designs. Of this there is evidence in the promptitude with which he acted upon hearing that the King of France, contrary to the liberties of Gascony, levied an impost [2] of ten shillings of Tours upon every cask of wine brought down the Gironde to Langon by merchants of lands subject to the English Crown. In general, however, the Gascon customs were manipulated for the attainment of fiscal and political ends. Thus in 1343 by a charter [3] of 'great fee' Bordeaux received permission to exact two shillings of Tours on every tun of wine brought from St.-Macaire. The case is the more noteworthy as it was only in 1338 that this town had received [4] exemption from the customs of wine at Bordeaux, and this had been confirmed [5] in 1340. This want of stability which characterised the customs became more marked when the charter of 1343 was annulled [6] shortly after, only to be renewed [7] with its application extended to the wines of both St.-Macaire and Libourne in 1348. That the motives which produced these changes were political is probable from the later history of St.-Macaire. In 1373 its wines became subject to a levy [8] of two "sous petits tournois" per tun levied in Bordeaux for the repair of the walls and towers of that city, while the wines of the Bazadais and Agenais, then hostile to the English Crown, were to pay not less than four sous. It is still further significant of the nature of the policy pursued that with the object of precluding enemies from "première vente" it was decreed [9] in the same year that even if it were found that the wines of these districts were already under

---

1. Jullian, *Hist. de Bord.*, ch. xiv.
2. *Foed.*, II, pt. ii, 838. Also *C.C.R.* 1330–3, p. 561; 1332, p. 561.
3. *A.M.Bord.*, I, 189; *C.C.R.* 1343–6; p. 284.
4. *I.S.Gironde*, E. Suppl., p. 346, § 3,100.   5. *Ib*
6. Michel, I, 218, with ref. to *Rot. Vasc.* 17 Edw. III, m. 3.
7. Michel, I, ch. 8.   8. *A.M.Bord.*, I, 149.
9. *Ib.*, I, 180.

prohibition from passing to Bordeaux before the feast of St. Martin they should not in future so long as rebellion continued, descend before Christmas. In the case of Bazas a policy not really dissimilar in motive had been tried [1] in 1342, and again twenty years later, when its wines had been exempted from the customs taken at Bordeaux castle "to make the citizens more ready to assist the King," the manipulation of customs for political as distinct from commercial purposes being in this case obvious.

Like Bordeaux, the town of La Réole was of considerable political importance, with great commercial privileges, and between the two the keenest commercial jealousy [2] existed. In the struggle which took place between them even Bordeaux could maintain no real superiority. In 1347 La Réole received confirmation [3] of a privilege by which it exacted twenty pence per tun on wine passing on the Garonne, while in 1355 it obtained exemption [4] from the " custom " of Bordeaux, a privilege which sufficiently indicates its great bargaining power. In 1406 further evidence of the same fact occurred, for in the year upon complaint being made that Bordeaux exacted one tun of wine from cargoes of ten tuns or more descending from La Réole, and from other merchandise two sous (shillings) in the pound, the latter city was authorised [5] by the Duke of Berry to make a similar levy upon the goods of the citizens of Bordeaux.

The case of other towns whose political importance recommended them to royal favour was very similar. In 1337 St.-Emilion was urged [6] to be faithful against France, while in 1341 the appeal was followed by the exemption [7] of the inhabitants of that town from all tolls and customs both in Gascony and in England. At the same time they were assured [8] of immunity from unjust arrest for debts, while next year they received exemption [9] when the rest of Gascony was made subject to an imposition of a halfpenny in the pound levied upon merchandise for the repair of the frontier

1. *Foed.*, Feb. 28th 1342.
2. And this apparently from an early date; *I.S.Gironde*, E. Suppl., p. 191, § 2,774 (A.D. 1230).
3. *I.S.Gironde*, E. Suppl., p. 263.   4. *Ib.*, p. 190.
5. *Ib.*, p. 191.   6. *Ib.*, p. 229, § 4,400.
7. *Ib.*   8. *Ib.*, 25 Nov., 15 Edw. III.
9. *Ib.*, E. Suppl., p. 281, § 462.

fortresses. The temporary nature of the privilege of Caudrot, which in 1349 received permission[1] to exact for ten years fifteen pence Bordelais on every tun of wine descending from Toulouse, Albi, Cahors, Agen, and other parts outside the dominion of the Crown is suggestive of a like motive.

It is thus clear that great instability and a general tendency to increase both in severity and in number characterised the customs as they existed in the reign of Edward III. These conditions, both of them due to political circumstances for which the Crown was mainly responsible, would in themselves have presented a serious obstacle to the development of the wine trade. The manner in which the customs were collected, however, was perhaps an even greater impediment. Efforts had been made, it is true, to remedy[2] this branch of the administration in the reign of Edward II, but it was still so unsatisfactory in the reign of his successor as frequently to occasion[3] the threat on the part of Gascon importers never again to visit certain ports. For this there is no doubt that the frequency with which the English customs were farmed[4] or assigned[5] was largely responsible, but the removal[6] of the Butler's deputies in 1333 and the prohibition[7] in 1339 and again in 1345 of extortions committed by that official under pretence of purveyance shows that they were great offenders. Merchants, however, continued to be thus annoyed throughout the reign, and in 1351 and again in 1369 it was found necessary to forbid[8] by statute the evil practices of the King's butler and his deputies. From this statute it appears that these officials, and with them the Constable[9] of the Tower, took more wine than the satisfaction of the King's needs demanded, delivered to him the worst and either made profit on the rest or demanded a fine as a condition of its being restored to its

1. Michel, I, p. 219, with ref. to *Rot. Vasc.*, 22 Edw. III, m. 11.
2. *A.M.Bord.*, I, 169; *cf. C.C.R.* 1333–7, p. 74.
3. *Ib.* 1339–41, p. 290. The greatest dissatisfaction was with London and Bristol.
4. *E.g., Ib.* 1327–30, p. 141.   5. *E.g., C.P.R.* 1340–3, p. 274.
6. *C.C.R.* 1333–7, p. 74.
7. *C.C.R.* 1339–41, p. 290; and *Ib.*, 1343–6, p. 492.
8. 25 Edw. III, St. 5. Confirmed in 1353 by 27 Edw. III, St 2, c. 2; also *Rot. Parl.*, II, 239, 242, and 43 Edw. III, c. 3.
9. *C.C.R.* 1360–4, p. 169.

owner.   It was this fraud which was known as the 'mala-prisa.'

Besides deliberate extortion, the errors and delays occasioned by the King's officers caused further injury to many traders.   Not infrequently it happened that enfranchised Gascons and natives resident in Gascony were regarded [1] as aliens and required to pay the higher duties exacted from these.   In other cases by an infraction of the ordinance that customs should only be charged upon goods landed for sale, merchants who touched at a port on their way to their true destination or who landed goods from the same ship at two different ports, had frequently occasion to appeal [2] against a double demand for customs on the cargo or portion of cargo landed at the second port.   The same misfortune often befel the goods of ships putting to port from stress of weather even though they were not taken ashore, and to the end of the reign the cargoes of ships bound from Gascony to Flanders suffered [3] from illegal exactions of this nature.   So great was the disregard for the rights of traders that even when goods were landed before reaching the port to which they were consigned, in consequence of the arrest of the ship for the King's service customs were often demanded.[4]   A last illegal demand for customs on imported wine was the exaction [5] of threepence in the pound in addition to that of two shillings per tun.   On exports, too, customs were frequently illegally demanded.   In the case of ships for the King's service, danger of attack at sea, or other reasons for which the Crown was responsible, the return of the customs paid was always subject to lengthy delays,[6] while they were sometimes demanded [7] a second time upon re-exportation when the receipts of the first levy had not been returned.

Not inferior to the customs in its influence on the trade with Gascony was the condition of the seas, a fact which was fully recognised when it was ordained that municipal authori-

1. *C.C.R.* 1327–30, p. 487.
2. *E.g.*, *C.P.R.* 1338–40, p. 328; also *C.C.R.* 1341–3, p. 617; *Ib.*, 1364–8, p. 227.   (A good case with regard to exports is *Ib.* 1339–41, p. 180.)
3. *E.g.*, *Ib.* Aug. 16, 1333, p. 74; *C.P.R.* 1338–40, p. 441; *Ib.*, 1358–61, p. 567; *Foed.*, II, pt. ii, 879.
4. *C.C.R.* 1330–3, pp. 42, 47.
5. *E.g.*, *Ib.* 1364–8, p. 334; *Ib.* 1369–74, p. 275.
6. *E.g.*, *Ib.* 1346–9, p. 307.   7.   *E.g.*, *Ib.* 1339–41, p. 132.

ties making assize of wines should have regard to the peril of the seas when fixing retail prices. In the case of the Gascon trade this condition was of unusual importance not only because, according to fourteenth century ideas the voyage to and from Gascony was long, but also because it was always attended with great danger. Throughout the Hundred Years' War traders suffered not only from piracy which was then unusually rife, but, during the periods of actual warfare, from the attacks of the armed fleets of France and Spain which awaited them off the coast of France.

In the early days of the wine-trade it was the Gascons who had been most actively engaged in the work of importation, and even to the end of the reign of Edward III they brought[1] the purchases of English vintners from Gascony to England. The numerous shipowners of Bayonne provided freightage[2] for the wines of Bordeaux merchants who wealthy as they often were, disliked to expose their capital unduly to the risks of the sea. It is probable that few[3] of the ships which sailed from Bordeaux were owned by inhabitants of that city, who preferred either to sell their wines to the English or to pay freights. By the reign of Edward III no small proportion of the wine of Gascon and English merchants was conveyed in English ships whose owners suffered with the Bayonnese from the increased dangers at sea. It has indeed been maintained[4] that if the English created the demand for Bordeaux wine, the wine trade of Bordeaux assisted in the creation of the English strength at sea. In early times Irish merchants traded with Gascony through England. Later they gained permission to trade direct, but were often at some disadvantage, especially, as has been seen at the time of the institution of the Calais staple. Even greater disadvantages hindered the Scots, who, owing to the enmity of England, were for long almost excluded from the Gascon trade. These therefore suffered at sea to a less extent than the English and Gascons, whose risks are sufficiently reflected in the fact that the

1. *C.P.R.* 1338–40, p. 321; *C.C.R.* 1369–74, p. 404.
2. *E.g., Ib.* 1339–41, pp. 304–5.
3. Jullian, *Hist. de Bord.*, ch. xiv.
4. *Ib.*, ch. xiv.

U

freights [1] from Bordeaux to the various English ports were from ten shillings to a pound per tun.

The most constant danger to shipping was the ceaseless piracy which prevailed at sea, and from the responsibility for this none of the seafaring nations of the age can be considered free. The attacks of seamen were not directed against the ships of other nations only; they regularly attacked and plundered those of their own countrymen. Even the King's merchants [2] were not spared by the inhabitants of the English coast, who lost no opportunity of pillaging stranded vessels, despite a law [3] of wreck which declared illegal the appropriation of goods from such vessels if any person or animal escaped alive.

Still more piratical than the English were the Bayonnese. An energetic people, actively engaged in shipping, with interests conflicting with those of their neighbours the French and Castilians, they did great damage to the shipping of both, who in turn made reprisals not only upon the Bayonnese but also upon English merchantmen. The extent of the injuries committed by the Bayonnese was very great, as they were intensely devoted to this form of plunder, while their shipping, which contributed substantially [4] to English sea-power, was a powerful instrument to this end. The prominent part which they took against the French marine and their exposed position on land gave occasion for the undertaking [5] made by Edward III at the beginning of the Hundred Years' War that they should be indemnified for all losses and no treaty should be made with the French in which they were not included. Like the English, the Bayonnese did not confine their attacks to enemies. In the reign of Edward II they had taken part in bitter disputes with the men of the Cinque Ports, and not infrequently in the reign of his successor it was found advisable that they should be notified [6] of royal grants of letters of safe conduct and protection.

---

1. The King paid £69 2s. 6d. freight on 112 tuns of wine from Bordeaux to London, and 19s. 2d. for the safe conduct of the same; *Bk. D.*, p. 227; *cf.* Michel, I, p. 123.
2. *C.P.R.* 1327–30, p. 212.   3. *Foed.* III, pt. ii, 766, 937.
4. *Ib.*, III, pt. ii, 1,173.   5. *C.P.R.* 1334–8, p. 410.
6. *E.g., Ib.* 1350–4, p. 472; see also *C.C.R.* 1343–6, p. 257.

The reign of Edward III was not marked by any real improvement in the conditions of the seas. The efforts that were made to remedy the evils that existed did no more than counteract the increased anarchy that the war tended to produce. The system of reprisals merely perpetuated piracy, and little improvement was made when in 1327 the merchants and mariners of English towns became responsible[1] for the doings of their fellow townsmen. The mere assertion of a claim to the " Sovereignty of the Seas " was of little actual assistance to the traders, though the victories of Sluys and Espagnols sur Mer doubtless did much to afford temporary relief in those parts of the sea near Calais and Brittany, where traders with Gascony were most molested. A number of treaties made with Castile, Arragon, and Portugal, having for their object the mutual suppression of piracy, appear to have had some effect, and were persistently published in the Gascon ports. In 1347 a tribunal [2] was established in Bayonne, consisting of the Lord of Albret, the Mayor and Constable of Bordeaux, and other lieges of the King, together with the commissary of the King of Castile, their purpose being to hear complaints of men of Castile, Gascony, and England, and to do justice. By these efforts some little order at sea was secured during the middle years of the reign, but it was only for a short period after which traders again became exposed to their former risks, which were yet to continue for more than a century.

The war not only hindered trade by encouraging piracy, it also increased the frequency with which ships were arrested for the royal service. Arrests were often made considerably [3] before the service of the ships concerned was strictly necessary, and cargoes were forcibly discharged before reaching the port to which they were consigned.[4] Wines for Hull, Yarmouth, and Harwich were frequently brought to shore at the ports of the south coast, and in this way the east coast towns suffered not indeed alone but most heavily from the increased number of arrests in this reign.

1. *C.P.R.* 1327–30, p. 98.
2. *A.M.Bord.*, I, p. 158; *C.C.R.* 1346–9, pp. 405, 690; *Foed.*, III, pt. i, 266; *C.P.R.* 1358–61, p. 255; *Foed.*, III, pt. i, 229, 266, 270; *Ib.*, pt. ii, 600, 607, 611.
3. *C.P.R.* 1334–8, pp. 201, 567.   4. *C.C.R.* 1360–4, p. 17.

There was yet another direction in which by its effect on shipping war proved harmful to the traders with Gascony. At the beginning of Edward's reign the importation of wine had been carried on both in annual[1] fleets and in ships voyaging alone. The military value which merchant shipping acquired in time of war during an age when there was little difference between the mercantile marine and the navy led to the discouragement of the latter mode of trading. During the later years of the reign of Edward III the ships trading with Gascony often appear to have had the dual[2] character of merchant ship and ship of war, and carried both seamen and armed forces. In periods of actual warfare, when the armaments of the French were at sea, attempts were made to restrict the trading with Gascony to the visit of the fleet, which was accompanied by an armed convoy.[3] Thus it became usual in making grants of letters of protection and in issuing trading licences to require[4] that the journey to and from Gascony should be made in company with the fleet. These attempts to concentrate English shipping with Gascony into the passage of the fleet were strengthened by an important statute[5] of 1353 and by the proclamation[6] that the vessels of shipmasters refusing to join the fleet would be forfeited.

The fleet sailed with royal licence at the end of summer or the beginning of autumn, and deprived the country of so great a portion[7] of her naval strength for so long a period that its sailing was a matter of national concern. The naval value of the wine fleet became increasingly important in the reign of Edward III. In 1336 and 1338 upon licence for the fleet being granted it was ordained that it should be equipped for war, part of its duty being 'to repel[8] and destroy the galleys and ships of war gathered at sea for the King's annoyance.' The officer in charge was empowered to imprison those disobeying his orders, an essential condition of command, since the seamen of the Cinque Ports and Yarmouth were ever ready to break out into dissensions,

---

1. *C.C.R.* 1337–9, pp. 283, 526; *C.P.R.* 1334–8, pp. 2, 566, 567, 569.
2. *E.g., C.C.R.* 1369–74, p. 51.   3. *C.P.R.* 1370–4, p. 204.
4. *Ib.* 1334–8, p. 339.   5. 27 Edw. III, St. 1, c. vii.
6. *Rot. Scot.*, I, 467, 468.
7. *C.P.R.* 1338–40, p. 2; *Ib.* 1350–4, p. 376.
8. *C.C.R.* 1337–9, pp. 283, 526.

while the presence of the Scots, Welsh, and Spaniards tended to make control still more difficult. They were to keep together under pain of forfeiture of those separating themselves, and in case loss was sustained by the flight of some members, the fugitives were to make satisfaction [1] according to the size and value of their ships.

The economic difficulties which resulted from this restriction of trade to one season made themselves felt most after the year 1350, when other difficulties of the same character also began to appear. Between the years 1337 and 1351 no statute had been passed making any general change in the conditions under which the wine trade was carried on, but there was a great development in the power and wealth of the vintners and a great extension of their activities in Gascony. In this connection we hear the name of William Talbot,[2] while Vincent of Barnstaple [3] and William of Wakefield [4] were citizens of Bordeaux during this period. In Toulouse, Saintonge, Périgord, and the Agenais there were many English subjects,[5] while the Gascon town of Libourne was a great resort of English merchants. If other evidence were wanting an important statute [6] of 1353 affords ample proof that by that time English merchants had settled in Gascony in such numbers as to raise grave suspicion at home.

At no previous time had the vintners included among their number so many persons of such influence as John Malewayn, John Stodeye, Henry Picard, John Michel, Henry Vannere, Henry Palmere, William Clapitus, Henry del Strete, John and Richard de Rothyng, and Richard Chaucer. The magnitude and variety of the enterprises of these and other vintners of this time were very remarkable. Picard, in addition to his work as a vintner, was a merchant of the Staple at Bruges and served the City of London as alderman,[7] mayor,[8] and sheriff.[9] The King also profited by his services as butler,[10] merchant,[11] and financier,[12] and it was probably as

1. *Rot. Parl.*, IV, 85.
3. *C.P.R.* 1340–3, p. 162.
5. *Ib.*, R. II, pt. ii, p. 874.
7. *Bk. F.*, p. 205.
9. *Ib.* 1345–8, p. 388.
11. *C.C.R.* 1346–9, p. 66.
12. *C.P.R.* 1345–8, pp. 69, 70, 441; *C.C.R.* 1343–6, pp. 410, 600, 601, 627; *Ib.* 1346–9, p. 5; *Ib.* 1349–54, p. 128.

2 *C.C.R.* 1333–7, p. 42.
4. *Foed.*, R. III, pt. i, p. 432.
6. 27 Edw. III, St. 1, c. vii.
8. *C.P.R.* 1354–8, p. 490.
10. *Ib.* 1348–50, p. 570.

a reward for these that he received knighthood and a life annuity of fifty pounds upon the customs of London.   As a financier he advanced to the Crown enormous sums which were devoted to the prosecution of the war, receiving payment from the tenths and fifteenths granted by parliament, the subsidy on wool, and by licences for its export free of custom.   On occasion he and his fellows advanced loans of as much as 35,000 marks,[1] while the Crown [2] is known to have been offered to him as a pledge for repayment.   His dealings with private merchants were also large, as when in company with Stodeye and Wesenham he became indebted [3] to two merchants of Bristol to the extent of £1,614. Stodeye, who also was a knight [4] and a vintner, occupied the same posts [5] in the service of the Crown and the City as Picard.   He was one of the merchants appointed [6] in 1349 to see that the new coinage was of the standard ordained. As in the case of Picard [7] the intimacy of his relationships with Gascony may be inferred from the frequency with which he was chosen to be attorney [8] in England for influential Gascons.   Thus his services were secured [9] by the Gascon executors of the will of the Lord of Albret for the settlement of the affairs of the deceased in England.   His debts to the Archbishop [10] of Canterbury and Sir Walter Manny [11] afford some evidence of the variety of his dealings, while their extent is indicated by numerous recognisances made by persons who were indebted to him for merchandise in sums frequently amounting [12] to £400.   The extensive nature of his premises [13] in the City is further evidence of the same fact, while his gift [14] to the vintners of the site of their Hall affords some sign of the wealth he derived from his transactions. Malewayn too continued in the service of the Crown with dealings in wine.   Like most vintners [15] he had interests in the wool trade also previous to 1363, and for a time held the

1.   *C.P.R.* 1345–8, p. 69.   2.   *C.C.R.* 1346–9, p. 40.
3.   *Ib.* 1343–6, p. 551.   4.   *C.P.R.* 1370–4, p. 161.
5.   *Ib.* 1345–8, p. 253; *C.C.R.* 1354–60, p. 458; *Ib.* 1369–74, p. 536.
6.   *Ib.* 1349–54, p. 63.   7.   *C.P.R.* 1361–4, p. 25.
8.   *Ib.* 1354–8, p. 95; *Ib.* 1361–4, p. 25; *C.C.R.* 1374–7, p. 114.
9.   *C.P.R.* 1354–8, p. 274.   10. *C.C.R.* 1343–6, p. 667.
11. *Ib.* 1346–9, p. 416.   12. *E.g.,* *Ib.* 1349–54, p. 509.
13. "Winchester Selde."
14. Herbert. *Twelve Great Livery Companies,* II, 635.
15. *E.g., C.C.R.* 1354–60, p. 116; *C.P.R.* 1358–61, p. 75

ferm[1] of the King's customs of wool in London; in 1349 he received for life the office[2] of the tronage and pesage of wool in London; in 1359 he was governor[3] of the liberties and privileges of English merchants in Flanders, Holland, and Zeeland; and in 1360 obtained a like office[4] in Bruges. He was also the King's alnager,[5] and served the City as alderman. Though his dealings in wine were not on the scale of Stodeye and Picard, they were not inconsiderable.[6] A remarkable instance of the great capital of some merchants at this time is that of William of Wakefield, who during a truce with France lost wine to the value of £5,000 at the hands of the latter.[7] Another London vintner of great repute at this time was William Clapitus, who with Henry del Strete became creditor[8] in 1346 to Walter de Chiriton and his fellows in the sum of £1,027 6s. 8d., while the assessment[9] of the latter in 1345 and 1346 in connection with the collection of the fifteenth at ten marks sufficiently indicated his wealth. In 1346 Richard Chaucer became creditor[10] to Walter de Chiriton to the extent of £420, while John Osekyn, at one time[11] a vintner of comparatively small importance was able to join[12] a London Spicer in 1347 in lending Thomas Flemyng of Newcastle on Tyne £500. Richard Lyons was another merchant who, if not exclusively a vintner, frequently traded in wine. He played a great part in the financial affairs of the Crown and in the civic life of London at this time. In 1373 he obtained[13] the lease of the subsidy of two shillings per tun on wine, and sixpence in the pound on merchandise, while in February, 1374, in company with Richard Franceys, he lent[14] the King 8,354 marks, and in August[15] of the same year, with John Pyel, £10,000. He rented[16] from Picard's widow the cellars which Picard had once used, and shared for a time a monopoly[17] of the sale of sweet wine in London. He was

1. *Ib.* 1348–50, p. 448. 2. *Ib.* 1348–50, p. 571.
3. *Ib.* 1358–61, p. 285; *C.C.R.* 1354–60, p. 592.
4. *Ib.* 1360–4, p. 10. 5. *C.P.R.* 1358–61, p. 283.
6. *E.g., Ib.* 1358–61, p. 75. 7. *Foed.,* July 16 1359.
8. *C.C.R.* 1346–9, p. 40. 9. *Ib.,* p. 130.
10. *Ib.,* p. 36.
11. For subsidy of 1339 he was assessed at 16d.
12. *C.C.R.* 1346–9, p. 240. 13 *C.P.R.* 1370–4, p. 382.
14. *Ib.* 1370–4. p. 411. 15. *C.C.R.* 1374–7, p. 41.
16. *Ib.* 1374–7, p. 415. 17. *Rot. Parl.,* II, 328.

at one time sheriff[1] of the city, and in 1371 was one of the
lieutenants[2] of ' the King's fleet toward the west.' The
nature of the dealings of John Michel, a merchant who
appears to have been exclusively a vintner, may be seen from
the fact that he was on one[3] occasion debtor to three
Gascons in £666 13s. 4d., and on another[4] owed a Bristol
trader £200. Not to add to the number of examples, the
very numerous loans,[5] debts, and purchases of quit rents,[6]
manors,[7] and rights[8] in land made by the vintners at this
time clearly testify to the growing wealth and influence of
the vintners.

It was doubtless in opposition to the activities of these,
especially in London, that in 1351 a series of commercial
enactments was initiated which affected the wine trade during
the remainder of the reign. In that year the Statute of York
(1335) was re-enacted[9] and it remained[10] in force until 1376,
despite repeated demands for its repeal. Moreover, on this
occasion its operation was not restricted by any exceptions
in favour of London, so that full liberty of trade
throughout England was accorded to all, aliens as
well as natives, and even in their own City the merchants of
London were to enjoy no advantage over aliens. In pro-
ducing this change many causes acted together, the most
important of which was the high price of wine at this period,
and the consequent popular demand for such legislation. In
November, 1342, an ordinance[11] had been made that wine
should be sold at what had become in London the usual rate
of fourpence per gallon, but in 1353 the necessity arose for a
royal injunction[12] to limit the price to sixpence. The public
became alarmed at the rise in prices, and in 1349 complained[13]
that the vintners and fishmongers forestalled the market,
while in March, 1351, outcry[14] was again raised against
victuallers, wholesale and retail, who advanced the price of

1.   *C.C.R.* 1374–7, p. 259.   2.   *C.P.R.* 1370–4, p. 180.
3.   *C.C.R.* 1360–4, p. 408.   4.   *Ib.* 1364–8, p. 44.
5.   *Ib.* 1354–60, pp. 60, 99; *Bk. F.*, pp. 149, 235, loans to King.
6.   *Ib.* 1346–9, p. 504; and 1364–60, pp. 99, 224, 335.
7.   *Ib.* 1343–6, p. 198.
8.   *Ib.* 1349–54, p. 509; 1354–60, pp. 99, 224, 308; and 1360–4, pp. 399, 533, etc.
9.   25 Edw. III, St. 3; *Rot. Parl.*, II, 232a.
10. *Ib.*, II, 347b.   11. *Bk. F.*, p. 83.
12. *Bk. G.*, pp. 4, 41.   13. *Bk. F.*, p. 201.
14. *Ib.*, p. 230; *Rot. Parl.*, II, 232a.

victuals. It cannot be doubted that the free-trade enactment of 1351 was the result of the same popular outcry.

Two years later this enactment was followed by others equally important. Early in 1353, despite frequent petitions[1] in the City for its repeal, the Statute of 1351 was confirmed,[2] together with an ordinance forbidding all exportation of wine from England, as this it was stated was carried on with the specific purpose of raising the price of what remained. The same year moreover witnessed the enactment[3] of what was probably the most important and certainly the most lasting[4] of all measures affecting this branch of trade. In this statute prohibition was made against the engrossing and forestalling of wine in Gascony by English merchants, and in order to prevent this more effectually it was declared that no English merchant nor any acting on his behalf should visit Gascony for the purchase of wine before the time of vintage, when common passage was made for that purpose; none should reside there; nor should any bargain for wine save in the ports of Bordeaux and Bayonne. On the other hand, Gascons were permitted and indeed encouraged to import wine from all parts of the Duchy.

The statute of 1353 was suggested by much the same considerations as produced that of 1351. Like that enactment it was an endeavour on the part of the consumers of wine to check the rise in prices by restricting and regulating the activities of English vintners who, it was believed, were the cause of it.[5] In 1351 the attempt had been made to lower the price of wine by emancipating the Gascon trader in London and preventing forestalling at home; in 1353 an attempt was made to secure the same result by restricting and regulating the operations of the English trader in Gascony and by preventing the forestalling of the Gascon market.[6]

Taken together the two statutes by granting freedom of trade in England to Gascons and by restricting the liberties of English traders in Gascony appeared to produce a transfer of the balance of privilege from the latter to the former, and

1. *Bk. F.*, pp. 229, 242.
2. *Bk. G.*, p. 4.
3. 27 Edw. III, St. 1.
4. *Rot. Parl.*, II, 114b.
5. 27 Edw. III, St. I.
6. *Rot. Parl.*, II, 249a.

in 1357 complaint [1] was made to this effect.   But though the Gascons as a whole thus obtained advantages over English merchants, the citizens of Bordeaux and Bayonne gained doubly, an effect which was in full agreement with the diplomatic needs of the Crown, its recent policy and that of the two cities.   The facility with which Bordeaux obtained privileges as regard the customs has already been noted.[2] Further, of all the natives of the Duchy, its inhabitants had the greatest liberty [3] of trade within Gascony, and they acquired a little later a strict monopoly of the right to retail wines [4] in their own city from Easter to Michaelmas annually. In 1366 they received [5] from the Duke of Lancaster the offer of this monopoly for the whole year, and in 1373 they secured an ordinance [6] forbidding the sale of wines of the Haut Pays in their city even by the porters of Bordeaux castle.   The natives of Gascon towns of the interior, La Réole, Bergerac, Ste-Foy, St.-Emilion, and Libourne, had occasion in the next century to complain [7] of the action of the Bordelais who opposed the entry into their city of the wines of other Gascons, while they denounced [8] as intolerable the action of certain wealthy merchants of Bordeaux, who not content with this, engrossed wine with the object of obtaining a monopoly of its sale.   In 1351 the municipal authorities had obtained from Edward III an ordinance [9] forbidding the loading of wine for foreign parts at any place between Crebat and Castillon other than at Bordeaux, and it was but the culmination of this policy and of the influence of that city when in 1353 even the right of the English to bargain in Gascony was restricted to the two towns of Bordeaux and Bayonne.

By these means, the emancipation of the Gascon trader in England, and the more rigid regulation of the dealings of English merchants in Gascony, it was sought to restrain the enhancement of prices which, it was believed, was artificially effected.   That these suspicions were justified appears certain, though doubtless other causes also contributed to this result.   A general rise in prices occurred after 1349 as

1. *Bk. G.*, p. 86.   2. *Vide supra*, p. 286.
3. *A.M.Bord.*, I, 25 June 1358.   4. *Ib.* I, 196 (A.D. 1358).
5. *Ib.*, I, 268.   6. *Ib.*, 20 March 1373.
7. *I.S. Gironde*, E. Suppl., 2,899, p. 294.   8. *Ib.*
9. *A.M.Bord.*, I, 178. Crebat (Crevat) was the north-western part of Bordeaux, on the left bank of the Garonne.

a result of the Black Death, and the debasement of the coinage. The war too, as has been seen, produced a rise in prices by entailing upon merchants the cost of convoy and by restricting importation to England to the passage of the fleet, thus enabling the Gascons to make great gains from their English customers, who after so long and costly a voyage would not return without purchase. Moreover, this tendency towards an abnormal demand in Gascony during vintage was only confirmed by the Statute of Wine, 1353, and though its ill effects were recognised some years later,[1] even then relief was not sought in a repeal of the statute. Still another cause of the enhanced prices is to be found in the deplorable condition of the Gascon coinage at this time. An attempt to deal with the evil was made in 1351 when it was ordained[2] that all Gascon coins should be of the same weight and alloy as those of Bordeaux. This measure, however, did not effect a remedy, and the evil was still great[3] in 1354. Accordingly in this year it was ordained[4] that the pound and not the florin should be used in all dealings in Aquitaine, and that any persons conducting transactions contrary to this decree should forfeit the goods involved. Next year a new coin, the silver leopard, was instituted,[5] and of this a fresh issue was made in the following year,[6] but it is improbable that these measures were more effective than those of 1351—and monetary conditions in Gascony appear to have been equally chaotic in 1361[7] and 1367.[8] There can be no doubt but that this evil was a real cause of the difficulties merchants experienced, and consequently of the high price of wines in England. Not only is this made highly probable by the persistence of the agitation respecting the coinage and mint of Gascony at this period, it is explicitly stated in the records.[9]

There is no reason to suppose that the statute of 1353, with its twofold policy of liberating the Gascon and regu-

---

1. *C.P.R.* 1364–7, pp. 6, 7. 2. *A.M.Bord.*, I, 272.
3. *I.S. Gironde*, G. Suppl., 1—920, p. 113, A.D. 1354. Also *Foed.*, III, pt. i, 272.
4. *Ib.*, 272. 5. *I.S.Gironde*, G. Suppl., 15—920, p. 114, A.D. 1355.
6. *Ib.*, p. 117, A.D. 1356. 7. *Ib.*, p. 121.
8. *A.M. Bord.*, I, 26 Jan. 1367–7. The Black Prince fixed for five years the value of money as a concession to the three estates of Gascony when negotiating with them for a hearth tax.
9. *Foed.*, III, pt. i, 272.

lating the activities of the native trader, achieved any considerable success.   It is however certain that the restriction of English trading activity in Gascony to two cities was injurious to several small Gascon towns.   Thus as early as May, 1355, the people of Libourne, a town which had been founded by Edward I in 1269 [1] and was a centre for English traders, complained [2] that since the passing of the statute of 1353 they had been reduced to destitution.   Their whole living, they declared, consisted in the sale of wine, for the most part to English exporters, and this commerce the statute of 1353 had destroyed.   As a result of this complaint it was found necessary to admit Libourne to equal privileges with Bordeaux and Bayonne.   The statute was, moreover, quite ineffectual to achieve its chief object, the lowering of the price of wine in England.   The ten years immediately succeeding its enactment were marked by repeated regulation [3] of prices, and in London wine sold at more than the regulated price was 'seised' [4] by the authorities, yet at the end [5] of that period a distinct rise in prices was noticeable, the retail price having doubled during a period of twenty years.   Even so early as December, 1354, it was found necessary to intervene on behalf of the consumer by royal proclamation, [6] limiting the price in London to sixpence, while so extensive did the evil of high prices become that the necessity arose, [7] apparently for the first time, for the specific regulation of prices by royal ordinance both in London and in several parts of the provinces. In 1357 the Chancellor, Justices, and King's Council were empowered [8] to deal with the matter, but no remedy was to be had from them. The fact that free-trade in wine had already existed in the provinces without disturbance for nearly twenty years suggests [9] that the restrictions now placed on native traders were the real cause of economic embarrassment at this time.   Regulation was not, however, confined to price alone.   It was ordained [10] that the purchaser should be allowed to see his wine drawn, and that new

1. Cunningham, I, 268.   2. *Foed.*, III, pt. i, 300.
3. *Bk. G.*, pp. 35, 41, 42, 77, 149; *C.C.R.* 1354–60, pp. 37, 111, 112, 134, 299, 540; *Ib.* 1360–4, pp. 95, 446.
4. *Bk. G.*, pp. 41, 42.   5. *Ib.*, p. 149.
6. *Ib.*, p. 42.   7. *C.C.R.* 1354–60, p. 299.
8. 31 Edw. III, St. 2, c. 3.   9. *C.C.R.* 1354–60, p. 37.
10. *Bk. G.*, pp. 102, 104, 138, 145.

wine should not be mixed with old for the purpose of rendering putrid wines suitable for sale, an object which was also sought in more frequent inspection of taverns and by legislation[1] against the retention of this commodity from sale until unfitted for use. Yet in spite of these precautions the King's Butler had occasion to license[2] the exportation of large quantities of wine of inferior quality, a proceeding which had been unnecessary or unusual at any previous time, while compulsion[3] was required to keep taverns open and to cause vintners and taverners to offer their wines for sale at the regulated prices. A highly important precaution in view of the amount of wine taken from England to Flanders at this period was the more rigid prohibition[4] of exportation without special licence, while the object which underlay this policy was still further sought in a proclamation[5] made in London against the importation of wines of Gascony elsewhere than to England. Even so late as 1444 the Commons petitioned[6] that English merchants should be allowed to buy Gascon wines at other towns of the Duchy as well as at Bordeaux and Bayonne.

The difficulties under which the wine trade suffered during the years 1353 to 1363 may therefore reasonably be considered as resulting chiefly from the statute of 1353, which sought to control the activities of English vintners in Gascony, creating as it did an abnormal demand at one season annually. This involved a stricter regulation of retail prices in England in order to prevent their making good their losses at the expense of the home consumer; while the decline in the importation of wine to England, the attempt to export wine once imported, and the refusal of retailers to sell at the regulated price, mark the dissatisfaction of dealers with this regulation. It is to the interaction of these causes that we must attribute the growth of the vintners' mistery in the immediately succeeding years.

The raising of the retail price of wine to eightpence[7] in 1363 was accompanied by renewed agitation on the part of the consumer. Already in 1362 a confirmation[8] of the

1. *Bk. G.*, p. 149; *C.C.R.* 1354–60, p. 37.
2. *C.P.R.* 1358–61, p. 44.   3. *Bk. G.*, p. 137.
4. *C.P.R.* 1358–61, p. 44.   5. *Bk. G.*, p. 52.
6. *Rot. Parl.*, V, 114b.   7. *Bk. G.*, p. 149.
8. *Rot. Parl.*, II, 270b.

statutes and ordinances against the monopoly of wines and victuals had been obtained, but further measures were now suggested for the restraint of prices. The Commons petitioned [1] for an investigation of the work of engrossers to be conducted by "foreign inquests," and carried a demand that importers should be required [2] to bring with their wine written evidence of their price in Gascony to aid local authorities in making the assize. Of still greater importance, however, was an enactment [3] forbidding merchants to deal in more than one commodity, which though it related to all kinds of merchandise, had special reference to wine where it had already been the subject of a petition [4] by consumers. Moreover, while these measures were being taken to prevent engrossing at home further action was taken to prevent its taking place in Gascony. The statute of 1353 was confirmed,[5] and it was provided [6] that the Crown should be informed of persons who visited or remained in Gascony contrary to this enactment.

The legislation of 1363 became the basis in the following year of a remarkable series of charters which accorded to several misteries exclusive powers of trade, each in a certain commodity,[7] the most important being those granted to the fishmongers, drapers, and vintners. By the charter of the last named the right of natives to trade with Gascony or to engage in the sale of wine in England was severely restricted —in London to those free of vintners' craft, in the provinces to those who could show an equal intimacy with the trade. Gascons might import wines as before, and sell them in gross to merchant vintners and others, chiefly nobles, who desired wine in large quantities for their own needs and not for resale, but they were strictly forbidden to retail them. At the same time the right to supervise and regulate retail prices was given to the more capitalistic element of the mistery by a provision enforcing the annual election for this purpose of four [8] persons of the most knowledgeable of the craft not

1. *Rot. Parl.*, II, 276b.   2. *Ib.*, II, 279b; St. 37 Edw. III.
3. St. 37 Edw. III.
4. *Rot. Parl.*, II, 278a; *C.C.R.* 1360–4, p. 284.
5. *Rot. Parl.*, II, 279b, 282b, St. 37, Edw. III.   6. *Ibid.*
7. *C.C.R.* 1364–8, pp. 74 et seq.
8. By this time engrossers were not prohibited from retailing as formerly. Riley, *Mem.*, p. 81; *C.P.R.* 1364–7, p. 687.

holding taverns in the City of London.' The persons elected were to receive public recognition and were empowered to punish offenders with the aid, if need be, of the mayor, bailiff, or president of the town. The prohibition against the re-exportation of wine without the King's licence already so often made was again repeated, and with the object of preventing the exportation of money, licence was given to native vintners to export cloth, and to Gascons to export cloth, herrings and dried fish of Cornwall and Devon with which they might purchase wines in Gascony. This encroachment of the activities of the vintners upon those of the fishmongers and drapers was carefully retricted to the purchase of fish and cloth equal in value to that of the wines imported. It was found necessary to make this exception in the vintners' favour in order to avoid the violation of a principle rapidly rising into prominence in mediæval economy—the retention of bullion [1]—and moreover it was peculiar to the vintners that of the three misteries then receiving charters theirs alone was concerned with a commodity imported from abroad.

There can be no doubt that this charter was accorded at the instance and in the interest of the native vintners. It conferred on the mistery, if not a monopoly, such a command of the whole trade in wines as was practically its equivalent. Among natives they alone could import, while the Gascons, their only rivals in this respect, were deprived of the fruit of their enterprise by their inability to retail and the consequent obligation under which they lay of selling to vintners at the purchasers' price the wine they imported unless indeed they were fortunate enough to secure in some noble, or person of wealth a purchaser who required wine in great quantities for the needs of a large household. Thus almost the entire wholesale supply of wine was at the command of the vintners, who could accordingly make easy purchases, while they possessed also the further advantage of controlling retail prices.

To obtain the grant of this charter, and more especially of the clause restricting to them the right of seeking wines in Gascony, the vintners brought forward [2] many reasons. They

1. 9 Edw. III, St. 2, c. i.   2. *C.P.R.* 1364–7, pp. 6–7.

stated that there was no other merchandise in Gascony which
was of profit in England, and hence English traders visiting
Gascony under any but carefully regulated conditions placed
both themselves and the trade in a disadvantageous position
at the hands of the Gascon dealers, who saw how necessary
for them it was to make purchases, and accordingly raised
prices.   They affirmed that the mere presence in Gascony
of great numbers of English people of divers trades afforded
the Gascons the opportunity to enhance prices.   The manner
of bargaining adopted by the non-vintner element, they
declared to be even more harmful. Large sums of money and
' earnests,' they said, were taken out by these, who being
unable or unwilling to wait ' so as to employ them reasonably,'
put a price on the wines by ' truk' or by exchanges which
amounted to an excessive sum.   Moreover, it was argued by
the vintners, these persons having other commercial interests
besides those in wine, had no need to sell except at will, and
therefore like the engrossers, whose activities so injured
retailers, they could await a time when higher prices prevailed.   It was also said to be impossible for dealers of this
character to be regulated as could those who made their living
solely by the sale of wine, and prices were enhanced by commodities passing through many hands.   Finally it was maintained by the vintners themselves, that they had been
' disturbed ' in their trade, and were unable to buy at a
reasonable price, while the Gascons, being able to sell in their
own country at so great a price, had no further need to
visit England.

Doubtless a prohibition of all but vintners visiting Gascony
would enable these to buy more cheaply, but this need not,
and in fact [2] did not, lead to greater abundance or cheapness
of wine in England.   For the moment, however, the vintners
were successful, and obtained the charter of 1363, and this
the more easily as it also afforded the Crown better opportunities for the regulation of this branch of trade.

Almost immediately it was enforced the charter produced
difficulties, chiefly in consequence of its prohibition of the
exportation of bullion. The issue of licences permitting the
violation of this rule were at once necessitated in order to

1. *C.P.R.* 1364-7, p. 6.   2. *Rot. Parl.*, II, 287.

render possible the mere continuance of the trade with Gascony. Great importance attaches to these licences, as nothing, not excepting even the licences for the direct exportation of wool to Gascony granted after the establishment of the staple of wools at Calais in 1363 indicates so clearly as these the enormous extent to which wine was imported by the English, the different parts of the country to which it was consigned, and the variety of purchase by which it was procured. From both, examples of the corporate or joint-stock undertaking may be given. In May, 1364, just three months before the Vintners' Charter was accorded, the town of Plymouth received licence [1] to export to Gascony and Spain " two thousand cloths of colour, and two thousand packs of cloth of Devon and Cornwall " with which to procure wines and other merchandise. Three months later, and as a direct result of the charter, a still more striking instance occurred. Twenty-five vintners of the City of London, whose names included those of Sir John Stodeye, and William Stodeye, John Michel, John Rothyng, and William de la More, received licence [2] to take to Gascony two thousand pounds with which to purchase wines, the sum being divided among them " according to their estates by the advice of the whole mistery of vintners," while by a similar licence they were permitted to take one thousand marks to the Rhine and Eastland with which to make like purchases. At the same time licences were issued for the exportation of cloth from the ports of Hull, Ipswich, and Colchester to Gascony and for the exportation of both cloth and fish from Plymouth, Fowey and Mousehole.

The main provisions of the charter did not, however, remain long in force. In little more than a year they were repealed " de facto," if not indeed " de iure " by the statute of 38 Edward III (1365). Already, apparently in November, 1364, the commonalty of London had claimed that enfranchised [3] persons should be free to sell wholesale any manner of merchandise upon which they could make a profit, though they should retail only those goods that belonged to their own mistery. In short, the smaller tradesmen sought in their

---

1. *C.P.R.* 1361-4, p. 496.   2. *Ib.* 1364-7, pp. 15.
3. *Bk. G.*, pp. 179, 187.

V

own interest to restrict the statute of 37 Edward III (1363) to the retail trade, and claimed the right to deal freely at wholesale in all commodities.   Their object was in part attained in the statute [1] of 1365, which, however, not only accorded to them full freedom of trade in all commodities, with liberty to seek wine in Gascony, but also conceded to Gascons freedom of sale in England.   By this return to the free-trade policy it was hoped to make greater abundance of this commodity in England.

Thus within eighteen months of its being granted the vintners' monopoly was withdrawn, only the right to control taverns and regulate retail prices remaining of all the privileges conferred on them by their charter.   Yet even now complaint was not less frequent than before.   In November, 1365, in consequence of such complaint the Mayor of London was authorised [2] to examine cellars for putrid wine, while during the two years succeeding the enactment of the statute of 1365 Gascons frequently obtained permission [3] to export unsound wine.   Prices did not fall, as might have been expected, but rather continued to rise.   In June, 1366, in London the Mayor of the City was required [4] to summon the vintners and merchants of London to deliberate with a view to removing the serious clamour occasioned by the price of wine.   In October the same year similar dissatisfaction existed in Beverley [5] as a result of the price of wine in that town, being twelve pence per gallon while in Hull it was eightpence.   In February, 1368, so serious was the position in London that the leading vintners were required [6] to undertake before the Mayor and Aldermen that wine should be sold at a reasonable price, while they also promised to notify the price before the Black Prince on his return from Gascony if need be.

By the statute of 1365 the conditions which had prevailed in the wine trade from 1353 to 1363 were restored.   All native merchants, excepting only artificers, became free to make the voyage to Gascony to purchase wine, while at the

1. St. 38 Edw. III; *cf. Bk. G.*, pp. 203, 206.
2. *Foed.*, III, pt. ii, p. 778; *C.P.R.* 1364–8, p. 280.
3. *Ib.* 1364–7, pp. 1, 104, 107, 27, 3075, 310, 324.
4. *C.C.R.* 1364–8, p. 280; *Bk. G.*, p. 208; *Foed.*, III, pt. ii, p. 795.
5. *C.C.R.* 1364–8, p. 299; also *Foed.*, III, pt. ii, 811.
6. *Bk. G.*, p. 222.

same time the Gascons received full liberty of sale in England. The policy of 1353 and that of 1363 were directly in opposition to each other, but in the statute of 1365 the former again won acceptance. From this time the policy adopted in regard to the wine trade was unstable in the extreme and admittedly tentative. Prices still continued to rise, and neither the policy of 1353 which favoured the Gascon, nor that of 1363-4 which favoured the native merchant, had proved successful in arresting their advance. Accordingly in 1368 a new attempt to deal with the difficulty was made. It was enacted[1] that natives should not visit Gascony with a view to the purchase of wine nor should they depute aliens to bring it on their behalf, but wine should be imported only by Gascons and other aliens. At the same time, moreover, the retail trade in wine was restricted to natives, and the Gascons thus lost, temporarily at least, what they had gained in 1365. Of the motives which produced this statute one of the most powerful was the desire to retain bullion within the country. This was sufficiently clearly stated[2] in 1368, but the idea found even more explicit expression[3] in 1559, when it was made one of the chief reasons for a proposed revival of the statute of 1368. It was also thought that by thus imposing the necessity of voyage upon the Gascons they could be compelled to sell cheap by reason of the great loss they would incur should they return without having negotiated a sale.

It was declared at the time of the repeal of this statute the following year (1369) that it had had good effects upon prices. Two reasons only were openly alleged as grounds for its repeal. The Black Prince, then Prince of Aquitaine, complained that by prohibiting the visits of English merchants to Gascony for the purchase of wine much remained unsold, while his receipts from customs had been much diminished. The outbreak of war made both these results particularly undesirable at this time. It was essential to confirm the bond between England and Gascony, and this could best be effected by economic changes which favoured the Gascons as a whole, since it was largely upon the economic tie that the loyalty of Gascony depended. Thus it

1. St. 42 Edw. III, c. 8.   2. *Rot. Parl.*, II, 296.
3. Hist. MSS. Com. Rep. on Salisbury, *MSS.* I, 163.

became necessary to remove the restriction by which only the wealthier Gascons who could afford to export on their own account had direct access to the English purchaser, and to afford facilities for sale to the smaller dealers who obtained their best prices from the English merchants who visited Gascony. At the same time, despite the alleged improvement of prices, there was a scarcity of wine in England, so that it was to the general advantage that wine should not remain unsold in Gascony for want of English buyers. As however the new statute [1] required merchants to give security not to import less than one hundred tuns " of their proper goods and of others " the trade, while opened to natives generally, was still confined to the wealthier class of English merchants. It cannot be doubted that this restriction was a real source of injury to native small dealers. In 1371 the Commons petitioned[2] for a definite repeal both of the statute of 1368 and that of 1369, and complained that they had made wine dearer and had checked the growth of English power at sea. Their petition was refused [3] in 1372, though both complaints appear to have been justified.

The last year of the reign was marked by a return to those forms of hostility to the alien which had been so familiar in the reign of Edward II. In 1376 complaint was made[4] by the civic authorities of London against the liberties of aliens who were said to be acting as brokers and retailers. They had also become householders, and as such were accused of harbouring spies, while they were also responsible, it was believed, for the impairing of the navy. These complaints were not unheeded, and in consequence the restriction under which they already lay of selling in gross only was made more severe by an ordinance [5] forbidding aliens to sell to aliens for resale, to act as brokers, or to hold hostel. In December, 1377, the Gascons received[6] exemption from the prohibition of aliens to trade among themselves, though the obligation upon aliens to lodge with hostellers and not to keep hostel on their own account was once more confirmed,

1. 43 Edw. III, c. 3.
2. *Rot. Parl.*, II, 206b.
3. *Ib.*, II, 315a.

4. *Rot. Parl.*, II, 347b.
5. *Bk. H.*, p. 53.
6. *Ib.*, p. 86.

in 1378. This return to the old attitude towards aliens was, however, no more permanent than in earlier times. Conditions still continued to vary, and in 1388 the citizens of London were deprived [1] by statute of the exclusive powers of trading they had sought to exercise to the prejudice of such as were not free of the City.

1. *Ib.*, p. 90.

F. SARGEANT.

CALAIS UNDER EDWARD III.

Calais in the twentieth century is a typical port and manufacturing town of modern times, with its extensive harbour,
partly of natural formation partly of special construction, huge
factories for the manufacture of silk and cotton net and other
products, and canals and railways linking up its various districts.[1] There do not seem to be any maps of the town in
the fourteenth century extant, if indeed any ever existed, so
that to obtain information of it as it was nearly 600 years
ago one is dependent upon such slight descriptions as the
chronicler or records afford, and with these as a basis one
must endeavour by comparison with later maps to form some
idea of the mediæval town. For this purpose the map and
the general view during the time of Henry VIII., published
by the editor of Turpin's " Chronicle of Calais," are the most
useful.

Apparently, when conquered by Edward III., it covered
an area of about 200 acres, corresponding to the district of the
modern town known as Calais-Nord.[2] It was defended by
two walls and two ditches, the latter of which could be flooded
by sea-water,[3] whilst the harbour, formed by a piece of land
jutting east, was an additional defence to the north. At the
extreme north-west was the castle, the fortifications of which
were merged in the town walls. In the centre was the market
place. There was also a suburb beyond the walls stretching
east, south and west,[4] which coincided to some extent with a
part of the modern St. Pierre, or Calais-Sud.

On the 4th of August, 1347,[5] after eleven months' heroic
resistance which has made it famous in the annals of history,
Calais surrendered to Edward III., and thus became for two
hundred years a centre for the English wool trade with the

1. P. Joanne, *Dictionnaire Géographique et Administratif de la France*, II,
681–683.
2. *Ib.*, II, 681–683; Nichols, map bet. pp. xxviii and xxix.
3. Baker, p. 90.
4. *Foed.*, III, i, 142; *Rot. Parl.*, II, 359; Nichols, map bet. pp. xxviii
and xxix.
5. Baker, p. 91; Knighton, II, 51.

continent, and a convenient landing place for English armies. During that period the King of England did indeed in the words of Geoffrey Harcourt " carry the keys of the kingdom of France " [1] at his girdle.

Having taken the town, Edward ordered the Chancellor, the Treasurer and the Archbishop of Canterbury [2] to summon John de Pulteney, William de la Pole, Roger Norman, and any other wealthy merchants whom they chose, and to require them to go to Calais for a month or six weeks, taking with them merchants and others suitable for giving aid and counsel with regard to its administration. He also issued a proclamation throughout England that houses would be assigned to all English persons wishing to reside there who crossed over before a certain date, such houses to be granted for a reasonable rent to the new burgesses, who should have " liberties, privileges and immunities, so that with their families and goods they may be able to remain and live there safely." [3]

In consequence nearly two hundred men received grants of lands and tenements, [4] variously designated as inns, houses, messuages, cottages, shops and cellars, bakeries, gardens, void places and walls. Amongst the recipients were a number of well-known financiers of the king. Peter de Melchebourn was granted an inn, Walter de Chiriton messuages and gardens, Gilbert de Wendlyngburgh inns, Thomas de Swanlond, Henry Picard, John Golbeter and John Stodeye received messuages, and Matthew Canaceon inns and shops. There is little information about the occupations of the new burgesses or the places from which they went. Three leather workers, three mercers, two clerks, two serjeants-at-arms, a vintner, a goldsmith, a locksmith, a merchant, a taverner, a saddler, a barber, a spicer of the queen, and a porter of the king are mentioned. Towns in various parts of England, and Gascony and Pavia occur as the original homes of the immigrants in a few cases.

As a result many of the native inhabitants were expelled. According to Froissart, [5] after prisoners had been taken all the rest of the people were driven out except a priest and two

1. Froissart, IV, 242.
2. Le Bel, II, 349.
3. *Foed.*, III, i, 130.

4. *C.P.R.*, 1345–8, pp. 549, 561–568
5. Froissart, IV, 63, 64.

other old men who knew the ancient laws, and who were retained to assign the heritages. Other chroniclers [1] give similar accounts. The expulsion can hardly have been so indiscriminate as the chroniclers state however, for although a charter, which may be called for the purpose of distinction Edward III.'s charter, granted at an early date, ordered the removal of all natives, there was a saving clause " except those who have special leave of the king to remain there," [2] and the fact that three months after the conquest Edward confirmed the charter granted previously by the Countess of Artois seems to prove that a considerable number did remain.

From the outset there were two distinct branches of government, one consisting of royal officials, and the other consisting of representatives of the burgesses—the municipality. It seems advisable to deal first with the question of the royal officials and their authority, as they formed the pivot round which the administration revolved.

Immediately after the conquest there is reference to four royal officials, the captain, marshal, seneschal and constable,[3] the last three of whom are not mentioned at a later period. In Edward III's charter [4] certain duties pertaining to the offices of captain, marshal and seneschal were laid down. These were of a judicial character for the most part. It was ordained that in cases arising between the king's soldiers, the captain and the marshal should be judges, and in those arising between the king's soldiers and the inhabitants, the captain, marshal, and seneschal should share the jurisdiction. The seneschal was also given cognizance of all cases between inhabitants, and of those in connection with lands and tenements, and of all other royal pleas. How far his jurisdiction over the inhabitants extended is not clear, as the municipality had both civil and criminal jurisdiction. In addition to his judicial power the seneschal was given the con-

1. Le Bel, II, 168; Baker, pp. 92, 103; *Chronique Normande*, p. 90; Le Muisit, p. 187.

2. *Foed*, III, i, 139. Eustace de St. Pierre, the chief of the renowned "six burgesses," remained; *Foed.*, III, i, 138.

3. *C.C.R.* 1346–9, p. 518; *Foed.*, III, i, 139; *C.P.R.*, 1345–8, p. 562.

4. *Foed.*, III, i, 139. This charter is dated 1347, and immediately succeeds a letter dated the 8th of October. The Close Rolls of the 20th of June, 1348, record an order to the keeper of the hanaper of chancery " to deliver to the burgesses of Caleys quit of the fee due thereon, a charter by which the King grants to them certain laws and customs "; *C.C.R.* 1346–9, p. 462.

trol " of the houses of the king's herring-women, and of the lands, rents, and all other profits belonging to the king within the town and without, to make the king's profit of them." He also shared with the captain supervision of the marshes, in order " to ordain that all the defaults be redressed and repaired at all times that it shall be necessary, in the manner which shall be to the greatest profit of the king and 'the town." [1] From this it appears that during the very earliest period of Edward III's administration the seneschal was the chief royal official. The first captain, John de Montgomery, who only held that office for a short time,[2] was apparently merely given the judicial power and control of the marshes mentioned above. Whether that judicial power was exercised by his successors is not clear, as there is no mention of it in the letters of nomination to the position.

The authority of the captain however gradually increased, and from 1349 onwards certain powers were with one exception always conferred on him.[3] These were the right to punish all who were rebels to him in things pertaining to the salvation and defence of the town, and the right to remove all servants of the king found neglecting their duty in its fortification, and put other men in their places.[4] This authority was often supplemented. For example, Robert de Herle when captain was authorised to receive and hear all appeals made to the king.[5] During part of the time the captain was controller of all payments made by the treasurer,[6] and also held the office of constable of the castle.[7] Evidently to be captain was no sinecure, for in 1351 Edward III. made

---

1. There is no further mention of a seneschal after this very early period, and in August, 1349, the captain and bailiffs were given power to let for rent or in fee " all our houses in the same town, and our lands, meadows and pastures within our dominion there," and also "lands and tenements in our town and dominion aforesaid laid waste and in ruins" ; *Foed.*, III, i, 187.

2. *Ib.*, III, i, 138, 142.

3. *Ib.*, III, i, 186, 193, 226, 259, 294, 316, 346, 389; *Ib.*, III, ii, 914, 941, 975, 992, 1042.

4. In most cases the right to send those dismissed to the Tower of London was added.

5. In 1350: *Ib.*, III, i, 201.

6. From 1353 to 1361, and from 1370 to 1372; *Ib.*, III, i, 259, 294, 316, 389; *Ib.*, III, ii, 914. In 1373 and 1375 that position was given to the wardens of the castle, Thomas de Banfeld and Ralph de Sutton respectively; *Ib.*, III, ii, 992, 1036.

7. From 1355 to 1361, and from 1369–1372; *Ib.*, III, i, 294, 316, 346, 389; *Ib.*, III, ii, 881, 882, 914.

certain promises to Herle whom he re-appointed to the office for the duration of a year.[1] He promised that the wages of Herle and that part of the garrison which was apparently his retinue should be paid beforehand each quarter of the year, and that the town should always be victualled for at least six months in advance. If the king failed in this after he had been warned, and suitable amendment was not made at the end of the quarter, he granted that it should be " lawful for the said Sir Robert to depart from the said town with his men, horses and their equipment, without hindrance or challenge of our said lord the king, his heirs, his council, or of any other in time to come." Moreover, if the town were besieged, the King promised within a month after he was informed of it, to send a relieving army of a hundred men at arms and a hundred archers. A similar agreement was made later with John de Beauchamp.[2]

In the year 1361[3] the title of captain was changed to governor, and the office was endowed with powers of supervision, and full jurisdiction of all kinds high and low, in all causes both civil and criminal. The governor had all the powers held by the captain except that he was not given the wardenship of the castle. Later however that too was added,[4] and he retained it until almost the end of his governorship.[5] Only two men, Henry Lescrope and Bartholomew de Burghersh, seem to have been given the title of governor, the former of whom held it from 1361 to 1365, and from 1366 to 1369, whilst the latter seems to have held it for a few months between these two periods.[6] In 1369 Lescrope was appointed captain, apparently with merely military authority, and received his command shorn of the wide powers of jurisdiction in all civil and criminal cases which had characterised his period as governor.[7] His successors to the captaincy were given authority similar to that exercised by previous captains.

1. *Foed.*, III, i, 222.
2. In 1356; *Ib.*, III, i, 324.
3. On the 3rd of February, 1362, Henry Lescrope was made governor; *Ib.*, III, ii, 636. He was governor, however, as early as the 16th of May, 1361; *Ib.*, III, ii, 618; *C.C.R.* 1360-4, p. 267; *Scrope and Grosvenor Roll*, ed. N. H. Nicolas, II, p. 115.
4. *Foed.*, III, ii, 723, 724, 761, 774, 795, 847.
5. *Ib.*, III, ii, 865.
6. *Cal. Papal Registers, Letters*, IV, 18.
7. *Foed.*, III, ii, 881, 882.

Apparently during the years 1361–1369, therefore, the royal power reached its climax. The title of the chief royal official during that period, " gubernator," itself implies more real authority than " capitaneus," and the fact that the power of civil and criminal jurisdiction was conferred on the governor must have given him considerable authority. Apparently he exercised his power in conjunction with the municipality, for that body, or one or more special members of it, had also civil and criminal jurisdiction.

Other royal officials besides the captain or governor were the treasurer, the master of the mint, the captain, warden or constable of the castle, the keeper or receiver of the victuals, to whom provisions were sent for the fortifications, and the bailiffs. In the charter of the Countess of Artois,[1] which describes the municipal constitution before the conquest, and which Edward III. confirmed soon after the town fell, there is frequent reference to a bailiff. His duty was to represent the lord, and to attend to the lord's interest in the administration of the laws. Under Edward III. there was more than one bailiff, for on the 4th of December, 1347, William Stury besides being appointed to the office of seneschal, was made chief bailiff,[2] and later mention is made of bailiffs.[3] Evidently there were officials possessing this title throughout Edward III's reign, for at a later date when the French laws were swept away, reference is made in 1368 to the bailiffs,[4] and in 1370 to the bailiff.[5]

Having considered the royal officials and the part they played in the administration of Calais, we may now turn to the ordinary inhabitants, the duties devolving upon them, the privileges the king granted to them, and the various councils by which they were represented to a greater or lesser degree. The history of the town from this point of view can be divided into four periods, marked off distinctly from one another by changes in the municipal constitution.

The first period covers the years from the conquest to 1363, and is characterised by the fact that the town retained its old French municipal constitution by which it had been governed

1. *Foed.*, III, i, 142–144.   2. *Ib.*, III, i, 145.
3. *Ib.*, III, i, 187; *C.C.R.* 1346–9, p. 518; 1354–60, pp. 32, 42, 44, 49.
4. *C.P.R.* 1367–70, p. 90.   5. *Ib.*, p. 469.

before the conquest. In Edward III's charter several grants were made for the benefit of the townsmen. It was promised that the ancient customs and franchises should be kept in every detail, that all foreign merchants going to the town by sea or land to sell their merchandise should be free from all manner of customs and tolls as long as it pleased the king, that the captain and marshal should not take any wages from any man for anything concerning the safe keeping of the town, nor for default, but that transgressors should be punished " by their body and in no other manner," and that the watch should be kept by the king's soldiers as well as by the burgesses. The question of the watch is constantly cropping up. The tenements granted to the inhabitants immediately after the conquest were held " on condition that they bear themselves faithfully towards the king and do what shall be due for the safe-keeping and munition of the town and that the heirs render yearly a reasonable farm."

On the 3rd of December, 1347, Edward III. confirmed the charter of the Countess of Artois,[1] which described the laws and constitution previously to the conquest. The municipality consisted of thirteen échevins. Every year the outgoing officials elected five of those for the ensuing year,[2] and the five thus chosen co-opted the remaining eight. The échevins made laws, raised the " taille "[3] and " assise "[4] with the counsel of the other good men and true, and had judicial authority together with thirteen cormans [5] elected in the same manner as themselves.[6] If one inhabitant of the échevinage committed an assault against another outside the échevinage, and the deed was not redressed where it was done, it was tried at Calais. In connection with jurisdiction there was also each year a court of " frank verity " to enquire into

1. *Foed.*, III, i, 142–144.
2. In Edward III's charter tne captain, marshal and seneschal were commanded to elect the first five aldermen for the first time.
3. An impost upon people; Godefroy, *Dictionnaire de l'Ancienne Langue Française*, X, 739.
4. An indirect tax paid by the seller upon merchandise sold, and a direct tax upon renters and proprietors; Giry, *Histoire de la Ville de Saint-Omer*, pp. 244, 245; Godefroy, *Dictionnaire*, I, 446.
5. Hommes de loi; Godefroy, *Dictionnaire*, II, 302.
6. From the *French Roll*, 21 *Edw. III*, pt. 2, m. 7, a copy of which is found among similar notes on the subject of Calais made by Miss Bateson, it appears that the échevins had civil jurisdiction, and that the cormans tried criminal cases.

"all things concealed"[1] during the previous year. The members of this court were apparently nominated by the échevins. Many transgressions were punished by fines paid to the lord of the town, an additional fine sometimes being paid to the injured party. The most serious crimes, such as murder and arson by night, were punishable by death and forfeiture of goods to the lord. Larceny of the value of two sous and upwards was punishable in the same way, larceny of the value of less than two sous by the loss of an ear, and for a second offence by death and forfeiture of goods. The offender who broke laws made by the échevins lost his service for a year and a day, and paid a fine to the lord. One or two glimpses into the ordinary life of the burgess can be seen. Saturday was market day. The lord of the land had two annual festivals, one from the last day of Easter to the 24th of June, the other from the 29th of September to the 30th of November.

M. Daumet in "Calais sous la Domination Anglaise"[2] thinks that under Edward III. the cormans were abolished, and the power of the échevins was limited to administration, criminal jurisdiction and jurisdiction over foreigners, as a result of the granting of judicial functions to the captain, marshal and seneschal. As Edward III. confirmed the charter of the Countess of Artois without reservation, however, a fact which M. Daumet himself seems to imply, are we not more justified in thinking that there was a dual jurisdiction of municipal and royal officials, which indeed seems to have been the case throughout the reign?

Apparently Edward III. kept good control over the aldermen, if the following entry in the Close Rolls[3] is illustrative of his general policy. "To the constable of the Tower of London or to him who supplies his place. Order to release Richard Atte Wode, the king's serjeant-at-arms and échevin of Calais, from prison, as the king, on learning that Richard made several illicit meetings with the men of that town to the terror and disturbance of the people there and the danger of the loss of the town, appointed Thomas de Kingston,

---

1. Miss Bateson's notes state that this refers to fines which were owing to the lord.
2. Pp. 70, 71, 87.   3. *C.C.R.* 1349-54, p. 196.

constable of Calais castle, to take Richard's key from him and to send him to the Tower to be detained there, and the king has pardoned Richard at the request of certain magnates and because he submitted himself to the king's favour, and by a security found before the king." He was released on the mainprise of a certain serjeant-at-arms " that he would behave faithfully henceforward in that town and if he should hold meetings or commit other like delict there that he should incur forfeiture of life and members and of his lands goods and chattels." The king had been informed of Richard Atte Wode's offence by the captain.[1]

But the burgesses were by no means oppressed by the rule of Edward III. It was to Edward III.'s interest that they should be friendly disposed towards him, and with this intent his policy towards them was directed. A few months after the fall of the town letters were issued to the mayor and bailiffs of Dover and several other ports, as well as to the captain of Calais,[2] stating that it was the king's will that the common landing place for traffic between England and France should be Calais, and not Whitsand or Boulogne or elsewhere, and instructing those officials to take measures for the carrying out of that intention. Although this attempt to make traffic with France all go through one channel was obviously not initiated in the interests of the inhabitants, yet it is equally certain that the plan would benefit them considerably. In 1348 a similar ordinance was made, promulgated in a letter to the captain,[3] with the difference that " a true merchant with his merchandise " was exempt from the regulation. At the same time the burgesses were declared free from exactions of goods and money granted to the king by the commonalty of the kingdom of England, and from pontage and all other payments through the whole of the kingdom of England for a period of three years, saving the usual customs and subsidies.[4] In this year also a more important concession was gained. Edward III. granted that a staple should be held for cloth, feathers, tin and lead for a period of seven years.[5] In 1358 the burgesses petitioned the

1. *C.P.R.* 1348–50, p. 59c.   2. *Foed.,* III, i, 142.
3. *Ib.,* III, i, 150.   4. *Ib.,* III, i, 158.
5. *Ib.,* III, i, 158

king concerning a tenement question.[1] They asked that when tenements held in fee simple became vacant, the bailiffs[2] and échevins might have the administration of them for a year, if the heirs were absent or if there were no heirs, " since it often happens that those holding houses in the same town granted to them and their heirs. . . . die suddenly, at sea or elsewhere," the ordinary proceeding in such cases being of course their immediate transference into the king's hands. Edward granted this demand as a reward for keeping the watch, " considering the various cares and great labours which those burgesses by continuous vigils for the guardianship of the aforesaid town thence sustain, and that they may sustain more willingly in the future cares and labours of this kind."

Although Edward III. granted many privileges it is not to be supposed that the advantage was all on the side of the townsmen. In 1363 an order concerning the restitution of a tenement to a certain burgess, of which he had been deprived by mistake, mentions " burdens, so for the guard and fortification of the aforesaid town, as other burdens whatsoever incumbent on the same tenement in times of war and peace. . . . which burdens indeed far exceeded the annual value of the aforesaid tenement before this time."[3]

In 1361 [4] the king ordered the bailiffs, échevins and commonalty to elect six men to come to him at Westminster, and discuss how the town might be governed to the best advantage of the townsmen and the king, and what profit accrued to the kings of France and other lords before the king of England possessed it. Six representatives came to England and were apparently interviewed by the king on these subjects, " probably at the conference of representatives of the eleven staples summoned for the end of May." [5]

In the early part of 1363 the great staple for wool, woolfells and leather, which had been removed from the continent to

1. *Foed.*, III, i, 413.
2. These bailiffs do not seem to be the royal bailiffs, for Edward granted to the " ballivi and scabini dictæ villæ " the above-mentioned concession " absque eo quod capitaneus, ballivi, seu aliquis alius minister noster ibidem, se inde intromittat."
3. *Ib.*, III, ii, 689.
4. *C.P.R.* 1361–4, p. 29; *C.C.R.* 1360–4, pp. 267, 268; *Foed.*, III, ii, 617, 618.
5. *Chronica Johannis de Reading*, etc., edited J. Tait, p. 297.

England in 1353,[1] was established at Calais.[2] This begins the second period of the history of the municipal constitution under Edward III., for until the next year the town council was in the hands of the merchants of the staple. A letter patent of the 1st of March,[3] issued from Westminster, ordained that twenty-six English merchants chosen by the king and mentioned by name " be there to govern the town and the people and merchandises which shall come here, and that of the said twenty-six English merchants be two mayors and twenty-four aldermen, by whom the burgesses and others who shall come to the said town shall be received and governed ; and that they be between them a community and have a common seal."[4] The organisation of this company was simple. The members had to elect two mayors from themselves yearly. They could expel anyone from their number for sufficient reason, and elect a successor in his place from English merchants resident in Calais or England, and similarly if any member died they had to elect another from such English merchants. Amongst the members of this corporation was Adam de Bury, who played an important part elsewhere in the economic history of the reign of Edward III.

Further details of the powers given to the company were contained in the letter of the 1st of March. All franchises and charters granted to the town before that time were declared null and void. The mayors and aldermen could make laws for its administration, and the old laws were not to be in force unless re-enacted by them. They, or four, three, or two of them could hold civil and criminal pleas, but, if complaint arose about their judgment, suitors were allowed to go to a higher court, which would sit once a year in March, and be composed of the governor, the treasurer, the two mayors, and two merchants apparently not members of the company, chosen by the aldermen. If anyone objected to the inclusion of the mayors on a plea of wrong done by them, their places

1. *S.R.*, I, 332
2. *Foed.*, III, ii, 688, 689.
3. *Ibid.*, III, ii, 690–692.
4. The mayors and aldermen governed Calais before the 1st of March, however. There is mention of a charter granted to them previously ; *Ib.*, III, ii, 688, 692. Moreover there is a reference later to their government before they farmed the revenues, which they undertook to do on the 1st of March ; *Ib.*, III, ii, 745.

W

might be taken by two merchants elected in the same manner as the two previous ones. Apparently civil and criminal jurisdiction had to be administered on the same lines for both burgesses and merchants according to merchant law, with the exception that pleas of lands, rents and tenements had to be tried according to the laws of England or the usage of the country. If any burgess or merchant in Calais or the March were imprisoned or his goods seized on any pretext, such a man or his goods had to be presented to the company in order that the case might be tried before them by jury. If this were between denizens, or between denizen and foreigner, and done within the franchise of Calais, it must be tried by denizens : if between denizen and foreigner, and committed outside the franchise, by both denizens and foreigners in equal numbers, in which case the sovereigns of the place where the deed was done might be present if they so desired. The mayors were given power to take recognizances of debts of all people, to make obligatory letters according to statute merchant, and to make execution of them according to staple law. The town, échevinage and haven with all profits except those obtained from the mint, were handed over to the mayors, aldermen and burgesses in return for the payment of a fixed sum, 500 marks a year. They were also granted forfeitures of staple merchandise, which had apparently been coketted but had not been taken direct to Calais, afterwards found in the town, and half such merchandise found elsewhere in the king's possessions.[1]

The company was given complete control of lands and tenements, and no one could hold a tenement without its consent, and then he must be English.[2] Descent of property had to be in accordance with the law of England, "and if any alienation or devise by testament or infeudation be made to others than to Englishmen, be the same lands, tenements, and rents so alienated or devised seized into the hands of the said

1. Forfeitures of goods not coketted belonged to the King wherever they were found; *Foed.*, III, ii, 693.
2. In February the King ordered the governor, treasurer and two mayors to take into his hands " all ruinous houses and tenements, and those not built up nor inhabited, and vacant places in the same town," and rent and let them out to farm; *Ib.*, III, ii, 689. In July the governor, treasurer, and five other nominees, of whom four were members of the company, were given complete control over lands and tenements; Daumet, pp. 156, 157.

mayors and aldermen, to hold to them and their successors, to the common profit of themselves and of the burgesses of the community aforesaid." No land or tenement could be sold or leased except to Englishmen on the same penalty.[1] The company could elect the bailiff and certain other ministers,[2] and change them at will. The same franchises, quittances and immunities which were enjoyed by the citizens of London were granted to the mayors, aldermen and burgesses, together with those granted to merchants by the Statute of the Staple. They were freed from all kinds of tolls upon their goods and merchandise throughout the king's realm and power, saving the usual customs and subsidies. The letter ended with the promise that if the king failed in his word with regard to the above concessions "then the said mayors, aldermen and burgesses can safely depart from there with their goods and merchandises, without hindrance of us or of our heirs, and without bearing the charge of the farm, or of other things belonging to the said town, haven and échevinage, from that day forward : saving always to us that if default be found after this time in the above mentioned things, it shall be quite lawful for us and our heirs by advice of our council to amend, repeal and adjust at our will; and if the said mayors, aldermen and burgesses will not assent to what shall be thus amended, repealed or adjusted, then it shall be quite lawful for them to depart with all their goods and chattels, women and children, out of the said town of Calais, and to return to England discharged of the farm and of all other charges of the said town from that hour forward, without challenge, hindrance or disturbance of us or of our heirs, or of our ministers whomsoever, on this side the sea or over- seas."

A letter of the same date as the previous one released the governor and treasurer from the guardianship of the town, and commanded them to hand it over with all its belongings to the mayors and aldermen.[3]

1. Apparently aliens could reside there, but had to obtain the royal permission; *Ib.*, pp. 156, 157. Probably too the old French inhabitants, who had been permitted to remain in the first case, would still be allowed to stay.

2. The clause says that the company could elect the bailiff and all other ministers, and change them at will. This must refer to subordinate officials, such as the wardens and changer of the mint. The chief officials, such as the governor, were appointed by the King.

3. *Ib.*, III, ii, 692, 693.

In spite of all these elaborate regulations the union of town and staple government did not last long. It seems to have worked unsatisfactorily. The mayors and aldermen quarrelled with the other merchants,[1] and by the end of the year Edward III. found it necessary to order the governor and treasurer to assemble mayors, aldermen, merchants and others whom they thought fit, in order that arrangements should be made until the king could devise a new form of administration. In the early part of 1364 the governor and treasurer, together with Adam de Bury, three other nominees of the king, and those whom they thought suitable to join them, were appointed to assemble on the 1st March,[2] in order to survey the state of the town and the fortifications, to discover whether the mayors and aldermen had undertaken their duties faithfully, and to hear and terminate complaints against those officials. The reason given by the crown for this step was that " by the very grievous complaint of the prelates, lords, and others of the commonalty of our realm of England, we have heard that diverse unsuitable impositions, customs and charges are put upon the wools and other merchandises of our said kingdom, by the said mayors and aldermen in the said town of Calais : and several wrongs and grievances done to the merchants and others, who come to the said town for the cause of trading, to the great impoverishment of the peers and commons of our kingdom aforesaid."

M. Daumet summarises the text of the resulting inquest, the original of which he has seen in the Public Record Office. From this it appears that in addition to excessive impositions upon merchandise, the mayors and aldermen had issued troublesome rules, had concerned themselves with their own interests to the neglect of those of the king and townsmen, had raised taxes for their own profit, and had allowed foreigners to hold inns, with the result that the town had decreased in prosperity, that it had a bad reputation, and that if things were not altered both English and foreign traders would cease to congregate there. The inquisitors stated that they could not prove whether the wrongs had been done by indi-

---

1. *Foed.*, III, ii, 719.   2. *Ib.*, III, ii, **722, 723**

vidual members or by all, and could not value the damage done.[1]

Soon after this the town council and staple were separated, and thus terminates the second period of the history of the municipal body. After March there is mention of a mayor of the staple[2] and a mayor of the town.[3] In July the treasurer was ordered to pay the wages of the mayors and aldermen from the 1st of March " to the time of the last ordination concerning the town of Calais made by us."[4] At the same time twenty-one merchants of the company of twenty-six were exonerated from all money received from the profits, the farm, and the imposition of 40d. on each sack of wool ordained by the king and council, and from all kinds of transgressions against the king during the past year,[5] for £600 which the company paid over and above the farm;[6] but "those of the aforesaid aldermen who lately were ordained by us and our council to delay in the said town of Calais in the fortification of the same. . . . we will not in any way have excused." M. Daumet suggests that the payment of £600 was the means employed by the mayors and aldermen to extricate themselves from their position after the charges brought against them in the inquest.[7]

Details of a new municipal constitution are found in an ordinance of 1365.[8] It was decreed in that year that the council should consist of one mayor and twelve aldermen. The mayor was given jurisdiction in all actions and complaints except those belonging to staple merchandise, which had to be settled by the mayor and commonalty of the staple, and he was made comptroller of the treasurer. One wonders to what extent he really enjoyed these powers, as the governor was endowed with the same authority. The mayor must also have eight men sufficiently armed for the search-watch, and for the cost of these and for his own wages must be paid £200 a year. Of the twelve aldermen one must be the

---

1. Daumet, pp. 73, 74.   2. *Foed.*, III, ii, 732.
3. *Ib.*, III, ii, 739.   4. *Ib.*, III, ii, 745.
5. *Ib.*, III, ii, 745, 746.
6. John Wroth was also pardoned his portion of the £600, because he remitted his daily wages, and money spent in connection with the town before it was committed to farm, which far exceeded his portion of the £600.
7. Daumet, p. 74.
8. *Foed.*, III, ii, 768, 769.

marshal, and have a valet under him to summon the watch, the payment for himself and the valet being £20 a year, and another be the water-bailiff, taking "for himself and a valet guarding the high tower [1] £20 a year." Of the other ten aldermen six had to be "merchants of good renown," of whom one must be the mayor of the staple, and take for all cost £50 each a year, whilst the remaining four had to be "the more important burgesses," and take for all costs £40 each. Each of these ten aldermen had to provide six men sufficiently armed for the search-watch. Three of the six merchants mentioned in the letter were members of the company of 1363. Apparently the usual method of appointment of these officials was nomination by the king for an indefinite period,[2] although the corporation could appoint a successor to any alderman found inefficient, or who withdrew from his office. A number of less important municipal officials and their wages were also specified in the ordinance of 1365. There had to be a recorder taking £20 a year, a common clerk taking 100s., two serjeants and fourteen valet porters for the mayor, the wages of the former being 40s. a year, those of the latter 5d. a day, eight valets for the scout-watch taking 6d. a day, a valet day-watch under the mayor paid 5d. a day, and a town crier paid 2d. a day. Also there must be two clerks under the treasurer, one "to receive the 4d. on each sack entering the said town, and all the other tolls and customs on all manner of merchandise," and the other "to receive the 8d. on each sack of wool going out," each to receive £10 a year. These exactions were levied for the payment of the above mentioned wages and the works of the town and haven, and must not be confused with the ordinary customs and subsidies levied in England. The assize of wine, ale and beer had to be received from denizens and foreigners as in times past. The mayor and aldermen were freed from the 500 marks of fee farm specified in their previous charter,[3] because the revenues were taken into the king's hands.

As time went on the judicial power of the mayor was more particularly defined. Questions of lands and tenements were

1. This was apparently a tower on the quay.
2. *Foed.*, III, ii, 767, 769, 900; *C.C.R.* 1364–8, p. 179.
3. This must refer to a charter granted after the separation of the municipality and the staple in 1364, and previously to this letter.

settled according to the English law and custom, other pleas and quarrels according to the law and custom used in Calais before that time.[1] Cases arising between a merchant or officer of the staple and a burgess, unconnected with merchandise, were tried before the mayor of the town in the presence of the mayor of the staple, those connected with merchandise or debt, before the mayor of the staple in the presence of the mayor of the town.[2] Apparently it was intended that trial by jury should be used. The mayor appointed in 1370 was Adam de Bury,[3] and he retained the office until 1372.[4] Of the twelve aldermen appointed that year [5] one was made mayor and five were made aldermen in 1365, whilst one of the latter also had been alderman in 1363.

The municipal council established in 1364 was the least independent of all the municipal bodies under Edward III.'s administration. He apparently nominated its members, and took the control of taxation directly into his own hands, instead of leaving it in the hands of the representatives of the burgesses.

In the parliament of 1372 the burgesses of Calais made numerous petitions to the king.[6] They asked that they might devise freely by will to English people their lands and tenements as the burgesses in the city of London did, that property should only be inherited by English heirs, that each burgess should be inhabited in the town within a year and a day after he had made oath, and that no alien should become a burgess nor purchase a heritage. They complained that several houses had fallen down and been destroyed, some of which had come into the king's hands, so that he had lost their rent and watches, and they petitioned that he would allow the lands, tenements and void places belonging to the king to be granted in fee by the captain and treasurer to English people for a reasonable rent. They demanded that all houses should be granted on condition that the holders bore the charge of the watch, or did the watch themselves. Edward

---

1 *Foed.*, III, ii, 794, 900, 921, 957.   2. *Ib.*, III, ii, 795.
3. *Ib.*, III, ii, 900.
4. *Ib.*, III, ii, 920, 921, 957. Reference is made to him once in 1371 as the mayor of both town and staple.
5. *Ib.*, III, ii, 900.   6. *Ib.*, III, ii, 966, 967.

III.'s reply to most of these requests was in the affirmative, but he declared that any true and loyal man could inherit by purchase or otherwise, whilst the demand that aliens should not become burgesses was ignored. The further petitions made by the burgesses that they might buy and sell victuals and merchandise in England, Ireland, Wales, Berwick, Calais, and its march free from all kinds of exactions, and that they might have common pasture for their cattle in the échevinage between Calais and Wale, and Calais and Sangatte, Edward III. declared should be granted if such were the case before the conquest. The burgesses also asked that the king would hand over to them " the lands in the échevinage of Calais, and in the lands of Merk, of those who were sworn to him in time of peace, and now are turned and become his enemies in France, for the same rent and service that they bore anciently to their lords." The king's answer concerning this seems strange, " It is granted that they have the fishery, and all other profits belonging to the town in ancient times before the conquest." These petitions and answers were quoted in a letter to the ministers, and the answers were given the force of a decree.

It appears that at this time the burgesses also demanded the restoration of Edward III.'s charter, except that the law of land and tenements might be as in the city of London.[1] As that charter contained the ratification of the Countess of Artois' charter, they were evidently demanding a return to the state of affairs immediately succeeding the conquest, when the municipal council consisted of a bailiff, échevins and cormans. Edward III. therefore appointed a commission of five, amongst whom were the governor and treasurer, to consider the advisability of such a proceeding. The request seems peculiar side by side with the anti-French petition concerning property, but perhaps it was merely a protest against Edward III.'s autocratic nomination of the chief municipal officials, and a desire to get back some share in their appointment.

There seems to be no further information concerning the commission, but in 1376 the Calaisiens petitioned the king in parliament a second time.[2] Almost all the demands of 1372

1. *Foed.*, III, ii, 967.   2. *Rot. Parl.*, II, 358–360.

were repeated, including the request for the confirmation of the charter of the Countess of Artois, with the exception that the law of lands and tenements might be amended according to English law. In addition they now demanded government by a mayor and twelve aldermen, instead of by a bailiff, échevins and cormans, with "the mayor at their election from one of the said aldermen as they do in the city of London," that the mayor might take £100 a year from the king, and bear the charge of six men for watch and ward as the aldermen did at that time, instead of taking £200 a year, and bearing no expense for watch and ward as mayors had done in the past,[1] that no burgess should be taken from the franchise for any plea by writ of the king or otherwise, that no plea of lands, tenements or of any other contract, civil or criminal, should be adjudged in any court except that of the mayor and aldermen, and that the mayor, aldermen and burgesses should have power to make ordinances for the good government of the town which should be considered firm and stable.[2]

Letters of July and October, the one patent, the other to the burgesses of Calais,[3] with some slight alterations embodied almost all the answers to these petitions, and gave them authoritative force. The first letter decreed that the town council should consist of a mayor and twelve aldermen. The aldermen, who must be English, had to be elected by the

1. M. Daumet finds a difficulty in the demand for a mayor and twelve aldermen instead of a bailiff, échevins and cormans, on the grounds that the old municipal organisation could hardly have been restored between 1365 and 1376, that there were no cormans under Edward III, and that there was a demand for the reduction in wages of the mayor. His explanation (p. 76) is that there was "a confusion borne in the mind of the compilers of this document," and that what was really demanded was liberty of municipal elections. He seems, however, to have ignored the fact which removes the difficulty, namely, that the burgesses were demanding the restoration of their old French charter with the exception that they wished for a mayor and aldermen instead of a bailiff, échevins and cormans.

2. In this parliament Adam de Bury was impeached "of several deceits and other evil deeds to the King and to his people" when he was mayor of Calais; *Rot. Parl.*, II, 330. In the parliament of 1377 the Commons asked that Adam de Bury, "who was by violence and by great malice" impeached in the previous parliament, might be included in the general pardon granted in that parliament; *Ib.*, II, 374.

3. *Foed.*, III, ii, 1057, 1058, 1062, 1063. Previously to these letters a commission was granted to the captain, treasurer and controller to lease the King's lands and tenements, together with those laid waste and destroyed, in fee or for a term; *Ib.*, III, ii, 1057.

burgesses from themselves as often as it was necessary,[1] and on election take an oath to the king. Every year they had to elect a mayor from themselves, who likewise took an oath to the king on election. All officers and ministers must bear their share of all costs for which burgesses were liable. The mayor was given jurisdiction in all causes, civil and criminal, pleas of lands and tenements to be judged according to the law of England, other pleas according to the law henceforth used in the town, saving pleas between soldiers which must be settled by the captain, pleas between soldiers and burgesses which must be judged by the captain and mayor together, and staple jurisdiction. In order to help the burgesses to bear financial burdens, " namely, in the maintenance of the mayor and aldermen and the other officers aforesaid, as in the repairing of the pavement and the common fountains and the gutters. . . . . which need great reparation as we have learned," they were granted " the assise of bread, wine and beer, and the stallage of the drapers and butchers, and the toll for fixing stalls of other merchants there in the market place, ... and also the exits and amercements and other profits arising from our court held before the said mayor and aldermen, ... saving always to us and our heirs fines for blows, spilling blood, escheats, and all lands, tenements, goods and chattels there confiscated." The mayor and aldermen were exonerated from the watches of six armati and archers which were due from each of them by virtue of their offices, on condition of course that they did the watches due from their tenements.

The second letter included almost all the contents of the first, and further decreed that burgesses could devise their lands and tenements by will to English people as in London, that they could buy victuals in England and the March of Calais and take them to the town free from toll and custom, that questions of lands, tenements, debts or other contracts should not be tried by any other court than that of the mayor and aldermen, except by way of error, or unless the quarrel concerned the king, and that no alien or anyone unless he was English could become a burgess without special permission

1. According to the second letter it must be each year and as often as it was necessary; *Foed.*, III, ii, 1062.

from the king. It is noticeable that Edward III. did not grant to the mayors, aldermen and burgesses the power to make laws. In spite of this omission, however, the fact remains that by the year 1376 the principle of self-government had been introduced into the administration. After a period of twenty-nine years the burgesses had gained the right to elect their representative body.

A few words may be said here with regard to the finance of the town. There were various sources of revenue. There were the taxes levied by the municipal council, the rents from the land and houses, the profits from the mint and exchanges, and various other sources, such as the customs duties mentioned in 1365, and the profits from the municipal court mentioned in 1376. On the assumption that all the revenue obtained was used for expenses in connection with the administration, the town was unable to support itself. In 1363 certain forfeitures of staple merchandise were granted to the mayors, aldermen and burgesses. When the company of twenty-six merchants was dissolved there was mention of a tax of 40d. levied at Calais on each sack of wool, which appears to have been levied " for repair of the said town."[1] In 1363 the Commons petitioned in parliament against this tax, which was an extra impost over and above the usual customs and subsidies, on the plea that it was used to enrich the merchants of the staple,[2] but it was evidently continued until 1365, for in that year the Commons again petitioned in parliament that it might be removed.[3] In the same year and later reference was made in parliament to the large sums of money which had been used for the town.[4]

Many regulations were made with regard to the coinage. Soon after the conquest the king appointed a certain William de Salop as warden of the mint,[5] with power to make the assay of the money as often as was necessary. In 1348 the moneyers were ordered to coin silver money corresponding

1. *C.C.R.* 1364–8, p. 37.
2. *Rot. Parl.*, II, 276.   3. *Ib.*, II, 287.
4. *Ib.*, II, 285, 295. In 1361 Edward III granted land in England to a certain Richard Englis " for good service and in recompense for the pontage of the town of Caleys and the bailiwick of the water there to him late granted and after for sure causes taken again into the King's hand "; *C.C.R.* 1360–4, pp. 3, 4.
5. *Foed.*, III, i, 140; Le Bel, II, 351, 352.

with that made in England,[1] but in the next year Edward III. informed the captain and council[2] that they might give orders for the coining of such money as they thought advisable.

In 1363 fresh regulations were made. In the early part of that year an exchange of money, gold and silver plate, and broken silver was set up at Calais,[3] and as a result a certain Adam de Saint Ive of London, who had been granted the farm of the exchanges of England, was released from part of the farm, because "profit which used to arise of the exchanges in England is rather taken at Calais to the king's use." The letter of the 1st March establishing the staple company ordained that the master of the mint should be chosen by the king and council, that the mayors and aldermen could appoint the wardens and changer, and with the assent of the governor and treasurer remove them if found guilty of default, and that the master, wardens and changer must be laymen. The same day an indenture was made between the king and a certain Henry de Brisele,[4] witnessing that the king had made the latter master of the mint, and embodying certain regulations. The master had to coin gold and silver money agreeing with that coined in the Tower of London. There must be three kinds of gold money, nobles, half nobles and ferlings, valued at 6s. 8d., 40d., and 20d. each, respectively, and four kinds of silver money, groats, half groats, sterlings and mailles, valuing 4d., 2d., 1d., and half a sterling each, respectively. Of every pound of gold by weight four ounces had to be coined in nobles, six ounces in half nobles, and two ounces in ferlings of nobles; of every pound of silver by weight three ounces must be made in groats, four ounces in half groats, four ounces in sterlings, and one ounce in mailles, and "for the common profit," each year one hundred pounds of silver by weight had to be made in silver ferlings, four of them worth a sterling. The coinage had to be tested every three months before the governor, treasurer and two mayors, in the presence of the wardens and master, who must notify the king and council in England

1. *Foed.*, III, i, 150; Le Bel, II, 352.
2. *Foed.*, III, i, 185. This council doubtless consisted of the chief royal officials.
3. *C.C.R.* 1360-4, p. 495.   4. *Ib.*, pp. 535, 536.

what was the result. This did not satisfy Edward III. however. A part of each kind of money thus tested must be sent under the seal of the above officials to England, and again tried before the king and council. The king undertook " to cause proclamation to be made once every month in the town of Caleys and the échevinage forbidding any man, rich or poor, for any sort of merchandise great or small, victual, labour or aught else, openly or privily to receive or pay any money but the king's money made in the said town on pain of losing the value thereof and his body at the king's will, or to bring to Caleys or the seigneurie round about any sort of false or counterfeit money on the same pain, the informer to have one third of money found counterfeit." The charters of liberties previously granted to the moneyers were confirmed, and the master took oath before the king's council to do his duty, finding mainpernors before the governor and treasurer of Calais for 1,000 marks to recompense the merchants who took gold and silver to the mint. Three days after this indenture the officers of the exchanges were given privileges similar to those of the officers of the London and Canterbury exchanges.[1] They must not be placed on assizes, juries or any recognitions, if guilty of wrong doing they must be tried by the master and wardens, except with regard to pleas belonging to free tenement and the crown, and they must be free from all taxation upon themselves or their property in England or Calais.

The regulation that no money should be used except that which was specified was evaded.[2] In June Edward III. informed the company that people had made " subtle exchanges of moneys, so of our kingdom of England as of other parts, with money made in the said town of Calais," ordered a proclamation to be issued that this must be stopped, and stated that he was going to appoint a commission to make a scrutiny and that after eight days from the proclamation all money not made in the town would be cut in two parts and returned to the owners. A few days later the treasurer and master of the mint were ordered to execute this,[3] but to leave enough money in the hands of travellers to take them where they wished to go.

1. *Foed.*, III, ii, 693. 2. *Ib.*, III, ii, 704.
3. *Ib.*, III, ii, 705.

The next year lending for interest was prohibited,[1] the reward for anyone who brought an offender to law being the fourth penny of what was forfeited as punishment. In that year too [2] the king complained that although he had established a mint and caused the coinage to be made like that of England for the advantage of the merchants, the merchants were selling their goods "by way of loan, without paying anything of gold or silver," in order to destroy the coinage. "Seeing how the moneys of gold and silver, which are much better than the moneys of other countries, are from day to day taken and carried out of our kingdom because of the gain of the merchants, and if no bullion of gold and silver be taken to our coinages our said kingdom will be destitute within a short time of moneys," all men buying wool and other merchandise of England, Wales and Ireland, sold in Calais or taken outside it, had to take a certain amount of bullion, assessed on the quantity of goods bought, to the mint, sufficient security to be taken from buyers by the survey of the treasurer and master of the mint, before the mayors and aldermen. The treasurer and master of the mint had likewise to see that the merchants bartering "wools of simple price or refuse of wools" for other merchandise took bullion to the coinage.[3]

In 1365 [4] a proclamation was ordered to be made to the effect that no one must exchange money except with known merchants and for trading purposes, after which no ordinances concerning fresh regulations for the coinage were made throughout the reign. Indentures made after 1363 between the king and the master of the mint [5] corresponded in all important details with that made between Edward III. and Brisele in 1363.

With regard to religious matters. The town was situated in the diocese of Thérouanne.[6] At the time of the conquest there were three churches,[7] those of St. Mary, St. Nicholas and St. John or Maison Dieu, the two latter of which had

---

1. *Foed.*, III, ii, 724.   2. *Ib.*, III, ii, 725, 727.
3. *Ib.*, III, ii, 727.   4. *Ib.*, III, ii, 773.
5. *C.C.R.* 1369–74, pp. 303–306, 449, 450; *Foed.*, III, ii, 727, 772, 811, 915, 916.
6. *Ib.*, III, i, 138, 511.
7. *C.P.R.* 1345–8, pp. 561, 563, 566; 1364–7, p. 411; Nichols, p. 37.

hospitals attached, and a house of Carmelite Friars.[1] During the period of repopulation "all the Calais chaplains and clerks" were driven out,[2] "on account of the peril which might happen from them," and it was decreed that two chaplains should be ordained as priests of the churches. At the same period [3] certain dwellings kept vacant by the departure of their original holders, were granted to the Carmelite Friars for the extension of their premises. In 1351 a house of Augustinian Friars was established,[4] a habitation in mortmain being granted to them in the parish of St. Mary, on condition that they should not cause any houses to be thrown down there without the consent of the captain and treasurer, and that the prior provincial of the order in England should place only English friars in the monastery.

As the town was situated in a French diocese it is not surprising that there was friction between the king of England and the bishop of Thérouanne. In 1372 Edward III. presented a certain Geoffrey de Westwyk to the church of St. Mary.[5] Two years later we find the king complaining that owing to the war between France and England the bishop had not yet confirmed his nominee, Geoffrey de Westwyk being afraid to approach the bishop on the subject, "on account of fear of death." Edward III. therefore ordered the captain, treasurer, mayor and aldermen to hand over to his protegé all the fruits and issues of the church, which had been seized into the king's hands owing to the war, and to allow him to collect such in the future, until he had obtained the church "canonically and pacifically," on condition that he did his duty faithfully as pastor.

Various religious bodies had considerable rights. There were "rents and services due to the church and the hospital of St. Nicholas,"[6] rents and profits due to the Abbot of Boulogne and the Master of the Charterhouse of St. Omer,[7] "a quit-rent to the Masendewe,"[8] and a yearly rent of 107s. 3d. due to the Carthusian convent of St. Omer,[9] all which profits apparently were drawn "from the common purse as from the

1. *C.P.R.* 1345–8, p. 558.   2. *Foed.*, III, i, 139.
3. *C.P.R.* 1345–8, p. 558.   4. *Ib.* 1350–4, pp. 174, 175.
5. *Foed.*, III, ii, 1016, 1017.
6. *C.P.R.* 1345–8, p. 563.   7. *Foed.*, III, ii, 713.
8. Nichols, p. 37.   9. *C.C.R.* 1364–8, p. 111.

other lands and tenements." In 1352 Edward III. decreed that the Carmelite Friars should receive a grant " of 20 marks yearly of the king's alms to be taken by the hands of the treasurer of the town." [1]

The church was prohibited from acquiring more land than it possessed at the conquest. The retention of what it held at that time was guaranteed by the Treaty of Calais,[2] but in 1363, 1372, and 1376 alienation in mortmain of land and tenements was forbidden.[3]

The arrangements for defence were twofold, those dealing with the food supply, and those dealing with the fortifications. Every facility for exporting food stuffs from England to Calais was given. When free export of corn and victuals was forbidden, licences were granted to take them to the town, or it was exempted from the regulation.[4] Provisions were bought and purveyed in England,[5] and dispatched to a special officer deputed to receive them, the receiver or keeper of the victuals.[6] In spite of all the care taken to keep a good supply of provisions there was a shortage of corn in the summer of 1355,[7] for in July of that year an order addressed to the sheriffs of London, and the mayors and bailiffs of a large number of other towns, commanded " proclamation to be made that all merchants and others who have any corn and especially oats, and wish to sell it, shall bring the same with all speed to Calais, where there is now a great scarcity of corn, and where they will find numerous buyers and prompt payment, as the king has learned that there is a great scarcity of corn and especially of oats at Calais, whereby a great peril may come to the town."

Great efforts were made to keep the fortifications in repair, and to defend them properly. Soon after the conquest it was decreed that all people except those who had the liberty of the town, or who were employed in its fortifications, should pay on entering or leaving a tax of 3d., one penny for murage, and the remaining two pennies for the repairing of the har-

---

1. *C.P.R.* 1350–4, p. 215.   2. *Foed.*, III, i, 515
3. *Ib.*, III, ii, 691, 967, 1063.
4. *Foed.*, III, i, 139, 199, 207, 298; *C.P.R.* 1348–50, pp. 311, 513, 556.
5. *Foed.*, III, i, 149; *C.P.R.* 1367–70, p. 243. In 1352 and 1354 the Commons petitioned in parliament that payment might be made for provisions taken to victual Calais; *Rot. Parl.*, II, 240, 258.
6. *Foed.*, III, i, 149, 157; *C.C.R.* 1354–60, p. 168.   7. *Ib.*, p. 223.

bour.[1] The king bought and purveyed materials such as timber, lime and stone for the works, and stones for the war machines, as he bought and purveyed victuals for the inhabitants.[2] It is certain that some of the war machines at least were discharged by means of gunpowder, for in 1363 there is mention of "*attilium pulverum*."[3]

No one who was an inhabitant could be a member of the garrison, "lest the soldiers there should be overwhelmed."[4] How many men constituted the garrison is unknown. When Robert de Herle was made captain of the town in 1351, there were in his retinue alone ten knights, forty-nine esquires, and sixty archers on foot,[5] in that of John de Beauchamp[6] in 1356, nine knights, forty esquires, and thirty archers on horseback. When Henry Lescrope was made captain of the town and castle in 1369,[7] it was ordained that there should be in his company[8] or retinue forty-nine men-at-arms and fifty archers. His wages should be 4s., those of "forty-one esquire men-at-arms" 12d. each, and those of the fifty archers 6d. each a day. It was decreed at the same time that a knight of the captain's company must always remain in the castle with fourteen of the men-at-arms and twenty archers, and the remainder be at the disposition of the captain, over and above eighty men-at-arms, two hundred archers, and the retinues of the mayor and aldermen of the town already in the garrison. The captain and his men, together with those remaining on garrison duty during war, were granted the gains of war as they were accustomed in times past. The captain and his men-at-arms were granted also the accustomed regard.

From time to time persons were appointed to supervise the fortifications,[9] to see that they were well supplied with victuals, to take sufficient security from the men of the garrison that they would remain at their posts, to remove those found to be inefficient, and to imprison deserters.

In connection with the defence of the town the watch of the burgesses should be mentioned, and the part played by

1. J. J. Champollion-Figeac, *Lettres des Rois*, II, p. 101.
2. *Foed.*, III, i, 293, 315; *C.P.R.* 1350-4, pp. 68, 168, 405; *Ib.* 1364-7, p. 349.
3. *Foed.*, III, ii, 705.　　4. *Ib.*, III, i, 158.　　5. *Ib.*, III, i, 222.
6. *Ib.*, III, i, 324.　　7. *Ib.*, III, ii, 881, 882.
8. The treasurer seems to have had a "company" as well as the captain; *C.P.R.* 1370-4, p. 133.
9. *Foed.*, III, ii, 713, 723, 841, 862, 1078.

X

the great staple when established there, which consisted in the provision of a number of men-at-arms and archers by each staple merchant, amounting in all to one hundred swordsmen and two hundred archers,[1] to act as a guard when the captain had withdrawn the usual garrison on a hostile expedition.

In addition to the land defences there was also at the beginning of the reign a small fleet of seven ships stationed in the harbour,[2] under the control of the captain of the castle.

One of the greatest benefits that Edward III. conferred on the town was the establishment of staples. In 1348 " certain men " of Calais persuaded the king that it would be to his own and the town's advantage if the staple for cloth was set up there, and accordingly a grant of a staple for cloth, feathers, tin and lead, to last for a period of seven years, was issued on the 5th of April.[3] This was not pleasing to the English people, and before the end of the year they complained that it was injurious to the king and themselves, and petitioned for its removal. So on the 1st of December Edward III. summoned the men, or at least four of them, by whom he had been encouraged originally to fix the staple at Calais, to come to London in the ensuing February, and show him and his council the advantage accruing to himself and the town from the staple, and what that advantage was likely to be in the future, " wishing to be done what might be of more advantage so to us and the said town of Calais as to our same people." Already he had attempted to conciliate his subjects by granting special licences to take goods elsewhere,[4] but apparently the result of the February conference was the removal of the staple, for licences cease after the 1st of April, 1349.

When parliament met in 1362 [5] part of its chief business was to discuss whether Calais, "which belongs to our said lord the king, and where he has full jurisdiction, would be a good and suitable place for the wools and residence of the merchants." Complaint was made that previously when the staple had been in the dominions of a foreign power, the

1. *Foed.*, III, ii, 713, 723, 967.   2. *Ib.*, III, i, 165.
3. *Ib.*, III, i, 158, 178.
4. *C.C.R.* 1346–9, pp. 476, 482, 560; *C.P.R.* 1348–50, pp. 136, 137.
5. *Rot. Parl.*, II, 268, 269.

wools had been greatly reduced in value owing to misdeeds and outrages perpetrated on English subjects, which could not be remedied because the king had no authority, and also owing to the feebleness of the money received for the goods, and the unsatisfactory exchanges. The lords gave their opinion "that the said town would be a good and suitable place, if it were inhabited with good merchants and well governed. And the knights of the shires examined on this matter before the lords said that they had spoken to several merchants about the matter, of whom some said that the repair would be good for the said town, and others the reverse. And therefore they prayed that they might be excused from saying one or the other, since knowledge of that matter lay with merchants more than with any other. And so this article remains pending the opinion of and agreement with merchants and others." From a letter to the mayors and aldermen two years later[1] it appears that all merchants advised the fixing of the staple at Calais.

Accordingly on the 9th of February, 1363,[2] an ordinance was made by the king and council complying with this advice. It was decreed that the town should be the staple for wool, woolfells, leather, cloth, tin, lead, worsted, cheese, butter, honey, feathers, felt, woad, grindstones, sea coal, " and other merchandise whatsoever, ... except namely lead which we will to be retained in our kingdom for a certain time, and tin and cloths, which if they be not taken to the said town of Calais, we will permit to be carried to the parts of Gascony, and to other parts in the west and south subjected to our dominion, and not elsewhere." Both aliens and natives might export. As a check to evasion of the decree all ships-masters and merchants taking staple merchandise out of the kingdom, must take oath in the presence of the collectors of customs in the ports assigned for export, that they would take their goods to Calais, and obey the mayors and aldermen in all things. Letters patent, indented under the coket seal had to be made, one part of which must remain in the hands of the collectors of customs, and the other be delivered to the mayors and aldermen by the ships-masters.

The words " other merchandise whatsoever," lead to the

---

1. *Foed.*, III, ii, 725.   2. *Ib.*, III, ii, 688, 689.

supposition that there was an attempt at this time to accomplish some new enterprise, and to make Calais the sole mart for all English exports whatsoever, with the two exceptions mentioned above. The evidence on this point is unsatisfactory. In April,[1] horses, falcons, woollen and linen thread, and in May,[2] wine, corn, beer, animals, flesh and fish, were forbidden to be taken from the kingdom without special licence, the commons having petitioned in parliament that the latter commodities, that is the food stuffs, might remain in the kingdom.[3] A prohibition of the unrestricted export of so many articles, together with the fact that there is no mention of Calais either as the sole mart for these commodities, or the only place to which licences could be issued, seems to contradict the statement that the town was the staple for all exports from England. Moreover in July [4] the men of Sandwich and the sea coast near, complained that Flemish traders importing victuals had ceased to export chalk, lime, brushwood, tan, bacon, pigs, and honey to their own land, because of the ordinance, "to the damage of the men of the coast aforesaid." The Flemish traders were allowed to continue exporting these goods, "as by the coming of the men of Flanders great advantage and profit arose, whereof the whole country of the said coast had great part of their living; and the goods aforesaid are not among the merchandise specified in the proclamation to be taken to Calais, nor was it the king's intention that the passage of goods of small value should be restrained by colour of the proclamation."[5] On the other hand next year Calais is again referred to as the mart for "all wool, hides and other merchandise."[6]

The staple was restricted in two ways, by the granting of licences to take staple goods elsewhere than to Calais,[7] and by the prohibition of export of some of those goods without licence, which meant that a licence would be required to take them to the staple. The first restriction of the latter kind was the one with regard to woollen thread, which apparently

1. *Foed.*, III, ii, 694, 695.   2. *Ib.*, III, ii, 698.
3. *Rot. Parl.*, II, 277.   4. *C.C.R.* 1360-4, pp. 482, 483.
5. The last part of this quotation seems contradictory, for honey and pigs were staple articles; *Foed.*, III, ii, 688, 689, 691.
6. *C.C.R.* 1364-8, p. 8.   7. *Ib.* 1360-4, p. 474; *Ib.* 1364-8, p. 8.

included worsted, mentioned above.[1] A further restriction was the result of the petition of the Commons against the exportation of food, for in October [2] aliens and natives were prohibited from taking red herrings, cloth, corn, malt and beer out of the kingdom without special licence, except " cloths of worsted, and other narrow cloths by merchants of Germany to Germany, and herrings and certain woollen cloths by the merchants of Gascony bringing wines to England, to whom it shall be lawful to buy herrings and cloths below or up to the value of their wines which they shall have led thus into England, having made oath that the herrings and cloths thus bought by them are being taken to Gascony and not elsewhere." This was a serious reservation, for whilst now cloth could be taken to Germany and Gascony under certain conditions without licence, it could only be taken to the staple with one.[3] Later, merchants wishing to take cloth from the county of Devon to Gascony could do so without licence.[4] In 1367[5] a further regulation was made with regard to cloth. It was decreed that no native should take worsted cloth, and that no native or alien should take sea-coals, millstones or felware outside the kingdom without special licence, except only to Calais.

It has already been shown how after the location of the staple at Calais the government of town and staple was put into the hands of the two mayors and twenty-four aldermen, how the mayors and aldermen quarrelled with the other merchants, and how in 1364 owing to a complaint of the English people that those officials had been putting extortionate impositions upon staple merchandise, Edward III. appointed a commission to enquire into the matter, with the result that the municipality and the staple each came into existence as a separate body. From the details in connection with all

1. This prohibition was renewed in 1364 ; *Foed.*, III, ii, 724.
2. *Ib.*, III, ii, 710; *Rot. Parl.*, II, 275, 276.
3. *C.P.R.*, 1361–4, pp. 495, 500, 522.
4. *Foed.*, III, ii, 737.
5. *Ib.*, III, ii, 823; *C.C.R.* 1364–8, p. 376.

this it is obvious that there were two divisions of merchants bringing goods to the staple, the actual merchants of the staple, that is the staple company, and the merchants who were not of the company, but under its control. It does not transpire whether the company, although not known as two mayors and twenty-four aldermen, still numbered twenty-six after 1364.

The ordinance of 1365 which described the new municipal constitution laid down certain regulations about the staple.[1] The mayor of the staple must have cognizance of all quarrels touching the staple. He must take as wages £40 a year, and for his regard what was decreed by the staple company from their own goods or the profits of their court, without any tax upon merchandise for the purpose. The wages of all staple officials except those of the mayor had likewise to be paid from court profits, and the constables ·had not to be paid more than they had formerly received at Bruges. All officials must be appointed and dismissed by the company. John de Norfolk was appointed by the king as searcher of forfeitures,[2] his wages being 12d. a day, and Richard de Cayton was elected by the merchants as weigher of wools for the usual wages. The wools had to be weighed " in the house near the moneyage, which house was ordained and directed for that cause at the commencement of the staple there, on account of peril of fire, and for several other reasonable causes." Four Lombards were mentioned as correctors of wools for the men of Lombardy.[3]

Further details of the staple are· recorded in a letter patent of the succeeding year.[4] The company was given free election yearly of all its officials, including the mayor and two constables, the three latter to be chosen from the company, and to have recognition in all pleas concerning staple merchandise between merchant and merchant. The company must have a gaol to guard prisoners, or otherwise hand them over

1. *Foed.*, III, ii, 768, 769.
2. All forfeitures belonging to the King had to be sold from time to time by the view and testimony of the mayor of the staple and the treasurer; *Ib.*, III, ii, 768.
3. Foreign merchants who wanted to take staple merchandise to Italy "beyond the mountains" were exempted from selling their goods at Calais, "so that they and all other merchant strangers pay for their merchandise there, in the same manner as do the merchants of England "; *Foed.*, III, ii, 692.   4. *Ib.*, III, ii, 795.

to the gaoler of the town, who must " find sufficient security to them concerning replying for those prisoners at the mandate of the same mayor and constables." The mayor could receive recognitions of debts of merchants or others, in the presence of one or both of the constables, who must do execution with regard to the recognitions according to the ordinance of the staples. The merchants of the staple could sell all their merchandise and other possessions wholesale, but not retail or by parts. The mayor and constables had power to grant houses necessary for the households and merchandise of the merchants of the staple, from merchants and burgesses, in the staple court, by the common consent of merchants specially elected for this purpose.

In 1367 [1] it was ordained that wools which had to be weighed on the suspicion that they were not properly coketted, should be weighed before the treasurer and the mayor of the staple, and the defects be certified in chancery under the seals of those officials [2] and the searcher of forfeitures. The same year [3] Edward III. promised that the English merchants of the staple should be free from the custom and subsidy on all cloth sent to Calais, to be used for their own and their servants' livery. Evidently merchants of the staple wore a distinctive dress.

In this year too there were dissensions between the merchants of Lombardy and the merchants of the staple. [4] The former complained that from the time of the establishment of the staple at Calais, certain of their number, together with certain of the latter, had been brokers, but that now a number of the English brokers were preventing their Lombard fellow officials from doing their duty. Edward III. commanded the governor, treasurer and mayor of the staple, or two of them, to end the dispute if possible, but if they were unable to do so to send the parties to Westminster, where the king and his council would settle it, in which case each party would be under the penalty of £200.

The customs and subsidies payable on staple merchandise

---

1. *Ib.*, III, ii, 836.
2. The treasurer had some authority in connection with the staple. In 1371 and 1373 the treasurer and the King's searchers together arrested wool as forfeit; *C.C.R.* 1369–74, pp. 227, 228, 525.
3. *Foed.*, III, ii, 836.   4. *Ib.*, III, ii, 839

were collected at the English ports from which the goods were shipped,[1] specified by the letter patent of 1363 as those towns assigned for export by the statute of the staple. The customs fixed by that statute [2] were 6s. 8d. on each sack of wool, 6s. 8d. on every three hundred woolfells, and 13s. 4d. on each last of hides, for natives, and 10s., 10s., and 20s., respectively, for aliens. The subsidies varied. From 1363 to 1365 they were 20s. on each sack of wool, 20s. on every three hundred fells, and 40s. on each last of hides,[3] from 1365 to 1368 40s., 40s., and 80s., respectively,[4] and from 1368 to 1369, 36s. 8d., 36s. 8d., and 80s., respectively.[5]

In 1369,[6] on the petition of parliament, the staple was removed from Calais, on account of the risk to the goods at sea, as a result of the renewed outbreak of war with France.

As early as 1370,[7] however, the mart for wool, woolfells and leather was set up a second time, although it seems to have been removed the next year.[8] After Whitsuntide in 1372 [9] it was re-established, and apparently remained until the end of the reign.[10] How far these staples of 1370 and 1372 were staples for other exports besides the three chief products of England is not quite clear. Together with the various petitions made in parliament by the Calais burgesses towards the end of 1372,[11] was one that wools and other little merchandise might " be sold there and not elsewhere, ... for when the staple was entire. . . . at Calais, and the captain made any chevauchée upon our enemies, the mayor of the staple made watch within the said town with about a

1. *Foed.*, III, ii, 688, 692.   2. *S.R.*, I, 333.
3. *Rot. Parl.*, II, 273.   4. *Ib.*, II, 285.
5. *Ib.*, II, 295. The number of woolfells on which the specified customs and subsidies had to be paid is here stated as twelve twenties, "dusze vintz." As the custom of 6s. 8d. on every 240 fells is referred to as the ancient custom, it is obvious that twelve twenties must equal 300. Probably twenty was reckoned as twenty-five, on the analogy of the "baker's dozen," which seems to have been the case later, for in the Rolls of Parliament for 1372 the subsidy for natives assessed on each last of hides is referred to in one place as £4, and in another as 100s.; *Ib.*, II, 310.
6. *S.R.*, I, 390; *Rot. Parl.*, II, 301.
7. *C.C.R.* 1369–74, pp. 192, 193.
8. There is no mention of it after the 3rd of August, 1371; *C.P.R.* 1370–4, p. 131; until its re-establishment in 1372, which seems to have been not merely a renewal of the grant of 1370, but a fresh location; *C.C.R.* 1369–74, pp. 390, 391.
9. *Ib.* 1369–74, p. 434.
10. *Ib.* 1369–74, p. 399; *Ib.* 1374–77, p. 499; *Foed.*, III, ii, 1058, 1068.
11. *Ib.*, III, ii, 967.

hundred swordsmen and about two hundred archers of the merchants and their servants, who do not take any wages of the king. And now they are gone to the great peril of the said town." The same request was made in the petitions of 1376.[1] It was decreed in reply to the first petition that the mart for wools, woolfells and leather should be there " as shall please the king, and of the remainder be as has been accustomed before this hour," which appears to have authorised a return to the state of affairs before 1369.[2] In reply to the second petition it was ordained that the town should be the mart for wools, hides, woolfells, lead, tin, cloth called worsted, cheese, butter, feathers, woad, honey, felperie, and tallow.[3] It is evident that both demands requested measures against the infringement of the staple, which seems to have been a particular evil at this time. In 1373 the Commons protested in parliament against it,[4] and in 1376[5] one of the charges against Latimer and Lyons in the impeachment of those ministers, was, that together with a number of privy councillors, they had persuaded the king to grant licences to export goods elsewhere than to Calais, and had levied extortionate impositions to their own profit on those taking out such licences.

In December of 1376 there is again a reference to Calais as the staple for all exports from England, with the exception of a few specified articles.[6] An ordinance was made to the effect that all merchants, native and alien, exporting the above mentioned articles, " and other merchandise whatsoever," except woollen cloths made in England, dried herrings, grindstones, sea coals, corn and logs of wood, must take their goods to Calais and not elsewhere.

M. Daumet shows that in 1376 the staple organization was established on the same lines as it had been previously. An ordinance of July renewed the privileges granted formerly to the company, and granted others. Amongst the latter, power

1. *Rot. Parl.*, II, 358.
2. Calais was mentioned in the parliament of 1376 as the staple for wools, woolfells, and other merchandise, but the burgesses in their petitions only refer to wools, fells, hides and tin, as if only those commodities were staple articles; *Ib.*, II, 323, 358, 359.
3. *Foed.*, III, ii, 1057, 1058, 1062; *C.C.R.* 1374-7, pp. 441, 442.
4. *Rot. Parl.*, II, 318. 5. *Ib.*, II, 323-326.
6. *Foed.*, III, ii, 1068.

Y

was given to the mayor and constables to make ordinances
which they judged necessary for good order, and to fix with
the common consent the tax to be paid upon goods entering
the mart,[1] which must be used to pay the wages of the
employees.   All the members of the company when going
to Calais were exempted from personal tolls collected at Dover,
and from taxes upon bread, wine, beer and other victuals
bought for their own consumption at Calais.   An ordinance
of December confirmed that of July, with the addition that all
traders going to the town were excused from personal tolls
at Dover.   It was also specially decreed that Italians could
buy wools in the town and take them to Italy, after giving
security that they would not sell them in Flanders, or in any
other country this side the mountains,[2] so that the privileges
of English merchants might be safeguarded in the north-west
of Europe.

DOROTHY GREAVES.

1. In 1365 taxation by the company for payment of officials was forbidden; see above, p. 328.
2. Daumet, pp. 123–125.

LIST OF OFFICERS.

The dates are the earliest references to the men in their official capacity. It is presumed that each man held office until the earliest reference to his successor.

CAPTAINS.
1347 John de Montgomery. *Foed.*, III, i, 138.
1347 John de Chivereston. *Ib.*, III, i, 142.
1349 John de Beauchamp. *Ib.*, III, i, 181.
1350 Robert de Herle. *Ib.*, III, i, 193.
1351 John de Beauchamp. Nichols, p. xxxiii.
1351 Robert de Herle. *Foed.*, III, i, 222.
1353 Reginald de Cobham. *Ib.*, III, i, 276, 277.
1355 Roger de Beauchamp. *Ib.*, III, i, 294.
1356 John de Beauchamp. *Ib.*, III, i, 315.
1358-1361 Ralph de Ferrers. *Ib.*, III, i, 389
1369 Henry Lescrope. *Ib.*, III, ii, 881, 882.
1370 Nicholas de Tamworth. Nichols, p. xxxiv.
1372 Roger de Beauchamp. *Foed.*, III, ii, 941.
1373 John de Beurle. *Ib.*, III, ii, 992.
1375 Hugh de Calvyle. *Ib.*, III, ii, 1042.

GOVERNERS.
1361 Henry Lescrope. *C.C.R.*, 1360-4, p. 267.
1365 Bartholomew de Burghersh. *Cal. Pap. Registers*, Letters, iv, 1362-1404, p. 18.
1366-1369 Henry Lescrope. *Foed.*, III, ii, 787.
1370 Henry Lescrope. Nichols, p. xxxiv.

WARDENS OF THE CASTLE.
1348 John de Beauchamp. *Foed.*, III, i, 165.
1350 Thomas de Kingston. *Ib.*, III, i, 197.
1353 Reginald de Cobham. *Ib.*, III, i, 259.
1353 Thomas de Hoggeshaue. Nichols, p. xxxiii.
1355 Roger de Beauchamp. *Foed.*, III, i, 294.
1356 John de Beauchamp. *Ib.*, III, i, 316.
1358 Ralph de Ferrers. *Ib.*, III, i, 389
1361 Thomas de Kingston. *Ib.*, III, ii, 619.
1364 Henry Lescrope. *Ib.*, III, ii, 724.
1369 John Tirel. *Ib.*, III, ii, 865.
1369 Stephen de Valence. *Ib.*, III, ii, 865.
1369 Henry Lescrope. Nichols, p. xxxiv.

1370   Nicholas de Tamworth. Nichols, p. **xxxiv**
1372   William de Risceby. *Foed.*, III, ii, 941.
1373   Thomas de Banfeld. *Ib.*, III, ii, 992.
1375   Ralph de Sutton. *Ib.*, III, ii, 1036.
1376   Thomas Fogg. *Ib.* III, ii, 1066.

TREASURERS.

1348   William de Salop. *Ib.*, III, i, 150.
1356   Richard de Eccleshale. *C.P.R.*, 1354–8, p. 477.
1361   Thomas de Brantingham. *Foed.*, III, ii, 612.
1368   William de Gunthorpe. *Ib.*, III, ii, 844.
1373   John de Romeseye. *Ib.*, III, ii, 992.
1376   William de Eyrmyn. *Ib.*, III, ii, 1051.

MASTERS OF THE MINT.

1363   Henry de Brisele. *C.P.R.*, 1361–4, p. 313.
1364   Walter de Barde. *Foed.*, III, ii, 727.
1365   Thomas King. *Ib.*, III, ii, 772.
1366   Walter de Barde. *Ib.*, III, ii, 811.
1371   Bardet de Malepilys. *C.C.R.*, 1369–74, p. 303.

MAYORS.

1363–1364   John Wroth and John de Wesenham. *Foed.*, III, ii, 691.
1365   Richard de Preston. *Ib.*, III, ii, 767.
1370   Adam de Bury. *Ib.*, III, ii, 900.

INDEX.

Printed and bound by PG in the USA